Gender, Companionship, and Travel

T0331455

Over the last couple of decades there has been a strong academic interest in how individuals interact with each other while en route. Yet, even if various studies have informed us about present-day realities of travel companionships, we know little about the influence of gender both on these realities, as well as on the discourse in which these are being narrated.

This book aims to establish an agenda for the study of companionship in travel writing by offering a collection of new essays which study texts that belong to the broad category of pre-modern and modern travel literature. Chapters explore the differences and similarities in the ways that women and men in the past chose to describe their experiences with, and/or their ideas about companionship, and specifically reveals the influence of gender norms, conventions, restrictions, and stereotypes.

This is the first book which looks at the long-term, interdisciplinary, and genuinely international history of gendered discourses on companionship in travel writing. It will be of interest to scholars and students from a wide variety of disciplines, including cultural and social history, as well as cultural, literary, gender, travel, and tourism studies.

Floris Meens is Assistant Professor of Cultural History at Radboud University, Nijmegen, the Netherlands. During the last couple of years, his broad interest in cultural history has resulted in publications on European travel cultures, European *Lieux de mémoire*, the history of private music cultures, and on modern intellectual and cultural networks.

Tom Sintobin is Assistant Professor of Cultural Studies at Radboud University, Nijmegen, the Netherlands. His research interests include Dutch literature from the nineteenth and twentieth century, Dutch and Belgian culture around 1900, and cultures of tourism.

Routledge International Studies of Women and Place

Series Editors: Janet Henshall Momsen, *University of California, USA* and **Janice Monk**, *University of Arizona, USA*

Who Will Mind the Baby?
Geographies of Childcare and Working Mothers
Edited by Kim England

Feminist Political Ecology
Global Issues and Local Experience
Edited by Dianne Rocheleau, Barbara Thomas-Slayter, and Esther Wangari

Women Divided
Gender, Religion and Politics in Northern Ireland
Rosemary Sales

Women's Lifeworlds
Women's Narratives on Shaping their Realities
Edited by Edith Sizoo

Gender, Planning and Human Rights
Edited by Tovi Fenster

Gender, Ethnicity and Place
Women and Identity in Guyana
Linda Peake and D. Alissa Trotz

Reproductive Geographies
Bodies, Places and Politics
Edited by Marcia R. England, Maria Fannin and Helen Hazen

Gender, Companionship, and Travel
Discourses in Pre-modern and Modern Travel Literature
Edited by Floris Meens and Tom Sintobin

For more information about this series, please visit: www.routledge.com/Routledge-International-Studies-of-Women-and-Place/book-series/SE0406

Gender, Companionship, and Travel

Discourses in Pre-modern and Modern Travel Literature

Edited by Floris Meens and Tom Sintobin

LONDON AND NEW YORK

First published 2019
by Routledge
2 Park Square, Milton Park, Abingdon, Oxon OX14 4RN

and by Routledge
52 Vanderbilt Avenue, New York, NY 10017

First issued in paperback 2020

Routledge is an imprint of the Taylor & Francis Group, an informa business

British Library Cataloguing-in-Publication Data
A catalogue record for this book is available from the British Library

Library of Congress Cataloging-in-Publication Data
A catalog record has been requested for this book

ISBN 13: 978-0-367-58308-8 (pbk)
ISBN 13: 978-1-138-57992-7 (hbk)

Typeset in Times New Roman
by Integra Software Services Pvt. Ltd.

Contents

Figures

Contributors

Dick de Boer studied History and Dutch Language and Literature in Leiden, where he started his academic career in 1971. After several years as researcher and high school teacher, he became Assistant Professor in Medieval History in 1976, acquired the doctorate in 1978 and became senior lecturer in 1985. In 1992, he was appointed Full Professor in Medieval History at the University of Groningen, which he remained until his retirement in 2012. Until September 2013, he kept a partial position as coordinator of the European Science Foundation project *Cuius Regio*, on regional dynamics as a historical phenomenon. In 2002, he was Visiting Professor at the University of Michigan in Ann Arbor. From 2006, until his retirement he was Director of the National Research School of Medieval Studies in the Netherlands. Abroad he functioned as member of the Programming Committee of the International Medieval Congress in Leeds, and as cofounder and first Academic Director of C.A.R.M.E.N. (Cooperative for the Advancement of Research through a Medieval European Network). His research and publications cover a wide range of subjects from Hanseatic Studies to Miracle Narratives and Urban studies to Medieval Travelling.

Babs Boter is Assistant Professor at the Humanities Faculty of the Vrije Universiteit Amsterdam. She teaches BA and MA courses on Travel Writing, Diaspora Literature, (Trans)nationalism, American Literature and World Literature offered by the Department of Language, Literature & Communication. She also contributes to other programs offered by the Humanities Faculty, such as the Research MA Program of the History Department and the Minor Program Gender & Diversity. Boter is writing a biography of the Dutch travel journalist Mary Pos (1904–1987). In addition, she is initiator and convener of the international and interdisciplinary expert group "Unhinging the National Framework: Platform for the Study of Life-Writing and Transnationalism," which is VU-based and affiliated with CLUE+, Research Institute for Culture, Cognition, History and Heritage. Boter has a background in History (Leiden University), American Studies (University of Minnesota) and Cultural Studies (Amsterdam School for Cultural Analysis, University of Amsterdam), and has previously worked for Humanities programs at various Dutch and American universities.

Margherita Carucci was a Research Fellow at the Helsinki Collegium for Advanced Studies, Finland, where she worked on a multidisciplinary project on ideas and workings of privacy in the Roman imperial house. She has edited a volume *Revealing Privacy: Debating the Understandings of Privacy* (2012), which collects a number of contributions written by an international group of scholars from the fields of humanities and social sciences to contribute toward and discuss how privacy is understood today. She has published also a book on the *Romano-African domus: Studies in space, decoration, and function* (2007) along with a number of articles on a variety of aspects of the Graeco-Roman society, such as visual art, gender studies, sculpture, and urbanism, with particular focus on social and cultural history. However, her main interest is on every aspect related to the domestic and public experience of ancient Roman women that she explores with the support of textual and archaeological evidence along with modern critical theories in sociology, anthropology, and visual art. She has recently published an article on the "The Dangers of Female Mobility in Roman Imperial Times" (2017).

Tara Kathleen Kelly received her Ph.D. in History from Johns Hopkins University. She has been a Mayer Fellow at the Huntington Library and has taught at Emmanuel College as well as in Duke University's Writing Program. Her first book, *The Hunter Elite: Hunting Narratives, Manly Sport, and American Conservation, 1880–1925*, was published by the University of Kansas Press in March 2018.

Martyn Lyons was born in London and currently is Emeritus Professor of History in the School of Humanities and Languages at the University of New South Wales in Sydney. His main research interests are in the history of reading and writing in Europe and Australia, and he recently published *The Writing Culture of Ordinary People in Europe, c. 1860–1920* (2013). His study of the Pyrenees in the nineteenth and twentieth centuries was published in 2017, entitled: *The Pyrenees in the Modern Era: Reinventions of a Landscape, 1775–2012*.

Alan Moss completed a BA in Dutch Language and Culture and a MPhil in Literary Studies at the Radboud University Nijmegen. As a PhD Candidate, he is currently researching the formation of national and religious identities in Dutch educational travel accounts in the seventeenth century.

Ipshita Nath is an Assistant Professor of English at University of Delhi, India. She is working towards her doctoral thesis on the post-colonial representations of memsahibs in various literatures at the Department of English, Jamia Millia Islamia. She was the IES Abroad scholar to Loyola University Chicago, in 2012.

Fabia Neuerburg is a research assistant working on travelling philosophers and scientists in Greek antiquity at Trier University, Germany.

Rosella Perugi received her MA in Modern Languages and Literatures at the Faculty of Humanities, University of Genoa, Italy. She attended post-graduate courses in Didactics of Foreign Languages at Tor Vergata University, Rome, and at the University of Siena. In 2010, she received her MA in Italian at the University of Siena. She worked as a teacher of foreign languages in her country for more than twenty years. From 2008 to 2016, she worked as Lecturer of Italian in Tehran (Iran), Turku (Finland), and Alexandria (Egypt). Since 2012, she is a doctoral student at Turku University, Department of Italian, researching about Italian women travellers in the Nordic countries.

Peter Rietbergen is Emeritus Professor of Cultural History at Radboud University, Nijmegen, the Netherlands. He published fourteen monographs and approximately 300 scholarly articles. He is interested in the history of early modern papacy and the culture of Rome and in the relation between Europe and other Eurasian worlds, more specifically India and Japan. His book *Europe: A Cultural History* (1998) has been translated in Chinese, Korean, and Polish. His book *Short History of The Netherlands* was reprinted 7 times and was translated in German and Japanese.

Joachim Schätz is a film scholar and critic, currently working at Ludwig Boltzmann Institute for History and Society in Vienna. His research interests include mass culture and political theory, sponsored films, concepts of the detail and the politics of comedy.

Rob van de Schoor is Assistant Professor of nineteeth-century Dutch Literature at Radboud University, Nijmegen, The Netherlands.

Ute Sonnleitner is Head of the Department of Education of "ÖGB-Steiermark" (Austrian Federation of Trade Unions – Styria) and Lecturer at Karl-Franzens-University Graz. She studied history and classical archaeology. Her PhD thesis dedicated to the "Resistance against Austrofascism in Styria 1933–1938" was finished in 2008. Since then until 2015, she worked as a Researcher and Lecturer, was engaged in various projects and coordinated the PhD programme "Migration-Diversity-Global Societies" at University Graz. Main research interests are: Education, migration, and theatre history, women, and gender studies, labour history (and their various interactions).

Katalin Teller is Assistant Professor at the Department of Aesthetics, Institute for Art Theory and Media Studies of ELTE in Budapest and former research associate at Ludwig Boltzmann Institute for History and Society in Vienna. Her research interests include political aesthetics and the history of popular and urban culture in Austria and Hungary in the first half of the twentieth century.

Gerrit Verhoeven teaches early modern history at the universities of Antwerp and Brussels. He has published widely on seventeenth- and eighteenth-century social and cultural history. In 2015, his book *Europe within reach: Netherlandish travellers on the Grand Tour and beyond (1585–1750)* was published by Brill, while he coedited a volume *Beyond the Grand Tour: Northern metropolises and early modern travel behaviour* for Routledge in 2017. He is an associated editor of *Urban History*.

Acknowledgements

The idea for this book originated at the conference "The Europe of Women" (Nijmegen, The Netherlands, Autumn 2015), which hosted a panel on companionship en route organized by the research group Tourism, Travel and Text. The editors wish to thank the Institute for Historical, Literary and Cultural Studies at the said university for its continuous support. We are particularly grateful to the series editors Janet Momsen and Janice Monk, as well as the anonymous reviewers, for their expertise and trust. Our thanks also go to Ruth Anderson and Faye Leerink from Routledge for their very professional and friendly help. Last but not least, we thank Lien Foubert and Carlijn Cober from the Radboud University, the first for her involvement in the early stages of this project, the second for her invaluable help with editing and proofreading this book.

Who is carrying the luggage?

Gendered discourses on companionship in travel writing: an introduction

Floris Meens and Tom Sintobin

> We two ladies [...] have found out and will maintain that ladies alone get on in travelling much better than with gentlemen [...] The only use of a gentleman in travelling is to look after the luggage, and we take care to have no luggage.
>
> (Emily Lowe, *Unprotected Females in Norway: Or, The Pleasantest Way of Travelling There*, 1857)[1]

New perspectives

The topic of companionship has been explored both by social scientists as well as historians and cultural and literary scholars. Functioning as a reflection of the mobilising processes that characterise and deeply influence modern societies both spatially as well as socially, ever since its beginnings in the 1990s the mobility turn in the social sciences has created a strong academic interest in the various ways in which individuals interact with each other while en route.[2] The fields of tourism and transport studies and cultural anthropology have developed a particular interest in the interactions between tourists and "other" travelling people – as well as their encounters with locals. A wide array of subtopics has thus already been explored, ranging from encounters between tourists in remote regions of present-day Australia,[3] to the effects of visitors' interactions with their companions on their satisfaction and revisit intentions.[4]

Yet, even if these studies inform us about present-day realities of travel companionships, they have little to say about the influence of gender both on this reality as well as on the discourse in which these travelled companionships are being narrated. Within the social sciences there have been successful efforts to combine the mobility and gender paradigms, though. In their volume *Gendered Journeys, Mobile Emotions* (2009), for instance, Gayle Letherby and Gillian Reynolds even touched upon the topic of companionship.[5] Arguing that "all passengers do engage more or less contently with other travellers in the same space" and that "many of them may have to engage with the emotions of others,"[6] they introduce the eloquent concept of a "community of occasion" to analyse the encounters of those individuals who, willingly or unwillingly, share a journey (for instance a train ride) but would not run into each other otherwise

(Cfr. Pettinger's "contact zone").[7] Their analysis, however, omits the role of gender in companionships of men and women who deliberately travel together. Also, it uses various "'real' travel stories" to reconstruct the – in itself important and interesting – reality of mobility. As Tanu Priya Uteng and Tim Cresswell remind us in the introduction to their volume *Gendered Mobilities* (2008), however:

> the meanings given to mobility through narrative, discourse and representation have [...] been clearly differentiated by gender. Similarly, narratives of mobility and immobility play a central role in the construction of gender as a social and cultural construct.[8]

Priya Uteng and Cresswell's remarks fit perfectly with the latest insights on travel practices and cultures from the humanities. Cultural and literary scholars as well as historians have, however, taken another path to recognise the importance of the topic of companionship in travel (writing). For a long time these scholars generally assumed that, at least until modern times, travel texts had predominantly been written by men because they moved more freely in the public sphere than women, who in these male-gazed narratives thus only functioned as objects of desire or as someone to return home to. Since the 1970s in particular, however, the absence of women in the mobile societies of Europe and beyond has, by and large, been questioned. Scholars have left behind what Janet Wolff has called the "cul-de-sac of complaints about women's absence from (and invisibility in) the public sphere."[9] Influenced by the burgeoning of gender studies and the spatial turn in the humanities, various studies have revealed the liminality, porosity, and ambiguity of spaces. The reappraisal of diaries, letters, travel writings, and scientific reports by women from different periods of time has rendered visible that many of them undertook and reflected upon voyages of their own.[10]

As Carl Thompson has indicated, while at first many scholars emphasised the differences between men's and women's travel practices and writings, most "now recognize that an individual's experience and representation of travel is shaped by multiple, intersectional factors, including not only gender, but also race, age, class, wealth and status, education, political and religious views, ideals and beliefs."[11] Focusing on the role of travel companions might be an effective strategy for revealing these intersectionalities, and indeed some scholars have pointed at its importance in past travel praxes and discourses.[12] Only a few of them, however, have addressed companionship in travel writing as their central topic. An important exception is an article in which Amrita Sen traces the interactions between European and Mughal Indian female travellers by analysing the personal bonds between three women who were closely connected to both the East India Company as well as various Mughal officers.[13] Sen is more interested in reconstructing the past reality of such friendships rather than analysing their functions in travel discourses and unveiling the complex relationships between text and reality.

Such an approach to the study of companionship has been put on the research agenda recently by Eva Johanna Holmberg.[14] Her examination of the ways in which travel companions were described in two early-modern English texts on journeys to the Ottoman Empire reveals much about the social values and practices of that time. As she argues "the portrayals of travel companions provide us with an interesting perspective not just on the strategies of self-narrating of [...] travellers, but also on how their social life shaped the traveller's presentation of himself, his travels and his writing."[15] Holmberg reveals the multilayered meaning of companionship in early modern travel culture by analysing both its role in travel realities as well as in its narratives. She notes that early modern English men who took to the road, when choosing a comrade – a process that was deeply influenced by intimates – proved to be well aware of possibilities and restrictions based on gender, nationality, social class, and ethnic, political, and religious identities. Focusing on the writings themselves and by quoting from the work of Natalie Zemon Davis, Holmberg reminds us that:

> the author's choice of audience and genre shapes the channels in which her voice can sound, enlarging possibilities in some directions, limiting them in others.[16]

Referring to Adam Smyth's work on early modern English autobiographies, she thus invites us to leave the question of truthfulness behind and concentrate on how these travel texts "work as documents," and "how [...] the conventions of each form ... shape what is being recorded."[17] Doing so, Holmberg is able to reveal the ways in which companions enabled her two early modern English male authors to justify and verify their accounts, and helped them in the process of self-fashioning by emphasising their "honesty," "reliability," and "ability to recognise these qualities in others."[18]

Our volume aims at taking Holmberg's completely new perspective on companionship even some steps further. Bearing in mind the many insights that both the social studies and humanities have provided us about the reciprocal relationships between space, mobility, gender, and discourse, we study the role of companionship to reveal travel both as a gendered discourse as well as a practice in reality. Diachronically examining how both related to each other by analysing cases from different parts of the world, this book reveals that from antiquity onwards travelling together has always been a structural part of men's and women's social lives, cultures, and worldviews.

More specifically, we aim to expose the differences and similarities in the ways that women and men in the past chose to describe their experiences with, and/or their ideas about companionship. We reveal how their texts were influenced by, and itself influenced time- and place-specific gender conventions, norms, restrictions, and stereotypes. In doing so, we elaborate on Holmberg's analysis of genre conventions and supplement it with gender-sensitive readings of these narratives. Did travel writings simply represent, or did they subversively counter the given social order and its related views on and formation processes of masculinity and femininity? Various studies have shown that women in particular had to be extremely cautious not to trespass the line when entering the public sphere, while this concern was less pressing in the private domain. But then again, as Carl Thompson reminds us, "women travel writers were undoubtedly often received and treated differently by editors, publishers, reviewers and readers" than men.[19] Our volume reveals the strategies women employed to make both their journeys and their female gaze acceptable for their reading audiences in a male-dominated world. Some of them travelled on their own, but stressed their ability to open up new territories, often meaning the private domain of a "strange" culture. In other cases, female travellers emphasised the harmless, often religious character of their male companions, thereby desexualising them, a notion to which we will return. Rather than choosing plainly between subverting or affirming dominant views and narratives, many women, but men as well, engaged with social norms and literary conventions, sometimes upturning or even changing them gradually. This insight not only elucidates the difference between the role of companionship in the texts that were (intended to be) published, and those that were for private use only; it also challenges the suggestion that women's travel in reality radically differed from men's. Thus, this volume corroborates the idea that the ideology of the separate spheres was strongly discursive (Chapter 4), while it also questions how this ideology eventually influenced the male monopoly on travel related memory.

In order to understand the role that companionship in travel writing played in the affirmation or disavowal of time-related conventions, this volume further explores the concept of liminality, here understood both in its spatial, temporal as well as ideological meaning. The scholarly record on travel as a liminal place is already quite large,[20] and a special issue of *Tourism Geographies* is in preparation (scheduled for publication in the second half of 2019), but the concept has so far never been used to understand the meaning of companionship. While for women especially travelling always had the danger of blurring the borders of decency, the "other place" of shared mobility itself could also function as a "secure" space – somewhere between the private and public (Chapter 10). We question how it brought individuals from different social backgrounds together, and how it forged, empowered, and disempowered various masculinities and femininities – and the dynamics between them – that were strongly influenced by other signifiers of social difference such as class, wealth, nationality, ethnicity, age, religion, etc. Here the means of transportation, the journeyed geography, and the political circumstances all prove to be essential. Often, companionship was shaped against the background of confrontations with difference and Otherness. Therefore, some of the chapters on the (early)modern period specifically question the influence of colonial and racial ideas in the narration of these encounters. (How) did companionship function in the portrayal of moments of tension and conflict? But also, how did it function in moments of peace and understanding? In all cases, companionship in this liminal space and time ratified hegemonies, or functioned as a means of breaking taboos and creating sub- or contra-narratives. Focusing on their individual agency, we aim to analyse the narrative strategies that the authors of these travel writings employed to avoid, adapt, or adopt traditions and/or modernity. Letherby and Reynolds have reminded us that travel encounters themselves "are always structured by the time and space in which they occur."[21] By studying companionship in different places and periods, we therefore further rethink liminal space (and time) as a dynamic component in human life, and elaborate on Phillip Wegner's idea that space is:

> both a *production*, shaped through a diverse range of social processes and human interventions, and a *force* that, in turn, influences, directs and delimits possibilities of actions and ways of being in the world.[22]

This volume establishes an agenda for the study of companionship in travel writing by offering a collection of new essays that all study one particular, or a group of texts that belong to the broad category of pre-modern and modern travel literature from different parts of the world. These include real and fictional travel journals, travelogues, and travel guides, as well as pilgrim stories and classical texts. The notion of travel itself has been much contested in recent academic debates. Some of our chapters interpret travel as the journey only; others include the traveller's life as experienced at the destination, even if this might be longer than a year. The full scope of companionship is studied and problematised as well. While most of the authors focus on texts that encompass companionships between men and women, some of them analyse the tales of those who journeyed with a same-sex comrade. Yet others, inspired by the work of Rachel Jennings who revealed the companionship(s) between women and cars,[23] question how we should define a companion, incorporating analyses of the emotional connectedness with the home front, with past travellers, the unknown reading public or even with the luggage.

This book offers the first systematic, diachronic, interdisciplinary, and genuinely international history of gendered discourses on companionship in travel writing. Two primary narratives, or lines of interpretation, run through the chapters.

Narrative 1: home sweet home

It has been written before and it will be written again in the future: the mobility of women seems to have been very strictly regulated since time immemorial. They were supposed to lead domestic lives, limited to the private sphere, as "angels of the hearth" (Chapter 11). To leave that sphere was considered irresponsible and something that would inevitably lead to misfortune. Women, thus ran the *communis opinio* for many centuries, were unable to deal with both the physical and moral ordeals along the road, which at times seemed to be intertwined. Women's "natural weakness," as a bishop called it in the late Antique period, could only be solved by counting on a man to put the women on their horses or lift them down again – and that inevitably amounts to blameable conduct (Chapter 2). Because they were the "weaker vessel" they were unable to deal with the harsh realities of travelling, according to the physician Johannes van Beverwijck in 1639. If one takes the male dominated discourse for granted, one cannot but conclude that women had indeed stayed at home for centuries.

However, such opinions did not mean that women did not travel in reality; on the contrary, as becomes clear from all contributions to this volume. Data from the High and Late Middle Ages suggest that up to 39% of the pilgrims in those days were in fact female (Chapter 3). More and more women got the chance to travel from the second half of the seventeenth century onward; interestingly, these new patterns of travel can be connected to infrastructural changes that made travelling safer, such as the development of a network of canals and the construction of paved roads (Chapter 4). Women consequently travelled even for non-religious purposes: leisure (Chapter 4 and 6); finding a partner or a job (Chapter 7); as professional writers (Chapter 9 and 12); for business (Chapter 15). It is clear that there is a large discrepancy between this dominant male discourse and everyday reality. Although in theory, women should not and did not travel, they were on the road anyhow. It was up to the hegemonic power discourse to try and deal with this discrepancy.

Companionship played a crucial role in this. Although it was preferable if women stayed at home, their mobility was less harmful if they were properly accompanied by men. In other words, women who did travel needed honourable male companionship to assist them. Groups of women in medieval times travelled accompanied by male protectors. The very fact that Tryphaena wanders around as a "free woman," accompanied by a man who is not her husband nor her owner, makes her suspicious. As is shown in Chapter 1, she is, indeed, met with deprecatory remarks and calls to "lash" her as an "accursed woman." The narrators of the texts discussed in this volume take care to describe the men, if unrelated, accompanying the "decent" women as worthy. Some have respectable, unsuspicious professions: they are schoolteachers (Chapter 3), or theologians and priests (Chapter 5). Others deserve to be respected and trusted due to their age, or poor health ("Monsieur. M." in Chapter 9), or behave according to the codes of gentlemen (Chapter 13). An intriguing example is Egeria, a nun travelling to the Holy Land in late Antiquity. In what is preserved of her travelogue she does not elaborate on her companions and even seems to suggest that she is the one in charge of the group. She does interact, however, with another type of companion: local people on whom she depends to show her around. They are invariably male. Much emphasis is placed on the fact that these men do not pose a threat to her in any way: they are "old, truly religious" and their conversations were not "about anything else than God's Scriptures or the deeds of great monks." Almost sixteen centuries later, Mary Pos, the first female travel journalist in the Netherlands, travels on her own, but constantly depends formally and informally on the men she meets to assist her (Chapter 15).

Even after the said changes in infrastructure, unaccompanied trips were hardly imaginable for women (Chapter 4). Chapter 8 describes the case of "Mademoiselle Rachel," doomed to travel despite being ill, whose male companions do their utmost to shelter her from the threats of the "masculine" world outside.

Lilla von Bulyovszky, as described in Chapter 10, systematically emphasises the weaknesses of her male companions, thereby stressing that she always kept her distance. Notwithstanding, some parts of the world remained no-go areas for women, even if they were accompanied by men; an interesting example of such an ideological structuring of space is described in Chapter 9, which argues that high altitudes were an exclusively male territory.

Men, on the other hand did not necessarily need to bring female companions. If they needed a woman, they could find one along the road. A rare example of a linguistic aid for travellers from the Middle Ages contains the translation of typical sentences having to do with the practicalities of a journey: how to ask for one's horse or gloves, a drink, more food or less. Interestingly, it also includes the sentence: "You have slept with the woman in your bed" (Chapter 3). Before setting out to a journey from the Crimea to China, a traveller could take an interpreter, men-servants and, if he wished, a woman with him. Many men, however, only travelled with other men. The celibate abbot Emo, for instance, despite the fact that he was trying to save a contested mixed-gender monastery, travelled with a trusted male friend. Men who did travel with female companions, more often than not depicted them (if at all) as dependent and in need of protection – which, evidently, does not necessarily reveal reality, but the male need to construct an identity as courageous adventurers (Chapter 4). In this sense, paradoxically, male travellers were dependent on female companions as well.

Narrative 2: beyond the discourse

To a certain extent, the first narrative above in fact repeats and reinforces the masculine hegemonic discourse. It implies that women *were* constrained: they either did not travel, or if they did, they generally obeyed the limitations put upon them by men. When they did disobey these rules, they suffered the consequences. In other words: according to this narrative, women had to remain within the boundaries fixed by men. Since the majority of travel accounts throughout history were written by men – at least: the official ones – this representation should not come as a surprise. It also warns us that we have to be careful to distinguish between discourse and reality (as pointed out in several chapters, for instance Chapter 1, 4, 9 and 12), despite the fact that some accounts by female travellers, such as the one by Ignatia Geertruida Timmers (Chapter 6), seem to conform to the same stereotypes. There may have been more women on the road than we will ever know, simply because many of them did not write themselves, and male travellers often did not feel the need to mention them in their travelogues (Chapter 6 and 9). We will never be able to conclude whether Rachel left the ship or not when berthing at Key West, for the two travelogues analyzed in Chapter 8 offer conflicting renderings of that moment: in one she does, at the arm of a captain – where a woman should be according to etiquette – but in the other she refuses to leave the ship, showing unexpected agency in doing so, "livrée sans doute à de tristes réflexions" (overwhelmed by sad reflections). Chéry's explanation is a typical example of what we want to argue in this section: within his masculine discourse, he claims to know with certainty why Rachel stays aboard, thus rendering her in the conventional position of a passive being, who is not in control of her emotional self. Within this narrative, he is unable to dwell on the remarkable fact that this woman has decided for herself that she will not go out. Through Chéry's words, or rather: despite his words, we perhaps see the vague contours of a stronger woman, escaping the male monopoly on the narrative and the representation of gender. Especially since she herself in one of her own letters, indirectly compares herself to Napoleon Bonaparte while gazing at the pyramids.

Several chapters in this book are dedicated to women who nevertheless seem to have escaped the male-dominated discourse. Although Adriana de la Court is accompanied by men, she constructs a very unusual identity for herself in her journals: that of a free woman who engages in all sorts of conventionally male activities. As is concluded in Chapter 4, she could probably do so because her diary was strictly meant for private use. On the other hand, the very fact that such an identity was imaginable and in no way represented as something outrageous, is telling. It was at least a discursive possibility that may well have had its counterpart in reality. The Marquise described in Chapter 5 was made of stern stuff, at least, according to her own depiction in her letters. For her trip to her daughter, 500 kilometres away, it is she who has to convince one of her male companions to join her because he "fears the perils," and on the way back, the 47-year-old woman wonders whether she had not done better to travel on "horseback, as some ladies do," since the roads are so dangerous that she sometimes has to walk next to the carriage. Her letters are full of spectacular obstacles that she and her companions had to overcome: horses drowning, or dying due to the heat, barges running aground, rain pouring, and carriages getting stuck in the mud. The image of her we get from her letters to her daughter is that of a brave, adventurous and very energetic woman – contrary to the traditional depiction of women as fragile and unable to deal with the hardships of travelling. The fact that on the last occasion boys from a neighbouring village come to carry her to the hostelry does not diminish that impression, since her companions have to be carried as well. A final point of interest, is that the Marquise seems to have travelled on her own as well, with just her staff. Another woman whose travel account challenges conventional gender roles to a certain extent, is Agnes Herbert (Chapter 12). Additionally, Ann Lister is a spectacular example of a woman venturing into the heart of male territory, as she was the first to reach the summit of the Vignemale (Chapter 9). These women precisely represent adventurous and independent female travellers – an image the male discourse often tried to neutralise by describing them as eccentric and dangerous outsiders (Chapter 6).

Interestingly some women omitted male companions in their travelogues to stress the idea that they travelled alone, as was the case with Mary Eyre (Chapter 9). This act points towards a feminine counterpart of the masculine hegemonic discourse: women, just like men, did not necessarily consider their texts as historiographical, but rather as an important tool in their identity politics. The first Dutch travel journalist Mary Pos (Chapter 15) may well be an example of this. In the 1930's she published an essay under the title "Why do so few Dutch girls travel on their own?". It is unclear whether this was indeed the case – there definitely were and had been some others, including Alexandrine Tinne (1835–1869) and Elisabeth "Lizzy" van Dorp (1872–1945) – but what is obvious is that this claim gives her the perfect opportunity to shape her own identity as a courageous pioneer, and, consequently, to inscribe herself in a fashionable worldwide trend of those days.[24]

What all these cases have in common, is that these women occupied exceptional social positions: they did not depend on men for their living. Adriana, the Marquise and Herbert were wealthy and single (unmarried or widowed). The openly lesbian Lister, already rich herself, married the even-wealthier Anne Walker, with whom she travelled. This volume contains other examples, however, of married women showing characteristics that are traditionally seen as masculine. Fanny Parkes, for instance, rather seemed to like travelling – considering it as a sport even – and appears just as courageous and clever as her husband. As a self-proclaimed ethnographer, Parkes toured India, even on her own (Chapter 7). In 1850, after returning to Europe, Parkes published her memoirs. This is a highly relevant fact: in doing so her views made it outside the private sphere into the typically male realm of the public sphere as well. Several of the women studied in this volume (Chapter 9 and 12) were professional writers and supported themselves through their writing – a position usually associated with men. Mary Pos eventually managed to finance her trips (partly) by selling her texts to magazines and newspapers (Chapter 15). Lister was an exception: she did not publish about her ascent and was eventually omitted in the travel account of the second traveller to reach the top, the Prince of Moskova (Chapter 9).

These examples suggest that there was a female counter discourse that valued female independency. This view was present in private documents, but also in the public sphere, as we saw, since a surprising number of travelogues written by women *did* get published – sometimes, but not always, with sufficient disclaimers to make the practice less suspicious. Often this counter discourse is characterised by ambiguity: it is not a full-blown attack or overthrowing of male hegemonic discourse, but a process of negotiation. Chapter 9 shows how the widow Selina Bunbury presented herself as an independent traveller on the one hand (one of her companions is even assigned the frailty usually associated with women), but on the other hand realised that her "freedom" was framed by male norms. The same ambiguity plays in the travel journal of Lilla von Bulyovszky (Chapter 10) as well: it is subversive and conforming at the same time. Both male and female characters in *Two Dianas in Alaska* deviate from and confirm conventional norms (Chapter 12). A very important finding from this particular chapter is that this case suggests that travelling women were perhaps not all as problematic in reality as the hegemonic discourse has us believe. Herbert's book became a popular and well-reviewed bestseller, like many similar books, and her hunting trip was sponsored by her uncle, which suggests male approval of what she did and the way she did it.

Interestingly, one of the reviewers even minimalised Herbert's subversivity, denouncing it as "only a few simple conventions."

As pointed out in Chapter 12, the hunting trip is the setting where such an otherwise unimaginable negotiation of traditional gender roles and social expectations becomes possible. The characters enter a kind of unknown, a-cultural space where existing norm systems lose their restrictive power, which we could thus call liminal. As we already argued, liminality can be defined in spatial, temporal, and ideological terms, and all three are closely intertwined. In some ways, travelling can be said to echo the carnivalesque frame of mind as described by Michael Bakhtin in *Rabelais and His World* (1984): people venture outside their familiar realm, with its well-known and tightly regulated set of norms and behavioural scripts, into the unknown, the different space of the Other. In many respects, the liminal space of the journey fits into Said's reconstruction of the discourse on the Oriental Other. The bishop quoted in Chapter 2 knows exactly why female pilgrims will end up morally corrupted if they travel: "the inns and caravanserays and cities in the east are so free and indifferent towards vice." This concept of liminal space has proven to be very important in this volume. The norms of companionship are redefined en route, in vehicles of all sorts (in cars and carriages, on boats), through "wild" landscapes (in the mountains, in the woods, in the arctic, in the colony). These first types could be described as "in between" spaces (in between domestic and public), the second as "undefined" spaces, which, at least in public imagination, were not yet charted and structured. For both, in a way, behavioural scripts were not (yet) available.

Another finding is that, at least in some cases, gender distinctions, in fact, did not seem to play a role at all, since they occur in what one could call an asexual constellation. The question of gendered companionship is not the right one, then. The example of Egeria could also be interpreted in another way than as above, as suggested in Chapter 2: not as a woman conforming to male norms and therefore attempting to neutralise the masculinity of her male companions, but as evidence of a reality that women like her apparently were free to travel, and that the entire enterprise was not necessarily to be understood in gendered terms. Her world was an asexual one, in which the men she meets remain vague, anonymous – reduced to a very specific role: to represent biblical figures who meet a late antique/early Christian ideal of an asexual brother- and sisterhood, even within marriages. Another example of this constellation of asexual companionship is the case described in Chapter 7, which analyses the way in which couples served their country in India. Despite the fact that the conventional separation of the spheres was enforced in official discourse, in reality, in many ways the difference between some memsahibs and their husbands seems to have been blurred. Men and women were colleagues and companions at the service of the Empire, rather than individuals of the opposite sex; they both participated in each other's "traditional" duties and sometimes even wore the same clothes. In a way, despite its apparent naughtiness, something similar is the case with Herbert's group of four (Chapter 12): these men and women share a social circle, class, and nationality, they have the same passion for adventure and they need each other's company to make it more enjoyable and even safe – and all these factors seem to be more important than their sex. They are fellows, rather than lovers – pretty much like Colin and Lisa Ross are called "Kamerads" in his writings (Chapter 14), androgynous beings who, in line with certain contemporaneous theories on modern families, are in a way each other's equals. If this is true, it means that not all phenomena having to do with men and women going on a journey together need to be interpreted along gender lines. We hope that our volume can function as a first step on the long road towards "the new history that may yet emerge as we begin to explore the pleasures men and women found in travelling together, in conflict and companionship" – to use Kelly's words in Chapter 12.

A journey through the volume

In the first chapter, Margherita Carucci suggests a new reading of Petronius' *Satyrica*: not as a satire of the social, religious, educational, rhetorical, and poetic concerns of his time, but as an opportunity to study the discourse on travel and gender, dominated by the male ruling class, in the early period of the Roman empire. On the one hand, she shows how the trope of a ship at sea constitutes a liminal space in which conventional Roman morality constantly seems to be transgressed by a set of characters whose behaviour does not conform to dominant social views on gender. On the other hand, however, Carucci argues that in the end this does not lead to the destruction of the dominant male ideology, quite the opposite. Despite their unconventionality, both men and women are characterised according to the established distribution of gender roles as expected in a patriarchal society: travelling women are fickle, lose control over themselves and are passive in cases of emergency; whereas men are depicted as travellers, courageous and, after all, in command. Carucci stresses the fact that this unconventional world becomes imaginable in the liminal situation of a sea journey, in a space lacking specificity and concreteness, geographically and ideologically. Since an authoritative narrator is lacking, it is up to the reader to evaluate the events and characters himself, according to his own value system.

In the second chapter Fabia Neuerburg studies a rare example of a travelogue written by a woman in late antiquity: *Itinerarium Egeriae*. En route, she visits historical and biblical sites and depends on the monks living nearby to guide her around. Interestingly, all characters in the story seem to be described in asexual terms: no one's gender is addressed, and the monks that accompany her on site are only described in a very sketchy way. They are systematically called "holy," which suggests that to Egeria the difference between biblical figures and living clerics is small, just like her depiction of the Holy Land is informed by biblical representations instead of a harsher reality that we are familiar with from other texts from that period. In other words, her travelling companions are literary constructions instead of real people.

The third chapter, by Dick de Boer, discusses medieval forms of companionship. Women were not supposed to travel, unless there were very good reasons (for instance religious) and they were accompanied by male guards. Men's mobility was regulated as well. Although they were allowed to travel for several reasons – religious, mercantile, diplomatic – their mobility had certain limitations. There was a taboo on clerics travelling with women, and it was strongly advised to never travel on one's own. De Boer describes a journey undertaken by Emo of Witte-wierum, a Frisian abbot, who travelled to Rome in the early thirteenth century, accompanied by a male friend from his youth. Tracing their itinerary and revealing how they succeeded in reaching their goals, De Boer uses this case study to reveal the importance of companionship in medieval travel writings.

Gerrit Verhoeven in the fourth chapter discusses gender differences in travel behaviour and discourse in Dutch and Flemish travel journals from the early modern period. Although the early seventeenth century offered few opportunities for women to travel, that changed from 1650 onwards, when due to several factors (new visions on masculine identity; new infrastructure; rise of family based leisure culture) new travel patterns emerged – family and leisure trips –, which left more room for women, be it within certain limits: they needed male supervision, stayed within clear geographical boundaries and had to conform to traditional role models. However, since most travelogues were written by men, it is questionable whether there was more to this last aspect than discursive othering: men depicted women in traditional ways to be able to bolster their own male identity. Verhoeven analyses one possible exception: Adriana de la Court. Although accompanied by men, in her journals she constructs a very unusual identity for herself: that of a free woman who engages in all sorts of conventionally male activities. She could probably do so because her diary was strictly meant for private use.

The fifth chapter, by Peter Rietbergen, studies the letters written during the second half of the seventeenth century by Mme de Sévigné when travelling through France. This offers the reader a view on numerous aspects of early modern travelling by an aristocratic widow, both material and cultural: making use of an aristocratic network for lodgings and dinners she usually but not always travelled with companions (family, servants, friends, among them a theologian and an abbot). Some of these "real" companions were not that interesting to the Marquise, however, prompting her to search for alternatives that, at least according to her letters, she seems to have found in the books that she read while en route. Tracing companions in texts in this chapter thus evolves into the analysis of texts as companions. Rietbergen also suggests that the downright impressive, not to say pathological number of letters Mme de Sévigné wrote to her child turns this daughter into a virtual companion on the road.

In the sixth chapter Alan Moss delves deeper into the new phenomenon Verhoeven identified: leisure trips in the Dutch Republic, which he identifies as "the missing link" between the practice of the Grand Tour and tourism. He analyses six case studies between 1669 and 1748, some written by men and some by women. Whereas the travel literature by men contains many precise observa-tions of the surroundings and either relegates female companions to the margins or employs them as a literary vehicle to showcase male bravery, the female counterparts tend to focus on the social aspects of a journey.

Chapter 7, by Ipshita Nath, concentrates on spousal behaviour during travels documented in the writings of memsahibs in colonial India from the late eighteenth century onwards. She finds that these women, depicted in official history as limited to the domestic sphere and entirely dependent on their husbands, are ascribed a different position in their own (epistolary) writings. Due to the very specific circumstances of the Raj (among others the necessity to travel), traditional roles for both genders remained fluid. Women seem to have held an insider-outsider position, from which they managed to contribute to the Empire without officially leaving the institution of marriage or family. Nath identifies them as "chroniclers" of an alternative or supplementary history of the Empire.

In the eighth chapter, Rob van de Schoor analyses the tour that the French tragedienne Rachel undertook overseas in the middle of the nineteenth century, as documented in the travelogues by two of her male companions, Jules Chéry and Léon Beauvallet. Van de Schoor shows how the two men act as chaperones to Rachel in a presumably threatening world that was clearly governed by a different etiquette and unimpressed by Rachel's art or celebrity in Europe.

In chapter 9 Martyn Lyons considers travellers and their travel writing in the mid-nineteenth-century Pyrenees. He first sketches important changes over three phases: firstly, the Enlightenment Pyrenees, when male geologists wrote scientific accounts for their male peer group; secondly, the Romantic Pyrenees, when travel writing became more impressionistic, and the genre allowed a space for female authors as well as female readers; thirdly, the rising vogue for mountaineering in mid-century, which celebrated masculinity and once again relegated female companions (and competitors) to obscurity. Lyons focuses on three British women in particular. The cases of Selina Bunbury, Georgiana Chatterton, and Ann Lister all reveal different aspects of female self-representation in a mountainous landscape, as companions, dependants, or competitors with male fellow travellers.

In the tenth chapter Ute Sonnleiter studies the travelogue Lilla von Bulyovszky wrote after her journey from Pest to Paris and back. The vehicles she used functioned as "other places," in which she could meet strangers in a safe and – to a certain extent – socially accepted way. In fact, they formed a kind of hybrid space, domestic and public at the same time. Von Bulyovszky cleverly made use of that ambiguity, avoiding all suspicion by ridiculing men, thereby simultaneously confirming to as well as undermining male hegemonic discourse.

Chapter eleven, by Rosella Perugi, is dedicated to the phenomenon of upper-class female travellers from Italy who visited Northern Europe from the end of the nineteenth century until the 1920's and reported on their trip. Perugi concentrates on the case of Elisa Cappelli, travelling with her former student and friend Ebba, a Swedish girl who lived in Italy for a long time. The two companions meet many people during their trip to Sweden and Cappelli cleverly sketches the country as an example for her own country to follow, without rejecting it.

In chapter twelve Tara Kathleen Kelly takes a closer look at gender, conflict and companionship in *Two Dianas in Somaliland*. Cowritten by well-known hunter Agnes Herbert and an anonymous male companion, the book raises provocative questions about current conceptions both of Edwardian travel and of gendered discourses in travel literature. Both authors repeatedly defied traditional gender conventions, in particular by assigning Herbert the "hero" role during two dramatic bear attacks. This offers a challenge to historiographical arguments that women travel writers in this period were constrained by gender from adopting the persona of the adventure hero, but also suggests that men may have experienced contemporaneous discourses of masculinity as more flexible than is usually assumed. The enthusiastic reviews that greeted the book also indicate that there was a variety of acceptable ways to construct gendered wilderness travel for both women and men. Unlike gendered discourse, however, racial constructions appear to have been far more stable, especially in terms of both authors' representations of native Alaskans. Even as they challenged conventional gender elements of masculine and feminine discourses, then, the cowriters also exposed the commonalities of class, race and imperial power that underlay their journey together.

Tom Sintobin analyzes the travelogue Cyriel Buysse wrote on a trip through France with three ladies. He shows how the rather dominant I-narrator systematically depicts his female companions as tourists, keen on comfort, conventional sights and limited in space. This allows him to construct his own identity as an autonomous traveller, as opposed to his luggage-like companions.

The fourteenth chapter, by Joachim Schätz and Katalin Teller, is dedicated to an immensely popular travelogue author in interwar Germany: Colin Ross. More specifically, they analyze the significance of the author's wife Lisa against the background of Weimar era culture. Three roles can be distinguished. In real life, she functioned behind the scenes as a mother and caregiver of the family. Since that household was redefined as a travelling unit in which the distinction between the private and the public collapsed, her largely uncredited conjugal labour included several organizational and editorial tasks as well. Second, she functions as a character in her husband's travelogues, fulfilling an array of functions: a guarantor of travel safety and smooth logistics, a coauthor – to a certain extent – of certain episodes, a brave (and often more rational and disciplined) companion, a point of reference for his thoughts on gender relations or family. Third, her presence, as is that of the children, is essential for several reasons. On the one hand, she (and the children) form the unique selling proposition of the Colin Ross brand in a crowded marketplace for travel media. On the other, travelling with his family allows him to "truly" get access to the cultures of the Others he meets without ever radically leaving his native land, even when on foreign soil: they embody the idea of the new German family as emissaries of a superior German ethos, as envisioned by National Socialism.

The volume concludes with a case study from the interwar period by Babs Boter. She examines the ways in which the Dutch "business girl" Mary Pos presented her travelling self in various texts. The reader gets the ambivalent image of a courageous, autonomous and witty young woman traveller on the one hand, who depends on men and blunders at times as well on the other. With this curious hybrid self-image she successfully negotiates en route with the (gendered) colonial, national, and class discourses of her time.

Notes

1 Lowe, E. 1857, *Unprotected Females in Norway: Or, The Pleasantest Way of Travelling There, Passing Through Denmark and Sweden, With Scandinavian Sketches From Nature* (London: G. Routledge & Co.): 3.
2 Kesselring, S. (2008), "The Mobile Risk Society," in: Canzler, W., Kaufmann, V., & Kesselring, S. (eds.) *Tracing Mobilities* (Aldershot: Ashgate): 77–102.
3 White, N.R., & White, P.B. (2008), "Travel as Interaction: Encountering Place and Others," in: *Journal of Hospitality and Tourism Management*, Volume 15, Issue 1: 42–48.
4 Choo, H., & Petrick, J. (2015), "The Importance of Travel Companionship and We-Intentions at Tourism Service Encounters," in: *Journal of Quality Assurance in Hospitality & Tourism*, Volume 16, Issue 1: 1–23.
5 Leterby, G., & Reynolds, G. (2009) "Preface. Gendered Journeys, Mobile Emotions," in: Leterby, G., & Reynolds, G. (eds.), *Gendered Journeys, Mobile Emotions* (Aldershot: Ashgate): xvii–xxi.
6 Leterby & Reynolds (2009): xix.
7 Leterby, G., & Reynolds, G. (2009), "Section 4. Introduction: Making the Journey – Travel and Travellers," in: Leterby, G., & Reynolds, G. (eds.), *Gendered Journeys, Mobile Emotions* (Aldershot: Ashgate): 159–164. Cfr. Pettinger, A. (2002), "Trains and Boats and Planes: Some Reflections on Travel Writing and Public Transport," in: Borm, J., & Le Disez, J-Y. (eds.), *Seuils et Traverses: enjeux de l'écriture de voyage* (Brest and Versailles), Volume 1: 107–115.
8 Cresswell, T., & Priya Uteng, T. (2008), "Gendered Mobilities: Towards a Holistic Understanding," in: Priya Uteng, T., & Cresswell, T. (eds.), *Gendered Mobilities* (Aldershot: Ashgate), 1–15: 2.
9 Wolff, J. (2008), "Foreword," in: Gómez Reus, T., & Usandizaga, A. (eds.), *Inside Out. Women Negotiating, Subverting, Appropriating Public and Private Space* (Amsterdam/New York: Rodopi): 15–18, 15.
10 See, for instance and among others: Foster, S., & Mills, S. (eds.) (2002), *An Anthology of Women's Travel Writing* (Manchester/New York: Manchester University Press); Amoia, A., & Knapp, B. (eds.) (2006), *Great Women Travel Writers. From 1750 to the Present* (New York/London: Continuum); Broome Saunders, C. (ed.) (2014), *Women, Travel Writing and Truth* (New York/London: Routledge); McKenzie Stearns, P. (ed.), *Women Rewriting Boundaries: Victorian Women Travel Writers* (Newcastle upon Tyne: Cambridge Scholars Publishing); O'Loughlin, K. (2018), *Women, Writing and Travel in the Eighteenth Century* (Cambridge: Cambridge University Press).
11 Thompson, C. (2017), "Journeys to Authority: Reassessing Women's Early Travel Writing 1763–1862," in: *Women's Writing*, Volume 24, Issue 2: 131–150.
12 See, among others: Thompson, C. (2011), *Travel Writing* (London/New York: Routledge); Shiba, K. (2012), *Literary Creations on the Road. Women's Travel Diaries in Early Modern Japan* (Lanham: University Press of America); Robinson-Tomsett, E. (2013), *Women, Travel and Identity: Journeys by Rail and Sea, 1870–1940* (Manchester/New York: Manchester University Press); Broome Saunders, C. (ed.) (2014), *Women, Travel Writing and Truth* (New York/London: Routledge).
13 Sen, A. (2015), "Traveling Companions: Women, Trade, and the Early East India Company," in: *Genre*, Volume 48, Issue 2: 193–214.
14 Holmberg, E.J. (2015), "Writing the Travel Companion in Seventeenth-Century English Texts about the Ottoman Empire," in: Hecket, H. (ed.), *Early Modern Exchanges. Dialogues between Nations and Cultures, 1550–1750* (London/New York: Routledge): 183–200.
15 Holmberg (2015): 184.
16 Zemon Davis as quoted in Holmberg (2015): 195.

17 Smyth as quoted in Holmberg (2015): 192.

18 Holmberg (2015): 197.

19 Thompson (2017): 132.

20 See, for instance: Crouch, D. (2000), "Places Around Us: Embodied Geographies in Leisure and Tourism," in: *Leisure Studies*, Volume 19, Issue 1: 63–76; White, N.R., & White, P.B. (2004), "Travel as Transition: Identity and Place," in: *Annals of Tourism Research*, Volume 31, Issue 1: 200–218; Andrews, H., & Roberts, L. (eds.) (2012), *Liminal Landscapes: Travel, Experience and Spaces In-between* (London/New York: Routledge); Gómez Reus, T., & Gifford, T. (eds.) (2013), *Women in Transit through Literary Liminal Spaces* (Basingstoke/New York: Palgrave Macmillan); Brooker, E., & Joppe, M. (2014), "Developing a Tourism Innovation Typology: Leveraging Liminal Insights," in: *Journal of Travel Research*, Volume 53, Issue 4: 500–508.

21 Leterby & Reynolds (2009): 160.

22 Wegner, P.E. (2002), *Imaginary Communities: Utopia, the Nation, and the Spatial Histories of Modernity* (Berkeley/Los Angeles, London: University of California Press): 11.

23 Jennings, R.A. (2004), "Women Writers and the Internal Combustion Engine: Passing Penelope Pitstop," in: Siegel, K. (ed.), *Gender, Genre & Identity in Women's Travel Writing* (New York/Bern: Peter Lang): 97–122.

24 See for instance Galletly, S. (2018) "The Spectacular Traveling Woman. Australian and Canadian Visions of Women, Modernity, and Mobility between the Wars," in: *Transfers. Interdisciplinary Journal of Mobility Studies*, Volume 7, Issue 1: 70–87.

1   On the ship in Petronius' *Satyrica*

Gender roles on the move in the early Roman Empire

Margherita Carucci

Adhuc loquebatur, cum crepuit ostium impulsum, stetique in limine barbis hor-rentibus nauta et: « Moraris, inquit, Eumolpe, tanquam properandum ignores». Haud mora, omnes consurgimus, et Eumolpus quidem mercennarium suum iam olim dormientem exire cum sarcinia iubet. Ego cum Gitone quicquid erat in alutam compono, et adoratis sideribus intro navigium.

He was still talking when the door was pushed open with a creaking sound and a sailor with a shaggy beard stood on the threshold and said: "You are wasting time, Eumolpus, as if you don't know we have to haste." Without any further delay, we all stand up and Eumolpus orders a certain hired servant of his, who at that time was sleeping, to go out with the baggage. Giton and I put together whatever was in the sack and, after praying the stars, we boarded the ship.[1]

Petronius, *Satyrica*, 99

With these few lines on the preparations of a sea journey, the Latin writer Petronius introduces the episode on a ship (99–115) in his novel *Satyrica*. The *Satyrica* is a first-person narrative told by Encolpius, a young man who moves from place to place together with his boy-love, Giton. He has various encounters with all kinds of people mostly living on the fringes of society, and has several adventures in his search for a free meal and sex. In the passage quoted above, the couple is described boarding a ship with the poetaster Eumolpus, who Encolpius had previously met in an art gallery of a Greek town in South Italy. Only after embarking do Encolpius and Giton discover that they have boarded the ship of Lichas, and are travelling with Tryphaena, who had good reasons to hate both the two young men. This unforeseen, unhappy encounter leads to a series of events on ship until the final shipwreck.

In the reading of this episode, modern scholars often highlight the parallels with the traditional epic wanderings of classical heroes,[2] the plots of romantic Greek novels,[3] or the conventions of dramatic scenes[4] and rhetorical speeches[5] that Petronius uses as a means of satirising social, religious, educational, rhetorical, and poetic concerns of his time. However, this tale of a fictional sea journey, in which men and women happen to travel together and interact with each other while *en route*, also contains significant elements for articulating a gendered discourse on travel in ancient Roman society that modern scholarship seems not to take into account. In this chapter I want to emphasise the way in which the novel both proclaims and problematises gender as a structuring category for the definition of social norms. Central to my argument is the notion of liminality as a spatial and ideological dimension in which the characters move and act. I will try to show how the lack of geographical or historical specificity and concreteness of the marine area, where the episode on the ship is set, contributes to create a narrative experience outside the boundaries of Roman morality. However, at the centre of this travel experience of freedom and indeterminacy remains the dominant male ideology with its gendered norms as the internal organising centre for seeing and evaluating the main characters on board the ship. Thus, while departing from expected models of male-female relationships by the standards of the early Empire, Petronius' fictional travelogue does reinforce ancient male ideas about female conduct and male behaviour. But, before any discussion of this fictional sea journey, it could be useful to outline the main questions that anyone approaching the *Satyrica* will inevitably end up asking. Firstly, who is the author of this novel?

In search of the author, or: La Questione Petroniana

The manuscripts containing the text of the *Satyrica* identify the author by the name of "Petronius," which remains just a name on the title page. Many scholars from the sixteenth century onwards have been tempted to identify the writer of the *Satyrica* with the Caius Petronius that the Roman historian Tacitus describes in his *Annales* (16.18–19). The first-century C.E. historian sketches a vivid portrait of this refined voluptuary, who had been governor of Bithynia (a region in modern Turkey) and later consul until he was admitted into the small circle of Nero's intimates as Arbiter of Taste; fallen in disgrace with the emperor and arrested at Cumae in 66 C.E., Petronius committed suicide. This courtier of Nero as described by Tacitus in his obituary notice might be the same Petronius that Pliny the Elder (*Historia Naturalis*, 37.20) and Plutarch (*Moralia*, 60 d-e) mention in a similar light, though the two writers give "Titus" as his first name. The initial C., short of Caius, as appears in Tacitus, may be a corruption of the text in the later process of copying the manuscripts of the historian. However, is Petronius as described by Tacitus, Pliny, and Plutarch the author of the *Satyrica*? Nowhere in the ancient tradition it is said that this T. or C. Petronius is the author of a work titled *Satyrica*; nor are there many testimonies for this novel. The first reference to the work of Petronius appears in Terentianus Maurus writing around 200 C.E.[6] The work is also mentioned by Marius Victorinus in his *Ars Grammatica* (6.143) dated to the fourth century. These references provide no more than a *terminus post quem* that does not answer the question "When was the *Satyrica* written?" Lacking secure external references to the date of the *Satyrica*, scholars look at many elements inside the work that may support a particular date. Most scholars have tried to place the action of the novel, the characters, and the events against the historical and cultural evidence of the Neronian age, anchoring both author and novel in the 60s.[7] Some other scholars prefer to follow Enzo

Marmorale's proposal to date the novel to the second century on linguistic grounds.[8] Marmorale's suggested date has been rejected by René Martin and François Ripoll, who place the text in the Flavian period (69–98).[9] A secure identification of the author and dating proves to be very difficult given the novel's fragmentary state of conservation. In fact, the 141 chapters forming the *Satyrica* in our modern editions are a collection of larger and smaller fragments and excerpts, which have been transmitted in various manuscripts and assembled into one text by scholars between 1482 and 1669. We do not know how many books or chapters the original *Satyrica* included: The calculation of a 24-book structure analogous to that of the *Odyssey* because of the number of allusions to Homer's poem in Encolpius' narrative[10] remains guesswork without additional evidence.

This essay is not about supporting or rejecting a date of composition or identity of the author through a combination of external and internal evidence. I will accept the general consensus that ascribes the *Satyrica* to a writer named Petronius, probably belonging to the Roman elite class, and I will place the novel in the social context of the early Empire, leaving aside the question of a more precise date. Depriving the *Satyrica* of a historically situated author and date may puzzle the reader who is accustomed to making sense of what s/he is reading through a continuous reference to the historical times and social conditions in which the author lived. In the case of the *Satyrica*, however, this lack of secure references may help the reader to change the perspective from which to read the novel.

Representing and voicing reality

The realism of Petronius and the use of his novel as a potential document of Roman social life have been widely discussed in modern scholarship.[11] Populated by characters that go through bizarre sufferings and grotesque experiences, the world of the *Satyrica* cannot certainly be visualised as a simple mirror of historical reality. Leaving aside the question as to whether narrative imagination is somehow less truthful about lived experiences than historical writings as the product of elite males and their ideologies, I interpret the *Satyrica* as a document of the ways in which the male ruling class of imperial Roman society constructed their models of normative behaviours. In other words, the episode on the ship will be not read as offering an authentic background against which to document the travel practices in the Roman Empire. This essay is not so much about reality as about the ways of representing reality, more specifically in the context of gender roles and norms in the early imperial period. But who is representing reality? From whose point of view is reality to be viewed? And, since this essay focuses on ideal norms of gender, what ideology is the narrator aligned with? This brings us to the discussion of the voice and authority of the author and the narrator.

The narratorship of the *Satyrica* is a hotly debated topic whose complexity lies in the structure of the narrative.[12] The novel, in fact, is a first-person

narrative told by Encolpius at a later date, as explicit references to remembering or retelling in the text make clear.[13] Encolpius thus plays the dual role of
the young protagonist of the adventures told in the book and of the I-narrator
as the old man who recounts those episodes. A further complexity lies in the
lack of development for Encolpius' character: We expect the older I-narrator
to comment on the events in which his former self acted and thus provide
us with an interpretive framework expressing the evaluative stance of the
author of the work. In the *Satyrica*, however, these expectations are not met,
because there is no clear dividing line between the young character and the
supposedly mature narrator. The result is a polyphony – or, one might say,
cacophony – that makes it difficult to distinguish between narrative levels and
therefore deprives us of a extradiegetic narrator of the highest level who
guides us while reading and interpreting the story. The reader experiences a
sort of full immersion in the narrative world that continuously challenges his
position as somebody outside the story who looks down on the Petronian
characters.

What makes a man and a woman

The passage quoted at the beginning of this chapter briefly describes how
Encolpius and Giton ended up boarding ship together with the older Eumolpus.
The arrival of the sailor, who warns Eumolpus that the ship is about to leave
soon, suggests that the old man had made some travel arrangements before
encountering Encolpius in the art gallery, which is confirmed later in the novel
when Eumolpus states that his decision to sail on the ship had been taken long
before meeting the two young men.[14] Since the sea voyage with its pirates,
tempests, and shipwrecks is a stock motif that often occurs in the plot of ancient
novels as a narrative strategy for the description of new adventures, the briefly
described preparations of the sea trip in Petronius' *Satyrica* seem to promise
further incidents for the protagonist. On board the ship, Encolpius, Giton, and
Eumolpus find "a very secluded spot below deck"[15] for rolling themselves up in
rugs and sleeping when two familiar voices are heard from the poop deck.[16]
Encolpius and Giton wake the drowsing Eumolpus, who confirms their fears: The
ship belongs to Lichas of Tarentum and he is conveying Tryphaena to his native
town. From the surviving fragments and internal references we may reconstruct
the first encounter between these four characters, though lacunae can be filled
only with academic conjecture. Lichas was on very intimate terms with
Encolpius,[17] but the relationship ended when Encolpius seduced Lichas' wife
Hedyle[18] and stole the sacred rattle and robe of Isis as the tutelary deity of
Lichas' ship.[19] Tryphaena had been Encolpius' lover[20] before turning her attentions to Giton.[21] Encolpius and Giton had outrageously insulted Lichas in the
colonnade of Hercules and Tryphaena in the presence of a crowd,[22] though the
specific details of these insults are difficult to reconstruct. Eumolpus describes
Lichas and Tryphaena as follows:

Lichas Tarentinus, homo verecundissimus et non tantum huius navigii dominus, quod regit, sed fundorum etiam aliquot et familiae negotiantis, onus deferendum ad mercatum conducit. Hic est Cyclops ille et archipirata, cui vecturam debemus; et praeter hunc Tryphaena, omnium feminarum formosissima quae voluptatis causa hic atque illuc vectatur.

Lichas of Tarentum is a very respectful man and owner of not only this ship that he sails, but also of a certain number of farms and servants in business; he's carrying cargo that needs to be delivered to the market. This is your Cyclops, the pirate-chief, to whom we owe our transportation. And beside him Tryphaena, the most beautiful of all women, who travels to and fro for pleasure.[23]

Eumolpus' initial assessment of Lichas and Tryphaena is based on a set of well-defined attitudes and expectations surrounding gender roles in Roman society. The male character is outlined by his position in society in terms of possessions (ship, farms, and servants) and authority (the expression *navigii dominus, qui regit* – "owner of the ship that he sails" – suggests the idea of command), which demand and guarantee high respect. Though Roman aristocrats considered commerce unworthy and senators were banned from owning merchant ships,[24] wealthy merchants enjoyed respectability and were positively described by elite authors.[25] A number of monuments and inscriptions also commemorate, in positive terms, businessmen who conducted business in distant places, such as Lichas. Thryphaena, by contrast, is characterised by her femaleness in terms of physicality and appearance (*omnium feminarum formosissima*: "the most beautiful of all women"), though she too is wealthy, as the number of servants accompanying her in her sea journey suggests. The noun *femina* (from the Greek verb *phuo*, "to produce") refers to sex and can be applied to animals, plants, and minerals while in grammar it is used to indicate the feminine gender. Its sexual connotation is reinforced by the term *formosissima*, the superlative form of the adjective *formosa* which is mostly used to denote the fine exterior forms of visible objects. The reason for Tryphaena's travels is equally linked to physicality: The term *voluptas* refers to pleasure or satisfaction in sensual terms. The dominant trait of her character is emphasised also by the etymology of her name, from the Greek noun *tryphé* to describe delicate living or self-indulgence and the verb *truphao* meaning "to live luxuriously or in pleasure." The image of Tryphaena reminds us of other travelling ladies of luxury in Latin literature, such as Cynthia and Eppia. In his references to Cynthia's travels, the Augustan poet Propertius fears that his mistress' whereabouts may distract the woman from her love for the poet and give young men occasions for seducing his lover.[26] In one of his satires, the late first-/ early second-century C.E. poet Juvenal describes Eppia, the senator's wife who left behind her home, husband, children, and sister and accompanied a troop of gladiators to Alexandria. The Latin satirist adds that in her pursuit of pleasure Eppia was not much concerned by her reputation or the difficulties of the sea voyage.[27] The fragmentary status of the *Satyrica* makes it difficult to conjecture whether Tryphaena, like Cynthia and Eppia, had left her husband or lover for travelling around.

The lack of specific references or allusions to a husband or marital status in the surviving portion of the novel would suggest that Tryphaena was a free woman, which makes her position as a female traveller more ambiguous. Accounts of Roman women's journeys in ancient non-fictional writings show that most ancient women travelled mainly to accompany a male member of their family or their owner, if slaves; they may also have travelled in the company of servants, hired protectors, or other female companions.[28] Regardless of the travel arrangements, the main purpose of Roman women's journeys were not for their own but for a man's sake, even when ancient record seems to suggest that women may have travelled without a man as an escort.[29] Tryphaena, by contrast, is described as being in the socially ambiguous position of travelling with a man (Lichas), who is not her husband or relative or hired protector; nor does it seems that she has embarked on a sea journey in order to meet a male relative. Tryphaena, however, is not the only protagonist to be characterised by ambiguity according to the gendered norms of Roman society. Social and gender ambiguity is a shared feature, which is prominent in all of the main Petronian characters, as will be discussed in the next section.

Social and gender ambiguity

We find Lichas and Tryphaena the next morning discussing the dreams they had the night before.[30] The captain has been informed by Priapus that Neptune led Encolpius onto his boat and Tryphaena dreamt that the statue of the god, which she had seen at Baiae, told her that she would find Giton aboard Lichas' ship. The message of these parallel dreams is clear and delivered in direct speech without danger of misinterpretation. Nevertheless, Eumolpus, who happens to be with the captain and his friend, tries to ridicule these visions by invoking the teachings of Epicurus, who denied to dreams any transcendental significance. The location in the ship where this scene takes place is not specified; nor is it clear why Eumolpus is with the captain and his privileged passenger. Notwithstanding, it is clear that, after their conversation on the poop deck the night before, Lichas and Tryphaena retired in two separate cabins. In fact, when the captain talks about his dream the next morning, Tryphaena shudders at the similarity to her dream and says: "You would think we've slept together."[31] While assuring the reader that the captain and his female friend are not involved in any romantic or sexual relationship, this line highlights Tryphaena's licentious character rather than her moral integrity. A good woman would not find it appropriate to even allude to the possibility of sleeping in the same room with a man who is of no relation; an allusion that Tryphaena makes in plain terms in the presence of two other men with whom she seems not to be on intimate terms: The poet Eumolpus and, as we will apprehend later in the text, Hesus as another passenger of Lichas' ship. Not convinced by the Epicurean views expressed by Eumolpus, Lichas suggests searching the boat so as not to disregard the manifestations of the divine mind. The search is also instigated by Hesus who informed the captain that the night before, while leaning over the ship's side vomiting, he had caught the unknown Encolpius and Giton shaving their heads in the moonlight,[32] certainly a bad omen for the captain who believes in this particular superstition of not allowing the cutting of hair or nails during a sea trip. The search leads to the recognition of Encolpius and Giton, who, in their plans to escape from the boat, had been convinced by Eumolpus to shave their heads, trace brandmarks on their foreheads with ink, and pretend to be recaptured runaway slaves. After the set-up of an impromptu mock court that risked escalating into physical violence, peace is restored and celebrated with a banquet, during which Eumolpus tells the story of the *matrona* of Ephesus.

In these scenes of recognition, fight, and final peace all the characters onboard gather together and take part in the action either as active agents or as spectators. Their characterization is apparently well defined by the role that they play in this tale of a fictional sea journey: The superstitious captain Lichas and his crew; the luxurious Tryphaena and her servants; the creative Eumolpus and his hired servant; the jealous Encolpius and his lover Giton; and the indefinite number of anonymous passengers from whom only Hesus is singled out. However, the fanciful character of the story and its marine location in an uncertain space between two coastal towns of South Italy contribute to create a paradoxical and a-normative world, in which recognised social norms are turned upside down. This is evident, for instance, in the scene of the mock court that was set up following the recognition of the homosexual couple. The court consists of Encolpius and Giton as the accused, Eumolpus as their defence counsel, and Lichas as both the accuser and the judge. During the mock trial, Eumolpus presents the two accused as freeborn persons,[33] but their legal status is contradicted by their current disguise as branded fugitives. Moreover, a freeborn man has the right and privilege of having control over what he says or happens to his body, even when he is charged with some accusation: Encolpius and Giton do not enjoy this privilege or claim their right while Lichas and Eumolpus deliver their speeches in the mock court.[34]

Lichas is represented as a successful merchant who shows his ability in the command of a naval vessel and speech (in the mock trial, his response to Eumolpus' arguments is clearly articulated and structured[35]). However, his image as a man-in-command contrasts starkly with his excessively superstitious beliefs and reverence of gods that Lichas is not able to control with rationality and wisdom as expected from a man of his position. Lichas' characterization as a superstitious man adds to the ambiguity of his character. In his decision to inflict punishment on the disguised fugitives as a ritual that the captain deems as necessary for appeasing the tutelary divinity of the ship, Lichas acts as the captain of the ship, who has religious responsibility toward his crew and passengers.[36] However, Lichas' death at the end of the episode reinforces the ambiguous state of the world in which the Petronian characters live: Prudent people, such as Lichas, who show much reverence to the gods, are not rewarded nor live longer than individuals, such as Encolpius and his friends, who seem to be oblivious to the insights and demands of religion.

The social ambiguity surrounding the Petronian characters appears more evidently in overtly sexual contexts and relationships. Within the specific framework of the episode on ship, the bi-sexual Encolpius is represented as excessively jealous of his lover Giton who, by contrast, does not refuse Tryphaena's attentions. Encolpius is unable to decide whether to be angrier with the boy for robbing him from his ex-girlfriend or with the woman for seducing his current lover. Lichas is described as a man with a strong sense of right and wrong who appeals to rights or a sense of justice for a punitive action against Encolpius' earlier injuries to him; the fierce captain is never shown engaged in a promiscuous relation with either Tryphaena or any of his other passengers.[37] However, Lichas is no paragon of virtue: The fierce captain had known Encolpius so intimately in the past that he can easily recognise his ex-lover disguised as a fugitive slave by only touching his genitals.[38]

The twisted world of Petronius' *Satyrica* is filled with figures who do not conform to recognised social and gender categories and who trouble the categories themselves with the result of a fluid and ambiguous society, where the codes of conventionally respectable behaviour are constantly transgressed.

Notwithstanding, I would like to argue in the next section that in the *Satyrica* gender remains a powerful structuring category for the definition of social norms, including those governing travel. Particularly useful for the purpose of my discussion is the inset-tale of the *Matrona* of Ephesus.[39]

Clearly, all women are the same

During the banquet following the mock trial, Eumolpus tells the story of the *Matrona* of Ephesus as a form of amusing entertainment for the crew and the passengers celebrating the peace restored on the ship. The story of the *Matrona* of Ephesus seems not to be related to the whole episode on the ship in which it is inserted. The tale, in fact, can be isolated from the narrative context of the *Satyrica* without disrupting the sequence of events. Nevertheless, the story adds to the characterization of the main characters of the episode on the ship; it also reinforces traditional ideas about gendered roles and expectations. The story tells of a married woman from Ephesus, who was widely known for her *pudicitia* ("chastity, modesty"). She superbly proved her faithfulness and marital virtues when her husband died and she moved with her maidservant into the tomb with the intention of starving to death. The lamp lighting in the tomb attracted the curiosity of a soldier, who was guarding some crucified robbers nearby. With the help of the maidservant, the man persuaded the widow to eat and then successfully mounted an attack on her virtue. The two lovers bedded down together in the tomb for two days, but on the third night the parents of one of the robbers removed their son's body for proper burial. Terrified and fearing capital punishment for neglect of duty, the soldier resolved to kill himself, but the widow refused to weep over another loved one and ordered the soldier to fix her husband's corpse up on an empty cross. The story provokes different reactions in the audience: The sailors laugh; Tryphaena blushes and leans her cheek on

Giton's neck; and Lichas comments disapprovingly upon the behaviour of the governor who should have replaced the husband's body in the tomb and crucified the woman.

The story prompts an association between the *matrona* of Ephesus and Tryphaena as the only female passenger on Lichas' ship.[40] At first reading, the two female characters seem to represent two opposite models of female behaviour, starting with the terms used to name them. Tryphaena is named after the Greek word *tryphé* to highlight her role and character as a licentious and luxurious woman; the unnamed woman in the inset-tale, by contrast, is significantly described as *matrona*, a Latin term meaning "married woman" but that very early acquired the additional idea of moral dignity and rank: The word *matrona* signified not only an upper-class woman, who was the wife of an elite male, but also female virtues, such as chastity and modesty, that a good woman was required to embody.[41] Whilst the *matrona* carefully stages her own image as the most renowned example of *pudicitia* to display as a theatrical spectacle for a wide audience,[42] Tryphaena constructs her image of a sensual woman that uses her beauty and charm for her own pleasure within a restricted circle of spectators. However, the more evident element of contrast between the two female characters is in the dichotomy between staticity and mobility. In the ancient male construction of ideal womanhood, the natural place for women and femininity was to be found within the private world of house and family. This idea is expressed in a number of Roman writings. For example, in a funerary epitaph from Rome, Amymone, wife of Marcus, is praised for being *lanifica, pia, pudica, frugi, casta*, and *domiseda* ("a woolworker, dutiful, modest, temperate, chaste, and one who stays at home").[43] Another funerary inscription from the African town of Mactar commemorates a wife and mother *nihil potius cupiens quam ut sua gauderet domus* ("who desired nothing more than to rejoice in her house").[44] The *matrona* of Ephesus seems to embody this traditional male ideal perfectly well: She is shown as confined within the boundaries of a town (Ephesus) and the closed space of a tomb. Tryphaena, by contrast, is represented as a wanderer who resists being pinned down to an exact location and challenges the male association between femininity and domesticity. Her character may reflect a new image of the Roman woman in imperial times, when the changing political and social circumstances gave, especially upper-class women, more opportunities for stepping into the more public (and male) sphere of politics and power. Yet, the image of the woman who centres her life on her family and restricts her daily activities to those within the domestic walls was an ideal that never lost its power and attraction in Roman society. Nor did the greater opportunities for women to step out of the house and travel on a short or long journey change the male belief that being away from the male-controlled domestic sphere could have exposed a woman to the danger of moral corruption.[45] These traditional male ideas of what and where a woman ought to be form the backdrop against which Petronius constructs his female characters.[46] In fact, the main female characters of the *Satyrica* (Quartilla, Tryphaena, and Circe) are shown to move in public spaces[47] where they act as amoral and sexually predatory women according to the moral standards of correct female behaviour. The only exception is Fortunata, the wife of the rich *libertus* Trimalchio, who is significantly never portrayed outside the premises of her domestic building. In the paradoxical world of the novel, Fortunata embodies the male ideal of what ought to be a good woman: A caring wife who stays at home, is able to run her husband's business affairs, and accepts her husband's authority when beaten by him.[48]

The *matrona* of Ephesus too is described as the perfect wife who shapes her social identity around the domestic virtues of chastity and modesty. However, as soon as her husband's death sets her free from marital control and authority, the *matrona* gives in to the soldier's blandishments in the semi-public area of a tomb from which her parents, relatives, and even magistrates had departed after their vain attempts at taking her back home.[49] A further element that the *matrona* and Tryphaena seem to have in common is the fickleness that was considered as a typical characteristic of the female sex. In Eumolpus' words, in fact, the short story serves to exemplify women's fickle character, a motif that occurs very often in male-written Latin texts, where the terms *infirmitas sexus* or *infirmitas consilii, levitas animi, imbecillitas sexus,* and *fragilitas sexus* were interchangeably used to describe the biologically determined vulnerability or incapacity of women. The *matrona* proves the emotional instability of her sex when, for the joys of love and life, she gives up the idea of starving to death over her husband's corpse. Tryphaena is often portrayed as a woman who is unable to make up her mind with regards to her feelings toward Giton. Her swinging between anger for the injury inflicted on her in the past and attraction toward the young boy irritates the more emotionally stable Lichas, who addresses Tryphaena as a "naïve woman."[50] In the portrayal of women who appear as sexually unrestrained or promiscuous in public spaces, Petronius, the irreverent author of absurd themes, characters, and situations, proves to comply with accepted standards of Roman morality by reiterating the common belief among the male members of Roman society that women were naturally prone to dangerous excesses and unable to control themselves, hence the need for their seclusion in the domestic realm of home where it would have been easier for their kinsmen to monitor them.

The travelling man

Petronius shows the same conformity to the dominant male ideology in the characterization of the male characters. Though they are as promiscuous as their female counterparts, their patterns of behaviour are not influenced by the domestic or public dimension of the space in which they move. Lichas, for instance, is portrayed as a married man who allows himself every licence, while he is deeply pained by any breach of wifely decorum; the *demimondain* Encolpius behaves similarly in both private and public spaces. Following long-standing male ideologies which see a close association of men and masculinity with public spaces and mobility, Petronius portrays his male characters as frequent travellers who comfortably wander about the known Graeco-Roman world. Eumolpus, for instance, appears to be a regular traveller: Earlier in the novel, the poet tells that he had been taken to Asia as a paid assistant to the *quaestor* and was given accommodation in Pergamum;[51] on the ship, while discussing various schemes of escape, he seems to show some knowledge of the ship's structure and sailors' normal duties.[52] The departure scene does not specify the reason why Eumolpus had to sail to Tarentum, where the ship was heading to, but it is evident that the main reason of his frequent journeys was a lucrative one, that is, to find occasions for getting some money and seducing young boys. In his first encounter in the art gallery, Encolpius is left in no doubt, from his look of concentration and shabby outfit, that Eumolpus is a man of letters that rich people hate; an impression that is confirmed when the poet is pelted with stones by bystanders as he declaims his lines.[53] Later, after the shipwreck, on the road to Croton that a countryman describes as a place whose inhabitants' main occupation is legacy hunting, Eumolpus proclaimed that such a means of getting rich was quite attractive to him.[54] In his decision to stop in the Greek town, he seems to have forgotten his initial plan of sailing to Tarentum, where he probably did not have any specific business to carry out. His questionable activities must have been somewhat lucrative if he could afford to hire a servant who followed him in his wanderings.[55] As travel companions of the poet, Encolpius and Giton too were used to travelling very often. Evidence gathered from references in the text and in the fragments suggests that Encolpius had been in Massilia and, along with Giton, in a town in the Bay of Naples[56] before both being shipwrecked in Croton. A fragment makes reference to a religious ceremony at Memphis in Egypt, which might be another place of Encolpius' wanderings.[57] Unlike Eumolpus, the two young lovers had not planned to sail to Tarentum but readily accept the poet's invitation to follow him and remain in Croton after the shipwreck. As the captain of a merchant ship, Lichas is the only character whose purpose of sailing is specified: "he's carrying cargo that needs to be delivered to the market".[58] However, this detail, which is inserted in Encolpius' brief introduction of the captain and Tryphaena, seems to aim at highlighting and reiterating the natural juxtaposition between male and female gender: While Lichas is representative of the males who travel for honourable purposes such as commercial transactions, Tryphaena exemplifies the category of female travellers whose purpose for stepping out of the home can only be the pursuit of sensual pleasures.

The double standard

Petronius' characterization of the male and female *en route* is thus based on a "double standard"[59] whereby the men are not criticised for their loose behaviour in public, while the women are judged with explicitly deprecatory remarks. When the mock trial turns violent, the narrator Encolpius addresses Tryphaena as an "accursed woman and the only person in the whole ship who deserved to be lashed."[60] His angry outburst is justified by his noble intentions to protect his lover Giton from the lecherous woman, but nowhere in the surviving portion of this episode does Encolpius (or the other characters) make similarly offensive remarks about the hot-tempered Lichas, though the latter does not hide nor suppress his contempt toward the young man. This more benevolent attitude toward the fierce captain is attested again when a storm suddenly interrupts the sea journey and causes Lichas' death by drowning. When the next morning Lichas' corpse is washed ashore, Encolpius cries over the man, who shortly before had been so fearsome and relentless, and prepares a pyre for his cremation and burial.[61]

The narrative of the sudden storm and the passengers' reaction seems to further support my argument that Petronius uses the confusing and contradictory portraits of men and women as a means to advocate the male constructions of masculine and feminine ideals:

> *Postquam manifesta convaluit, Lichas trepidans ad me supinas porrigit manus et: "Tu, inquit, Encolpi, succurre periclitantibus, et vestem illam divinam sistrumque redde navigio. Per fidem, miserere, quemadmodum quidem soles." Et illum quidem vociferantem in mare ventus excussit, repetitumque infesto gurgite procella circumegit atque hausit. Tryphaenam autem propem iam fidelissimi rapuerunt servi, scaphaeque impositam cum maxima sarcinarum parte abduxere certissimae morti.*

> When the storm grew clearly strong, Lichas stretched out imploring hands in panic toward me and said: "You, Encolpius, help us who are in danger, and give back to the ship the sacred robe and rattle. I implore you, have pity, as you were used to." As he was crying out, the wind swept him into the sea; he rose again from the raging whirlpool, then a hurricane whirled him round and sucked him down. Tryphaena, on the contrary, was grabbed by her very devoted servants, placed in the ship's boat along with most of her luggage and rescued from certain death.[62]

In this final scene, Lichas' death may appear as the ironic outcome of excessively superstitious beliefs and fears.[63] Even his burial by his enemy Encolpius in a foreign land, where no relative or friend could mourn him, contrasts with the idealised image of the man who has control over his body and dies at home with his nearest and dearest nearby to catch his last breath with a kiss.[64] Yet, paradoxically, in the very moment preceding his drowning, when he makes the last attempt at saving his life and that of the people on board his ship, Lichas proves to possess some of those qualities that in Roman male ideology defined manhood, that is, command and courage. His ultimate action, that is, imploring Encolpius to return the stolen rattle and robe of Isis as the tutelary divinity of the ship, may appear as the foolish attempt of a superstitious man. Nevertheless, his last deed prompts an association with the ideal of the male as an active agent, which is further emphasised by the contrast with the description of Tryphaena as passive. In peril Tryphaena seems able to take no action but to let her servants manage the dangerous situation by placing her and her luggage in the ship's boat. The servants' prompt action may reflect the expectations of a class which expects servants to do whatever is necessary to make their owner's life run smoothly. The stereotyped image of the woman as passive and helpless is highlighted by the structure of the sentence, which opens with Tryphaena's name in the accusative (*Tryphaenam*), that is, the case indicating the direct object, and ends with *servi* in the nominative as the subjects of the verb *rapuerunt* to signify the action of being carried off by force. The mention of the luggage adds to the standardised portrayal of women as frivolous creatures, since the reader is promptly reminded of Tryphaena's wigs of different colour that her servants had used to conceal Encolpius' and Giton's baldness during the banquet.[65] Again, Petronius uses the favourite rhetorical motifs in patriarchal ideology for the portrayal of the female character of Tryphaena, though textual evidence shows that ancient women were capable of facing the dangers of the sea heroically. Seneca, for instance, praises his aunt for her very brave behaviour during a sea storm while she was travelling with her husband. In the very moment when her life was most at risk, the woman did not look for a way off the wrecked ship but resolved to rescue her husband's body and give him a proper burial.[66]

The last scene in the account of the shipwreck focuses on Encolpius and Giton, who tie themselves together to die in each other's arms after expressing their loving feelings in a sentimental dialogue.[67] The rhetorical heightening of the speeches made by the two lovers at a moment of stress serves to parody the heroes of Greek novels, who often lament that they will be separated from their lovers because of a terrible disaster.[68] However, what makes this melodramatic scene more farcical is the extent to which the two protagonists subvert traditional definitions of masculinity. In Roman ideology, death was perceived as a privileged moment, which had the capacity to reveal the true character of the dying person. Needless to say, the true character that was expected from a man was linked to masculine virtues, such as bravery and determination. The Petronian lovers in distress fail to manifest these highly moral virtues, when they surrender to the idea of death instead of fighting against it. The image of the couple tied together and waiting for death goes counter to what emerges often in the writings of Roman authors, for whom dying was fundamentally an active rather than a passive process.[69] Moreover, the triviality and emptiness of frequently used phrases as exemplified in the words of Encolpius and Giton are a far cry from the noble and elevated speeches that men are expected to make while facing death.

Travelling in liminal space

The motif of the journey, either by sea or land, occurs in almost all of the surviving Greek and Latin novels written under the Roman Empire. This stock motif is introduced in the plot mainly as a narrative device for more adventures and entertainment to come. In Petronius' *Satyrica*, for example, the protagonists' sea journey served to move the scene of action from the Bay of Naples to the Greek town of Croton, where Encolpius and his travelling companions will end up after the storm and the shipwreck. In spite of their fanciful character and use in ancient narrative, literary representations of travels are a reflection of Roman practice. As textual and archaeological evidence shows, the movement of people, goods, and ideas was deeply embedded in the lived experience of Roman society and facilitated by a highly sophisticated and extensive transport network, which was developed and sustained by the consolidation of the centralised Roman power over a vast area of the inhabitable world.

In the *Satyrica*, the protagonists move in the familiar area of the Graeco-Roman world. Notwithstanding, the indefinite and uncertain area of the unknown sea, where the episode of the sea journey is set, places the protagonists in a space which lacks specificity and concreteness not just geographically but also ideologically. In this space everything is indefinite, unknown, and free of the laws governing the social and cultural life of the homeland; the protagonists are private individuals deprived of any connection with their country, their social group, and their family. The only personal link they could claim as a group is the one with the past: Encolpius, Giton, and Eumolpus had met Lichas and Tryphaena before boarding the ship. Nevertheless, in the liminal space of the sea journey, even the terms of relationships established in the more definite past become loose and abstract. Though Lichas and Tryphaena had very good reasons for hating the homosexual couple and demanding justice for the offences committed in the past, the mock trial ends with a sudden reconciliation among the four protagonists. The liminality of the world in which the Petronian characters move may provide an explanation for their apparent departure from traditional gender roles; in the undefined space of sea they are even more free to deviate from normative gender behaviour. For, in this quintessentially marginal and abstract space, the travellers are not required to locate a meaning and hence an objective for their behaviour; the patriarchal ideology with its well-defined codes of conventionally respectable behaviour, through which to construct male and female identities, can lose its power and authority. Yet, the male-initiated order remains the internal organising principle for evaluating social and gendered behaviour and thus restoring its legitimacy. In fact, while undermining the traditional gender constructs, the fictional tale reaffirms the specific cultural values of the dominant male ideology. Bearing in mind that unconventionality establishes norms much as social codes do, the irreverent and non-normative behaviour of the Petronian characters is depicted against an implied background of the patriarchal ideology with which the author and his readers were familiar. For, in the construction of characters that are unable or unwilling to conform to the norms of the dominant male ideology, the author highlights the traditional masculine and feminine ideals as terms of reference for interpreting his characters. Those ideals are not completely missed or deprived of their force and legitimacy, even though the liminality of the world in which the Petronian characters move seems an invitation to depart from traditional gender roles. The protagonists on the ship seem to have immediate access to those ideals, which, however, remain just an idea. For instance, Tryphaena blushes after listening to the tale of the *Matrona* of Ephesus but continues seducing the younger Giton;

Lichas acknowledges his right to punish those who have betrayed his friendship, but, after the mock trial, the captain tries to restore the sexual relationship with his former enemy Encolpius. Yet, those traditional male ideas about female conduct and male character serve as foil for the departure from expected models of male-female relationships by the standards of the early Empire.

Conclusion

At first reading, the tale of a fictional sea journey seems to have served as a form of "pure" entertainment with its bizarre characters and grotesque situations. The ancient reader might equally have derived pleasure from a deliberately distorted version of ideal masculinity and femininity which makes sea travel a more exciting trope than any conventional or painless journey of reality. The liminality of the world in which the Petronian characters move may provide an explanation for their apparent departure from traditional gender roles; in the undefined space of the sea they are even freer to deviate from normative gender behaviour. However, as I hope I have demonstrated with a deeper analysis of this episode, while undermining the traditional gender constructs, the fictional tale reaffirms the specific cultural values of the elite class to which the author belonged.

The characterization of Tryphaena as a travelling lascivious woman reveals the tensions regarding women's acceptable behaviour outside the traditional confines of the home, which were generated by the male belief that a woman who steps out the male-controlled domestic sphere finds an opportunity for corrupt behaviour.[70] The construction of Encolpius' and Giton's characters is based on terms of opposition between the type of travellers, who make enquiries in advance of their journey and always know their destinations,[71] and of the heroes who face the hardships and uncertainties of travel with resolution and courage. Similarly, Lichas subverts the traditional definitions of masculine wisdom with his excessively superstitious beliefs and fears.[72] Thus the conventionality or conservatism that runs through the novel's gender assumptions reaffirms traditional definitions of femininity and masculinity and promotes the patriarchal ideology of the male elite of Roman imperial society.

Notes

1   Translations are my own.
2   The theory that the *Satyrica* is a parodical rewriting of the Odyssey goes back to Klebs, E. (1889) "Zur Composition von Petronius *Satirae*," in: *Philologus*, 47: 623–635. See also McDermott, M.H. (1983) "The Satyricon as a Parody of the Odyssey and Greek Romance," in: *Liverpool Classical Monthly*: 82–85; Jašková, N. (2010) "Parody and Irony in the Works of Petronius: Encolpius' Wandering," in: *Graeco-Latina Brunensia*, 15: 81–90.
3   The idea that in the *Satyrica* Petronius was parodying the ideal love of the Greek novel was introduced by Heinze, R. (1899) "Petron und der griechische Roman," *Hermes*, 34 (1899): 494–519. It has found wide acceptance.
4   Panayotakis, C. (1994) "Theatrical Elements in the Episode on Board Lichas' Ship (Petronius, *Satyrica* 99.5–115)," in: *Memnosyne*, 48 (5): 596–624.

5 Panayotakis, C. (2006) "Eumolpus' *Pro Encolpio* and Lichas' *In Encolpium*: Petr. *Sat.* 107," in *Authors, Authority, and Interpreters in the Ancient Novel: Essays in Honor of Gareth L. Schmeling. Ancient Narrative Supplementum vol.5.* S.N. Byrne, E.P. Cueva, and J. Alvares (eds.). Groningen: Barkhuis: 196–210.
6 Müller, K. (2003) *Petronius: Satyricon reliquiae*, 4th edition revised. Munich: De Gruyter: 181, fragment XX.
7 Rose, K.F.C. (1971) *The Date and Author of the Satyricon*, Mnemosyne, Suppl. 16. Leiden: Brill; Sullivan, J.P. (1968) *The Satyricon of Petronius: A Literary Study.* London/Bloomington: Indiana University Press: 21–33.
8 Marmorale, E.V. (1948) *La questione Petroniana*, Biblioteca di cultura moderna (Bari, 1948); Daviault, A. (2001) "Est-il ancore possible de remettre en question la datation néronienne du Satyricon de Pétrone?," in: *Phoenix*, 55: 327–342; Flobert, P. (2003) "Considérations intempestives sur l'auteur et la date du Satyricon sous Hadrien," in: *Petroniana. Gedenkschrift für Hubert Petersmann*, J. Herman and H. Rosén (eds.). Heidelberg: Universitätsverlag Winter: 109–122.
9 Martin, R. (1975) "Quelques remarques concernant la date du Satiricon," in: *REL*, 53: 182–224; Ripoll, F. (2002) "Le Bellum Ciuile de Pétrone: une épopée flavienne?," in: *REA*, 104: 185–210.
10 Sullivan (1968): 34–38, *op.cit.* no. 7.
11 Sullivan (1968): 98–106, *op. cit.* no. 7. See also contributions in *Petronius: A Handbook*, Jonathan Prag and Ian Repath (eds.). Chichester: Wiley-Blackwell. Such as: Vout, C. (2009) "The *Satyrica* and the Neronian Culture": 101–113; Andreau, J. "Freedmen in the Satyrica": 114–124; Verboven, K. "A Funny Thing Happened on My Way to the Market: Reading Petronius to Write Economic History": 125–139.
12 See, for example, Veyne, P. (1964) "Le 'je' dans le Satiricon," *REL*, 42: 301–324; Beck, R. (1973) "Some Observations on the Narrative Technique of Petronius," in: *Phoenix*, 27 (1): 42–61; Slater, N.W. (1990) *Reading Petronius*. Baltimore/London: John Hopkins University Press; Conte, G.B. (1997) *L'autore nascosto. Un'interpretazione del «Satyricon»*. Bologna: Il Mulino.
13 Petronius *Sat.* 30.3, 56.10, 65.1, 136.4. *Petronio, Satiricon* (1988) Piero Chiara [tr.] Milano: Oscar Mondadori, (1st edition 1969).
14 Petr. *Sat.* 101.
15 Petr. *Sat.* 100: "*super constratum navis occuparemus secretissimum locum.*"
16 Petr. *Sat.* 100: "*supra constratum puppis.*" The expression is analyzed in *Petronius: The Satyricon* (1923) John M. Mitchell [tr.] London: Routledge: 310 note C.
17 Petr. *Sat.* 105, 108.
18 Petr. *Sat.* 106, 113.
19 Petr. *Sat.* 114.
20 Petr. *Sat.* 113.
21 Petr. *Sat.* 105, 108.
22 Petr. *Sat.* 106.
23 Petr. *Sat.* 101.
24 Verboven (2009): 132, *op.cit.* no.11.
25 Cicero, *In Verrem*, 5.154. *Cicero The Verrine Orations* Vol. II (1935) Leonard H.G. Greenwood [tr] London: William Heinemann and Cambridge, MA.: Harvard University Press.
26 Propertius, *Elegiae*, 1.11; 2.19. *Propertius Elegies* (1990) George P. Goold [tr.] Cambridge, MA: Harvard University Press and London: William Heinemann.
27 Juvenal, *Satirae*, 6. 82–113. *Juvenal and Persius* (1961) George G. Ramsay [tr.] London: William Heinemann and Cambridge, MA: Harvard University Press and (first printed 1918).
28 In a private letter, which is dated to 296 and was found in the Fayum area of Roman Egypt, Paniskos gives his wife Ploutegenia precise instructions on her travel plans to

meet him in Koptos: The woman must be accompanied by good and trustworthy men. *P. Mich.* 2. 214; Rowlandson, J. (1998) *Women and Society in Greek and Roman Egypt: A Sourcebook.* Cambridge: Cambridge University Press: 148.

29 In a second- or third-century private letter found in the Arsinoite nome, Thermouthas and Valeria write about their hope to sail downriver to their brother Apollinarios along with Demetrous and her (sc. Demetrous') mother, once Herois has given birth: The purpose of their journey is to meet their brother Apollinarios (*BGU* 1. 261); Bagnall, R.S. & Cribiore, R. (2006) *Women's Letters from Ancient Egypt.* Ann Arbor: University of Michigan Press: 189–190.

30 Petr. *Sat.* 104.

31 Petr. *Sat.* 104.

32 Petr. *Sat.* 103.

33 Petr. *Sat.* 107, 108.

34 Andreau (2009): *op.cit.,* no.1 no. 11.

35 Panayotakis (2006): *op.cit.,* no.5.

36 Neilson, H.R. (2002) "A Terracotta Phallus from Pisa Ship E: More Evidence for the Priapus deity as Protector of Greek and Roman Navigators," in: *Journal of Nautical Archaeology,* 31: 248–253. Suggests that a captain was the religious head of a ship.

37 In the preserved portion of the banquet scene following the end of hostilities, Encolpius laments that with his shaved head and eyebrows he was so conspicuously hideous that even Lichas did not consider him worth addressing (*Sat.* 110).

38 Petr. *Sat.* 105.

39 Petr. *Sat.* 111–113.

40 Tryphaena's maidservants are minor characters who serve to further emphasise the wealthy status and licentious character of their mistress.

41 On the concept of *pudicitia* see Langlands, R. (2006) *Sexual Morality in Ancient Rome.* Cambridge: Cambridge University Press.

42 The theme of celebrity in the *Matrona* of Ephesus is discussed by Dickison, S.H. (2013) "A Note on Fame and the 'Widow of Ephesus'" in *Roman Literature, Gender and Reception: Domina Illustris*, D. Lateiner, B.K. Gold, and J. Perkins (eds.) New York/London: Routledge: 85–89.

43 *CIL* 6.11602. Henzen, W., Rossi, G. B., Bormann, E. and Hülsen, C. (1882) *Corpus inscriptionum latinarum. Vol 6, Inscriptiones urbis Romae latinae.* Berlin: Georgium Reimerum.

44 *CIL* 8.647. Wilmanns, G. (1881) *Corpus inscriptionum latinarum. Vol 8, Inscriptiones Africae latinae.* Berlin: Georgium Reimerum.

45 For a discussion of the dangers (real and perceived) of female mobility in the early Roman empire see Carucci, M. (2017) "The Dangers of Female Mobility in Roman Imperial Times," in *The impact of mobility and migration in the Roman Empire*, A. Giardina, E. LoCascio, & L.E. Tacoma (eds.). Leiden: Brill: 173–190. The effects that travelling in foreign nations may had on women's (and men's) Romanness are analyzed by Lien Foubert "The lure of an exotic destination: the politics of women's travel in the early Roman Empire," forthcoming: I thank Dr. Foubert for kindly giving me a copy of her manuscript.

46 For a deeper discussion of Petronius' female characters, see Cicu, L. (1992) *Donne petroniane: Personaggi femminili e tecniche di racconto nel Satyricon di Petronio.* Sassari: Carlo Delfino Editore.

47 In Encolpius' lodgings for Quartilla and in a laurel grove for Circe.

48 The scene of Fortunata beaten by her husband is discussed in Margherita Carucci, "Domestic violence in the Roman imperial society: Giving voice to the abused women," forthcoming.

49 Petr. *Sat.* 110.

50 Petr. *Sat.* 106: *feminam simplicem.*
51 Petr. *Sat.* 85.
52 Petr. *Sat.* 101–102.
53 Horace, *Ars Poetica*, 295–301 *Horace Satires, Epistles and Ars Poetica* (1961) Henry Rushton Fairclough [tr.] Cambridge, MA: Harvard University Press and London: William Heinemann (first printed 1926). Persius, *Satirae*, 1.13–30., 5.5–36. Harvey, R.A. (1981) *A Commentary on Persius.* Leiden: E.J. Brill. Juvenal, *Satirae*, 1.13–18 [*op.cit.* no.26].
54 Petr. *Sat.* 117.
55 The wage-earner (*mercennarius*) is mentioned in several places of the *Satyrica*: 95.12–15 and 99.6 (in Encolpius' lodgings); 103.1 and 108.4 (on the ship).
56 Scholars identify variously as Naples, Cumae, Misenum, Formiae, Minturno, and Puteoli. Rose (1971): 403–405, op.cit. n°. 7.
57 Petronius (1996) *The Satyricon*, Patrick Gerard Walsh [tr.] Oxford: Oxford University Press. Walsh (xvii) points out that evidence for an episode in Egypt is hardly compelling, since the Isiac worship with which Memphis is associated was popular in Campania.
58 Petr. *Sat.* 101: *onus deferendum ad mercatum conducit.*
59 Stone, L. (1977) *The family, sex and marriage in England 1500–1800.* Harmondsworth: Weidenfeld & Nicholson: 501–505; Thomas, K. (1959) "The Double Standard," in: *Journal of the History of Ideas* 20 (2): 195–216, 195.
60 Petr. *Sat.* 108: *mulier damnata et in toto navigio sola verberanda.*
61 Petr. *Sat.* 116.
62 Petr. *Sat.* 114.
63 Barchiesi, A. (1984) "Il nome di Lica e la poetica dei nomi in Petronio", in: *Materiali e discussioni per l'analisi dei testi classici* 12: 169–175. Barchiesi argues that Licha's name foreshadows the way the captain will die.
64 Hope, V.M. (2007) *Death in Ancient Rome: A Sourcebook.* London: Routledge: 93–96.
65 Petr. *Sat.* 110.
66 Sen. *Cons. ad Helv.* 19.4; 19.5, 7. *Seneca Moral Essays* Vol. 2 (1965) John W. Basore [tr.] Cambridge, MA: Harvard University Press and London: William Heinemann (first printed 1932).
67 Petr. *Sat.* 114.
68 See, for example, Clitophon's lamentation in Achilles Tatius, *Leucippe and Clitophon*, 3.5.4. *Achilles Tatius* (1917) Stephen Gaselee [tr.] London: William Heinemann and New York: G.P. Putnam's Sons.
69 Edwards, C. (2007) *Death in Ancient Rome.* New Haven/London: Yale University Press: 5. The active process of dying is evident also in the act of self-killing in sickness. See Carucci, M. (2014) "Self-killing as a Cure to Disease: Illness and Death in Roman Imperial Literature," in *Death in Literature*, S. Kivistö and Outi Hakola (eds.). Newcastle upon Tyne: Cambridge Scholars Publishing: 199–216.
70 The different trends in Roman social attitudes towards women's mobility are evident is a senatorial debate during the reign of Tiberius as reported by Tacitus in *Annales*, 3.33–34. The passage is analyzed by Carucci op.cit., no.45 and Foubert (*op.cit.* no.45.).
71 Petr. *Sat.* 107.
72 An interesting reading of the origin of superstition in Roman society is given by Polybius, *Histories*, 6.56.6–11 *Polybius The Histories*, Vol. 3 (1972) W R. Paton [tr.] London: William Heinemann and Cambridge, MA: Harvard University Press (first printed 1923).

2 Meeting the holy men

Self-perception of the female traveller and interaction between men and women in the late antique *Itinerarium Egeriae*

Fabia Neuerburg

In the late nineteenth century, a manuscript containing a late antique travel report was found by the Italian scholar Gian Francesco Gamurrini in the renowned abbey of Montecassino, where it had lain undiscovered for the last 700 years. Since its discovery, plenty of hypotheses have been formed with regard to the name and identity of the author as well as to the actual date of the pilgrimage. As the beginning and the end of the account (as well as some parts in between) are lost, these examinations have proved to be especially challenging.[1] For now, it suffices to say that in the early 380's a woman from Aquitaine or Galicia named Egeria[2] set out to travel to Palestine by land in order to visit the "holy places" (*loca sancta*) and the "holy men" (*viri sancti*) living there. After having visited most of the biblical sites on her way, like the tomb of Job and the shrine of St Thecla, she wrote an extensive letter to her *sorores venerabiles*, her beloved sisters at home. The manuscript containing the remaining parts of her letter consists of approximately 44 pages (35 lines each). It is impossible to estimate the original length of her letter, since a great deal of it is missing. Nowadays, it is known as the *itinerarium Egeriae* (IE), sometimes called *peregrinatio ad loca sancta* or *peregrinatio aetheriae*.

Few texts can be compared to this letter, even less from Egeria's time. Moreover, none of the texts that could come under consideration have been written by women. The Bordeaux Itinerary for example, the *Itinerarium Burdigalense*, is the oldest Christian itinerary of the Holy Land, written by an anonymous pilgrim around the year 333.[3] However, this account comprises little more than a sequence of cities, places, *mansiones* (stopping places), and *mutationes* (change of horses) occasionally interspersed with remarks about historical incidents or Christian legends. Compared to this itinerary Egeria's lengthy first-person report provides us with a vivid impression of her personality and striking enthusiasm. The account itself is divided into two parts of almost equal length. The first one includes the whole itinerary to Jerusalem, which starts with the ascension of Mount Sinai, her journey via Antioch, Edessa, Carrhae, Seleucia and Chalcedon, and ends with Egeria's return to Constantinople, where she finally wrote her letter. The second part contains detailed observations of the local liturgical procedures of Jerusalem, which seemed to be a matter of great importance to her readers.

Travelling Christian pilgrims were a new phenomenon in late antiquity, albeit by now a well-researched subject. As a report of a pilgrimage written by a female pilgrim, Egeria's account is especially valuable. Exploring gendered discourses in this particular text may provide insight into the perception of her and the people who accompany her on her way. Therefore, the aim of this contribution is to examine the way in which Egeria, as a female pilgrim, and men – in this case her possible companions as well as her local guides, the "holy men" – interacted en route. This chapter will illustrate Egeria's manner of representing her almost exclusively male acquaintances, as well as herself in respect of her gender. It is crucial to keep in mind that this report is ultimately a highly stylised text. Egeria, as the author, only makes her readers – and therefore us – "see" what she wants them to see. Hence, every part of the representations of herself, of her acquaintances and their interaction must be viewed against this background. Of course this does not imply that the portrayed characters are "reducible to words."[4] The characters, even though they are textual constructs, are still created by analogy to real human beings. Therefore, they possess features and characteristics that – to a certain extent – make them amendable to reception-oriented approaches.

Egeria and her readers

Little is known about the people accompanying Egeria on her long journey to the Holy Land. Moreover, references to the author herself are also scarce. References in medieval manuscripts entitling her *abbatissa* and *sanctimonialis*, as well as the fact that she bestows the term *sorores* upon her readers, have led to the assumption that Egeria was a nun. Considering that her plan to travel to Palestine and to stay there for an indefinite period of time had to be a rather costly venture, one must assume that she had a large amount of money at her disposal.[5] This and further considerations, such as her relative freedom of movement, refute a direct affiliation with a monastic institution, which most likely would not have paid for the expenses of a journey that obviously served no official purpose. Additionally, during Egeria's time the expression *soror/frater* (including additions like *venerabilis, sanctus*, etc.) was a common address among clerics and laymen alike.[6] Egeria's Latin language and style is by no means comparable to other erudite women of her time, such as Paula of Rome (who also went on a pilgrimage to the Holy Land) or Melania the Elder. Unfortunately, these women did not leave any self-penned travelogues. Unlike her famous contemporaries, Egeria seems to have had no knowledge of Latin classics at all. Instead, she is well-versed in the Bible, and probably other Christian literary texts as well. By classical standards her "vulgar Latin" is certainly poor, which is why it has been subject to criticism.[7]

For these reasons, Egeria was likely to originate from an urban middle- or high-class milieu, though any further specification remains speculative. Her readers were presumably a circle of laywomen of a similar social standing, avid readers of the Bible who were eager to get a picture of the land which they hitherto only knew by reading Christian texts. However, Egeria was by far not the first woman to go on a pilgrimage to Palestine. As mentioned above, during the fourth and fifth century pilgrimages to Jerusalem and other biblical sites became increasingly common, especially among Roman noblewomen. Some of them would return home eventually, others stayed abroad, establishing new *xenodochia* – hostels for pilgrims – and in doing so paved the way for future generations of pilgrims. At times, some of the women chose to remain in a state of monastic, almost ascetic wandering, neither returning to their home town, nor fully settling in the new country.[8] Ultimately, we cannot possibly know for sure if Egeria ever went back. Judging from what she wrote at the very end of her report, chances are she never did, and – to put it in the words of Edith and Victor Turner – decided to rather stay in this exact kind of "liminal" situation, wandering from one holy place to another.[9] All these ventures that were undertaken by women suggest the emergence of a new type of late antique spiritual travelling. By journeying to the Holy Land, Egeria and other women of her social status probably attempted to imitate trends set by Roman noblewomen, although female travel itself was already an established custom even before Christian pilgrims like Paula set out for Palestine.[10]

Egeria's company

We hardly know anything about the people who accompanied Egeria on her way, although it is certain that she did not expose herself to the various risks of travelling alone. Egeria was most certainly able to use the advantages of the Roman courier and transportation service, the *cursus publicus*.[11] On a specific and obviously dangerous part of her route she – and her companions? – is even escorted by Roman military personnel. Apart from that, her preferred means of transportation are horses and mules, except when situations require her to walk, like the ascension of Mount Sinai at the beginning of her account. Undoubtedly, she does not travel in a litter and does not seem to have a large entourage in general.

At times she uses the plural when talking about her actions.[12] The constant alternation of *ego/nos* (and *tu/vos* respectively) makes it difficult to identify the people she includes, since *nos* may comprise herself and her local monks as well as any other group of companions or pilgrims who travel with her. It is remarkable that among the people she is travelling with, Egeria often seems to be the one in charge of choosing the destinations and determining the itinerary. On a trip to the tomb of St Job, while knowing that her group is near the place where St John baptised according to the Bible, Egeria asks her local guide, a presbyter, whether this place is far away.[13] "If you want to (*si vis*), I will guide you there (*duco vos ibi*)."[14] Once again, Egeria is the only person to actively influence the route of her group. She gets to go wherever she wants to go – or at least this is what she wants her readers to believe. Astonishingly, everything she finds in this process seems to measure up to her expectations. There is no disappointment and no frustration in Egeria's Holy Land.[15]

The holy men

Next to the biblical places, Egeria's most important destinations consisted of monasteries and monks living in cells (called *monasteria*) throughout Palestine. In addition to the conversations with these monks, these men also serve as her personal guides to most of the historical and biblical sites on her way. It is possible that the monks also serve as "indication marks" on her journey: Wherever their cells are found, these places have to be located near a historical site and are, supposedly, special.[16] On one occasion she first finds a cell, and *ut sum satis curiosa* – "inquisitive as I am" she asks the monk why he built his cell in this place, since she assumes it must be a biblical site – and rightly so. The monks and their monasteries seem to serve as "landmarks," just like the sites themselves. For Egeria a region is therefore "ticked off" by the time she has seen all the holy places (*loca sancta*), and visited the "historical" sites as well as all the holy people dwelling there (*viri sancti*).[17]

A closer look at how the author depicts the holy men and her interaction with them is now warranted. Related to her visits to the cells, where she and her companions often spend the night,[18] the nature of her account is always the same. Usually, she stresses the hospitality and kindness of her hosts.[19] However, calling the holy men companions in the traditional sense may be a bit far-fetched. Technically, her real companions are the people who accompany her on her way – and of whom we know nothing (see above). Nevertheless, Egeria spends a significant part of her journey in the presence and company of the monks. The only times when she is without them, are her journeys from one city to another. Whenever she reaches a destination (especially the holy sites) or explores the surroundings during her stay in a *xenodochium*, where the monks act as hosts, she associates herself with them. Yet the monks also assume the role of guide, and accompany her over considerable distances. Thus, it may be possible to regard them as companions as well.

As mentioned before, the "holy men" also acted as local guides for the pilgrims – including the "holy Bishop of Arabia,"[20] who meets Egeria and her companions at Rameses and willingly shows them around, telling them everything about the historical and biblical background of the sites. Indeed, this bishop is the first person in (the extant parts of) Egeria's account to receive a more elaborate characterisation: "He is an old man, truly religious since he became a monk. He is affable and receives pilgrims really friendly, and he is also well versed in the Scriptures of God."[21] Egeria's visits of cells and other dwellings of "holy men" all over the region are too numerous to list them all. Everywhere she went, her routine essentially stayed the same: She sought out the cells where the resident monks showed her all of the important places in the area. When they visited the sites, someone read an appropriate passage of the Bible or a matching prayer, as was the custom. In many cases, Egeria and her group stayed overnight. At their departure, they usually received *eulogiae*, "blessings," mostly fruits, from the monks.

In Edessa, she meets another bishop – again a truly religious man – who welcomes her with the words "Since I see, my daughter, that you took the effort to come here from the other end of the world for the sake of faith, we will show you all the places, that Christians should visit."[22] He then proceeds to give Egeria a copy of his version of the letter of King Abgar, which she happily receives believing that the one she was given is longer than her own version at home. Abgar V, King of Osroene in the first century, was said to have exchanged letters with Jesus. There are two versions of the exchange: One in Greek by Eusebius, bishop of Caesarea, the other is contained in the Syrian *doctrina Addai*. Egeria was right about the length of the letter, for there are indeed some parts missing in Eusebius' tradition. The legend of King Abgar enjoyed great popularity during the Middle Ages. In Carrhae she meets yet another godly bishop to show her the city. Aside from the "historical facts," "he told us many other things, just like the other holy bishops and holy monks did, always about the Scriptures or the deeds of holy men." She adds:

> Because I do not want you, my love, to think that my conversations with the monks were about anything other than God's Scriptures or the deeds of great monks.[23]

This last comment is slightly confusing, as she places so much emphasis on it. It almost seems as if she wanted to let her sisters know that travelling alone and interacting with foreign men is by no means a threat to her virtue. Indeed, this kind of suspicion did exist. In a letter to Christian ascetics in Cappadocia, Bishop Gregory of Nyssa advised against all kinds of dangers that await women who embark on a pilgrimage to Palestine. Gregory, writing this letter in the 380s, i.e. in Egeria's time, is especially concerned about the pudicity of female pilgrims. The inevitable "meeting and mixing of persons of opposite sex" during a journey will be harmful to the morality of travelling women:

> For it is impracticable for a woman to pursue so long a journey unless she has a conductor, for on account of her natural weakness she has to be put on her horse and be lifted down again, and she has to be steadied in rough terrain. Whichever we suppose, that she has someone known to her to fulfil this service or a hired attendant – in either case such conduct cannot avoid blame. Whether she leans on a stranger or on her own servant, she fails to observe the law of modesty. Moreover, as the inns and caravanserays and cities in the east are so free and indifferent towards vice, how will it be possible for one passing through such fumes to escape without smarting eyes?[24]

Was Egeria possibly referring to this type of criticism when she reassured her sisters about the chasteness of her conversations? This would be a unique and non-recurring remark concerning possible tensions between men and women. Throughout Egeria's report, the relationships between herself and the men she encounters seem to be characterised by mutual respect and a kind of asexual distance. Asexual in the sense that neither Egeria's nor anyone's gender is addressed even in the slightest. The topic is completely cut out of her report. As a matter of fact, her femaleness seems to have no effect on her actions or experiences in the foreign country whatsoever. She never insinuates that the "weakness" of her sex is an issue or that her sex precludes her from anything she wants to see or do on her way. Even hardships like the – no doubt exhausting – ascension of Mount Sinai are dismissed by her, since these small "martyria" only serve a higher purpose. Perhaps these pilgrimages could even be seen as opportunities for Egeria and other pious women to give proof of their bravery or of their "masculinity." In fact, out of concern for their integrity, young women of the fourth century were sometimes advised to shield themselves by "adopting strict modes of sexual avoidance and by taking on the firm contours of a man."[25] To protect their virginity and to be able to associate with the opposite sex, they literally had to abandon their own sex and become a "male" virgin. Strangely enough, Saint Paulinus of Nola even went so far as to call Melania the Elder, another Roman noblewoman, "Melanius" in his letters to emphasise and praise her extraordinary courage and commitment.[26] Other Christian women left their families and children to go on a pilgrimage, thus discarding their standard role of the "loving mother" that was traditionally assigned to them in the Roman society. While pagan authors condemned this behavior, Christian writers considered this a kind of exceptional dedication.[27] Yet, Egeria never refers to these considerations. To her it is self-evident that the relationship and the interaction between pious men and women are confined to an idealistic asexual level. Her remark is probably just another way to exalt the monks and bishops by underlining their "holiness."

Egeria's depiction of the holy (wo)men

There is something odd about Egeria's depiction of the holy people in general. Nearly all of them remain sketchy and unreal as characters. The author depicts her male acquaintances as faceless and interchangeable figures. Consequently, the many monks and priests she encounters are ultimately bound to remain anonymous. Speaking in terms of a reception-oriented character analysis, there is a "categorization" of characters, which allows her readers to allocate the figures to the well-established category "monk/holy man."[28] The common second step in the process however, the "individuation" of the character, is omitted in most cases. Usually, the description of the *viri sancti* remains rather vague. Whenever Egeria becomes more precise about them, she refers to their age ("he was old," therefore wise), conduct of life ("he became a monk at an early age"/"he always lived a godly life") and of course their knowledge ("he was well versed in the Scriptures"), thus portraying them as the near image of an ideal monk. Egeria does not allow the holy men to become real characters; her descriptions of the meetings with the monks are therefore restrained and unemotional. In this respect, they reflect her own vision of a perfect and chaste relationship between pious men and women. This does not necessarily imply that the conventional sexual relationship between wife/mother and husband/father is condemned by

Egeria and other people of her mindset, but it is set on a different, more "worldly" level, which is somehow inferior to the asexual community of pious Christian men and women. A similar way of thinking is to be found in a lengthy letter to a young woman named Eustochium written by Jerome. He advises his addressee to refrain from marriage and a traditional life. Instead he calls on her to defend the virginal life by claiming "The life on which I have resolved is independent of sex. Let those who are wives keep the place and the time that properly belong to them. For me, virginity is consecrated in the persons of Mary and of Christ"[29] Ultimately, the strict religiosity of the holy men and Egeria's devotional depiction of them mirrors her admiration of this lifestyle and her own idea of her aim in life.

Egeria also visits female clerics. During her stay at the sanctuary of Holy Thecla, she visited "the holy monks and apotactites, the men as well as the women."[30] Elsewhere, when she informs her sisters about the daily services of the holy places she had been to, she tells them of the "monazontes and parthenae, as they are called here,"[31] i.e. the monks and nuns, who take part in the ceremonies. However, the nuns never constitute their own literary "category" the way the holy men do. Therefore, it is even more astonishing that the only character whose name is actually mentioned by Egeria and who seems to exhibit some human features is a woman: Her good friend Marthana – as she calls her *sancta diaconissa nomine Marthana*.[32] She is also one of the few people Egeria has met on her way before, according to her own report. They meet in Seleucia, where Egeria spent the night before visiting the martyrium (the actual shrine) of Saint Thecla. Remarkably, in Egeria's time women not only played an active part in the conveyance of the various legends and miracle stories of Saint Thecla, but also began to assume leadership roles at the sanctuary itself – as Marthana herself is in charge of some cells at the shrine.[33] Naturally, over the course of time the martyrium of Saint Thecla became popular with female pilgrims in particular. This is the reason why Egeria notices a large number of cells for men and women all around the local church.[34]

> There I met one of my dearest friends – everyone in the East gives testimony of her life – the holy deaconess called Marthana. I got to know her in Jerusalem, where she had come to pray. She was in charge of a monastery of apotactites or virgins. How happy we were to see each other – I simply cannot describe it to you. But to get back to the point...[35]

This rare emotional (non-religious) release feels strangely out of place compared to the monotonous descriptions of her male acquaintances. Marthana's character, although she also fits into the category "holy person," appears to be individualised – not in the least because of all the people Egeria meets on her way, Marthana alone bears a name. Regarding her remarks about her alleged freedom to go wherever she wants to, one could argue that this perceived liberty somehow contradicts her religiosity and the strict pureness of her journey. However, it is important to note that Egeria herself did not regard her religion as a restriction. It was not until the rise of Christianity and the emergence of "chaste virgins," who were basically on par with their male counterparts, that women like Egeria could dismiss the traditional role of wife/mother and set out independently on a journey like this one.

Altogether the people she meets in the East, namely the *viri sancti*, are – as characters – part of her literary fiction of the Holy Land. In Egeria's account, Jerusalem and its surroundings resemble some kind of "Christian wonderland," a collection of biblical attractions that she wanders through in awe. That an opposing view of Jerusalem and the Holy Land indeed existed in her time, is clearly shown by Gregory of Nyssa's scorching criticism of the city that he expressed in his letters after completing his own pilgrimage:

> Again, if grace were greater in the vicinity of Jerusalem than anywhere else, sin would not be so entrenched among those who dwell there. But as it is, there is no form of uncleanness that is not brazened among them: fornications, adulteries, thefts, idolatries, drugs, envies, murders. This last kind of evil especially is so entrenched that nowhere else are people so ready to murder each other as in those places.[36]

Remarkably, the bishop had travelled to Palestine – and was quite positive about this experience – a short time before he dispraised the city of Jerusalem in his letter.[37] Egeria's account of the Holy Land sounds quite different. It appears to be impossible that on this extensive pilgrimage, which took her more than three years, none of the things mentioned by Gregory ever occurred to her – even supposing that the letter at hand is not the first one Egeria sent to her sisters. All these things had to be omitted in her vision of the "Holy Land," otherwise she would have to refrain from calling it "holy."[38]

A glance at the historical circumstances of early Christianity might help in order to gain insight into this situation. For Egeria and other men and women of her time and origin, the new Christian religion might still have felt "disembodied," although it was spreading fast.[39] This means that the Scriptures were probably seen as cut off from their geographical context. In this situation writings like, Περὶ τῶν τοπικῶν ὀνομάτων τῶν ἐν τῇ θείαι γραφῇ, the "Onomasticon," a list of all the important biblical places in alphabetical order, written by Eusebius of Caesarea, served as an auxiliary means for western Christians to help them understand biblical scriptures. This handbook, soon revised and translated into Latin by Jerome, shows that a thorough knowledge of the biblical geography was somehow deemed necessary for the complete understanding of the Bible. Thus, journeys to Palestine and the travelogues and itineraries originating from them were suited to make the visitors delve into the biblical world. Egeria herself suggests to her readers that her descriptions of the places Moses was said to have visited could help her audience gain a more thorough understanding of the books of Moses.[40] It would certainly be interesting to compare her depiction of the Holy Land to other parts of her account, e.g. her journey via Constantinople. Unfortunately the beginning of her letter is lost completely and only begins with her ascension of Mount Sinai. Although she completes her letter in Constantinople, Egeria does not include too much information about her stay, since she most likely described the city in the lost beginning. She only mentions the many churches and "tombs of the apostles" where she thanked God for her safe return to the city (23.9). But since Constantine strove to turn the city into a sumptuous Christian capital it is unlikely that Egeria made the city look any worse than the Holy Land itself.

Conclusion

Then what is the exact role and meaning of the "holy men"? It is not surprising that figures of the Old Testament are called *sanctus* Moyses and *sancta* Rebecca. Yet she constantly uses the same epithet to describe every monk and bishop she meets on her way, a fact that is rightly emphasised by Dietz.[41] This may be due to the fact that to Egeria, the difference between the biblical figures and the living clerics is indeed a small one. Egeria and other pilgrims of her time do not consider the places she visits holy by their very nature. They become sanctified only by the continuity of holy people living in these places. The holy people are part of her fictional literary land of the Bible.[42] Apart from the second part of her account, the general population, pagans as well as laypeople, hardly make an appearance.[43] Holy men and women alone populate her vision of the Holy Land. It seems as if, in her opinion, the asexual relationship between the monks, the nuns, and herself is the ideal mode of living together. Since at least the sixth century even married Christian couples ideally morphed into some kind of chaste "brothers" and "sisters" who lived in a joint household while at the same time abstaining from any form of physical contact.[44]

To Egeria, the monks are probably the successors of the biblical figures. Travelling the Holy Land is her way of fully immersing herself into the "historical" past of the Scriptures. Unlike church fathers like Gregory of Nyssa, who draw a clear distinction between heavenly Jerusalem and its physical counterpart, Egeria is interested in painting the portrait of a perfect "Holy Land." The description of the people she met on her way is therefore just part of this exact narration. Hence, the monks are almost treated as actual historical or biblical characters. Since they ultimately have to fit her vision of the Holy Land, they remain shadowy, thus revealing the literary character of the place and the figures of her account. The same is true for the relationship between men and women, which is completely defined by the late antique/early Christian ideal of an asexual brother- and sisterhood, partly by simply omitting everyone who is not a cleric like pagans and laypeople. Everything and everyone in her account can only be seen through her particular view, her "eyes of faith."[45]

Notes

1 In this chapter I am referring to the standard edition of this text which is Franceschini, E.A. & Weber, R. (1965) *Itinerarium Egeriae*, Corpus Christianorum, Series Latina, clxxv. Turnhout: Brepols: 27–103. Another convenient edition is the one of Maraval, P. (1982) *Égérie. Journal de voyage (Itinéraire)*, Sources Chrétiennes 296. Paris: Editions du Cherf. Wilkinson, J. (1981) *Egeria's Travels to the Holy Land*. Jerusalem/

Warminster: Ariel Publishing House provided us with an English translation, including several supporting documents and valuable notes.

2 Gamurrini himself identified the author as an Aquitanian woman called Silvia, the sister of Rufus, a magistrate of emperor Flavius Arcadius. In 1903 Marius Férotin finally related her to the letter of a Spanish hermit calling her *sanctimonialis Etheria* (other versions suggesting Aetheria, Eucheria, Egeria, etc.). These days the *communis opinio* seems to prefer the name Egeria. See Férotin, M. (1903) "Le véritable auteur de la Peregrinatio Silviae: La vierge espagniole Etheria," *Revue des questions historique* 74: 367–397; Mountford, J.F. (1923) "Silvia, Aetheria or Egeria?" *The Classical Quarterly* 17: 40–41.

3 Based on several observations, some suppose the author could have been a female pilgrim, although ultimately these are mere speculations. For the discussion see: Weingarten, S. (1999) "Was the pilgrim from Bordeaux a Woman? A reply to Laurie Douglass," *Journal of Early Christian Studies* 7: 291–297.

4 Margolin, U. (1990) "The what, the when, and the how of being a character in literary narrative," *Style* 24 (3): 453–468, 453.

5 According to her report it was already three years since her arrival in Jerusalem, IE 17, 1.

6 As to whether or not the term *sorores venerabiles* may refer to members of a monastery, see: Sivan, H. (1988) "Holy Land pilgrimage and western audiences: Some reflections on Egeria and her circle," *The Classical Quarterly* 38 (2): 528–535, 528.

7 Wölfflin, E. (1887) "Über die Latinität der Peregrinatio ad loca sancta," *Archiv für lateinische Lexikographie und Grammatik* 4: 259–276, 259. Other critics even tried to assign her language a certain epic sublimity, cf. Spitzer, L. (1949) "The epic style of the pilgrim Aetheria," *Comparative Literature* 1: 225–258, 230. In 1945 Benvenuto Terracini even thought of Egeria's grammaticalised use of reflexives as a stylistic expression of her femininity, assuming that her female frailty made her emphasise her fatigue all throughout her text: Terracini, B. (1945) "Sobre el verbo reflexivo y el problema de los orígenes románicos," *Revista de filología hispánica* 7 (1): 1–22, 14–15.

8 Dietz, M. (2004) "Itinerant Spirituality and the Late Antique Origins of Christian Pilgrimage," in *Travel, Communication and Geography in Late Antiquity: Sacred and Profane*, ed. L. Ellis and F. Kidner. Aldershot: Ashgate: 125–134, 126ff.

9 Turner, E. and Turner, V. (1978) *Image and Pilgrimage in Christian Culture: Anthropological Perspectives*. New York: Columbia University Press: 3.

10 Foubert, F. (2013) "Female travellers in Roman Britain: Vibia Pacata and Julia Lucilla," in *Women and the Roman City in the Latin West*, ed. E. Hemelrijk and G. Woolf. Leiden/Boston: Brill: 401.

11 Dietz, M. (2005) *Wandering Monks, Virgins, and Pilgrims. Ascetic Travel in the Mediterranean World, A.D. 300–800*. Philadelphia: Pennsylvania State University Press: 19.

12 Such as in Franceschini & Weber (1965): 15, 1.

13 At this point – on her way from Jerusalem to the land of Uz – her group consisted (in whole or in part) of "holy men" from Jerusalem "who had the kindness to keep me company on my way and also wanted to go there to pray," Franceschini & Weber (1965): 1.

14 Franceschini & Weber (1965): 15, 1.

15 Except for one time, when Egeria sets out to see the pillar of salt that Lot's wife was turned into according to the Book of Genesis. Although she is not able to find the pillar, Egeria is still convinced that the place is right, but the pillar simply submerged in the sea – since this is what the monks, again serving as her local guides, tell her. Franceschini & Weber (1965): 12, 7.

16 Franceschini & Weber (1965): 16, 3.

17 As stated by her in Franceschini & Weber (1965): 5, 11.

18 In most cases the cells of the monks served as harbourages, especially in the more remote regions which Egeria travels through. The holy men and their *monasteria* thus became the means and the destinations of her pilgrimage, just like for many other pilgrims of her time, see Chitty, D.J. (1966) *The Desert a City. An Introduction to the Study of Egyptian and Palestinian Monasticism under the Christian Empire.* Oxford: Blackwell: 46ff. It must be assumed that some kind of reciprocal effect evolved between the growing number of pilgrims visiting the eastern regions and the growing number of monasteries/ harbourages (making money out of the pilgrims), which again facilitated travelling.

19 Franceschini & Weber (1965): 3, 1 *susceperunt nos* [...] *humane* "received us hospitably," *prebentes nobis omnem humanitatem* "granted us every kindness"; 5, 10 *qui tamen nos dignati sunt valde humane suscipere* "they received us most hospitably."

20 Franceschini & Weber (1965): 8, 4. He is most probably the bishop of the city of Arabia (not the region), which Wilkinson identifies as the city of Phacusa (216).

21 Franceschini & Weber (1965): 8, 4: *Nam est iam senior vir, vere satis religiosus ex monacho et affabilis, suscipiens peregrinos valde bene; nam et in scripturis Dei valde eruditus est.* Again, her description is somewhat formulaic. In Sedima/Salim she is welcomed by the presbyter and clergy of the city. This "sanctus presbyter" is old and well versed in the Scriptures and had been the keeper of this place ever since he was a monk, Franceschini & Weber (1965): 14, 2.

22 Franceschini & Weber (1965): 19, 5: *Quoniam video te, filia, gratia religionis tam magnum laborem tibi imposuisse, ut de extremis porro terris venires ad haec loca, itaque ergo, si libenter habes, quaecumque loca sunt hic grata ad videndum Christianis, ostendimus tibi.*

23 Franceschini & Weber (1965): 20, 13: *Et cetera plura referre dignatus est, sicut et ceteri sancti episcopi vel sancti monachi facere dignabantur, omnia tamen de Scripturis Dei vel sanctis viris gesta* [...]. *Nam nolo estimet affectio vestra monachorum aliquando alias fabulas esse nisi aut de Scripturis Dei aut gesta monachorum maiorum.*

24 Greg. Nyss. (2007) epist. 2, 6–7, Letter 2: 'To Kensitor on pilgrimages', in: Anna M. Silvas [tr.] *Gregory of Nyssa: The Letters. Introduction, Translation and Commentary.* Leiden/Boston: Brill: 119.

25 Brown, P. (2008) *The Body and Society. Men, Women, and Sexual Renunciation in Early Christianity.* New York: Columbia University Press: 268. Rpt.

26 Paul. Nol. epist. 29, 5; 31, 1.

27 Zwingmann, N. (2014) "Reisen von Frauen im literarischen Diskurs der Antike unter besonderer Berücksichtigung der loca-sancta-Pilgerin der christlichen Spätantike," in *Mobilität in den Kulturen der antiken Mittelmeerwelt*, eds. E. Olshausen and V. Sauer. Stuttgart: Franz Steiner Verlag: 533.

28 See Schneider, R. (2001) "Toward a cognitive theory of literary character: the dynamics of mental-model construction," *Style* 35 (4): 607–640, 617–627.

29 Hier. epist. 22, 18, (1893) W.H. Fremantle, G. Lewis, W.G. Martle [trs.] *Nicene and Post-Nicene Fathers*, Philip Schaff (ed.), 2nd ser., vol. 6. Oxford: Christian Literature Company.

30 Franceschini & Weber (1965): 23, 6.

31 Franceschini & Weber (1965): 24, 1.

32 Franceschini & Weber (1965): 23, 3.

33 Davis, S. J. (2008) *The Cult of St. Thecla.* Oxford: Oxford University Press: 56.

34 This is in fact the first-time women are mentioned at all in her report. In the second part of her account (the description of the services) references to nuns and laywomen are more frequent.

35 Franceschini & Weber (1965): 23, 3: *nam inveni ibi aliquam amicissimam michi, et cui omnes in oriente testimonium ferebant vitae ipsius, sancta diaconissa nomine Marthana, quam ego apud Ierusolimam noveram, ubi illa gratia orationis ascenderat;*

haec autem monasteria aputactitum seu virginum regebat. Quae me cum vidisset, quod gaudium illius vel meum esse potuerit, nunquid vel scribere possum? Sed ut redeam at rem, [...].

36 Greg. Nyss (2007) "epist. 2, 10." Anna M. Silvas [tr.] *Gregory of Nyssa: The Letters. Introduction, Translation and Commentary*. Leiden/Boston: Brill: 120.

37 Ulrich, J. (1999) "Wallfahrt und Wallfahrtskritik bei Gregor von Nyssa," *Zeitschrift für Antikes Christentum*, 3: 87–96, 87.

38 As Palmer noted, this also applies to her emotions: "Another 'fiction' is that the pilgrim herself experienced only the appropriate emotions of gratitude and satisfaction, or of sorrow at Passion tide, never annoyance, scepticism, suspicion, fear, homesickness, loneliness, physical attraction [...]." Although he explicitly marked it as "fiction," he later states that Egeria was "journeying towards the centre of her universe. This, surely, rather than the filter of decorum, is the explanation for her lack of homesickness, of paranoia, of xenophobia." I disagree with him on this point. The lack of (the description of) negative emotions is not due to the fact that she is "feeling at home," nor to a "filter of decorum," but if anything is due to the "literariness" of her account. Palmer, A. (1994) "Egeria the Voyager, or the technology of remote sensing in Late Antiquity," in *Travel Fact and Travel Fiction*, ed. Martels Leiden, New York, and Cologne: Brill: 45–52.

39 Matthews, J. (2010) "Travel, diplomacy and the diffusion of ideas in the Roman Mediterranean and Near East" in *Roman Perspectives. Studies in the Social, Political and Cultural History of the First to Fifth Centuries*. Swansea: L'Antiquité Classique: 173.

40 Franceschini & Weber (1965): 5, 8: *sed cum leget affectio vestra libros sanctos Moysi, omnia diligentius pervidet, quae ibi facta sunt.*

41 See Dietz, M. (2005) *Wandering Monks, Virgins, and Pilgrims. Ascetic Travel in the Mediterranean World, A.D. 300–800*. Philadelphia: Pennsylvania State University Press: 50.

42 Much has been written about the complex process of the "sanctification" of Palestine in the 4th century. With the increasing popularity and spreading of the Christian religion, people in power like Constantine or bishop Cyril of Jerusalem began to play their part in the creation of the "Holy Land" as the origin of Christianity. Pilgrims like Egeria, who literally travelled with their Bible at hand started covering the land with a "literary topography, thus creation a close connection of text and geography. See Taylor, J.E. (1992) *Christians and the Holy Places. The Myth of Jewish-Christian Origins*. Oxford: Clarendon Press; Markus, R.A. (1994) "How on earth could places become holy? Origins of the Christian idea of holy places," *Journal of Early Christian Studies* 2: 257–271, 268.

43 One of the few exceptions is the city of Carrhae, about which she states: "In this city [...] I found absolutely no Christians, they are all pagans" Franceschini & Weber (1965): 20, 8. It is to be assumed, that in Egeria's time the pagan population in Jerusalem and elsewhere in this region was not insignificant. The urban population was still much more heterogeneous than Egeria made her readers believe, see Walker, P.W.L. (1990) *Holy Cities, Holy Places? Christian Attitudes to Jerusalem and the Holy Land in the Fourth Century*. Oxford: Oxford University Press: 18.

44 Zeddies, N. (2001) "Getrennte Räume – gemeinsames Leben? Von der räumlichen Trennung zwischen Klerikern und Frauen in der Spätantike und im frühen Mittelalter," in *Geschlechter-Räume. Konstruktionen von "gender" in Geschichte, Literatur und Alltag*, ed. M. Hubrath. Cologne/Weimar/Vienna: Böhllau: 9–22, 20.

45 Hunt, E.D. (1982) *Holy Land Pilgrimage in the Later Roman Empire AD 312–360*. Oxford: Clarendon Press: 147.

3 "He proved to be an inseparable travel companion"

Emo of Wittewierum and his Rome journey in 1211–1212

Dick de Boer

To Rome we go

From time immemorial the Eternal City has been the goal of travellers, especially since Rome changed from being the centre of an Empire into the heart of a faith that stretched far beyond the borders of its realm. Aristocrats and soldiers, merchants, and diplomats came and went. After the fall of the Roman Empire the numbers of normal inhabitants of Rome declined dramatically, from some 1,000,000 within the imperial, Aurelian, walls to between 20,000 to 30,000 at its lowest within the same boundaries.[1] The first abrupt drop was connected with the sack of Rome by the Visigoths in 410, followed by a nearly continuous decline over the ages. This drastic reduction of population mirrored the reduction of central functions and the consequent shrinking of economic activities. It also went hand in hand with a re-ruralisation of the Roman noble elites. However, it would be an error to deny this medieval Rome her dynamics. In his survey of Rome in the communal period, Vigeur points out that from the twelfth or thirteenth century onwards Rome benefited from a strong dynamism, which was reflected in a population size of some 50,000 in the early fourteenth century.[2] Although the reasons to visit the petrified memory of power changed and diversified, the numbers of visitors from across the world sometimes mounted to many hundreds of thousands per annum. This upsurge was by virtue of a new type of visitor the Roman Era had not known as such: The Christian pilgrim.

Flourishing – after a decline in the twelfth century due to a complex variety of reasons – from the papacy of Innocent III (1198–1216) onwards and reaching its apogee thanks to the development of the concept of Jubilee in 1300, already during the period of the large-scale migratory movements of the early Middle Ages, Christians from all over the world had started to visit Rome.[3] The "tertiary sector" boomed, since all these visitors, ranging from diplomats to pilgrims, merchants to artists had to be nourished and lodged. Moreover, since building materials were extremely cheap, the recycling and building sectors also thrived. Gradually city blocks were demolished, whereas churches and monasteries were built. Especially from the tenth century onward dozens of new churches and chapels were constructed. This was caused by a new practice of the veneration of saints within the Catholic

Church, attributing a manifest importance to their role as intermediaries between man and God. This veneration demanded a larger visibility and tangibility of the saints. Consequently, the relics of the saintly martyrs, which once found their "eternal" resting place in the Catacombs, were moved to churches (both in crypts and above ground level) – as did the veneration of these saints. And of course the machinery of papal government increasingly demanded space.

The voyage that offers the central theme of this contribution took place during the reign of pope Innocent III (1198–1216), who – being elected as an energetic man of just 38 years young – executed an ambitious program of administrative and moral reform, and at the same time favoured many building and restoration activities. Nevertheless, even his Rome was an urban landscape with huge empty spaces, where cattle was pastured and vineyards and vegetable gardens were maintained. The population gradually preferred to concentrate in the bend of the River Tiber, the Lateran complex and the Vatican developing as two eccentric poles.[4]

More than ever before, Innocent's *Curia* became the centre of a huge administrative machinery. The Fourth Crusade, papal ambitions of over-lordship over the kingdoms of Poland, Hungary, Portugal, Aragon, and Sicily, the fate of Christian prisoners in Islamic countries, Moorish efforts to start a new conquest of Southern Spain, the wars against the Albigensians, Waldensians, and Cathars, the efforts to prevent the new voluntary-poverty-movements of the *patarini* and the fresh efforts of Francis of Assisi and Dominic Guzman to develop in the same and fatal direction, the functioning of the *Curia* as court of appeal for conflicts large and small all over the Christian world; all of this led to a constant coming and going of diplomats and messengers, abbots and bishops, holy men and harlots to Rome.[5] Innocent's drive to clean up the Augean stables – into which he believed the papal administration had turned – inevitably created an elaborate bureaucracy that soon turned into a self-supporting, money-devouring beast.

One of the best testimonies of this is an anonymous poem, written during Innocent's reign and first published by Peter Herde.[6] In this *Dialogus inter euntem ad Curiam et venientem a Roma, de malis moribus Curie* (Dialogue between someone going to the Curia and someone coming from Rome, about the bad habits of the Curia) a man – obviously in a tavern north of Rome – sees a ragged traveller entering. At his question of why he travels alone and what happened to him, the other answers:

> Brother, I return from the Roman Curia, after having suffered tortures about which I prefer not to speak. I ran out of presents, have nothing left to eat, and in my misery miss a companion.

The man going to Rome, naively, wonders if some villain in a bad neighbourhood harassed him, or some highwayman robbed him in a silent forest. But no, it was the papal system itself:

The whole Curia is filled with rancidity. Every loving respect of good manners, science or honour is lacking here. Only money can help those who furnish it.

As to the cardinals the maxim is valid: If you give those people something, they call you "my son." They sell their support to whoever docks for it, and their barking is not without bite...

Above anything money rules. Helped by it the notaries do their job. Pennies are the ABC to the readers, he who gives richly, may count upon a preferential treatment....

A gang of robbers serves the masters. They charge heavily to transmit notices. And they too have "in battle" their purses always at hand. And at night they sleep with the money-bag under their mattress.

It was to this Rome that our abbot Emo, about 38 years of age, turned in despair when the year 1211 was running to its end. On November 9th he left "home" – home being a young, yet almost doomed little monastery in *Frisia* – to seek papal support. This meant that he chose to travel in a difficult season, through a turbulent world, crossing rough landscapes, to the administrative centre of Christianity. In such a situation travelling with a companion was more than ever necessary, both on the road, and to cope with the problems encountered in Rome, as the events would prove.

Travel and companions

The golden rule of travelling in historical times was: Avoid travelling alone. This rule had as a consequence that – unless a group was composed only of mounted men – the speed and distance of movement were dictated by the pedestrian part of the group. Next to this, in case of travelling on horseback or by other riding animals (ass, mule, camel), the speed and range of action depended on the natural capacities of the animals and the possibility to change mount regularly. Consequently, between 30 and 40 kilometres per day would be the average distance covered by people travelling in groups, be it merchants, be it pilgrims, be it missionaries, be it princely households. Indeed when in 1370–1371 the count of Holland, duke Albert of Bavaria, and his spouse Margaret of Legnica-Brzeg travelled to Nuremberg to marry off their daughter Johanna to the future king Wenzel of Bohemia, the princely company covered some 33 to 37 kilometres per day on the road south, and back home from Bavaria.[7] The Frisian abbot Emo arrived in Rome on 19 January 1212. This means that he covered the ca. 2215 kilometres of his journey in 72 days. With a short interruption in Prémontré this means an average of ca. 31 kilometres per day.[8]

One of the most well-documented travelling groups of the Middle Ages was the Bohemian nobleman Leo of Rozmital and his retinue, who travelled through most of Europe during the years 1465–1467, on a journey with the manifest objective of communicating the dynastic crisis around the Hussite king George Podiebrad to the European courts.[9] Rozmital was accompanied by some forty men. Two members of the retinue left highly interesting travelogues in which the landscapes, customs, and manners of the different countries were described. At many places festivities are mentioned at which local beauties were invited and dancing – even with nuns – took place.[10] No women, however, accompanied this male group while travelling. This does not mean that women did not travel at all, as we can learn from Femke Prinsen's study of female mobility that she based on a critical reading of the account books of the Counts of Holland.[11] When courts as such were on the move, and especially when queens, duchesses, or countesses moved, separated from their husbands and accompanied by their ladies in waiting, from one residence to another – as in the bridal journey mentioned above – women travelled in large groups, accompanied by male protectors.

Choosing a female companion would have been considered highly inadvisable for a travelling cleric, unless he was accompanying her as her guardian. This had to do with medieval opinions on female frailty, chastity, and what could be labelled as the "patriarchal (dis-) equilibrium."[12] No wonder women are lacking in Emo's travelogue. Yet, on his journey he most certainly encountered women, mainly as pilgrims, since substantial numbers of women are recorded to have taken part in pilgrimages during the medieval period.[13] For the Early Middle Ages information is scarce, and restricted to individual cases as the enterprise by a woman named Thigris or Thecla, a native of Valloires in the Maurienne-region, who "in the days of the most splendid king Guntram (from 567 until his death in 592 king of Burgundy)" travelled to the funeral church of St John the Baptist in Alexandria.[14] But in the High and Late Middle Ages data become abundant. One may deduce from miracle stories that in the twelfth century women and children constituted a substantial part of the flocks of pilgrims that travelled through Europe. Estimations mount up to one-quarter to one-third.[15] Finucane, looking at some 2300 miracle stories from France and England, found 61% of them referring to male and 39% referring to female pilgrims.[16] The Miracle-book of Our Lady of 's-Hertogenbosch (The Netherlands) starting in 1381 allows the conclusion that 32% of those who benefitted from miracles was female.[17] Out of the 542 miracles registered in the Miracle-book of Our Lady in Amersfoort (The Netherlands) some 26% had happened to women, and of those who came as pilgrims to thank Our Lady for this benefaction even 36% was female.[18] Often the miracle books narrate how these women travelled in groups to the place of worship, accompanied by both men and women.[19]

Nevertheless, there were doubts about the mobility of women too, and they were increasingly expressed. The church was opposed to wandering about by nuns and semi-religious women, and theologians, canonists, and other authors formulated their opposition against women going on (long-distance) pilgrimage.[20] However, women were sentenced to perform penitentiary pilgrimages in great numbers.[21] Maybe this contributed to establishing a *communis opinio* that travelling women were to be mistrusted and that especially women would fall victim to the many threats to their honour when travelling. There is a manifest internal contradiction between the obvious success of female voluntary travelling as a result of devotion, and male mistrust of this practice.

A nice example of this is a poem in the tradition of Reynaert the Fox, composed shortly before 1400 by the Dutch freelance poet, and favourite guest at court, Willem van Hildegaersberch. In this poem *Dit is van Reyer die Vos* he tells his audience how the fox somewhere during summer met his aunt, the she-wolf, in the Hesbaye, on a pilgrimage to Aachen.[22] She explains to him that she had promised this pilgrimage in her illness. The fox however says that:

> Moeye, soe en gave ic niet een kaff
> [. . .]
> om u bedevaert,
> soe dicke varet hindervaert,
> dat vrouwen veel after lande lopen:
> sy gaen om aflaet; maer sy vercopen
> dicwijl siel ende salicheijt.
> (Aunt, I would not give a bit [. . .] for your pilgrimage, since too often it turns wrong, when women travel around in the country: they go for indulgence; but often they sell their soul and salvation).[23]

To her objection that it would be foolish of her to break her vow, since "goede ghelofte is goet gehouden" (a good vow is rightly kept), the fox replies that she might contact God just as well in her parish church, even if she never came to Aachen, and he repeats that her pilgrimage could only bring her disgrace, and would make her vulnerable as a lame horse. Pleij and Meder read this poem as a rare example of a text in which the fox speaks wise words.[24] They see Reinaert here as the mouthpiece of a public opinion that condemned travelling by women. Jan van Herwaarden referred to this aspect of the poem, when putting it that "excessively zealous women [. . .] provoked criticism and laughter."[25] Contrary to their opinion I believe that one has to be aware of the story's false bottom. Even when – as is the case – the poet ends with the words *"Dat sprac Reynaert ende hi was vroet"* (thus spoke Reynaert and wise he was), one must be aware that finding an uttering of a personage that is known for his total unreliability qualified as "wise," especially when this runs completely against a widely spread, contemporary practice, this could imply the opposite intention. Here an internal moral contradiction becomes visible between male-dominated, mainly clerical-juridical opposition (although not founded in canonical law) against female travelling and the reality of travelling, mainly for devotional reasons by women of all layers of society.

To underline the positive approach during the same period, I have to restrict to one short example. On 1 August 1383 an *"eersam vrouwe Herborch, Jan Conincs wijf"* (honourable woman Herborch, wife of Jan Conincs) came from the town of Groningen, where she belonged to the patriciate, to the statute of St Mary in 's-Hertogenbosch. She covered the distance of 230 kilometres together with *"scoelmeyster vander stat en ander gebure"* (schoolteacher of the town and other neighbours) after a miracle that healed the severe wound in her left leg, from which she had suffered for a year and a half.[26] As a sign of her gratitude she moreover offered *"een silveren been ghehangen mit eenre silveren ketelen aen een silveren beelt*" (a silver leg, hanging with a silver chain from a silver statue).[27] Indeed, an honourable gesture by an honourable woman, travelling in honourable company.

Strange company, company as stranger

Travelling with companions of different origin, predominantly in haphazardly formed groups, sharing company when meeting in a tavern, and going in the same direction the next morning, may have offered a solution to possible linguistic problems, at least within Europe. These problems may have been less severe than in modern times, since the development of standardised languages largely matching the division into nation-states sharpened the divisions between and within the major linguistic groups. Travelling through Europe at a pedestrian's speed allowed any medieval traveller with some linguistic versatility to adapt to the gradual changes of dialect and "regiolect" in the regions he or she traversed. Yet, especially from the eleventh century onward, when the general mobility of almost all social classes increased, the need of linguistic aids must have been felt. Where travellers from the lay elite and the clerical professions had the advantage of sharing a Latin linguistic culture (although Cato and the medieval equals of *Winnie ille Pu*, especially when spoken, must have differed already by then quite a lot), merchants, sailors, cart-drivers and pilgrims needed help.

A rare example of such an instrument is preserved in the Vatican Library, as Ms. Christ. 566, and – because of its origin – known as the "Parisian Dialogues" (Pariser Gespräche).[28] A short selection shows how in Old-High-German and in Latin essential conversation was presented:

Guer is tin erro	*Ubi est senior tuus*	(Where is your boss?)
Guaz guildo	*Quid vis tu*	(What do you want?)
Gimer min ros	*Da mihi meum equum*	(Give me my horse)
Gimer min ansco	*Da mihi meos guantos*	(Give me my gloves)
Ger ensclephen mitte	*Tu iacuisti ad feminam*	(You have slept with
wip in ore bette	*in tuo lecto*	the woman in your bed)
Erro e guille trenchen	*Ego volo bibere*	(Lord, I want to have a drink)
Haben e genego/luzzil	*Habeo satis/parum ego*	(I have had enough/too little)[29]

For a man like Emo, such a tool does not seem to have been necessary to make his Rome journey successful. After being educated at a parish school and in a monastery in his homeland Frisia – in the part that nowadays is the Dutch province of Groningen, between 1190 and 1195 with his elderly brother Addo, he went to Oxford to finish the academic studies that they had started in Paris and Orleans.[30] This means that he had already got his proper part of the tower of Babel; he was trained in Latin and had lived in communities where the spoken vernacular was Frisian, Middle-Low German, French, and English. Many other travellers, however, did need either such a written tool, or the help of interpreters. A very explicit example is the Franciscan monk-missionary-diplomat

William of Rubruck, when travelling to the headquarters of the Mongolian khan Möngke in 1253–1255, carrying letters from the French king Louis IX that were translated in Arabic and Syriac in Acre already before leaving.[31] When breaking up from Soldaia (Crimea) his company was (in his words) composed of

> I and my colleague, friar Bartholomeo of Cremona; Gosset, the bearer of this letter; the interpreter Homo Dei; and a boy, Nicholas, whom I had bought at Constantinople with the alms you gave me. They (i.e. the Tatar leaders of Soldaia) supplied us in addition with two men who drove the wagons and tended the oxen and the horses.[32]

The necessity of having a trustworthy interpreter as company is repeatedly expressed in William of Rubruck's narrative. This is fully in line with the advice given some 80 years later, around 1335, by Francesco Balducci Pegolotti. This Florentine merchant and politician (ca. 1290–1347), after having lived for a while in England, applied in December 1321 to king Edward II for safe conduct for one year *"going beyond the seas"*; and between 1324 and 1327 he stayed at least two years on Cyprus.[33] His experiences were compiled in the work known as the *Pratica della Mercatura*. Starting with a short merchant's dictionary, the author, especially when describing the road to China, underlines the importance of having a good interpreter as company:

> ...at Tana (Crimea) he should furnish himself with dragomans (= interpreters), and he should not try to save by hiring a poor one instead of a good one ... and besides dragomans he ought to take along at least two good menservants who know the Cumanic tongue well.[34]

For the subject of this volume it is interesting that this advice is immediately followed by some remarks about women as travel companions. Pegolotti writes:

> ..if the merchant wishes to take along from Tana any woman with him, he may do so – and if he does not wish to take one, there is no obligation; yet if he takes one, he will be regarded [by the Asian communities which he visits; DEHdB] as a man of higher condition than if he does not take one. If he takes one, however, she ought to know the Cumanic tongue as well as the manservant.

A concern like this certainly had not been an issue for abbot Emo of Wittewierum. For a celibate abbot like him and only travelling in Europe, having a male companion would have been much more acceptable than having a female servant, who would have caused at least some frowning and probably suspicion.

Emo and his companion

After this short sketch of medieval travelling with companions, it is time to discuss Emo's case in more detail. We know about his whereabouts thanks to personal details in the Chronicle of his Premonstratensian monastery that he started writing around 1219, and thanks to the comments on his person by his successor Menko, who continued the Chronicle.[35] Emo was born between ca. 1170–1175 in the part of Frisia known as Fivelgo, from a family that obviously belonged to the Frisian gentry: The son of his father's brother, and equally named Emo, is mentioned as being "nobilis."[36]

This first cousin had founded a monastery shortly after 1200 on the family property in the village of Jukwerd, called Romerswerf, against the wish of his (female) next of kin and opposed by neighbouring monasteries that feared competition. The main problems, however, to make this foundation successful, were the stubborn character of the founder, and the fact that (although only indirectly mentioned) he persisted in a preference for a double monastery, inhabited by both monks and nuns. In the early Middle Ages this had been a widespread phenomenon. Already around 1150 the foundation of double monasteries in which both monks and nuns were living together in one abbey – albeit in separate buildings – had come under severe criticism.[37] As the consequence of this neither the Cistercians nor the Premonstratensians were willing to accept paternity over the young monastery. Although in 1204 the first *oratorium* was consecrated by the bishop of Münster – to whose diocese this part of Frisia belonged – the initiative was doomed to fail.

Our Emo decided to rescue his cousin's foundation. After his study of law in Oxford, around ca.1197–1198, he first was appointed schoolmaster in the parish of Westeremden, where his brother Addo had become the parish-priest (a clear sign that the family had its roots there), and several years later – at the request of the parishioners – he had become the parish priest of Huizinge himself, another basis of the family's status. But seeing the young monastery at Romerswerf in its exhausting near-death struggle, in 1207–1208 he decided to commit himself to rescuing it. He did so after a long discussion, during a walk in the fields with (in the translated words of the Chronicle) a man

> ...who was very close to him and who in a special way cared for the adornment of God by building and decorating churches; already in his youth and also later on this was what he loved to do most.[38]

Both friends decided to enter the monastery in 1209. For Emo it was a final choice, his friend soon discovered that life as a monk was not for him and that his vocation was a life as an architect. They remained, however, close friends. It was this friend, with the name Henricus (Hendrik/Henry), whose company would be essential during Emo's journey to Rome.

Fighting injustice

Emo's first rescue action, already before he entered the monastery at Romerswerf, was comparing the rules of Benedictines, Cistercians and Premonstratensians. When he had finally chosen for the last order at the end of March 1209, he travelled some 190 kilometres with his cousin to the bishop in Münster and to the Premonstratensian monastery of Varlar, 36 kilometres west of the episcopal see. Varlar was the oldest Premonstratensian monastery in the diocese, and the perfect anchor point for the little Frisian foundation. Although Varlar's abbot, Jordanus, symbolically accepted them within the Premonstratensian family by handing them over the white clothing of the order, the problems were not over yet. Varlar refused paternity, with the distance to Romerswerf as a pretext, but probably because the viability was all but guaranteed.

The year 1211 then seemingly offered a turning point, when the church of Wierum – meaning the office, the buildings, and all revenues connected with it – was donated to the monastery by the *"larger and wiser part of the patrons"* (a maiori et saniori parte patronum). This was common practice according to the Frisian law system, in which in most places the *"eigenerfden"* – members of the local elite who owned a substantial piece of land – had the say in the (rotation of) the local judge (or *redger*), and the right to take all major decisions in ecclesiastical affairs.[39] Only where powerful nobles had a superior seigneurial position, connected to a "stone house," this right could come (or remain) in one hand. On the 23rd of June, the parish priest of Wierum would resign and enter the Benedictine order, allowing Emo's Premonstratensians to take over the pastoral care, as was a common phenomenon in the order. This would change Wierum in Wittewierum (White Wierum), because of the white Premonstratensian clothing.

How bitter was the disappointment, how big the outrage, how strong the feeling of injustice of the idealistic Emo, when, contrary to logic and against expectations and Frisian law, on the 18th of September of the same year the bishop of Münster decided to recognise the claims of a certain *Ernestus prepotens*; a very powerful Ernest to his part of the church to cancel the donation and to convict the Premonstratensian canons. It has long been enigmatic why the bishop supported a man who overtly sought to reserve the position of parish priest for his own son (and showed not to loathe violence in another conflict about the church of Loppersum six years later), instead of helping out a young monastery in its struggle for existence.[40] Only when preparing the book in which I reconstructed Emo's Rome-journey, I found that on the 12th of September, not even one week before he gave his support to Ernestus, the bishop of Münster issued a charter in which, as a result of the activities of a special advisory committee, a delicate financial problem connected to the establishing of a new parish was solved.[41] All of the witnesses mentioned in this charter derive from the region, and are without doubt identical with the mentioned committee. The first layperson being... Ernestus Gerlenga. Finding the extremely rare name Ernestus twice within one week in the same context makes Emo's outrage even more understandable: It was an ordinary push-me-pull-you case in which the man who helped the bishop to solve a problem was rewarded with the recognition of his doubtful claim.

When an official appeal to the synodal court was turned down on the 23rd of September only an appeal to the Papal Curia might restore justice and could protect the monastery from total failure. The theoretical possibility of turning to the archbishop of Cologne, as the hierarchically next-higher layer in the apparatus of the Church, was useless already in advance, since the arch-episcopal see had become heavily involved in the struggle between Guelfs and Staufen that was growing towards a bloody climax, since pope Innocent III in November 1210 and March 1211 had excommunicated the "*tyrannus*" emperor Otto IV, and part of the Electors in the same month of September 1211 chose Fredrick II as "the other emperor" (*alium imperatorem*).[42] This meant that, while autumn had already started and winter approached rapidly, there was no other option but to travel first to Prémontré. There, true and unmistakable support of the head of the Premonstratensian order should finally be acquired before travelling to Rome. It indicated the prospect of an exhausting journey, in a severe season through lands in turmoil. It was a moment when trustworthy company was most needed. The company of a real friend.

Off to Rome

In his chronicle Emo, of course, pays attention to the birth pains of his monastery and the journey that he had to venture. It does not really develop into a full travelogue, but offers a rough description of the roads followed and essential places along these roads, mixed with some detailed passages about the events. Here, in translation, I quote the passage about his departure from Romerswerf, and the first stages to Prémontré:

> After having arranged for his expense, he left for Rome on the 9th of November. He was accompanied by his old friend Henricus who had left the monastery soon after his entering, but now on his own initiative proved to be an inseparable company, even postponing his own family-affairs.
>
> They travelled through Coevorden and several other places and crossed the Rhine near Duisburg. From there they went along Maastricht, Tongres, Heylissem, Villers, Bonne-Espérance, Hautmont, Clairfontaine, Foigny, Thenailles and Laon, before arriving in Prémontré.[43]

Short as this description might be, it gives some essential details about the nature of companionship and way of travelling. For the travelling abbot his male companion is already presented as a valuable factor: A trusted friend of old, who shares the dangers of the road with him. Female companionship was improbable for a cleric and indeed female company is not mentioned at all, just like women are the silent majority in this text. Mentioning Coevorden confirms the thought, already dictated by logic, that Emo and his friend Henricus going south would prefer to avoid the territories of "the enemy," the bishop of Münster, and moreover in the wet season would prefer the road over the higher, sandy ridge toward Coevorden, avoiding the wet peat district that laid east of it. That, several day marches further (probably on 16 November) they crossed the Rhine near Duisburg, indicates that they used the Premonstratensian itineraries: Since

1170 the Premonstratensian monastery of Hamborn served as the nodal point where most roads from Premonstratensians monasteries in the Frisian and North-German districts intertwined.[44] Of the mentioned places Heylissem, Bonne-Espérance, Clairfontaine, Thenailles, and Laon housed other Premonstratensian abbeys, while Villers-la-Ville and Foigny were Cistercians establishments and Hautmont was an old Benedictine monastery. So, the early details of the travel narrative as included in the Chronicle not only document the route chosen, but also an elementary principle of travelling – especially for an abbot/prior of a young and poor monastery, struggling for survival – seeking, whenever possible, lodging in religious houses. Primarily other Premonstratensian houses, or Augustinian priories, with almost the same rule, followed by the nearest of kin: Houses of the Cistercian order, and the other orders. If such an opportunity was lacking, chapters, parish priests, pilgrim-hospitals would be the normal places to turn to, when avoiding the more worldly and costly inns.

When reconstructing Emo's itinerary, applying these principles, a logical place to visit appeared to be the tiny village of Houthem (now in the ultimate south of the Dutch province of Limburg). Although not mentioned, it was the place where an equally young Premonstratensian monastery offered shelter. In Houthem a local saint was venerated, Saint Gerlach, a member of the lower nobility who had changed his life to become a hermit, living in or near an old oak tree, as a solitary near-equal of Saint Norbert. Having been venerated already as a "living saint," from his death in 1165 or 1166 onwards the place of his hermitage, the *loco qui vulgo Ad quercum dicitur*, became a place of worship.[45] In 1201 at that place, now indicated as the *locus sancti Gerlaci*, an *oratorium* was founded, soon to be changed into a small Premonstratensian monastery. And already around 1210 it became a flourishing community. The vita of St Gerlach – of course intended to support the veneration – mentions a miracle, to be dated around 1220, proving that immediately this young Premonstratensian foundation became part of the itinerary-network. It runs:

> A certain abbot from the Premonstratensian Order travelling from the Frisian provinces to the Chapter in Prémontré, left his horse that was given up and about to die at the sanctuary of the blessed Gerlach ...

> (Abbas quidam Praemonstratensis ordinis de Frisiae partibus ad capitulum Praemonstratum properans equum suum in cella beati Gerlaci moribundum et desoeratum dimisit ...).[46]

Besides the interesting aspect that this is a story about a mounted abbot (consequently from a well-established, rich monastery) who thanks to the miraculous powers of Gerlach receives his horse back, safe and sound, the narrative supports the thought that Emo and Henricus followed the same course heading for Prémontré. They, however, most probably went on foot, as most travellers; especially most pilgrims did, not being members of the higher nobility or clergy. There is no mention at all of horses, mules or donkeys, and the application of such animals either as mount or as beast of burden, would have been a serious problem when passing the

Alps mid-winter. The only information made about means of transport is on the way back when Emo and Henricus made the same choice as propagated shortly before or around 1240 by Albert, the Cistercian abbot of Stade, when describing an (imaginary) journey to Rome: "if you arrive in Basel, do good to your feet and take the boat to go downstream to Cologne" (*Cum veneris Basilem, bene fac pedibus tuis, et intrando navem descende usque Coloniam*).[47] Emo did this only halfway up North, when arriving in Strassburg: "there he joined a ship and, after passing Speyer, Worms, Mainz and quite a number of castles, he arrived in Cologne" (*ibi navi conducta, Sprea, Vurmatia, Maguncia et quamplurimis castris relitis, Coloniam venit*). The immediately following phrase: "After this he returned travelling on foot" (*Post hec pedestri itinere reversus est*) makes it highly probably that indeed the whole journey was made as pedestrians.[48]

We have already seen that the two friends left on 9 November 1211 for their almost impossible mission. It is inspiring to be aware that two pairs of eyes would travel through an early version of the "blue banana" of Europe. One pair of eyes belonged to Emo, an academic lawyer, later also trained as a theologian, with a strongly developed intellectual curiosity, a sharp awareness of the problems that endangered the church and the unity of faith. The other pair belonged to his friend Henricus, who, as a professional architect, not only may have been motivated by altruism when offering to accompany Emo on the long road to Rome, but also may have grabbed the opportunity with both hands to traverse towns and regions where church architecture was booming. Chapels, abbeys, parish churches and cathedrals were elevated in the young Gothic style, while in Italy a new, slender version of Romanesque building was applied. a less known, but highly interesting example of brand-new early gothic architecture they saw was the choir of Soissons cathedral, inaugurated in May 1212. See Fig. 3.1. Yet, saving the young monastery of Wittewierum remained the ultimate goal of the journey, and in realizing that goal friendship proved to be an indispensable tool.

Success and drama

After a short stay at the headquarters of the Order, Emo and Henricus left Prémontré probably on 1 December 1211, carrying a letter of recommendation by Gervase the Englishman, general abbot of the order from 1209 to 1220, and famous for his epistolary talents.[49] Following one of the main commercial and pilgrims roads along (i.a.) Troyes, Lyon, Susa, Pavia, Lucca, and Viterbo, they arrived in Rome on 19 January 1212, the feast day of the early Christian Persian martyrs Marius, Martha, Abachum, or Abacus, and Audifax, who supposedly were martyred on that day in 270, when coming to Rome as pilgrims.[50] This means that Emo indeed crossed the French-Italian Alps immediately after Christmas, using the Mt. Cenis-pass, and followed the Via Francigena through the Apennines during the second week of January, which might have been an even harsher challenge. (see Fig. 3.2.).

The two friends arrived in a Rome in turmoil, where pope Innocent III had cases to solve that were far more urgent than a conflict between a Frisian abbot and his bishop. The relation with the Muslim rulers in Egypt and Morocco,[51]

Figure 3.1 In Soissons Emo and Henricus saw the choir of the St Gervase and St Protase
cathedral that was about to be consecrated in May 1212

Source: *The author*.

problems in Portugal and Hungary, the Albigensian crusades and the preparation
for the battle of Las Navas de Tolosa, the success of the "Poor of Lyon" and the
patarini – even in Rome itself – and the question how to deal with the new poor
movements of Dominic Guzman and Francis of Assisi demanded his attention.[52]
Moreover, since Easter fell early that year, Rome was already preparing for Lent,
meaning that from 8 February onward until Easter (in 1212: 25 March) every day
a stationary mass would be read in one of the station churches of Rome.[53]

All these elements, and the usual struggles with bureaucracy, made Emo's stay in
Rome last 50 days. For the goal of my contribution it is only necessary to mention
that this long stay in Rome exhausted Emo's finances, yet that it led to a papal letter
of support, proposing an arrangement that would serve Emo's monastery well. These
two elements came together in a necessity to make a financial arrangement: In order
to borrow money temporarily to finance the journey back to Frisia Emo pawned his
papal letter to some merchants. They agreed to be paid back in Bologna. This
allowed Emo to arrange a formal loan on the first part of his way home, with one of
the young banking houses in Lucca, Siena, or Pavia; and it had as an extra advantage
that the papal letter might travel north more safely.[54] His conflict with the papacy
running to a climax, the excommunicated German emperor Otto IV had laid roadblocks with garrisons all over the Apennine roads.[55] There clerics carrying letters
from the Papal Curia were robbed, obviously in order to prevent messages of support

Figure 3.2 Immediately below the Mt Cenis pass the medieval road now runs through a reservoir, and is only visible during periods of extreme drought, such as in June 2017

Source: The author.

being delivered to Otto's opponents north of the Alps. It seemed the perfect solution for two of Emo's problems to have his letter follow its separate road to Bologna. The implicit detour was accepted as a necessary evil.

He would, however, see success change into drama very soon. Having arrived earlier than the merchants from Pavia in Bologna, Emo and Henricus had to wait many days before finally some of the merchants appeared. They admitted only after a long delay "that they themselves had lost the letter at one of these roadblocks" (*se perdidisse litteras ad quoddam presidium*). This disastrous news caused a mental breakdown in Emo, who was faced with a total failure after all his efforts, which had cost him all his money. Although the physical reaction was a fever for several days, he decided to return to Rome and submit the case to pope Innocent again. Here the value of friendship manifested itself to the full. In one of the most intimate, and detailed passages of the travel narrative Emo writes:

> But this companion of his, who was more concerned to save Emo's life than his own, offered on his own initiative that he would go. And he forbade Emo to return together with him, because of the danger caused by his fevers; and so he returned alone, led by God. And after chancellor had introduced him to

the pope, the pope listened to the letters of Emo's adversities, and ordered to write the letter again and hand it over to him. And with the support of God, he brought all of it, albeit very tired, to a good end.

(*Sed ille sodalist eius magis animam illius quam proprius salvare cupiens, sese ultro exhibuit; et ne cum eo redirect, propter periculim febrium prohubuit; sicque solus Deo duce rediit. Et a cancellario coram papa introductus, eut auditis litteris adversitatis adversitatis ipsius, iussit papa rescribi litteras et redid; et cooperante Deo licet fatigatus optato fine potitus est).*[56]

When Henricus returned in Bologna, "very worried about his friend's health" (*multum ... pro salutate sodalist sui sollicitus)* he found Emo safe and sound and healed by the best medicine an intellectual could wish for: The opportunity to the copy books of the library of the University of Bologna. Although the exact date is not given, the two friends most probably left Bologna immediately after Whitsuntide (which fell on 13 May 1212), to return triumphant to Frisian. The unlucky incident had as a hidden advantage that they did not encounter new problems with the armies of neither Otto IV, nor Frederick II, who probably had been received in a festive way in Rome around 10 April and had sailed north, to Genua, where he stayed until early July. It was sheer luck that the journey north had more or less the character of a quiet walk between two thunderstorms. But it was thanks to friendship that this remarkable quest was brought to a good end.

Notes

1 These are only rough estimations. Calculations for imperial Rome even differ from several hundreds of thousands to several millions, see Gregory S. Aldrete, *Daily Life in the Roman City: Rome, Pompeii and Ostia* (Greenwood Press: Westport, CO/ London, 2004), p. 22 ff. On Rome's population in the early sixteenth century only the census of 1526–1527 gives reliable information, see Peter Partner, *Renaissance Rome 1500–1559: A Portrait of a Society* (University of California Press: Berkeley etc., 1979), p. 82 ff, but even then the interpretations differ quite a lot.

2 Jean-Claude Marie Vigueur, *The Forgotten Story. Rome in the Communal Period* (Viella: Rome, 2016), p. 21 ff.

3 Debra J. Birch, *Pilgrimage to Rome in the Middle Ages: Continuity and Change.* (Studies in the History of Medieval Religion, 13) (Boydell & Brewer: Woodbridge/ Rochester, NY, 1998/2000), esp. p. 187 ff. For Pilgrims from the north of Europe especially during the Early and High Middle Ages see Jan van Herwaarden, '*Pilgrimages from the North to Rome,*' in: id., *Between Saint James and Erasmus: Studies in Late-Medieval Religious Life. Devotion and Pilgrimage in the Netherlands* (Brill: Leiden/Boston, 2003), pp. 211–241. On the upsurge of pilgrimage in 1300 see: Herbert L. Kessler and Johanna Zacharias, *Rome 1300. On the Path of the Pilgrim* (Yale University Press: New Haven and London, 2000).

4 Vigueur, *Forgotten Story.*

5 Catherine Cory and Michael Hollerich, *Christian Theological Tradition* (Prentice Hall: Englewood Cliffs, NJ, 3rd edition), p. 258.

6 Peter Herde, *Beiträge zum päpstlichen Kanzlei- und Urkundenwesen im dreizehnten Jahrhundert* (Verlag Michael Lassleben: Kallmünz, 1967). Here appendix I, pp. 181– 185, with a convincing argumentation for it being written during the papacy of

Innocent III. The poem is preserved in only one version, in the Bodleian library, Ms Add. A 44, fol. 46 r-v. Recently mentioned by Thomas Haye, "Zynische Empfehlungen für einen Besuch der Päpstlichen Kurie: Der Dialog De Quattuor Saccis Romanam Curiam Deportandis und die Briefe des Petrus Damiani," *Classica et Mediaevalia*, 65 (2014), pp. 283–321, esp. p. 297. No full translation exists. For my translation I am indebted to prof. Onno Kneepkens, emeritus Medieval Latin at Groningen University.

7 This could be calculated from the special account book that is preserved from this "honeymoon," the essentials of which I gave as an appendix to the text of my inaugural speech at Groningen University; Dick E.H. de Boer, *Over de binnengrenzen van de middeleeuwen. Verkenningen langs de regionale verbindingslijnen in het 14de-eeuwse Europa* (ICG Printing: Dordrecht, 1993), pp. 18–19 and 32.

8 A reconstruction of the daily stages is to be found in Dick E.H. de Boer, *Emo's Reis. Een historisch culturele ontdekkingstocht door Europa in 1212*. (Verloren: Hilversum, 2017, 8th edition; 1st edition Noordboek: Leeuwarden, 2011).

9 Malcolm Letts, F.S.A. (ed. and transl.), *The Travels of Leo of Rozmital through Germany, Flanders, England, France, Spain, Portugal and Italy, 1465–1467. Hakluyt Society*, Second Series No. CVIII (Hakluyt Society: Cambridge, 1955).

10 Ibidem e.g. pp. 23–24, 30–31.

11 Femke Prinsen, "Female Mobility in the Courtly Environment: The Evidence of Late Medieval Household Accounts," in: *Itineraria* 8–9 (2009–2010) (special issue: *Female Trails. Historical Sources on Mobility and Gender in the Low Countries (1200–1500)*, pp. 255–300.

12 See for instance Judith M. Bennett, *Medieval Women in Modern Perspective* (American Historical Association: Washington, 2000), p. 20.

13 See Diana Webb, *Medieval European Pilgrimage* (Palgrave Macmillan: Basingstoke 2005), pp. 90 ff. on female pilgrim: Leigh Ann Craig, *Wandering Women and Holy Matrons: Women as Pilgrims in the Later Middle Ages*. Studies in Medieval and Reformation Traditions 138. (Brill: Leiden, 2009),

14 She stayed there three years before receiving a relic of St John the Baptist, which she brought – probably shortly before 572 – to the place since then called St Jean-de-Maurienne, according to Gregory of Tours, *Liber in Gloria Martyrum*, published in Bruno Krusch (ed.), *Gregorii episcopi Turonensis Miracula et opera minora*. Scriptores rerum merovingicarum, 1, 2 (Hahnsche Buchhandlung: Hannover, 1969, 2nd edition), p. 47.

15 Renaat Gaspar, "Women on Pilgrimage to Jerusalem: The Evidence from Travellers' Tales," *Itineraria*, 8–9 (2009–2010) (special issue: *Female Trails. Historical Sources on Mobility and Gender in the Low Countries (1200–1500)*), p. 91.

16 Ronald C. Finucane, *Miracles and pilgrims. Popular Beliefs in Medieval England* (Saint Martin's Press: New York, 1995, 2nd edition), pp. 142–143.

17 H. Hens, H. van Bavel, G.C.M. van Dijck, and J.H.M. Frantzen, *Mirakelen van Onze Lieve Vrouw te 's-Hertogenbosch 1381–1603*. Transcription, annotation, and introduction by – Bijdragen tot de geschiedenis van het Zuiden van Nederland XLII (Stichting Zuidelijk Historisch Contact: Tilburg, 1978), pp. 93–94.

18 Calculation made by me based upon Dick E.H. de Boer en Ludo Jongen, m.m.v. Juliette Duisterwinkel, *In het water gevonden. Het Amersfoortse Mirakelboek naar het handschrift Brussel, Koninklijke Bibliotheek Albert I, 8179–8180*. Middeleeuwse Studies en Bronnen CLV (Verloren: Hilversum, 2015) and the numbers given there on p. 32.

19 Norbert Ohler, *Reisen im Mittelalter* (Artemis Verlag: München/Zürich, 1986) (also available in an updated English edition, translated by Caroline Hillier as *The Medieval Traveller* (Boydell and Brewer: Woodbridge/Rochester, NY, 2010) gives ample, yet random examples of travelling women.

20 Jan van Herwaarden, "Pilgrimages and Social prestige. Some Reflections on a Theme," in: Gunther Jaritz and Barbara Schuh (eds.), *Wallfahrt und Alltag im Mittelalter und früher Neuzeit* (Österreichische Akademie der Wissenschaften: Wien, 1992), pp. 25–79, esp. 76–78.

21 Many examples to be found in the study of penitential pilgrimages in the medieval Low by Jan van Herwaarden, *Opgelegde bedevaarten*. Een studie over de praktijk van opleggen van bedevaarten (met name in de stedelijke rechtspraak) in de Nederlanden gedurende de late Middeleeuwen (ca 1300–ca 1550) (Van Gorcum: Assen/Amsterdam, 1978), esp. pp. 406–407, who however explicitly did not try to make a statistic evaluation.

22 Willem Bisschop and Eelco Verwijs (eds.), *Gedichten van Willem van Hildegaersberch* (HES: Utrecht, 1981; reprint of the first edition of 1870), p. 21.

23 Bisschop and Verwijs, *Gedichten*, p. 21.

24 Hermn Pleij, *Het gilde van de Blauwe Schuit. Literatuur, volksfeest en burgermoraal in de late middeleeuwen* (Meulenhoff: Amsterdam, 1979), p. 151 and Theo Meder, *Sprookspreker in Holland. Leven en werk van Willem van Hildegaersberch (ca. 1400)* (Prometheus: Amsterdam, 1991), p. 393.

25 Van Herwaarden, *Between Saint James and Erasmus*, p. 97.

26 Dick E.H. de Boer, "Mirakels mooi. Groningers en wonderen in de dertiende tot vijftiende eeuw," in: Dick E.H. de Boer, Renée I.A. Nip, and Remi W.M. van Schaïk (eds.), *Het Noorden in het midden*. Groninger Historische Reeks, 17 (Van Gorcum: Assen, 1998), p. 212.

27 Hens, *Mirakelen*, p. 362.

28 Frank Jolles, "The hazard of travel in medieval Germany. An attempt at an interpretation of the altdeutsche Gespräche," *German Life and Letters* 21 (1968), pp. 309–319. Roberto Gusmani, "Medienverschiebung und Verwandtes in den 'Pariser Gesprächen,'" in: Alexander Lubotsky (ed.), *Sound Law and Analogy: Papers in Honor of Robert S.P. Beekes on the Occasion of his 60th Birthday*. Volume 9 of Leiden studies in Indo-European (Rodopi: Amsterdam, 1997), pp. 81–90.

29 Dick E.H. de Boer, 'Bûter, brea en griene tsiis. Langues et identités au Moyen Age, quelques observations,' in: Flocel Sabaté (ed.), *Identitats. Ruenio cientifica. XIV Curs d'Estiu Conmtat d'Urgell, celebrat a Balaguer els dies 1, 2 i 3 de juliol de 2009 sota la direcció de Flocel Sabaté i Maite Pedrol* (Pagès editors: Lleida, 2012), pp. 153–175.

30 Huub P.H. Jansen (†) and Antheun Janse (eds.), *Kroniek van het klooster Bloemhof te Wittewierum. Inleiding, editie en vertaling -*. Middeleeuwse Studies en Bronnen XX (Verloren: Hilversum, 1991), pp. X, and 10–11, doubting the sequence. De Boer, *Emo's Reis*, p. 17, chooses for Oxford as the final stage of their academic education. Oxford opts for the year 1190 of his arrival and sees him as the very first foreign student: http://oxford.openguides.org/wiki/?Emo_Of_Friesland, although it would be more proper to consider Addo as such; moreover in the same years other continental students came to Oxford, see: Joszef Laszlovszky, "Nicholaus clericus: A Hungarian student at Oxford University in the twelfth century," *Journal of Medieval History* 14 (1988–1989), pp. 217–231.

31 Peter Jackson (ed.), *The Mission of Friar William of Rubruck: His Journey to the Court of the Great Khan Möngke 1253–1255* (Hackluyt Society: London, 1990), p. 118. See also Ohler, *Reisen*, pp. 327–335 for a short version of the description of this journey.

32 Jackson, *Mission*, p. 69.

33 Allan Evans (ed.), *Francesco Balducci Pegolotti, La Pratica della Mercatura* (The Medieval Academy of America: Cambridge, MA, 1936), pp. XX–XXI.

34 Evans, *Pegolotti*, p. 21; translation available in Robert S. Lopez and Irving W. Raymond, *Medieval Trade in the Mediterranean World. Illustrative Documents, translated with Introductions and Notes by –* (Columbia University Press: New York, 1990, 2nd edition), p. 356. Italics mine.

64   *Dick de Boer*

35   Best to be consulted in the most recent edition of the Latin text with Dutch translation Jansen and Janse, *Kroniek*. The oldest copy of the Chronicle is a 13th c. manuscript, probably mainly in the hand of Menko, in the Groningen University Library, Hs 116. Birch, *Pilgrimage*, unfortunately seems only to know the 1874 edition in the MGH SS XXIII, and therefore makes him originating in Verum (which makes it completely vague for those who don't know that this is the Latin version of village Wierum, later called Wittewierum, and unfamiliar with the fact that there still is another village Wierum in Frisia).

36   On Emo, life and personality see, next to the introduction in Jansen and Janse, *Kroniek*: also Huub P.H. Jansen, *Emo tussen angst en ambitie*. Stad en Lande historische reeks 3 (Stichting Matrijs: Utrecht, 1984), passim, Dick E.H. de Boer, "De proost en de Paus. Hoe de wegen van twee fascinerende persoonlijkheden elkaar kruisten," *Groniek 180* (Stichting Groniek: Groningen, 2008), pp. 321–337 and Dick E. H. de Boer, "Sur les traces d'Emo. Le voyage d'un abbé curieux et furieux à Rome en l'an 1212," *Actes officiels des 38ᵉ et 39ᵉ Colloques du Centre d'Études et de Recherches Prémontrées. Amiens-1202, Troyes-2013* (Centre d'Études et de Recherches Prémontrées: Laon, 2018), pp. 9–19.

37   Basilius Franz Grassl OPräm, *Der Prämonstratenserorden, seine Geschichte und seine Ausbreitung bis zur Gegenwart*. Analecta Praemonstratensia 10 (Abbey of Averbode: Tongerloo, 1934), p. 18.

38   Jansen and Janse, *Kroniek*, pp. 14–15.

39   For the position of these "eigenerfden" see: Paul Noomen, "Eigenerfd of edel? Naar aanleiding van de afkomst van de Aytta's," *It Beaken*, 74 (Fryske Akademy: Leeuwarden, 2012), pp. 257–301.

40   Jansen and Janse, Kroniek, pp. 52–53.

41   Westfälisches Urkunden-Buch. Fortsetzung von Erhard's Regestae historiae Westfaliae. Hrsg. von dem Verein für Geschichte und Althertumskunde Westfalens. Dritter Band: Die Urkunden Westfalens vom J. 1201–1300.
      – Erste Abtheilung erstes Heft: Die Urkunden des Bisthums Münster von 1201–1250. Unter Mitwirkung von Ludwig Perger bearb. von Roger Wilmans (Regensberg'sche Buchhandlung: Münster, 1859), p. 35.

42   Olaf B. Rader, (C.H. Beck: München, 2012), p. 18.

43   Jansen en Janse, Kroniek, pp. 24–25.

44   Ludger Horstkötter, (Jahrhundert, MV-Verlag: Münster, 2012).

45   Anneke B. Mulder-Bakker, *De kluizenaar in de eik. Gerlach van Houthem en zijn verering* (Verloren: Hilversum, 1995), p. 9 ff.

46   Inibidem, pp. 204–207; Latin text and later Middle-Netherlandish translation.

47   [J.J. Lappenberg, ed.], *Annales Stadenses*. MGH SS, XVI (Hahn: Hannover, 1859), pp. 283–378 esp. 340.

48   Johann Martin and Janse, *Kroniek*, pp. 28–31.

49   Christopher R. Cheney, "Gervase, abbot of Prémontré, a medieval letter-writer," *Bulletin of the John Rylands Library,* 33 (1950), pp. 25–56; mentioning this letter on p. 46.

50   Jansen and Janse, *Kroniek*, 27, erroneously translate *Marii et Marthe* with Mary and Martha, suggesting the feast of the biblical Mary and Martha although Emo gives the 14th Kalend of February as the right day for the mentioned martyrs. The fact that since 1969, these martyrs are no longer included in the General Roman Calendar increases the confusion.

51   Exactly on the day of arrival of Emo and Henricus pope Innocent wrote a letter concerning Christian prisoners in Alexandria, Giulio Cipollone, *Cristianità–Islam: cattività e liberazione in nome di Dio: il tempo di Innocenzo III dopo 'il 1187'* (Pontificia Università Gregoriana: Roma, 2003, 2nd edition), p. 377.

52   On this last topic recently Werner Maleczek, "Franziskus von Assisi, Papst Innocenz III. und die römische Kurie im Jahr 1209. Ein folgenreiches Zusammentreffen,"

Mitteilungen des Instituts für Österreichische Geschichtsforschung, 118 (2010), pp. 323–343.

53 On the development of the stational liturgy in Rome, and the schedule of the churches see Sible de Blaauw, *Cultus et Décor Liturgie en architectuur in laatantiek en middeleeuws Rome. Basilica Salvatoris, Sanctae Mariae, Sancti Petri* (Eburon: Delft, 1987), pp. 16 ff. Also available in an (reworked) Italian translation as: *Cultus et decor: Liturgia e architettura nella Roma tardoantica e medievale: Basilica Salvatoris, Sanctae Mariae, Sancti Petri (Studi e testi)* (Biblioteca Apostolica Vaticana: Roma, 1994).

54 Still fundamental for the early history of Italian banking: Thomas W. Blomquist, *The Dawn of Banking in an Italian Commune: Thirteenth Century Lucca* (Yale University Press: New Haven, 1979), and id., "Some observations on early foreign exchange banking based upon new evidence from 13th-century Lucca," *Journal of European Economic History* 19 (1990), pp. 353–375, showing that indeed banking was still in its infancy.

55 Jansen and Janse, *Kroniek*, pp. 28–29.

56 Ibidem.

4 Not for weaker vessels?!

Travel and gender in the early modern low countries

Gerrit Verhoeven

Until recently, early modern travel was often portrayed as an all-male activity, yet a more subtle, gendered reality was uncovered by trailblazing British research. In this chapter, Flemish and Dutch travel journals will be analysed to provide a fresh perspective. From the late seventeenth century onwards, female travellers were no longer frowned upon in the Low Countries, as they cropped up in ever-growing numbers on *plaisierreijsjes* (leisure trips) and *somertogjes* (summer trips). Their elbow room was limited, however, both literally – Netherlandish women rarely if ever travelled beyond the familiar horizon of the Northern and Southern Netherlands and the rim of nearby metropolises – and metaphorically, as male chaperones – husbands, fathers, brothers, nephews, and other relatives – held sway over these mixed parties. Most of these men also kept a firm grip on the quill and inkwell, which makes it difficult to assess whether women really travelled differently. Female companions were usually portrayed as fearful and fretful, thereby serving as the ideal offset to emphasise masculine values of hardiness, stamina, and level-headedness. Apparently, these family trips and *somertogjes* were also used as an instrument to mould a male identity. Yet, travel journals written by Netherlandish women, such as Adriana de la Court, also suggest that these differences between male and female travel behaviour were all too often rather discourse than reality. Adriana engaged in all sorts of activities – sampling baroque art treasures, assessing industrial plants, and enjoying sublime landscapes – which were often deemed as exclusively male.

In 1639, the Dordrecht physician Johannes van Beverwijck published *the Uytnementheyt des vrouwelicken geslacht*, a much-vaunted treatise on women. Men were, in his opinion, made for public life, as they were virtually immune from cold, hunger, (sharp) rocks and travel, while women, with their weaker vessels – their *sachter vlees* – were bound to the private realm.[1] Beverwijck was not really exceptional in this regard; the *Uytnemendheyt* rather echoed a widespread opinion. Travel, and more specifically the long, wearying, and perilous *Grand Tour*, was considered a men's affair in the early seventeenth century, as a surge of guidebooks and *artes apodemici* (or treatise on the art of travel) served as evidence.[2] Ideas on the separate spheres not only loomed large in the minds of contemporaries, but also, slowly but surely, hardened into textbook-wisdom. As a consequence, the first academic books, exhibitions, and anthologies on the classic

Grand Tour portrayed the journey as an all-male activity.[3] It was not until recently, that research has moved beyond this stock image. Dolan, Sweet, and other experts have gathered compelling evidence on British female travellers, who embarked on the Italian *Grand Tour* in the late eighteenth century. Quite often, however, this information had to be gleaned from manuscripts that were written by men. Therefore, these sources have to be read against the grain.[4] Ladies also increasingly travelled to Paris, Amsterdam, or Brussels, in short to continental destinations within easy reach. Domestic "tourism" was also *en vogue*, as British women set off on trips to the Peak District, the Wye Valley, Salisbury, Bath, Mount Snowdon, or even to Scotland.[5] Apart from a surge in new studies on female travellers, the burgeoning interest in gender has also sparked a new line of research on masculinity and the *Grand Tour*.[6]

From a theme in the margins, gender has thus evolved into a hotly debated topic in early modern travel behaviour. Nonetheless, some issues remain unsolved.[7] It is, for instance, taxing to assess the ratio between the sexes. Women were obviously travelling in ever larger number in the late eighteenth and early nineteenth century, but it is much more complex to evaluate their presence in previous eras. Moreover, their freedom of action is still under discussion. Did female travellers always need a chaperone before the nineteenth century? Were they free to explore every nook and cranny of Europe, or was their range limited? Yet, the key question remains whether women really travel(led) differently. Whereas some experts tend to emphasise the disparities, others stress the similarities. It remains to be seen, whether these variations were real or imagined. Were they discourse rather than praxis?[8] Finally, it is doubtful whether the British experience was representative for other regions, as the elbow room of women varied considerably in early modern Europe.[9] Female travellers from the British Isles may have come into the limelight, yet less is known about other nationalities.

To solve some of these issues, this chapter delves into Dutch and Flemish travel journals to uncover gendered differences in travel behaviour and discourse. From the libraries and archives in Amsterdam, Antwerp, Brussels, Leiden, and The Hague a sample of 139 manuscripts – including travel diaries, journals, letters, receipt books, and other material – was selected, that sheds light on Netherlandish travel behaviour between 1585 and 1750.[10] Unfortunately, travel accounts written by Netherlandish women are as scarce as their British counterparts, so most of the information had to be gleaned from texts composed by men. The methodological flaws are obvious. Men were not always very informative about their female companions. Furthermore, it is difficult – not to say impossible – to look beyond the male discourse on women travellers. Yet, even with these caveats in mind, Dutch and Flemish sources provide a fresh perspective on early modern travel behaviour of women, especially as a setoff for the British experience.[11]

Venus' ascension: Netherlandish women on the move

In the autumn of 1622, Johan Berck, the future Dutch ambassador in Venice, embarked on a man-of-war in Den Briel to take up his new commission.

According to his journal, the voyage was long and unsafe, as the travelling party nearly fell prey to privateers on the North Sea, trembled with fear – and also from the blistering cold – at the crossing of the Alps near Mont Cenis, and barely escaped a raid of highwaymen near Savona. Berck did not travel alone, but was, as his high rank required, followed by a train of servants, officials, and family. Among his personal retinue were his wife, his son Hubert, and the sisters Cornelia and Antonina van den Corput.[12] It was not uncommon for ambassadors to take their family with them, but apart from this exception, there were few opportunities for female travelling in the early seventeenth century (Figure 4.1). Among the urban upper-crust of Netherlandish society, the classical *Grand Tour* to Italy, France, and Switzerland easily gained momentum as the acme of an aristocratic education. Young scions of bourgeois families – the offspring of well-heeled burgomasters, aldermen, merchants, and senior officials – were sent abroad with a stern pedagogical programme, including formal training in fencing, horsemanship, dancing, and fortification [applied arithmetic]. An academic degree of a renowned, foreign university served as the ultimate icing on the cake. Less formal goals were the mastering of languages (especially French and Italian), music, polite conversation, and even diplomatic skills. Last but not least, the classic *Grand Tour* also served as a *rite of passage* or a coming-to-age ritual, whereby the hardship, alienation, and loneliness served as a litmus test for masculinity.[13] Women were completely out of the picture in this educational programme.[14]

Even though the tide was already turning in the late seventeenth century, it was not until the eighteenth century that the slow-burn feminization of Netherlandish travel behaviour really gathered momentum (Figure 4.1). New travel patterns emerged, which left much more room for women. A textbook example is the *journaal van een voorjaarsreisjes gedaan naar Holland*, a manuscript written by the sixteen-year-old Zeeland boy Pieter Johan Macaré about a spring

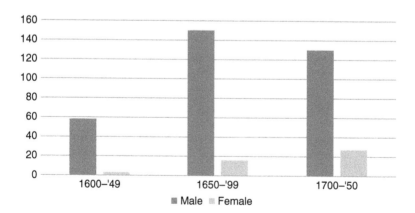

Figure 4.1 Netherlandish travellers and their gender (1600–1750) (n=384)[15]

trip to Holland. Besides his father, his two brothers and some other male relatives, the travelling party had a female touch. Macaré's mother was accompanied by her sister Johanna Marghareta Radeus, who also brought her daughter Johanna van Visvliet. There was also an anonymous maidservant.[16] Family trips were obviously on the rise from the late seventeenth century onwards.[17] These *plaisierreijsjes* (pleasure trips), *divertissante somertogjes* (pleasurable summer trips), or even *vacance* (vacation), as they were tagged by contemporaries, were poles apart from a classic *Grand Tour*. Not only were they powered by new motivations – leisure and art were in the ascendancy – they were also strikingly different in their timing and destinations. Neighbouring metropolises and regions were targeted, such as London, Paris, Aachen, or the Rhine valley, while "domestic tourism" was also *en vogue*. These trips were often concluded within some weeks and often scheduled during the summer months.[18] Netherlandish burgomasters, civil servants, and merchants increasingly took their wife along on these *speelreijsjes* and even the children – sons and daughters – were included.[19]

Flemish and Dutch travel behaviour thus evolved in a similar way as the British example. Yet, the quantitative analysis also evidences that the early modern feminization of travel behaviour should be taken with a grain of salt. Even in the eighteenth century, barely one out of five Netherlandish travellers were female (Figure 4.1).[20] What kindled this slow-burn, yet manifest, evolution? First and foremost, women obviously reaped the benefits of the rise of a new, family-based leisure culture. Dutch *burghers* took their wife to the opera and the theatre, to art auctions, to the coffeehouse, the *kermis*, and to pleasure gardens, as was the case with the London upper crust.[21] In the summer, elite families spent their time at their country house. There were some stunning examples along the river Vecht, yet, from the late seventeenth century onwards, virtually every Dutch town was girded with less luxurious country cottages.[22] Family trips served as a natural extension of this new leisure culture, which was, in itself, powered by the emergence of politeness. Female companionship played a vital role in this new masculine identity. Moreover, Netherlandish women also capitalised on an early modern transport (r)evolution. In the seventeenth century, an extensive network of track boat canals was dug out in the Dutch Republic. Barges were not only relatively cheap and fast, but they were also comfortable and safe, which enabled women to travel more frequently.[23] Later, in the early eighteenth century, the Austrian Netherlands were opened up by a dense grid of stone-slab paved roads. New roads and comfy *diligences* gave family trips and other *plaisierreijses* a kick-start.[24]

Venus in shackles: limits for female travelling

Netherlandish women were thus travelling more frequently in the eighteenth century, but their elbow room was often limited. Unaccompanied trips were, for example, out of the question, since male chaperones – spouses, fathers, brothers, uncles, nephews, and a motley crew of other relatives – were a *sine qua non*.[25] These male travelling companions also held sway over the paper and the ink, save for some notable exceptions such as Adriana de la Court. As a daughter of a Leiden textile baron, she set out on various *plaijsierreysjes* to London (1714), to Maastricht and Liège (1732), to Spa, Aix-La-Chapelle, and Düsseldorf (1733), to Brabant and Flanders (1740), and, finally, to Hamburg (1743).[26] In a legible hand, she held detailed notes of all her wanderings. Adriana remained single for most of her life, which might have given her much more freedom of action than her married peers. Yet, even in this rather exceptional case, male companions were never far away. When, for example, Adriana set out on a *somertogje* to the Austrian Netherlands in 1740, she was accompanied by her brother Allard and her nephew Adrien Bogaert, who were only evanescently mentioned in the journal. These gentlemen were outnumbered by female fellow travellers, such as Adriana's elder sister Catharina de la Court, her sister-in-law Catharina Backer, and her niece Esther van Roijen.[27] Apparently, this was a rather classic touring party, as Flemish and Dutch women on the move were often accompanied by female escorts. Families were on their occasional *somertogjes* and *speelreijsjes* accompanied by a motley crew of sisters(-in-law), nieces, cousins, or aunts, friends and acquaintances, as well as male relatives.[28] It is likely, that these trips were an important means to cement social relations, in addition to frequent visits, dinners, letters, balls, and other gatherings. Now and then, daughters were also taken along on these journeys. Maria Petronella and Anna Theresia, the offspring of Corneille van den Branden de Reet, a minor Brabant noble, travelled to Paris in the spring on 1736 with *mama* and *papa*.[29] Even though young ladies and girls were cropping up more frequently on family trips from the late seventeenth century onwards, Dutch and Flemish elites still favoured their male offspring.[30] On occasion, women also took their female staff with them. Manservants, valets, and footmen were often reinforced with maidservants, when the travelling party was mixed.[31]

Women's freedom to move was not only restricted in a figurative way, but also in a more literal sense. Even in the eighteenth century, the Netherlandish *Grand Tour* remained a male privilege, while the range of mixed *somertogjes* and family trips was often limited to London, Paris or Aix-la-Chapelle. More popular even were home tours through the Low Countries. Dutch *burghers* took their wife on day trips to the coast, on sightseeing tours to Amsterdam, Leiden or The Hague, and on small *picturesque tours* to eastern provinces of the Dutch Republic. Noordwijk, Scheveningen, and other Dutch seaside towns were for example a favourite destination of the Amsterdam wine merchant Isaac Pool and his wife. In the summer of 1673 they rode to Katwijk to stroll on the beach and to look at the bathers, both men and women, who rushed and plunged into the deep. In the *Halvemaan* inn, they took some fresh fish and delicious Rhenish.[32] Adrien van Assendelft, barrister in the Court of Holland, sallied forth on a one-week journey to Guelders and Kleef in the summer of 1696. Besides his wife Maria Magdalena van Beresteijn and their two daughters Maria and Catharina, the family was accompanied by Adriaen's younger brother Willem and his wife Maria. They sampled the – *incomparabele gesichten* – stunning landscape of the rolling hills, the impressive country estates, and the meandering river.[33] Trips to the Austrian Netherlands were also popular among Dutch *burghers*. Examples are legion. Pieter Hulft, a wealthy *regent* from Amsterdam set off on a *plaisier-reijsje* to Brussels, Mechlin, and Antwerp in 1682 together with his younger sister Johanna Hulft, his niece Johanna Hop, and some male relatives. Barely a fortnight later, they were back in Amsterdam again.[34] Adriana may have travelled to Hamburg in 1743, but most of her trips were limited to the Dutch Republic and the Austrian Netherlands.[35]

Flemish and Dutch women rarely travelled beyond this safe horizon and when they did it was rather out of necessity than for pleasure. In 1732 the Mechelen canon Charles Major set off to Rome to negotiate with the Holy See over the imminent dissolution of the Ursuline order. Major brought seven nuns along to press the argument. The journey was well documented, as Charles' *lettres* to his patron cardinal d'Alsace were supplemented by the daily notes of Anne Marie Thérèse de Saint-Bernard, an elderly Ursuline from Huy. Both documents enable to uncover some obvious differences in male versus female travel behaviour and discourse, although the balance of power was highly biased by the unbending hierarchy of the Catholic Church. Anne Marie Thérèse may have held sway over the younger nuns as she was the most senior, but it was Major who really held the reins. Barely departed from Brussels, he had to bar young Bernardine from speaking for her unruly behaviour. In Rome, Augustine needed a lesson in modesty, as she swaggered around.[36] Even though the imbalance was less obvious in other Netherlandish travelogues, it is likely that men wore the trousers on these family trips and *somertogjes*. Adriana was an exception to the rule, yet even in this unique case, it remains a moot question whether she was free to make her own choices in travel destinations, (leisure) activities, and other issues.

Mars meets Venus: gender differences in travel behaviour and writing

Most early modern travel journals evidence small, yet meaningful, differences in travel behaviour. Catharina and Elisabeth Backer set off on a three-week trip to Maastricht, Liège, and Aix-la-Chapelle in the summer of 1724 together with their respective husbands Allard de la Court and Adrien Boogaert. In most cases, the sisters followed in the footsteps of their men, including visits to the subterranean marl caves of Maastricht, the art collections of the prince-bishop of Liège, and the famous spa of Aix-la-Chapelle, but now and then their ways parted. After a tour of Den Bosch, Allard and Adriaen went for a bottle of wine, while the women were left to pack the suitcases.[37] British travel literature echoes these traditional role models, as women were supposed to care about the (un)packing of the luggage, the search for food, and other daily chores.[38] Manifest gender differences also crop up in the journal of Balthasar III Moretus, who set off to the sanctuary of Scherpenheuvel [in Brabant] in 1668 together with his family. Whereas the women were totally absorbed by the miraculous statue of the Blessed Virgin, the sumptuous Masses, and the Way of the Cross, Balthasar and his brother escaped as soon as possible. Together with a local guide, they spent some pleasant hours in a nearby forest by spotting *hares, deer, wolves, and bears*. It is likely, that this was an exaggeration, as big game was becoming rare in seventeenth-century Brabant, but it served the juxtaposition between male adventure versus female devotion rather well. Barely a week later, the touring party was split up in Turnhout. Bathasar's mother and sister returned to Antwerp, while the men continued their journey with a tour through the southern provinces of the Dutch Republic.[39]

A more subtle gendered discourse punctuated the travel journal of Pieter Hulft, who toured the Southern Netherlands in 1682 together with his brother and sister, uncle Hop, his niece, and nephew. When their yacht berthed in Antwerp, the men first explored the city to see how the land lay before allowing their womenfolk to go ashore.[40] In Brussels, the women were left in the hotel, while the men rode to the secluded monastery of Groendaal in the forest of Zoniën. The trip was described as a small-scale adventure, as the men ventured deep into the dense, gloomy woods, while the track led through deep valleys and over towering hills.[41] Clearly, the hyperbole endorsed the masculinity of Hulft and his companions, while the reluctance of the women to join them added a little extra. These (imagined) anxieties of the opposite sex were also used as a stage to bolster the male identity of courage, perseverance, and bravery on a later occasion.[42] On the return voyage, Hulft's yacht was caught in a gale near Rotterdam. While the men, evidently, held a stiff upper lip, the women were – *in groote benautheijt meenende daer haar leeven te moeten verliesen* – (terrified, as they thought that their final hour had come).[43]

Maybe, there was a germ of truth in these gendered responses, yet it is likely, that these role models were rather discourse than reality. The discrepancy between male adventurers and fearful women was also a well-worn chestnut in nineteenth-century travel literature and even lingers on today.[44] As Sarah Goldsmith has recently argued, similar tropes frequently cropped up in British journals, where young *Grand Tour* travellers used dogs and servants as a proxy to boost their own masculinity. Footmen in mortal fear functioned as an offset to the hardiness of their master.[45] Whether Dutch and Flemish women really travelled differently is hard to assess. Shopping was habitually depicted as a female activity. Pieter Johan Macaré, the sixteen-year-old boy from Middelburg, portrayed his *voorjaarsreijsje* (spring trip) to Holland in line with the traditional role model. Whereas *papa* was entangled in all sorts of serious business meetings, his *mama* was shopping her way from one city to another. The spoils included some books, two lacquered teacups, and precious textile.[46] Lace shopping was also described as a standard ingredient of tours to the Austrian Netherlands, at least, when a mixed touring party was involved.[47] Yet, this emphasis on (window-)shopping as a female activity referred rather to discursive "othering" than to a substantial reality. Netherlandish travel journals – and especially the receipts and running-accounts – evidence that consumption was every bit a men's as much as a women's affair.[48]

It remains thorny to look beyond this stock image of female travel behaviour, as most diaries were written by men. Yet, Adriana de la Court's journals debunk the idea of the separate spheres, as she engaged in all sorts of activities, that were often branded as exclusively male. On her trip in 1733, Adriana descended into the underground Maastricht marl-pit armed with a torch. From Liège she rode to Spa between – *eyselycke hoge style gebergtens* – (towering rock-faces,) while drily observing that the landscape was very diverting.[49] Adriana and her companions travelled to the Austrian Netherlands in 1740 to gaze at the baroque art treasures. In Antwerp, the collection of canon De Ligt was high upon the bucket list. Adriana exposed herself as a streetwise *connoisseur* or art buff, who was not only able to identify and assess the masterpieces of Rubens and Van Dyck, but also had an eye for the works of Barend van Orley, Hugo van der Goes, Jacob Swanenburg, and other lesser gods. In Aix-La-Chapelle, the party inspected the Stolberg copper forge. Thanks to its tangle of hammers, wheels, bellows and other machinery, Andriana was – *zeer gediverteert met alles te zien* – (delighted to see the factory).[50] That women spoke freely and frankly about serious matters, such as politics, science, industry, and the arts, which were part of the male realm, was all but evident in the early modern era. Nineteenth century British women always included a self-effacing clause when they were treating those subjects in their travel journals. Some assessed paintings or industrial technology, engaged in botany and other science, or evaluated political systems, but they all readily admitted that they, being female, lacked the expertise and erudition to discuss these issues in depth. In most cases, this was feigned modesty as women were well-informed, yet the disclaimer allowed them to trespass the line between the male and female spheres.[51] Adriana's diary does not include such a clause. Were Dutch women freer in this regard? Was it an attribute of her exceptional single status? Or was it the fact that her manuscript was never meant for publication?

Mars on his own: male identity and travel behaviour

Early modern travel – and more especially the classic Grand Tour to Rome – offered various opportunities to mould a male identity of courage, perseverance, level-headedness, and other qualities.[52] Family trips also opened some opportunities for bravery and bragging, as diaries were punctuated with tales of chicken-hearted women and valiant men. Yet, even in the travel diaries of men, who travelled to the Austrian Netherlands, to London, Paris or Berlin, or along the river Rhine the discourse of male heroism was lurking under the surface. In 1748, the young clerk Johannes Samuel Cassa travelled to Aix-la-Chapelle as a member of the staff of the Dutch ambassador Bentinck, who was appointed to sign the famous peace treaty. Cassa peppered his account with all sorts of exciting stories. Filthy inns, long rides on horseback, inedible food, bitter cold nights on haylofts, and other stories added to the image of male toughness and acted, in Johannes words, as a counterpoise to too much mothering, which had made Dutch boys frail and feeble.[53] Weakness was considered a national vice in the eighteenth-century Dutch Republic, as its declining supremacy in economic and political matters was often linked to loosening morals, softening education, and effeminate French manners. Travel – and especially the dangerous and uncomfortable journey – could serve as an antidote to reverse the decline.[54] Cassa also drew an epic self-portrait of his visit to the subterranean marl-pit of Maastricht. According to his journal, he had been in mortal danger as the guide tried to kill a mouse with his torch and thereby almost doused the fire. In the dark, it had been virtually impossible to find the exit of the caverns.[55] Apparently, Johannes saw no contradiction between this occasional bragging about his manhood and some earlier passages in his diary, where he admitted that he had wept *heete traenen* (bitter tears), when he bade farewell to his *papa* and *mama*, his brothers and sisters, nephews and nieces, and a motley crew of other relatives.[56]

Manhood, hardiness, and perseverance were also subthemes in the travel journal of Jason Bruijningh, a fourteen-year-old son of a prosperous Amsterdam wine merchant. In the winter of 1742, Jason embarked on *cours pittoresque* along the Rhine together with some other gilded youths. According to the travel journal, the boys had to cope with several ordeals on their way: Floating ice on the Rhine, scouring French soldiers, accidents, and endless woods. On several occasions, they were forced to sleep on straw and to nibble on a piece of stale bread, as decent inns were hard to find. Fresh horses and coaches were sometimes missing. In Andernach, their barge was nearly wrecked by a gathering storm.[57] There may have been a germ of truth in these tales, but it is likely, that these tall stories rather served as materials to create a strong, masculine identity. The *cours pittoresque* thus functioned as a coming-to-age ritual or a *rite de passage*, that transformed boys into men. *Divertissante somertogjes, plaisier-reijsjes* and other trips were in this regard not very different from the classical *Grand tour*, even if the former were also open for women.[58] Pieter de la Court van der Voort, a Leiden textile baron and father of Adriana, left for Paris in the summer of 1700 together with his twelve-year-old boy Allard, his brother-in-law Jan Poelaert, and his nephew Venlo. Barely had they crossed the border or Venlo became homesick in Antwerp. At night, the melancholy sent feverish shivers down his spine and almost forced him to return home. In the letters to his beloved wife, Pieter wrote smugly that young Allard had kept a stiff upper lip.[59] As melancholy was often deemed a female emotion, the plucky behaviour of his son served as an antidote of unfaltering masculinity.[60]

Conclusion

Flemish and Dutch travel journals on *plaisierreisjes, somertogjes*, and other family trips debunk – or rather refine – the idea of the separate spheres. Until recently, early modern travel was predominantly portrayed as an exclusive male activity, which is, upon closer examination, barely more than a myth. Netherlandish sources corroborate the British evidence, that women were already travelling in larger numbers in the eighteenth century. It is likely that this growing female participation was fuelled by an early modern transport revolution – including track boats, stone-slab paved roads, diligences, and turnpikes – by a new, family-based leisure culture, and by the relatively free position of women in the Dutch Republic and Great Britain. However, our research also shows the limits of female travel behaviour. Even though Dutch ladies and girls travelled more often in the eighteenth century, their participation was low in real numbers. Moreover, they were forced to take a chaperone along. Fathers, husbands, brothers, nephews, and other male relatives held the reins. Women's radius was also limited in a geographical sense, as female travel beyond the domestic setting and the nearby metropolises was frowned upon. For Dutch and Flemish ladies a classic *Grand Tour* to Italy was out of the question, even in the eighteenth century. Finally, *Plaisierreijses* and *somertogjes* rather affirmed than emasculated the traditional role patters. Women were in travel diaries, written by their men, often portrayed as fearful and fretful, which served as an ideal setoff to paint a male self-image of bravery, perseverance, and level-headedness.

Adriana de la Court's travel diaries suggest that such black-and-white opposition between male and female travel behaviour should not be taken at face value. Not only did Adriana engage in activities, that were usually tagged as dangerous, wearying, and therefore exclusively male, but she also fashioned herself as a *connoisseur* of baroque art, who could assess the merits and flaws in the paintings of Rubens, Van Dijck, and other masters. There was not the slightest trace of the disclaimers, that abound in the travel accounts of British women, who talked freely about politics, science, art, and other serious topics, yet hastened to say that they had no expert knowledge whatsoever. Maybe, Dutch women were freer to discuss such serious subjects in public, yet it is much more likely, that the striking difference in tenor and timbre was caused by the medium, as Zoë Kinsley persuasively argued in *Women Writing the Home Tour*. Whereas writings of British women were sometimes given in print, Adriana's diary was strictly meant for private use. Women had to be extremely cautious not to trespass the line between the role models when they entered the public sphere, while this concern was less pressing in private texts. Once again, these findings cast doubt on the suggestion that women really travel(led) differently. It corroborates the idea that the separate spheres were discourse rather than reality.

Notes

1 Quoted in: Haks, D. (1982) *Huwelijk en gezin in Holland in de 17de en 18de eeuw. Processtukken en moralisten over de aspecten van het laat 17de- en 18de-eeuwse gezinsleven*. Assen: Van Gorcum: p. 151.
2 For more literature on these pedagogic treatise, see: Warneke, S. (1995) *Images of the Educational Travellers in Early Modern England*. Leiden: EJ Brill, pp. 5–6.
3 Women are, for instance, almost invisible in classic studies: Kirby, P. (1952) *The Grand Tour in Italy (1700–1800)*. New York: S.F. Vanni; Black, J. (2003) *Italy and the Grand Tour*. New Haven: Yale University Press; Hibbert, C. (1987) *The Grand Tour*. London: Putnam.
4 Dolan, B. (2001) *Ladies on the Grand Tour. British Women in Pursuit of Enlightenment and Adventure in Eighteenth-Century Europe*. London: Harper Collins; Sweet, R. (2012) *Cities and the Grand Tour. The British in Italy, c. 1690–1820*. Cambridge:

Cambridge University Press, pp. 23–27; Wilton-Ely, J. (2004) "Classic Ground: Britain, Italy, and the Grand Tour," in: *Eighteenth-Century Life* 28, pp. 136–165.

5　Kinsley, Z. (2008) *Women Writing the Home Tour, 1682–1812*. Farnham: Ashgate Publishing, Ltd.: pp. 1–15; Proctor, T. (2009) "Home and Away. Popular Culture and Leisure," in: *The Routledge History of Women in Europe since 1700*. London: Routledge: pp. 299–340; Vickery, A. (1998) *The Gentleman's Daughter: Women's Lives in Georgian England*. New Haven: Yale Univeristy Press: pp. 251–252; Brewer, J. (1997) *The Pleasures of the Imagination: English Culture in the Eighteenth Century*. London: Fontana Press: p. 206.

6　Goldsmith, S. (2017) "Dogs, Servants, and Masculinities: Writing about Danger on the Grand Tour," in: *Journal of Eighteenth-Century Studies* 40, pp. 3–21; Goldsmith, S. (forthcoming) *Danger, Risk and Trust in Eighteenth-Century British Travel*; French, H. & Rothery, M. (2013) *Man's Estate: Landed Gentry Masculinities, 1660–1900*. Oxford: Oxford University Press: pp. 138–143.

7　An excellent historiographical overview is: Thompson, C. (2011) *Travel Writing: The New Critical Idiom*. London: Routledge: pp. 168–190.

8　Thompson, *Travel Writing*, pp. 171–172; Kinsley, *Women Writing*, pp. 7–9; For an interesting analysis of gender differences in contemporary travel writing and praxis see: Morgan, N. & Pritchard, A. (2000) "Privileging the Male Gaze: Gendered Tourism Landscapes," in: *Annals of Tourism Research* 27, pp. 884–905.

9　England was, together with the Dutch Republic, rather exceptional in this regard, as women's freedom of action was rather limited in other European countries. See: Prior, M. (1994) "Freedom and autonomy in England and the Netherlands: Women's lives and experience in the seventeenth century," in: *Women of the Golden Age. An International Debate on Women in Seventeenth-Century Holland, England, and Italy*, ed. Els Kloek, Nicole Teeuwen & Marijke Huisman. Hilversum: Uitgeverij Verloren: pp. 137–140; Gowing, L. (2000) "The freedom of the streets: Women and social space, 1560–1640," in *Londinopolis. Essays in the Cultural and Social History of Early Modern London*, ed. Paul Griffiths & Mark Jenner. Manchester: Manchester University Press: pp. 130–151; Van der Heijden, M. et al., (2009) "Terugkeer van het patriarchaat? Vrije vrouwen in de Republiek," in: *Tijdschrift voor Sociale en Economische Geschiedenis* 6, pp. 26–52.

10　More information on the original sample and research: Verhoeven, G. (2015) *Europe within Reach. Netherlandish Travellers on the Grand Tour and Beyond (1585–1750)*. Leiden: Brill: pp. 21–27; Verhoeven, G. (2013) "Foreshadowing tourism? Looking for modern and obsolete features – or a missing link – in early modern travel behaviour (1600–1750)," in: *Annals of Tourism Research* 42, pp. 262–283.

11　More details on these methodological flaws in: Thompson (2011): 169.

12　Colvius, A. (1622) *Cort verhael vander reijse van mijn Ed. Heere Johan Berck.* [National Archives, The Hague, Coll. Aanw. 1891 20c]

13　Goldsmith (2017): 3–21; French & Rothery (2013): 138–142.

14　On these educational goals of the *Grand Tour*: Warneke (1995); Ansell, R. (2015) "Educational travel in protestant families from post-Restoration Ireland," in: *Historical Journal* 58, pp. 931–958; Verhoeven (2015): 61–69. More information on the education of girls: Wiesner, M. (1993) *Women and Gender in Early Modern Europe*. Cambridge: Cambridge University Press: pp. 119–122

15　From the original sample of 139 manuscripts, 384 Netherlandish travellers were identified. 338 were male, 46 female. More details in: Verhoeven (2015): 125.

16　Macaré, P. (1749) *Journaal van een voorjaarsreisjes gedaan naar Holland* [Central Bureau for Genealogy, The Hague, FA Macaré 937]

17　Similar examples are: Van Assendelft, A. (1693) *Journaal van een reis door Holland* [High Council of the Nobility (The Hague), FA van der Lely 421]; Van den Branden, C.J.-M. (1763) *Voijage de Paris* (1736) [National Archives (Brussels) I 196:15b]; A very early example is: Balthasar III Moretus, *Reijse gedaan door Balthasar Moretus den jonghen in Compagnie* (1668) [Museum Plantin Moretus, M 90²: III-IV]

18 Verhoeven (2013): 262–283; Verhoeven, G. (2017) "In search of the new Rome? Creative cities and early modern travel behaviour," in: *Cities and Creativity from the Renaissance to the Present*, ed. Bert De Munck, Ilja Van Damme, & Andrew Miles. London: Routledge.

19 More information on these children: Verhoeven, G. (2017) "Young cosmopolitans. Flemish and Dutch youths and their travel behaviour (1585–1789)," in *Beyond the Grand Tour. Northern Metropolises and Early Modern Travel*, ed. Sarah Gold-smith, Rosemary Sweet, & Gerrit Verhoeven. London: Routledge: pp. 185–202.

20 Even in the nineteenth century men were much more common among Dutch travellers, see: Baggerman, A. & Dekker, R. (2017) "Changing places, shifting narratives. Nineteenth-century Dutch travellers in Germany," in *Travel Writing in Dutch and German, 1790–1930: Modernity, Regionality, Mobility*, ed. Alison Martin, Lut Missinne & Beatrix van Dam. New York/London: Routledge: pp. 159–181.

21 More background on women, family life, and leisure in the Dutch Republic: De Jong, J. (1987) *Een deftig bestaan. Het dagelijks leven van negentiende in de 17de en 18de eeuw*. Utrecht: Kosmos: pp. 85–88; Hokke, J. (1987) "Mijn alderliefste Jantielief. Vrouw en gezin in de Republiek: regentenvrouwen en hun relaties," in *Vrouwenlevens, 1500–1800*, ed. Ulla Jansz. Nijmegen: SUN: pp. 45–73. For a similar evolution in Great Britain: Brewer (1997): pp. 205–207.

22 Glaudemans, M. (2000) *Amsterdams Arcadia. De ontdekking van het achterland*. Nijmegen: SUN: pp. 74–92, 136–137.

23 De Vries, J. (1981) *Barges and capitalism. Passenger transportation in the Dutch Economy, 1632–1839*. Utrecht: HES: pp. 13–20.

24 Blondé, B. (2010) "At the cradle of the transport revolution? Paved roads, traffic flows, and economic development in eighteenth-century Brabant," in: *Journal of Transport History* 31: pp. 89–111. For the effects of this transport revolution on travelling: Verhoeven, G. (2009) "Een divertissant somertogje. Transport innovations and the rise of short-term pleasure trips in the Low Countries (1600–1750)," in: *Journal of Transport History* 30: pp. 87–97.

25 Netherlandish travel behaviour was, in this sense, not very different from its English counterpart. On the necessity of chaperones for British ladies: Thompson (2015): 169.

26 For these trips: De la Court, A. (1732) *De reys na Maestricht* [High Council of the Nobility, The Hague FA van Spaen 181]; De la Court, A. (1733) *Beschrijving van een reis naar Maastricht, Spa en Kleef*. [High Council of the Nobility, The Hague FA van Spaen 181]; De la Court, A. (1740) *Beschrijving van een reis door Brabant en Vlaanderen* [High Council of the Nobility, FA van Spaen 183]; De la Court, A. (1743) *Beschrijving van een reis naar Hamburg* [High Council of the Nobility, FA van Spaen 184.]

27 De la Court (1740).

28 Van Assendelft (1693); Hulft, P. (1682) *Verslag van een reis naar de Zuidelijke Nederlanden* [City Archives Amsterdam, HA Marquette 366].

29 Van den Branden (1736) *Voijage de Paris* [National Archives Brussels, I 196:15b] F.1r

30 Almost one out of three young travellers (under eighteen) in our sample were female. See: Verhoeven (2017): 190.

31 Some examples: Vollenhove, J. (1647) *Verslag van een reis naar Engeland*. [Library of the University of Leiden, BPL 2446:1–2]; Macaré (1794): 4.

32 Original quote: "Mannen en vrouwen die in zee loopen en doopten malkanderen wakker in zee," Isaac Pool, *Sjornaal* (1670-'75) 21r-22v.

33 Van Assendelft (1693): 5–8.

34 Hulft (1682).
35 De la Court (1732); De la Court (1733); De la Court (1740); De la Court (1743).
36 Major, C. & de Saint Bernard, A.M.T (1732) *Journal de voyage fait par le chanoine Major à Rome* [National Library Brussels, II.1274:1–2]: 87–88, 146.
37 Allard de la Court (1724) *Reis naar Luik, Keulen en Düsseldorf.* [University of Amsterdam Library, coll hss. IV J 10:2] 4.
38 Thompson (2011): 185–186.
39 Balthasar III Moretus, *Reijse gedaan door Balthasar Moretus den jonghen in Compagnie* (1668) 12r-20v. Pilgrimage was one of the types of early modern travel behaviour where female participation was at its height. Thompson (2011): 170.
40 Hulft (1682): 4
41 Hulft (1682): 15–16.
42 Danger is a common ingredient in travel journals to enhance masculinity: Thompson (2011): 175–177.
43 Hulft (1682): 19.
44 Thompson (2011): 175–177; Elsrud, T. (2001) "Risk creation in traveling: Backpacker adventure narration," in: *Annals of Tourism Research*, 28(3): 601–602.
45 Goldsmith, (2015): 3–21.
46 Macaré (1749): 27, 66.
47 Some examples: Hulft (1682):4, 10; Van den Branden (1736): 3v; De la Court (1740):, 7.
48 More information on consumption underway: Verhoeven (2015): 208–239.
49 De la Court (1733): 2^{r-v}.
50 De la Court (1740): 1.
51 More on politics in female private correspondence: Barnes, D. (2015) "Tenderness, tittle-tattle and truth in mother daughter letters: Lady Wortley Montagu, Mary Wortley Montagu-Stuart, Countess of Bute, and Lady Louisa Stuart," *Women's History Review*, 24: 570–590. About these rhetorical strategies: Thompson (2011): 182.
52 Goldsmith (2015): 3–21; Goldsmith (2017); Thompson (2011): 175–176; French & Rothery (2013): 138–142.
53 Johannes Cassa, *Journaal van het geene mij voorgekomen is, so op mijn reis na Aaken* (1748) [City Archives The Hague, Ov. Verz. Hs. 161a]: 29, 36.
54 A similar motive was also present in British travel literature. Thompson (2011):177. In Britain, there was also a lot of anxiety about the effeminate effect of the French manners: French & Rothery (2013): 139–140. For more literature about the link between economic and political decline, loosening morals, and effeminate manners in the Northern and Southern Netherlands: Anonymous (1735) "Abjurant mores patrios, peregrine sequuntur," *De Hollandsche Spectator* 349: 146–152; Anonymous (1731) "Caelum, non animum mutant, qui transmare current," *De Hollandsche Spectator* 1: 34–40; Van Damme, J. (2004) "Zotte verwaandheid. Over Franse verleiding en Zuid-Nederlands onbehagen, 1650–1750," in: *Het verderf van Parijs*, ed. Raf De Bont & Tom Verschaffel. Leuven: Universitaire Pers Leuven: pp. 187–203.
55 Cassa (1748): 107.
56 Cassa (1748): 1.
57 Bruijningh, J. (1742) *Rysbeschryving van Amsterdam naar Franfort en te rug* (1742) [City Archives The Hague, FA Heshuysen 364]: 5–9, 11.
58 More literature on the *Grand Tour* as a rite of passage: Thompson (2011): 175–177.
59 De la Court, P. (1700) *Letter of Pieter de la Court to Sara Poelaert* (3 June 1700) [Regional Archives Leiden, FA de la Court 64]
60 For the link between melancholy and masculinity see the lecture of Sarah Goldsmith *Nostalgia, melancholy, and elite masculine formation on the Grand Tour* at the *Cultures and Practices of Travel (1600–1800)* Conference (Leicester 2017).

5 The travels/travails of Mme de Sévigné

The companion(s) of an inveterate letter writer

Peter Rietbergen

Travel companion(s) wanted (f/m)

Judging its chronological spread to answer the main questions underlying this volume, there seems to be but scant material for the long period between the late fourteenth and the late eighteenth century. Of course, the texts left by the worlds of ancient Greece and Rome are readily available either in print or on the internet. The same applies to "medieval" texts, as far as they have been deemed of cultural merit. On the other hand, from the early nineteenth century onward mass printing has given us an abundance of material to study almost every historical topic; moreover, digitization and electronic retrieval techniques have made the historian's work easier and its results far more comprehensive. Does, then, the absence of research about precisely the period ca. 1400–1800 indicate a lack of suitable sources? Or does the fact these are mostly left in manuscript present too formidable a hurdle?

Luckily, the eleven hundred-something letters left by a seventeenth-century French noblewoman have been printed and edited. Since the Marquise de Sévigné (1626–1696) also wrote whenever she took to the road, I have been able to trace the role of travel and the presence of a variety of male and female travel companions throughout her correspondence. Yet, travel history research presents a problem that is often overlooked. It mostly addresses the traveller's relations with the exotic "other" and "otherness." Consequently, those studying female travel do so, too, perhaps feeling the need to redress a gender-biased view of travel as an expression of specifically male daring in, often, uncharted worlds.[1] Therefore, I also question which view of the world around her, and the people in it, transpires from an analysis of the Marquise's correspondence. The second problem is, perhaps, more complicated even. Do we define "travel" as the journey, only, or do we also study the traveller's life as experienced at the destination – even if, as in the case of Mme de Sévigné, she travelled to the Provence and then stayed there for more than a year?

Letter-writing as a life-necessity

Born the daughter of a noble family from Burgundy, Marie de Rabutin-Chantal was raised and educated mostly by her mother's brother, since both her parents and grandparents died when she was still young, leaving her the heiress of her maternal family's considerable possessions. At the age of sixteen, she married Henry de Sévigné (1623–1651), an impoverished nobleman and self-styled marquis from Brittany. Although not ideally suited, the couple produced a daughter and a son. Soon, however, and perhaps not to his wife's great chagrin, the Marquis died in a duel over an amourous affair, leaving Marie a widow of both standing and (some) fortune. Despite having many admirers, she never remarried.[2] Whatever the other reasons, she may well have felt that widowhood gave her an amount of independence that a position as a married wife certainly would not have allowed her.

Marie de Sévigné corresponded with a variety of friends and acquaintances. Some 126 letters of the 1155 that have been preserved were written to a Rabutin-cousin; others she wrote to a variety of people amongst whom was her son Charles; she cared for him well enough, even though she had to put up with his spendthrift habits, his many mistresses and his general inability to settle down.[3] Yet, the only person she ever wholeheartedly loved was her daughter, Françoise (1646–1705),[4] whom she dotingly referred to as "la plus jolie fille de France."[5]

Therefore, the climacteric moment in the Marquise's life came in 1671, when Françoise went to live in the Provence with her husband, the region's royal "lieutenant-general," François de Monteil, count of Grignan (1632–1714). Twice a widower, he seems to have married her for love though her marriage portion of some 300,000 *livres* was not to be despised, either. The situation explains why 764, i.e. 66%, of Mme de Sévigné's remaining letters are addressed to her daughter. Indeed, the painful long-distance relationship (which they both sharply felt), as well as the Marquise's overwhelming motherly feelings provided the main stimulus for her prolific writing. To put it differently, the grand corpus of "letters of Mme de Sévigné," extolled in every history of French culture as a prime example of the epistolary genre, probably would not have existed if the writer had not felt that without her almost daily correspondence with her beloved child her life would have been meaningless: "Lire vos lettres et vous écrire font la première affaire de ma vie."[6] The Marquise often asked her daughter whether she did not show her love to excess while, at the same time, confessing she yet expressed only a small part of it.[7] She admitted that thinking about Françoise even became what the French "dévots" – the pietist Catholics – would call a "pensée habituelle," the kind of spiritual exercise "qu'il faudrait avoir pour Dieu, si l'on faisait son devoir [. . .]."[8]

But what form did this duty take? During the Renaissance, with its Humanist stress on the heritage of Antiquity, writing letters, besides being a simple necessity, also became an art, a literary genre valued as much for its style – dictated by the Classics – as for its various content.[9] However, Mme de Sévigné certainly did not heed the conventions of her time.[10] Far more than producing stylishly wrought epistles, she wanted to keep the attention of her daughter through an avalanche of sociopolitical titbits about life in the political and cultural centre of France[11] – the "folies" that Françoise craved[12] and which enchant posterity as well. Alternatively, she showered her with often heavily emotional and, indeed, manipulative outbursts.[13] Maybe this, certainly to the "sentimental" eighteenth century attractive quality of the Marquise's letters caused their early fame which, within a few years after her death, led to the first printed editions and the beginning of a widespread fascination with her world that has never ceased.

The epistolary pattern was set when Françoise departed. In January 1671, constant rains caused the French rivers to overflow, the roads to be inundated and, generally, travel to be almost impossible.[14] Yet Françoise, newly wed, wants to join her husband in Aix, alone, if need be. Her mother cannot condone this plan. In the end, one of M. de Grignan's brothers will accompany his sister-in-law. When Françoise actually is en route, she starts writing her mother – at an almost daily rate – and receives her copious answers.

The French postal service, maintained by couriers who only departed/arrived twice a week, forced the two correspondents often to repeat – in letters sent via different routes, if they felt that political or seasonal circumstances dictated this – what they wanted to say and, indeed, had said already. Consequently, theirs was not a simple letter-for-letter exchange. They would voice questions that became obsolete due to the erratic arrival, if at all, of the answers. Moreover, since Françoise's letters have not been preserved, we must infer what she communicated through her mother's summaries. What with her need to reiterate her feelings over and over again, this makes the Marquise's letters, delightful though they often are, sometimes a bit boring as well. Even so, as mother and daughter become epistolary travel-companions, the letters reveal both their cultural and their emotional "baggage."

Since Françoise's journey takes almost three weeks, her mother is constantly having nightmares: About the perils of the roads, about the low quality of the food, about the torrential rains, about the wild, dangerous Rhone – "milles sources de sang forment cette rivière."[15] She follows her daughter's daily progress on the map, imagining when she will arrive at the post stations, admonishing her to use her own travel bed – a gift from her brother-in-law –, only to drink chocolate from her own jug, to wear her furs, etc. But Françoise enjoys both the boat trip down the Rhone – her husband allows her to take the helm herself, which makes him come in for an angry letter from the Marquise[16] – and the subsequent crossing of the mountain range separating the river from Avignon. She enjoys the sights. She writes about the people she meets. She laughs away her mother's fears about the treacherous eddies around the famous bridge. She likes the splendid receptions given in her honour at Arles and Aix.

In short, though Françoise seems to have written that her mother never leaves her thoughts, she also wonders whether during the previous years, the Marquise has not been "comme un rideau qui [me] cachait."[17] Yet, what might have been the most painful confession, viz. that her mother is more concerned about her than she is about her mother, is belied by her letters that seem to have been filled with constant questions about the Marquise's well-being as well as constant appeals for her love.[18]

Travelling – why and where?

Her journey finished, Françoise spent the better part of her life in the Provence. Yet, her mother never seems to have considered moving there as well. Indeed, Marie de Sévigné remained settled in Paris. There, she had her main residence. Changing addresses a number of times – always renting accommodation –, during the last decades of her life she inhabited the splendid "Hôtel Carnavalet."[19] In Paris – or at St Germain and, from the 1670s onwards, at court in Versailles – most of her relatives and friends lived as well.

However, concerned about what we would now call her peace of mind, the Marquise often escaped the bustle of the capital for the relative solitude of the abbey of Livry – "ce beau désert"[20] – over which her older cousin Christophe de Coulanges (1607–1687) held sway as commendatory abbot. It took her no more than a few hours to get there when she was "tired, and tired of Paris."[21] Also, having inherited the estates of her husband, every now and then the Marquise needed to visit faraway Brittany, living for a number of weeks or even months in the ancestral, gothic manor house of Rochers – near Vitré. This journey took at least nine full days, not counting the ones spent with friends along the road – visits that, sometimes, were more than simple overnight stays. To take the waters at the fashionable spa of Vichy,[22] as the Marquise did three times, required a slightly shorter trip of some six or seven days. But whether at home or on one of her journeys, her thoughts never strayed from the chateau at Grignan, the seat of the Monteil family perched atop a rock some fifty kilometers north of Avignon. There, her daughter lived with her husband and children – in according to her mother all too expensive splendour – almost as far from Paris as was possible within the confines of France.

In between years of contact by letter, only, Françoise sometimes came to visit, but her inevitable departure only served to increase her mother's sorrow.[23] When she returned to the Provence, the Marquise would "follow" her, again with the map on her desk, writing her, again, every day of the journey. Apparently, Françoise described the last stretch as being rather uncomfortable, for her mother commiserates with her: "Quelle fatigues pour y [sc. the chateau at Grignan] parvenir, que de nuits sur la paille, et sans dormir et sans manger rien de chaud."[24] Yet, inevitably, Mme de Sévigné herself made the journey South as well, though it was a strenuous trip indeed, lasting several weeks. She spent more than a year there, in 1672–1673. The second time, she stayed for sixteen months, from June 1690 till November 1691. Moreover, it was during a sojourn at Grignan which had begun in May 1694 that she died, there, on 17 April 1696.

Travelling – how and with who(m)?

Of course, in the seventeenth century public transport in the modern sense did not exist. But respectable persons – certainly women – did not walk. Therefore, even to go about town, a female aristocrat needed a carriage and horses, either private or rented ones. Once when, for reasons unexplained, the Marquise could command neither, she carried on a conversation with a Parisian friend by letter, delivered by a lackey.[25] When she did set out on a visit, there was a coachman to drive her. Whether there also was a groom to help her get in and out, and, perhaps, carry whatever luggage she was taking, I do not know, nor if, since she was a single lady, a female companion did "lend her countenance." I do know that on a trip to Livry she usually was accompanied by her valet, Philippe Hébert, by her "femme de chamber," Hélène, and by Marphise – her lapdog.[26] Maybe these three went with her whenever she embarked on a journey that included an overnight stay? Once, she went to Livry "all by myself"; this, apparently, was "not done," for she expressly mentions it to her daughter.[27] The one other time she – now with friends – decided to go there without maids was, as the Marquise wrote, because they did not want to be bothered by "toilette ni bonnet de nuit."[28]

Any journey beyond the capital or nearby Livry required a sizeable amount of organisation. For at least a decade, one M. d'Hacqueville took care of most arangements; indeed, during those years Madame de Sévigné would seldom embark on a longer trip without taking his advice on all practical matters involved.[29]

Reading about travel conditions in early modern times,[30] one shudders at the lack of comfort and, even more, hygiene most people had to put up with. However, for Madame and her companions the lodgings were always pleasant. Only seldom did she have to use a common inn.[31] As far as one can make out, en route she usually had dinner at, and spent the night in, the "manoirs" or castles of friends, or friends of friends, and, in the larger cities, in their comfortable town houses. She admonished her daughter to follow the same course when she came up to Paris: "certainement vous trouverez des amis, et le lendemain encore des amis, et ainsi, en relai d'amis, vous vous trouverez dans votre chambre [i.e. with her mother]."[32] Since this kind of (mutual) hospitality was considered a social as well as, in a way, cultural-moral obligation, it also meant a reduction of travel expenses, despite, perhaps, the cost of the drink money or other gifts one offered to one's host's servants. Moreover, embedded in such aristocratic networks, the Marquise always met people who would tell her the newest "on-dits" which then could be communicated to Françoise as she sat down to write her letters, sometimes twice a day.

About the state of the roads, which from our point of view was deplorable, the Marquise rarely complained; after all, they were what she and indeed all French-men/women were used to. Once, in a long and very evocative letter, she depicts conditions after many days of heavy rain – but rather as an adventure: When the carriage gets stuck in the mud, boys from a neighbouring village have to come and, by the light of torches, carry her and her companions to their hostelry.[33] The one time she describes the roads as "diabolique," one should bear in mind that she had a tendency to hyperbole.[34] Setting out for Bretagne in May 1671, the Marquise tells her daughter that she and the Abbé de Coulanges will sit comfortably in one carriage. Her son Charles, her maild Hélène, and one Dr Pierre de la Mousse – a theologian who had been Françoise's teacher and was now to help the Marquise get her dissolute son on the path of virtue again – will travel in the other. Moreover, there are to be seven horses, plus the four that young Sévigné takes with him, and a packing horse to boot.[35]

What conversations will they have? Madame assures her daughter that with the Abbé and La Mousse she'll mainly talk about her. Moreover, the "pensée habituelle," that thought of Françoise that is constantly with her, will be her travel companion, too.[36] When mother and son want to talk – about the writings of Corneille, for instance – he will change places with the Abbé.[37] In short, in a way the absent daughter is included in the physical family circle – a virtual travel companion even before the real travellers had started on their actual journey.

In 1675, on the road to Brittany again – with the Abbé and, because Hélène is pregnant, another maid, Marie – she tells her daughter she has six horses as well as two outriders. Whether this meant she travelled in one carriage, only, is not clear. Meanwhile, having to make do with an inexperienced servant does not bother her; it will be, she implies, character-building.[38]

The journey to Rochers in May 1680 follows the same pattern: The Abbé comes with her, and so does Charles, who lends her his horses; he returns to Paris halfway, taking the ordinary diligence.[39] Later, he joins her in Bretagne, and travels with her to Paris again in October.[40] The 1684-sojourn in Brittany runs along the same lines. But for what proved to be the Marquise's last visit to Rochers, in 1689, she chose – or, rather, was asked[41] – to accompany a high-placed old friend, the duchess of Chaulnes, whose husband represented the King in that province.

For the first trip to Vichy, in 1676, Mme de Sévigné writes she is taking her "grand carosse" to enable all travellers to sit without feeling cramped.[42] Maybe this meant the company existed of four people, only, viz. Madame herself, her young female companion Mademoiselle d'Escars – the daughter of an old friend – and, perhaps, two maids. The Abbé, who due to ill health did not accompany her, had offered her two of his own horses, to ensure she had six to rely on, as well as his coachman and a valet.[43] On the second journey, the Abbé does travel with her again, profiting from the trip to take the waters as well.[44] The weather is good and the coachman capable, though their carriage does not match the speed of the public "diligence."[45] Sometimes, they continue by night, which, the Marquise admits, is dangerous since it is pitch dark and one cannot see the ravines.[46] En route, they stay with a good friend, spending some days at his house, walking and talking.[47]

For their return trip, a number of friends who they meet at the spa decided to join them on the way to Paris. It must have been quite a cavalcade.[48]

During her third visit, that also took in Bourbon-le-Bains – another nearby spa –, for reasons unclear Mme de Sévigné does not travel by herself but accompanies the duchess of Chaulnes, who also wants to take a cure there.

On her first trip to the Provence, in 1672, the Marquise, and her two companions – the Abbé and La Mousse – travel together in one carriage, but there must have been another one, for she also brought two maids. This time, the lapdog is not mentioned. Of the six horses, one drowns in the Rhone.[49] The second journey to the South, in 1690, is barely documented, but the Marquise does write she uses a rented vehicle – not finding it as uncomfortable as she had been told.[50] Strangely, she does not seem to have had a companion at all; whether her servants came with her is not clear, either. During the third and last visit she is accompanied by a brother-in-law of her daughter; again she travelled in a "litière."[51]

Travelling, writing, talking: the complexities of companionship

Obviously, writing (letters) implies a reader, or, to put it otherwise, some kind of companionship. Inevitably, this creates situations wherein, wittingly or unwittingly, "the other" is burdened with all kinds of emotions about what is seen, experienced, felt, the more so since these are mediated through the written word rather than through direct speech. The Marquise herself once summarised the situation in a most perceptive way, writing to her daughter: "Ma bonne, votre commerce [i.e. exchange of letters] est divin. Ce sont des conversations que vos lettres: je vous parle, et vous me repondez."[52] If only therefore she continued this "commerce" unabatedly, even during her travels.

Of course, mother and daughter write about family affairs. Even when travelling, Mme de Sévigné constantly worries about the rather dissolute life of young Charles.[53] Françoise, for her part, discusses her plans for an advantageous marriage she wants her brother to conclude.[54] Also constantly, both worry about their (grand-)son, for young Grignan is a boy of a sickly nature.[55] And, every now and then, they write about the little daughter whom Françoise has left in Paris in her grandmother's care. Surprisingly, Marie-Blanche does not live with the Marquise but with a foster mother in the countryside. Hence, even Mme de Sévigné does not see the child all that often.[56]

Françoise's letters, reaching her mother en route, give many details about life both in Aix, the provincial capital, and at Grignan, where the comital couple are constantly carrying out costly improvements.[57] She also describes the complex politics of the Provence, where the regional elite is still trying to oppose the royal government. Especially in the 1670s, she also refers to international naval warfare in the Mediterranean.[58]

Well realizing that her daughter loves gossip about life in the capital, Mme de Sévigné goes out of her way to provide it even when she herself is travelling, by talking to people and reading letters from Paris as well as the gazettes that are available at the post stations.[59] Much of her writing is about persons they both know but also about the royal court, though it is clear that much of the latter information is second hand, since she herself does not frequent Versailles or the other non-Parisian royal residences. However, she always assures her daughter that her informants are reliable, high-placed persons rather than scandal-mongering journalists.[60] Moreover, she is a very astute analyst of the changes Louis XIV introduced: "La royauté est établi au dela de ce que vous pouvez vous imaginer. On ne se lève plus, et on ne regarde personne..." Indeed, the King ignores even the passionate pleas of those distressed persons who tearfully beg him for help.[61]

Last, but certainly not least, to judge by the Marquise's answers Françoise often sat down to write long monologues. Sometimes, these must have been painful for her mother to read, as when she said that because of "le désordre de mon esprit, de mon santé [...] je ne vaux rien du tout pour vous."[62] Such moments of self-recrimination, fundamental as equally many pleas for attention and love, did occur often indeed. The situation must, assumedly, have affected the conjugal life of the Comtesse as well. Though I have, perhaps, read too much between the lines, I feel M. de Grignan did not always appreciate the (emotional) intensity of his wife's correspondence with her mother.[63]

It is only through the Marquise' letters to her daughter that we learn anything about her actual travel companions. Whatever their contribution to Madame's voyages, we are barely informed about the "domestics" – beyond their gender and its consequences: The female(s) might travel in her carriage, the males would perform the more menial chores. As for Dr De la Mousse, his status is a bit problematic. From the letters I first inferred that, though not something of a superior servant, he yet only was a learned, but also somewhat dependent friend. However, at least one genealogy suggests he was related to the Marquise on her mother's side.[64] Obviously, as a travel companion he, a theologian and, indeed, a priest, was above suspicion. So was the Abbé de Coulanges – who, it has to be kept in mind, basically took care of all Mme de Sévigné's business affairs. Also, for many years, indeed even decades, he came with his niece on many of her trips. But though she loved him dearly, yet he quite evidently was not her "ideal" companion – he seems to have had, as one would say in those days, "little conversation," or, to put it otherwise, "little *esprit*." Finally, Madame's son sometimes accompanied her as well. He did not lack such *"esprit,"* for he certainly was a vivacious as well as well-educated and well-read man. Yet, as mothers often tend to do, the Marquise, at least in her letters to Françoise, Charles's elder sister by two years, could not refrain from also implying that he was somewhat – well, perhaps one should say: Immature?

Destinations, descriptions, discussions

To judge by the Marquise's letters, what one might term the Livry-routine which, basically, was a recurring vacation in the countryside outside Paris, evolved as follows. She often went there alone, to enjoy a solitary afternoon or a moonlit-evening walking in the gardens.[65] In Autumn 1677 she tells Françoise: "Je suis venue ici achever les beaux jours et dire adieu aux feuilles."[66] Sometimes, the Abbé joins her, or friends come on a day trip to enjoy a "promenade" and a good dinner.[67] Moreover, it is the place where she entertains her "philosophical" companions, specifically Jean Corbinelli, who is a friend of Françoise's as well, and La Mousse; both instruct her in this field.[68] Since Françoise was of a philosophical as well as moralistic bent, the Marquise often writes extensively about such topics. She also corresponds with her about her reading, for at Livry Mme de Sévigné lives with her books.[69] In November 1677, she opens the

Odyssey,[70] in Spring 1679 she is reading *La Vie du Grand Theodose*, in Autumn 1679 Montaigne, with great enthusiasm.[71]

Sometimes, Charles visits her.[72] Indeed, he even stayed with her there after, at long last, he had got married.[73] He did not bring his wife, but yet found time and pleasure in, amongst other things, playing an entire scene from Racine's *Mithridate* out for his mother and her friends, seated on a grassy hillock.[74] They discuss the *Confessions* of St Augustine – and he refers those conversations to his sister.[75] Meanwhile, his mother tells Françoise about their relationship, in an astonishingly revealing letter: "Mon fils me [. . .] dit qu'íl y a un *lui* qui m'adore, un autre qui m'étrangle et qu'ils se battaient tous deux."[76] I assume Françoise, knowing her mother's feelings, must have recognised her brother's emotions all too well. For indeed, in September 1679 the Marquise confesses: "Me voilà toute seule avec votre cher souvenir. C'est assez. C'est une fidèle compagnie qui ne m'abandonne jamais."[77] When, in later years, Françoise returns to Paris for a prolonged stay to enact all kinds of family business at court, she and her daughters, as well as other members of the Grignan-clan often join the Marquise in trips to Livry.[78] But the idyll that, obviously, was Livry came to an end when, in August 1687, the Abbé died. For after all, the "Bien Bon," as the Marquise tenderly called him, "qui était mon père et mon bienfaiteur,"[79] only had held the abbey "in commendam."[80]

The 1671-journey to Brittany was the first long one Mme de Sévigné made after Françoise had left for the South. Now, the memory of that traumatic separation was exacerbated, for both during the days on the road and the seven-month stay at Rochers, correspondence would be far more infrequent than between Paris and Grignan, if only because official regulations decreed that every letter had to be sent via the capital rather than directly. No wonder the Marquise had used her network, even asking the director-general of the French postal services to ensure that she would receive at least one letter a week.[81] Yet this did not work out. Complaints about packets of letters lost abound in the letters that remain.[82]

Setting out for what turns out to be an eight-day trip, the heat is almost insupportable: The company has to leave every morning before the crack of dawn. One of the horses succumbs. Still, the roads are passable, also due to the quality of the springs of the Marquise's carriage.[83] The travellers themselves – mother and son, the Abbé and the Doctor – while away the time with reading: Corneille but, as the Marquise writes, also La Fontaine, whom, apparently, her daughter does not like.[84] Indeed, they went through quite a lot of books, including some of the Classics, but also poets like Tasso and a few French writers. As the travel companions discussed their opinions of the various authors, I assume they recited them to each other aloud.[85]

Once she has arrived at Rochers, in her letters to Françoise Madame de Sévigné also relates the trips she takes to Vitré, where the States of Brittany meet to debate the fiscal demands made on the province by the King's government in Paris. Since it is a larger city, it offers plays as well as balls, which she describes in detail, as she does, daily and at great length, everything that passes at Rochers itself.

Returning to Paris in December, the Marquise takes a two-day detour to make sure that she passes through towns where she can collect Françoise's letters; once, she writes that she could have embraced the courier for joy in actually finding news from her.[86] Maybe this, even for her excessive emotion was caused by the fact that the Comtesse was expecting her first, long hoped-for son. The letter announcing his birth and the way the baby looked must have been so detailed that it enabled the Marquise, still on the road, to respond with a description as clear as if she held the infant in her own arms.[87] Generally, however, the Marquise felt that M. de Grignan should not get his wife pregnant as often as he did; she obviously feared for her daughter's life more than for the future of the Grignan-family.

In July, 1672 – with France and the rest of Europe embroiled in the "Guerre de Hollande," which the Marquise, the mother of a military son, condemns as total folly[88] – she herself embarks on her first trip to Grignan, a distance of some 500 kilometers, which, in the end, takes seventeen days. Again, the Abbé travels with her, looking forward to it. La Mousse comes too – Françoise had insisted on it[89] – but fears the perils.[90]

However, the weather turns out lovely, the roads are good, and the three of them read Virgil – the Marquise, apparently, with the help of an Italian translation.[91] Once arrived in Lyon, she does some sightseeing – amongst other things visiting a "cabinet of curiosities" – and she herself is being "shown" to sundry friends of her host and hostess,[92] which I think can be explained since she was, after all, a high-born lady from the capital as well as the mother-in-law of the man who was effectively royal governor of the Provence.

Alas, once she has settled at Grignan, the renewed closeness between mother and daughter certainly did not always work out. Indeed, even before the trip, the Marquise had spoken her fears that there might be some coldness on Françoise's part,[93] and this turned out to be all too true. Was this the reason why she accompanied her son-in-law on various trips through the Provence while Françoise stayed at home? From Montpellier, Madame very perceptively wrote:

> Comment vous portez-vous, ma belle petite? Mon absence ne vous a-t-elle point un peu réchauffée pour moi? Je souhaite de vous revoir comme s'il y avait longtemps que je vous eusse quittée [. . .].[94]

Meanwhile, even on these short trips she cannot desist from writing long letters. Coming to Marseilles, she is received with all the honours due to the status of M. de Grignan. The description she gives to her daughter – who, of course, had been there herself – is worth quoting. She visits the citadel and attends the parties that come with Carnival, at the beginning of Lent,[95] but, mostly, revels in the larger life of the town, far more populous than Paris, for it is picturesque, full of:

> des avonturiers, des épées, des chapeaux du bel air, des gens faits à peindre, d'une idée de guerre, de roman, d'embarquement, de chaines de fer,

d'esclaves, de servitude, de captivité: moi, qui aime les romans, tout cela me ravit et j'en suis transportée.[96]

Surely, few ever succeeded in bringing to life the caleidoscopic variety of a port town on the frontier of two worlds and cultures better and more succinct than did Mme de Sévigné.

After nearly ten months – during which Françoise gave birth to her third child – the Marquise leaves again. The farewell resulted in a number of letters written during the subsequent journey, full of tears and reflections on love and absence. From Montelimar: "en un mot, ma fille, je ne vis que pour vous." And, a day later, from Valence: "c'est mon unique plaisir que de vous écrire."[97] Nevertheless, the letters also give details about the roads – sometimes so dangerous that she has to walk alongside her carriage; she wonders whether she should not have travelled on horseback, as some ladies do. Again, she and, presumably, the Abbé – La Mousse is not mentioned – stay with friends or friends of friends. Thus, she sees lots of people and hears about all kinds of intrigues – who is going to succeed the deceased abbess of an ancient nunnery, etc.[98]

The return trip was enlivened by the reading of, among other authors, Quintilian. Also, the Marquise meets two priests and discusses with them some religious tracts she already had told Françoise about. However, before buying them herself, her daughter should consider a maxim that Mme de Sévigné held: "je trouve que le prix de la plupart des choses dépend de l'état òu nous sommes quand nous les recevrons"[99] – wise words indeed.

By taking the road from the Provence to Burgundy – an eleven-day journey – Mme de Sévigné allowed herself a prolonged stay at her own family's ancestral castle of Bourbilly, to put her affairs in order, there; the last time she had visited was in 1664. With the help of the Abbé, she manages to achieve what she had set out to do. Meanwhile she receives guests for dinner, and goes out to see neighbours whose magnificent seat she does not fail to describe for Françoise's delectation.[100] After nine days, she continues to Paris, by way of Auxerre, where all kinds of news from court await her, to be relayed, again, in a letter to her daughter – the tenth she writes since her departure![101] – for: "quand je ne suis pas avec vous, mon unique divertissement est de vous écrire."[102]

For the Marquise's 1675–1676-trip to Brittany, which started in September, the company travels via Orleans where, just for the fun of it, they leave their carriage and embark on a boat – the selection of a proper master boatsman is a droll story.[103] Yet, in the end, "la belle Loire," so much more tranquil than the Rhone, proves treacherous, too, since they repeatedly run aground due to the low water.[104] While Mme de Sévigné feels guilty exposing the old Abbé to such discomfort, it also appears that, good man though he is, he is not a great talker. Writing that she feels lucky to be "une substance qui pense et qui lit" – this time, she reads a "History of the Crusades" as well as a "Life of Origenes"[105] – yet she sighs that "il me faudrait un peu de conversation."[106]

But of course she tells Françoise about the interesting things she sees, such as, e.g., a pair of criminals hanging from the roadside gallows,[107] but also news about the French and, indeed, the English court, where a Frenchwoman now rules as one of the royal mistresses, though vying with an English competitor. En route they stay with aristocratic friends or acquaintances. At Nantes, where they remain for seven days, they are welcomed at the quay by the governor, with lackeys carrying torches: A festive sight. There are parties, and dinners, and stimulating conversations about politics and, inevitably, the ongoing war – the more so now that Charles is with his regiment.[108] When, after nearly three weeks, they finally arrive at Rochers, life resumes its normal routine.[109] The Marquise takes care of the estates, receives visitors, walks, reads – and, of course, writes to her daughter. However, she is now almost constantly pained by arthritis. Often, she dictates her letters to, apparently, a young girl. Though, on the way back to Paris in March 1676, the affliction is especially severe – spending hours in her carriage, she cannot take the walks that usually relieve her pain – she often manages to make even this an arresting point in her letters.[110]

Already in 1675, the Marquise starts making plans for a journey to Vichy, to take the waters that may offer a cure for her rheumatic complaints. Françoise has offered to meet her, there, travelling North from Grignan. Mme de Sévigné hopes she will return with her to Paris. That, however, Françoise refuses, and her mother then forbids her to come, since the danger and the expense do no justify such a short trip.[111] Another problem is the Abbé who, since 1674, has been living with the Marquise. He cannot join her for the journey. He has business to attend to – often, apparently, concerning the Marquise's affairs as well[112] – and, due to his age, fears the heat of the South. She really does not dare leave him for too long a time for she would never forgive herself if he were to die while she was away.[113] Moreover, he will miss her.[114]

Leaving in May 1676, she misses him too, though she is accompanied by Mademoiselle d'Escars. However, while her young companion takes good care of her,[115] she does not seem to have been a real conversation partner. During the trip – through a region so lovely that it is, as she writes, enough reason to start a letter[116] – Mme de Sévigné does a lot of reading, now delving into the contemporary politics of the Ottoman empire;[117] a week later, she dispatches the book to Françoise who, living on the Mediterranean coast, must be interested in it as well. She also discusses her daughter's scheme for getting a wealthy wife for Charles.[118] And she pities poor little Marie-Blanche, who now is a boarder with the nuns of Aix.[119] Along the road – staying, for example, with the unhappy Mme Foucquet who, the wife of the emprisoned former minister of finance, despite her incessant pleas still has not been given the King's permission to join her husband[120] – she picks up all kinds of news as well as gossip she shares with her daughter.

Arriving at Vichy, Mme de Sévigné is welcomed by a number of friends. Starting on her cure, she gives Françoise an almost day-to-day description of life in a fashionable spa that is amusing and pertinent even now.[121] The Marquise invites her daughter to laugh about the affectations and, indeed, antics of some of the "maladies." Reading her letters, Françoise can join in the daily, soon boring routines: Of drinking the hot, sulpherous water in the early morning – though it purges the body, the Marquise loathes it; of attending Mass; of taking long walks; of having dinner – consisting, mostly, of simple meat dishes and lots of chicken-broth[122] – with people who, after a few days, one knows all too well; of playing cards in the evening – which Mme de Sévigné does not like, so she reads Ariosto instead, with a friend; of going to bed very early, etc. But she loves the countryside around Vichy: When most of her friends have left, she is content, for "the scenery alone will make me healthy again."[123] She also enjoys the young farm boys and girls who come up to perform their quaint dances for an aristocratic audience. Apparently, Françoise voices her distaste, but her mother tells her every evening she actually invites two musicians as well as a few dancers, paying the paltry sum of four *sols* for this pleasure.[124]

After a week of drinking the odious water, the Marquise starts on the second part of her cure: A week of daily "showers," in which she retires to a cave where hot water soaks her entire, naked body; since this would be unsupportable for the two hours she is supposed to stay there, a young, clever medical doctor – not the usual charlatan[125] – sits behind a curtain and reads to her, or otherwise keeps her spirit up with pleasant stories. Again, the – very detailed – description is both informative and droll, and obviously helped Françoise to understand her mother's situation. But did the cure work out as Mme de Sévigné had hoped? Well, her knees get more supple again, but her hands still hinder her.[126]

In between all this talk about her health, about Françoise's sleeping problems, about international politics – the Marquise is rather critical of King Louis's predilection for warfare – mother and daughter also correspond about questions of ethics – the opposition between duty and desire – and about religion which, Mme de Sévigné confesses, is an emotion she lacks.[127] On the last leg of the return journey, when they have to travel by night because during the day the heat is insufferable and the horses need to rest, the company, not finding a friend's house to stay at, settles for a hotel – where they first hear about what became the infamous "Affaire des Poisons"[128] –, a complicated and long-drawn-out series of lawsuits following the discovery of secret plots involving a number of noble-women who were accused of having wanted to poison their husbands; in the end, the affair even implicated the (people surrounding the) King's current mistress, Madame de Montespan.

A year later, the second journey to Vichy – undertaken because Françoise insists that her mother take better care of her health[129] – passed much as the first one. The Marquise expressly assures her daughter that she is taking books with her – perhaps to relieve her of any concern that the Abbé will be a dull, non-conversationalist companion. She reads the *Alexiad*, as well as Lucianus and, also, *Don Quichotte*, which Françoise has enjoyed, too; consequently, they compare the merits of the various French translations. Like herself, Françoise is going through the *Iliad*, which results in a discussion whether a moral is best conveyed in an epic or a fable.[130] But, revealingly, Mme de Sévigné also brings some of her daughter's old letters, to peruse them again.

Once more she drolly summarises the boring regularity of life at Vichy as: "tout est reglé: tout dîne à midi; tout soupe à sept; tout dort à dix; tout boit a six."[131] Returning to Paris, en route the Marquise again stays with friends, such as her beloved Abbé Bayard – who suddenly dies a day after she has left his enchanting house and the terraced gardens she enjoyed so much. Along the Loire, they get lost in a community of people employed in the local ironworks. Mme de Sévigné admits that she and her companions, all "gens polis," find it difficult to watch the extremely hard labour these men are subjected to. Out of pity – or guilt? – on their departure they distribute alms.[132]

In May 1679, the Marquise departs for Brittany again. The Abbé comes with her, though he, now 73 years old, finds travel very tiring. But Charles accompanies her as well, and they spend much time reading and apparently discussing with some heat the books they bring. However, after Charles leaves them, at Blois, she is bored: "c'est mon écritoire qu'il me faut!"[133] Yet, she has taken precautions against what might have been too dull a trip. She has ordered the wheels of her carriage to be removed, and the carriage itself set up on the boat as a kind of "joli cabinet," wherein they sit "sur de bons coussins, bien à l'air, bien à notre aise." She admits that "tout le reste [sc. her servants] [sits] comme des cochons sur la paille." The views are enchanting – she feels they would have attracted any painter. But even so she is apathetic. The Abbé mostly indulges in pious talks, rather than in pleasant conversation. Therefore, she sings some of the songs she has brought – not surprisingly songs composed by Françoise![134] After a long stopover in Nantes where, despite all kinds of amusement, she yet feels spiritless, she writes Françoise she actually longs for the woods around Rochers, and the quiet, there.[135] And indeed, arriving at the house after this 22-day journey, she happily sits down to enjoy the books she has brought for her long sojourn – amongst them a shelf of edifying and religious texts.[136]

In September 1684, the Marquise accompanies her daughter – who has spent several months in Paris – on her return journey to the Provence. Leaving her at Etampes, she herself continues to Bretagne. The offer of an acquaintance to accompany her she politely declines, writing to Françoise: "je préferai l'ennui à la contrainte"[137] – even though now she will only have the Abbé as a companion. Again, they go down the Loire by boat, though heavy winds delay their progress and the rowers have a hard time. Yet, she enjoys the beauty of the riverscape, and, in dull hours, reads a number of biographies about which she writes to Françoise. In Angers, she is hosted by a dear friend, the 87-year old bishop who, despite his age, continues to be a good shepherd.[138] Arriving, finally, at Rochers, she stays for nearly a year. In September 1687, reluctantly leaving Françoise who has come to Paris again, Mme de Sévigné sets out for a third visit to the spas – Vichy and Bourbon. In her letters she outlines the regularity of her regime – wittily describing it as "le cérémonial de Bourbon"[139] – and, in a reversal of roles, now asks her daughter about news from life in the capital.[140] In April 1689, the Marquise travels to Bretagne again, accompanying the Duchess of Chaulnes who goes there to join her husband – on, apparently, the express invitation of the Duke, who is the King's commander-in-chief in the West. It means travelling in unaccustomed luxury but also at a slow pace, for the Duchess not only wants to spend a few days at her two country seats, she also is welcomed with grand, time-consuming ceremonies in the various cities of Normandy and Brittany – Amiens, Caen, Dol, Rennes. To her own surprise, the Marquise is enchanted by the countryside of Normandy, which she had not seen for forty years. In the end, interesting though, e.g., the political developments in the region are – there have been peasant rebellions[141] – and though she is met by Charles and his wife, she experiences the journey as tedious, longing for the solitude of Rochers.[142] She stays there for fourteen months.

While in Brittany, the Marquise decides to go and spend both the Winter of 1690 and the Spring and Summer of the subsequent year at Grignan – partly because the climate will help her bear her rheumatic pains, but also because Françoise is terribly jealous that she has lived so many months with Charles.[143] In a long and rather moving letter Mme de Sévigné anticipates each of the many days she will travel, and the emotions she will feel as she slowly approaches her destination.[144]

This time, she travels without a companion, or so it seems, for the letters from this period are scant.[145] On the road, she reads a number of "oraisons funebres" – a choice that may be indicative of her mood during these years – but, mainly, thinks about her daughter: "tous mes pas vous le disent [sc. que je vous aime].".[146] In Winter 1691, the Marquise is back in Paris. There are no letters to document the return trip. In 1694, Françoise joins her mother, again to take care of family matters at court. When she leaves for Grignan, Mme de Sévigné follows her with her letters, confessing that she loves her so much, and yet too little.[147] A few months later, she herself sets out for the South. To a friend she writes that she is now leaving Paris without much regret: Two of her oldest and best friends have died.[148] Nearly three weeks later, in June 1694, she arrived at Grignan. During the subsequent years, she travelled in the region, apparently accompanying her son-in-law on his official trips.[149] Meanwhile, Françoise seems to have stayed behind. Perhaps as during earlier visits, mother and daughter again experienced the reality of companionship as, sometimes, more difficult than the epistolary illusion: Two by now ageing ladies, each with various illnesses – and a mutual attachment that was problematic, to say the least. But we know little about the final years of Mme de Sévigné: At last united with her daughter, their compulsive letter writing was no longer necessary. Yet, when the Marquise died, the Comtesse, being unwell herself, was not with her.

Conclusion

Analyzing the Marquise's travel experiences, I note that she never writes about what, from the eighteenth century onwards, most travellers would put first: The "great" sights, recommended by travel guides. She rarely visited "stately homes" to explore their splendour – perhaps because she was used to them as the dwellings of many of her friends[150] – nor the remains of times past such as ancient churches and cathedrals. Yet, she is a precursor of the "modern tourist" in that she passionately loved the beauties of the countryside. Indeed, she favourably compares its naturalness with the "violence" that, at Versailles, had created the vast park Louis "le Grand" was so inordinately proud of and whose artfulness most of her contemporaries extolled as well.[151] She also liked the picturesque, as her description of Marseilles proves. On the road, the Marquise's most important companions were her books and the few trusted people she always travelled with. As to the real "others," people not of her own social group: They did enter her orbit, but she was but little interested in their way of life, except, again, for the picturesque peasants whose musical pastimes enlivened her weeks at Vichy.

Though to us the conditions under which Mme de Sévigné had to travel suggest a fair amount of *"travail,"* i.e. of hassle and problems, it seems that she did not find her journeys particularly strenuous. Rather, they helped her to, in a way, forget the greatest "travail" of her life: The painful absence of her most beloved and trusted companion, whose empty bedroom reminded her daily of her sorrows. She sought to annihilate the distances in space and time that separated her from her daughter by an incessant stream of letters, to ensure that: "vous aurez vu tout que je fais, tout ce que je dis, tout ce que je pense."[152] At the same time, the letters were an incessant plea for love. Whether Marie de Sévigné stayed at home, in Paris, or embarked on one of her long trips, it always was Françoise de Grignan who, emotionally, psychologically, had to carry her luggage.

However, since only the Marquise's side of the correspondence is left, this "judgement" may be one-sided, too. Indeed, reading between the lines of the hundreds of letters she wrote and, thus, picking up the clues as to what the Comtesse told her in what must have been hundreds of letters as well, one cannot escape the feeling that the daughter burdened the mother with her emotions, too. Indeed, her almost obsessive jealousy for her mother's sole attention is often painful to read. In short, carrying each other's "luggage," these two women created an emotional "double-bind" – both productive and restrictive – that has left us a correspondence that has few equals.

Notes

1 E.g. Birkett, D. (2004) *Off the Beaten Track: Three Centuries of Women Travellers.* London: National Portrait Gallery Publications. As English scholars often do, Birkett, too, writes about the British experience, only.
2 For a recent biography: Duchêne, R. (2002) *Madame de Sévigné.* Paris: Fayard.
3 E.g. C I, 210–211; 226; 227; 525. Also: C II, 683; 691; 721–722; 725. "The nicest girl in France."
4 Two good introductions: Bernet, A. (1996) *Madame de Sévigné, mère passion.* Paris: Perrin. and Farrell, M. (1991) *Performing Motherhood: The Sévigné Correspondence.* Hanover: University Press of New England.
5 C I, 101; 103.
6 C I, 189: "To read your letters and to write to you are the most important aspect of my life."
7 C I, 112–113.
8 C I, 151–152: [the kind of obligation] "one has to feel towards God, if one did one's duty."
9 E.g.: Mack, P. (2015) *A History of Renaissance Rhetoric, 1380–1620.* Oxford: Oxford University Press. Cfr. also: Craveri, B. (2001) *La civiltà della conversazione.* Milan: Adelphi. Especially Chapter X, about Mme de Sévigné.

10 Cfr. Duchene, R. (1982) *Écrire au temps de Mme de Sévigné: lettres et texte littéraire*. Paris: Vrin; Nies, F. (1992) *Les lettres de Madame de Sévigné, Conventions du genre et sociologie des publics*. Paris: Honoré Champion.

11 See for this aspect of the letters: Depretto, L. (2015) *Informer et Raconter dans la Correspondance de Madame de Sévigné*. Paris: Garnier.

12 C I, 232.

13 Few historians have analyzed the emotional burden the mother placed upon the daughter. See, however: Duchene, J. (1985) *Françoise de Grignan, ou le mal d'amour*. Paris: Fayard.

14 For the following; C I, 145–146; 149–150; 151–152; 153–154; 155; 157; 158; 161–162; 163 sqq.; 168–180.

15 C I, 172: "this river is formed of thousands of rivulets of blood."

16 C I, 175–176.

17 C I, 160: "like a curtain behind which I was hidden."

18 C I, 157.

19 C II, 544–546; 549; 567; 704.

20 C I, 21.

21 C II, 64; cfr. C II, 93.

22 Cfr. for a survey: Gordon, B. (2012) "Reinventions of a spa town: The unique case of Vichy," in: *Journal of Tourism History*, 4/1: 35–55.

23 C I, 716–717.

24 E.g. C II, 445–455 passim. Cfr. C II, 695: "How many exhausting days to finally arrive there, how many nights spent on a straw mattress, without sleep, without any hot dish to eat."

25 C I, 14.

26 C I, 199 sqq.

27 C I, 526.

28 C II, 626.

29 E.g. C I, 229; 256; C II, 95.

30 Cfr. Rietbergen, P. (2014) *Europe: A Cultural History*. London: Routledge, 3rd edition, 306–329.

31 C II, 525; 528; 531.

32 C II, 438: "You'll certainly find friends, there, and the next day other friends and thus, staying at friend's places every night, you'll find yourself in your own bedroom."

33 C II, 953.

34 C II, 541.

35 C I, 251; cfr. also; C I, 232; 237.

36 C I, 246–247.

37 C I, 251.

38 C II, 93; 94; 95

39 C II, 919.

40 C III, 43–44.

41 C III, 596.

42 C II, 291.

43 C II, 291.

44 C II, 551.

45 C II, 523; 525; 526; 527

46 C II, 531.

47 C II, 531–538.

48 C II, 550; 553; 558.

49 C I, 559

50 C III, 938–943.

51 C III, 1040–1041.
52 C II, 39: "My dear, your exchange of letters is divine. Your letters are true conversations: I talk to you and you answer me."
53 E.g. C I, 171; 210–211; 227. C II, 194.
54 C II, 292.
55 E.g. C II, 292; 366.
56 E.g. C I, 211–212; 257
57 E.g. C III, 1041.
58 E.g. C II, 314; 321.
59 C II, 97–98; cf. C II,105.
60 C II, 64–65.
61 C II, 69: "The kingly person now has made himself into a form which you cannot imagine. He never rises to meet one, never even looks at one."
62 C II, 521: "the chaos of my mind, the problems of my health [mean] I cannot mean anything to you."
63 E.g. C I, 464.
64 https://fr.wikipedia.org/wiki/Madame_de_S%C3%A9vign%C3%A9/ [last checked on 9/28/2018]
65 E.g. C II, 626.
66 C II, 584: "I've come here to experience the last beautiful days and say good-bye to the leaves."
67 E.g.: C II, 68; 70; 373.
68 C II, 364; 374; 378; 479–481.
69 E.g. C II, 368; 374; 382.
70 C II, 626. Cfr. C II, 689.
71 C II, 648; 715–716.
72 E.G. C III, 89–90.
73 C III, 132; 1216.
74 C III, 330, to M. de Moulceau.
75 C II, 431; 424; 437; 438; 450.
76 C II, 727: "My son tells me […] that there is one side of him that adores me and another that wants to strangle me, and that the two are constantly at loggerheads."
77 C II, 688: "You find me here all alone with the memory of you. It is enough for me. It is a faithful companion who never leaves me."
78 C III, 238; 261–262.
79 C III, 330.
80 C III, 324; 327; 330; 385.
81 C I, 256; 1088. Cfr. C I, 271.
82 C I, 271; 332.
83 C I, 264.
84 C I, 268.
85 C I, 258.
86 C I, 390–391.
87 C I, 392.
88 C I, 446; 448.
89 C I, 470.
90 C I, 550; 552; 554
91 C I, 555–559.
92 C I, 558.
93 C I, 483.
94 C I, 568: "How are you, my little darling? Has my absence not made you a little fonder of me? I do hope to see you again as if it has been a long time since I left you."
95 C I, 573; 574.

96 C I, 572: of adventurers, of swords, of elegant hats, of men one would love to paint, of a notion of war, of romance, of leaving port, of iron chains, of slaves, of servitude, of captivity: I, who love novels, am enchanted by it, enraptured by it.

97 C I, 593; 594: "In one word, my daughter, I only live for you." "My only pleasure is to write to you."

98 C I, 595; 599.

99 C I, 599–600: "I find that the value we attach to most things depends on the state of mind we are in when we receive them."

100 C I, 602; 503; 605.

101 C I, 604.

102 C I, 598: "if I'm not with you, the only thing that gives me pleasure is to write to you."

103 C II, 100.

104 C II, 99; 103.

105 C II, 103–104.

106 C II, 99, 104: "I do need a bit of conversation."

107 C II, 100.

108 C II, 104; 105; 106; 109; 110.

109 C II, 112.

110 C II, 255; 257; 258.

111 C II, 301; cfr. also C II, 323.

112 Cfr. e.g. C II, 312.

113 C II, 259; 262; 288; 289.

114 C II, 289; 312.

115 C II, 295; 305.

116 C II, 290.

117 C II, 293; cfr. C II, 309–310.

118 C II, 293; cfr. also C II, 324.

119 C II, 283; 294.

120 C II, 294.

121 C II, 295.

122 C II, 299; 306; 309.

123 C II, 308.

124 C II, 312; 318.

125 C II, 307.

126 C II, 308–309; 320.

127 C II, 312; 314; 317; 321; 545; 548; 551.

128 C II, 329.

129 C II, 524; 540.

130 C II, 523; 526; 535–536.

131 C II, 544.

132 C II, 561.

133 C II, 921: "I miss my writing-case."

134 C II, 919; 921; 922; 923; 925; 926. They sit "on nice cushions, in the open air, quite at our ease." But "all others [sit] like pigs in the straw."

135 C II, 931; 939.

136 C II, 943; 953.

137 C III, 136: "I do prefer boredom to constraint," viz. the constraint caused by having to travel with someone she does not feel comfortable with.

138 C III, 135–141.

139 C III, 327.

140 C III, 316–327.

141 Already C II, 193–194.

142 C III, 578–605.
143 C III, 944, to M. de Moulceau; C III, 945 and 949, to Bussy-Rabutin.
144 C III, 938.
145 C III, 927–928; 938–944.
146 C III, 943: "all my steps tell you [I love you]."
147 C III, 1026.
148 C III, 1041.
149 E.g. C III, 1031.
150 See: C I, 604; C II, 101.
151 C II, 319. Cfr. Rietbergen, P. (2018) "The political rhetoric of capitals: Rome and Versailles in the Baroque Period," in: Kaal, H., a. o. eds., *Repertoires of Representation* Leiden: Brill (= Radboud Studies in the Humanities) (at press).
152 C II, 298: "You will have seen everything that I do, everything that I say, everything that I think."

6 Female passengers and female voices in early modern Dutch travelogues of leisure trips (1669–1748)[*]

Alan Moss

Introduction

In recent years, scholars have increasingly focused on the much-neglected aspect of gender in early modern travel literature, identifying distinct female voices and analysing masculinity and masculine self-fashioning. In studies of the Grand Tour, the topic of gender has proved to be a fruitful angle of historical research, as it has enabled academics to counterbalance the extensive bulk of literature on education and status.[1] Studies of Romantic voyaging in the nineteenth century have highlighted the abundance of female authors and the feminine representation of nature.[2] Seventeenth-century travel, however, was a predominantly male activity. In case studies of the period, there is a large gap between male and female voices. According to the historian Gerrit Verhoeven, who has analysed mobility patterns in early modern travelogues from the Low Countries, throughout the seventeenth century female participation increased only gradually.[3] Dutch ego-documents and travelogues, both in print and in manuscript form, show a similar pattern.[4] For the whole of the seventeenth century, we have only one travel manuscript written by a Dutch woman. Elisabeth van der Woude (°1657) described a military expedition to in 1676–1677, where her father was to govern a Dutch colony on the banks of the Oiapoque river. Her account, spanning a period of almost four decades, elaborates on the mission's difficulties, but also mentions international politics and noteworthy family events.[5]

There are several reasons why women did not travel as much as men. Firstly, itinerant women did not fit within the contemporary system of male and female duties in the household. Men crossed the country's borders for utilitarian motives, while women stayed behind to run the household. Travel for travel's sake was uncommon. Even though leisure and curiosity were integral parts of travel, the main goal of a journey had to be framed in terms of trade, war, diplomacy, or education.[6] In the higher social classes, travel was seen as a mandatory part of a young man's education, whereas girls older than thirteen would remain home to prepare for domestic life.[7] As they did not pursue clear-cut utilitarian goals, itinerant women were scarce and often considered a threat. They were the eccentric outsiders, whose unique social position – e.g. wealthy, educated, and unmarried – enabled that kind of freedom.[8] Secondly, travel guides, which were often written for educational travellers, warned that a voyage could expose a traveller to a multitude of unforeseen dangers and obstacles that required swift and determined action.[9] This type of discourse was highly gendered. Since the supposed female fragility simply could not cope with rapid boat rides, steep mountain climbs, and bad-mannered innkeepers, women were barred entry to a journey abroad.[10] At the same time, a traveller's masculine identity was reinforced by encountering and bravely overcoming these ordeals, and subsequently recording them in his travelogue. Whether danger was real or fictitious was not necessarily important. By employing this type of discourse, the traveller-author could present his Grand Tour as a liminal experience that transformed him from a feeble youth into a battle-hardened young adult.[11] Within this framework used by contemporary travel literature, foreign women had to conform to a limited selection of topoi. Travel guides breathe life into the topos of the exotic temptress, who enticed, corrupted and tried to lead young, naive travellers astray. Moral growth was achieved by surpassing or ignoring those temptations.[12] On the other end of the spectrum, women appeared as *couleur locale*: They were enchanting sights, curiosities, or literary means to illustrate the strangeness of a yet unexplored city. The exotic representation of female beauty, often experienced in a company of fellow male travellers, was another way to frame a masculine identity.

In the late seventeenth-century Dutch Republic, a new mode of travel emerged, which, in comparison to the Grand Tour, started to blur the lines between male and female agency. On these so-called pleasure trips leisure became the new *vaut de voyage*.[13] The admonishments of travel guides lost their vigour, and utilitarian motivations became optional. This new mode of travel behaviour negated the usual difficulties for women. Compared to a long and arduous Grand Tour, a leisure trip to Brussels and Antwerp posed few hardships, nor did it impose on predominantly male activities. Although this change should not be overestimated, travel became a more female venture. Starting in the eighteenth century, female Dutch authors committed their experiences to paper.[14] In this chapter I investigate two types of travel literature: Early modern Dutch accounts of leisure trips written by female and male authors. Six travellers and their travelogues are explored, i.e. Cornelis de Jonge van Ellemeet (1669), Gerard Hinlopen (1683), Adriaan Gerrits van Assendelft (1696), Ignatia Geertruida Timmers (1729), Adriana Petronella de la Court (1732, 1733, 1740, 1743), and Cornelia Carolina de Vassy (1748).[15] The accounts of De Jonge van Ellemeet and Timmers will be highlighted. The first category offers insight into female representations of travel and travel activities. How did women reflect on their male companions? Which activities and which elements are highlighted in their journals? On the other end of the spectrum, how did male authors discuss their fellow passengers? Did male authors present a specific type of masculinity in their manuscripts, just as is often found in, for example, analyses of Grand Tour accounts? Before grappling with these questions, this new mode of travel is briefly explored.

The six accounts analysed in this chapter are all unpublished Dutch travel manuscripts written in the second half of the seventeenth and first half of the eighteenth century. They were shelved in family libraries and eventually moved to national archives and research institutes. In general, travelogues were meant as both a personal keepsake to reminisce about a past summer abroad, and as a means to inform and entertain a close circle of family and friends. They are also a means of self-fashioning, the conscious or unconscious representation of identity. Observations of nature and cityscapes are mixed with personal recollections of deeply-felt cultural, national, and religious differences. Traveller-authors either learned to appreciate other countries or were bolstered in their belief in persistent cultural stereotypes. Either way, these confrontations forced a traveller reflect on his or her ideas of faith and fatherland.

Leisure trips

According to Gerrit Verhoeven, who has meticulously investigated this new mode of travel, in the grand genealogy of mobility, leisure trips can be placed somewhere between the Grand Tour and modern tourism.[16] That intermediary position seems to bridge the glaring divide between these two opposing modes of travel. After all, it is difficult to consider the Grand Tour, its suggestive name notwithstanding, as a precursor to tourism. While many scholars have proposed such a direct link, these two types of travel appear to be polar opposites when considering aspects of social milieu (rich elite vs. middle-class), duration (years vs. weeks), and underlying goals (edification vs. leisure).[17] Espousing characteristics of both, the early modern leisure trip can be proposed as the missing link between the two. In light of female participation, this mode of familial travel falls between the era of male-dominated Grand Tours and nineteenth-century Romantic voyages, where female authorship came to the fore.

Leisure trips, referred to as *plaisierreisjes* (pleasure trips) or *somertogtjes* (summer jaunts) by contemporaries, first appeared in the last quarter of the seventeenth century.[18] Itinerant Dutchmen sojourned for a couple of weeks in nearby places, such as London, Paris, Brussels, and Antwerp, and German cities on the border of the Republic. Whereas the Grand Tour was a formative, once-in-a-lifetime experience, these trips were recurrent and seasonal.[19] Similar to Grand Tourists, travellers on a summer jaunt hailed from the upper crust, elite circles of the Republic, even though the reduced costs gave the less affluent some leeway. Travellers were generally older, however, and often journeyed with their wife and children in tow.[20] Sometimes travel accounts of a Grand Tour and leisure trips even appear next to one another. Gerard Hinlopen (1644–1691), for example, started off his manuscript with an exploration of the Greek isles and Istanbul in his mid-twenties, before settling for some short impressions of the lazy jaunts he made in his thirties.[21] In his elegant travel manuscript, Cornelis de Jonge van Ellemeet (1646–1727) elaborated on his journey to France before jotting down his report of a leisure trip.[22] With the advent of pleasure trips, travel no longer had purely utilitarian motivations. Recreation and relaxation became legitimate goals. Activities were varied. Churches, palaces, and city halls remained hotspots, but shops and theatres held an equal allure, as did outings to the coast or the countryside.[23]

The role of women changed. Daughters and wives could join their male counterparts on a short leisure trip. Leisure trips were a familial form of travel. While change was afoot, the gap between the sexes was still very much present in the eighteenth century: According to the statistics of Verhoeven, itinerant men outweighed women four to one.[24] Travel without a male companion was far from the norm. Dutch women also started to report on their journeys abroad. According to the compendium of early modern Dutch travelogues, in the first half of the eighteenth century six accounts were written by three female travellers.[25] While a number of travelogues might have been lost to us, it seems that female authorship was notably more marginal. Despite their scarcity, these memoirs enable us to investigate the role and agency of women in this mode of early modern mobility, where female participation gradually grew.

Reflections of male travellers: De Jonge van Ellemeet, Hinlopen, and Van Assendelft

Female travelling companions played a leading role in the 1669 account of Cornelis de Jonge van Ellemeet, one of the earliest recorded summer jaunts.[26] Cornelis was the scion of a notable family in the province of Zeeland, who would become one of the richest men of the Republic. He was able to amass a personal fortune of roughly two million guilders thanks to his lucrative appointment as tax collector general of the United Provinces in 1674, an office that financially buttressed the rule of stadholder William III.[27] As was customary to a man of his station, Cornelis had made a long educational journey to France in his early twenties, where he obtained a law degree at the prestigious university of Angers.[28] Two years later, Cornelis hired a yacht and departed for a brief leisure trip to Antwerp and Brussels. Joining him were his mother Margaretha Briel (1617–1685), his sisters Johanna (1643–1694) and Cecilia (1645–1686), family friend Agatha de Jong, and her young children. The trip had not been Cornelis' own idea:

> For two or three summers on end, the old women had promised their daughters some delights. All this time the young ladies had been most intent on a trip to the duchy of Brabant, a province worth looking at because of many things, but mostly of its religion, which differs greatly from the one we have in Holland.[29]

According to Cornelis, his mother and family friend Agatha de Jong had instigated their summer trip. Margaretha Briel had lost her husband, Jacob de Jonge van Ellemeet en Elkerzee (1610–1650), in her early thirties. Since then she had played a more dominant role in the family household, all the while raising her eldest son to become the future *pater familias*. Margaretha and her daughters wanted to satisfy their curiosity for the Catholic Low Countries, one of the main points of interests on a leisure trip. Interest in the religious "Other" was a recurring theme in early modern Dutch travelogues.[30] During the two-day trip to Antwerp alone, they visited ten churches, four monasteries and a *beguinage*. They admired the "many tasteful statues and paintings" in the Cathedral of Our Lady, bought flowers and handmade dolls from the Norbertines in St Michael's Abbey, and found some Catholic residents who were willing to guide them through the city.[31] Their trip was more varied however. The group visited fortifications, town halls, and an echoing well, observed the historical curiosities of Brussels' arsenal, and called on relatives and friends.

Despite this varied program, a large part of Cornelis' manuscript was allotted to the experiences of his fellow passengers. In Antwerp, the women from Zeeland became a recognisable sight due to their white clothing.[32] Cornelis' sister Johanna and Agatha de Jong chatted with the locals, enquired about the city, and separated from the group to visit some acquaintances. Their stopover went without a hitch, except for "some bad-mannered woman" who had bothered Agatha in the middle of the street.[33] The journey to Antwerp had been calm as well, as Cornelis teasingly wrote that only Agatha had been "a teeny, tiny, teensy bit" frightened.[34] The last stage of the trip had been equally pleasant: Cornelis was caught unawares by a large wave, which made Agatha's daughter Maria burst out in laughter.[35] In short, their trip was a cheerful one without many difficulties. Agatha received most of the author's attention. Since Cornelis was already familiar with Antwerp and Brussels, a trip to the Southern Netherlands could no longer please him. Instead he enjoyed conversing with Agatha during his spare hours. Cornelis made a long and flattering written portrait of his travelling companion. Adopting a lyrical tone, he admired "the unparalleled friendliness in her countenance," "her alabaster teeth," and "her rose-coloured lips."[36] Her eyes in particular caught his attention:

> Her eyes are not large, but filled with so much fire, and at the same time full of all sorts of charm, that it is impossible to conceive how such strong beacons, which like flickering suns emit a multitude of golden rays, could reveal the affability one can detect in her.[37]

Cornelis reserved three pages for his verbose appraisal of Agatha and came to the following conclusion: "Yes, she has so many pleasing features that one finds it difficult to get to know her without falling in love."[38] Agatha's ability to make men fall in love notwithstanding, Cornelis' lofty, Petrarchan depiction of his fellow traveller was most likely a poetic exercise to occupy his idle hours on deck. Cornelis settled down ten years later with his wife Maria Oyens (1647–1732), the daughter of a lawyer.[39] The author was no stranger to love poetry. He started off his manuscript with a poem dedicated to an anonymous woman from The Hague, in which he used the same superlatives: "There is no beauty as perfect/As yours, the only one to reach my heart."[40] That type of literature could fit perfectly in his neatly written, semi-private manuscript that most likely circulated in a close circle of family and friends.

Agatha was the subject of Cornelis' poetic observations, but during one particular event she and the other women on deck were also a means to express his masculinity. While the journey to the Southern Netherlands was hardly dangerous, the customs officers, one of whom was "a great impertinent beast," proved to be a persistent nuisance.[41] On the way to Brussels, they were assaulted by five or six soldiers who demanded toll. Cornelis' youngest sister Cecilia, affectionately called Cijltje, was especially frightened: "All of this upset our company enormously. Most notably it resulted in the skittishness of Cijltje, who displayed her fear just like her mama."[42] They stopped in the nearby town of Vilvoorden to drink some water and get over the shock. On the way back to the Republic, the travelling group was prepared to quarrel with the same border patrol. When they saw how a poor local woman was accosted and relieved of most of her money, the ladies prepared for the worst:

> In the third group [of customs officers] was the brute, that utter rogue who had snubbed us two days prior in a most ill-mannered way and had frightened the ladies so much that they immediately started to slide their rings and money in their shoes.[43]

Eventually the women hid below decks, while Cornelis confronted the rude soldiers. With some pride he mentioned that this was a good decision, since they avoided paying a higher tax.[44] Traditional gender roles are reiterated in this passage. While his mother initially called for a summer outing, it is Cornelis, the only male in the group, who has to take on a leading role when things seem to become more dire. At the same time, the women in his company are presented as frightened and skittish. According to Sarah Goldsmith, eighteenth-century British travel authors used several literary strategies to depict dangerous situations in order to fashion their masculine identity. The most common way is to neutrally and rather coolly observe exact details – the dimensions of a cascade, the diameter of a hailstone – while avoiding any mention of fear. Another tactic is to utilise emotional others against which the traveller's courage and steadfastness can be framed in a travelogue. On a Grand Tour, which was a rite of passage to adulthood in itself, the fear experienced by social inferiors was exacerbated in order to both illustrate the direness of a dangerous situation and to juxtapose the traveller's stoicism and supposed lack of fear. Usually those social inferiors came in the form of servants and animals, such as the traveller's horse.[45] The author of this travel account seems to adopt a comparable narrative strategy. While his sisters hide below decks, Cornelis acts miffed by the soldier's impoliteness. "The skittishness of Cijltje" is used to frame Cornelis' masculine identity and reaffirm traditional gender roles.[46] It goes to show that accounts of the Grand Tour and leisure trips are in line with one another. The level of danger differed, but travel literature was still a vehicle of masculine representation. While the account of Cornelis de Jonge van Ellemeet offers some insights into masculine representations and female travellers, it also seems to be an outlier of the genre. While women gradually stood on deck on a yacht to Antwerp and Brussels, travel accounts did not always acknowledge or elaborate on their presence.[47]

The women on the summer jaunts of Gerard Hinlopen and Adriaan Gerrits van Assendelft (1664–1742) are less visible than those described by Cornelis de Jonge van Ellemeet. On his summer jaunt in 1683, Gerard Hinlopen, a mid-level governor in the city council of Hoorn, made almost no mention of his wife, Margareta Hooghtwoudt (ca. 1648–1684).[48] Hinlopen was a seasoned traveller, with an adventurous exploration of Greece and Istanbul already under his belt, and sated his taste for travel on short summer jaunts aboard his own yacht, seven of which he committed to paper. Since he only married in 1681, fairly late in life, his previous trips had been in the company of friends and colleagues. In 1683, Gerard journeyed to Antwerp and Brussels in the company of his wife Margaretha, as well as the families of two of his colleagues. In Brussels they hired some local guides to explore the attractions of the city, including several churches, the arsenal, the ducal gardens, and a *beguinage*.[49] In Antwerp they observed a long line of floats, carrying a wondrous variety of whales, dolphins, elephants, lions, giants, and dwarves for the traditional pageant on Pentecost Sunday.[50] The account focuses on the various attractions the Southern Netherlands had to offer, but does not elaborate on the observations of Hinlopen's company. In fact, except for his introductory remarks, the women are only mentioned once. Returning to Hoorn, the group had a brief respite in Breda, where the men and women split up. The men spent their time observing the city's fortifications, while the "womenfolk" visited a cousin and made a short trip by carriage to a nearby forest.[51] While it is tempting to speculate about those opposing activities, the material in Hinlopen's descriptive account is rather scarce to suggest anything about the division of roles. A prominent detail, however, is that this was Hinlopen's last account. According to his biographer's speculations, Gerard did not recuperate from his wife's death one year later. He did not hold any public offices, nor did his manuscript report on any future trips.[52]

Women appear in a similar fashion in the account of Adriaan Gerrits van Assendelft. Adriaan, treasurer of the city of Delft, enjoyed a brief trip to the duchy of Cleves, the city of Nijmegen and palace Het Loo. According to his cash book, he spent 106 guilders on the whole affair.[53] Adriaan journeyed alongside his wife Maria Magdalena van Beresteyn (1667–1715), his daughters Catarina and Maria, his sister Maria (†1744), and his brother-in-law Willem (†1744), steward in the employ of stadholder William III. Their visit to the stadholder's palace in Apeldoorn was the high point of their voyage.[54] They enjoyed the many fountains in the garden, and in the palace they saw various tapestries, paintings, and a set of antlers of a deer shot by stadholder William III himself. The vistas around Nijmegen and Cleves garnered Adriaan's attention. The area around Nijmegen offered "incomparable sights" and Cleves had "several unbelievably pleasant views."[55] While his female travelling companions indubitably enjoyed the waterfalls, streams, gardens, and royal palaces along the way, Adriaan only briefly mentions his fellow passengers. During a visit to Roosendaal, the group paid a visit to a nearby paper mill, where Adriaan's youngest sister was shown how to make a sheet of paper. Since the sheet had to dry first and they had a later engagement in Roosendaal, she could not bring it along as a souvenir.[56]

While women gained a new role in early modern leisure trips, and the itinerary changed to accommodate their needs and interests, women appeared only in passing in the male accounts of those journeys. Women in the entourage of both Hinlopen and Van Assendelft are only mentioned in a single aside. The source material is usually too scarce to make any sweeping statements regarding male observations of female travellers. The account of Cornelis de Jonge van Ellemeet is the exception to that rule. Cornelis' manuscript and the curious addendum of a written, lyrical portrait offer some insights into the representation of his fellow travellers, as well as the representation of his own masculine identity.

Reflections of female travellers: De la Court, De Vassy, Timmers

Adriana de la Court (1696–1748), the daughter of a rich textile merchant from Leiden, is an interesting example of a female travel author.[57] The journeys and travel preferences of the De la Court family are preserved particularly well. Adriana's grandfather walked through London at the eve of the English Civil War, her father wrote some vitriolic letters to his wife in which he complained about unreliable French landladies, and her brother Allard critically observed the technical advancements of the linen industry during a business trip to England.[58] Adriana had that same taste for travel. Aged eighteen she joined her brother-in-law Johan Meerman (1687–1752) on his journey to England. Soon she committed her own journeys to paper.[59] Her unique social position allowed for that type of mobility: Adriana was unmarried for the largest part of her life and could draw on the vast family fortune.[60] Her travel account of a journey to Maastricht in 1733 offers a perfect example of Adriana's varied interests. In Maastricht she reported on a strict Catholic order which was not allowed a single piece of linen, while in Spa she enjoyed her time browsing shops and drinking chocolate milk. Near Arnhem she snacked on sweet cherries in the beautiful grotto of some luxurious gardens, and in Hardenberg she spent her time in the esteemed company of a local scholar.[61] Adriana enjoyed a pleasant summer jaunt. "We made this whole trip with beautiful weather and great pleasure, and without the least bit of trouble," she concluded.[62] While the others outings of women discussed in this paper were made in a purely familial setting, mostly organised by others, Adriana had a high level of agency in the preparation and itinerary of her journeys due to her special social standing. In the chapter of Gerrit Verhoeven in this book, Adriana's travel accounts and her particular motivations and interests are explored further.

The accounts of Ignatia Geertruida Timmers (1714–1733) and Cornelia Carolina de Vassy appear to be somewhat eccentric. In 1748, Cornelia joined on a short trip from Middelburg to The Hague in the company of Mr and Mrs Thibaut and their daughters, Leendert Bomme and his two sons, and Elias de Haze (1689–1752) and his wife Catharina (1715–1782).[63] The group made a brief detour for Bergen op Zoom and Wouw in order to observe the damage these towns had incurred a year earlier during the War of the Austrian Succession.[64] While Cornelia wrote down a very succinct, incomplete travel account, she did so in a very special format: She used verses to describe her leisure trip. Her decision to do so was apparently impulsive. Since she knew she was prone to forget otherwise, she looked for a journal "in one corner or another" to describe "the sweet things/we met along the way."[65] Although the journey was prepared for well in advance, the group had to rely on the services of one captain Claas van der Zalm. According to Cornelia, his ship was a disaster. The group could not find pillows or the chamber pot, had to hang their clothes on barrels of brandy, and were forced to use their suitcases as makeshift chairs. Their berths were equally uncomfortable: "When you looked at us then/we looked like sick people in the hospital."[66] Cornelia soon arrived in Goes, where an acquaintance managed to hire a carriage and ensured a more comfortable journey to castle Maelstede in nearby Kapelle. The author abruptly stopped her travel poem near Roosendaal, halfway between Middelburg and her destination. The rest of the manuscript was used as a later cash book. Possibly, the special form of this account ensured that this incomplete manuscript was kept for posterity as a sort of family curiosity. This special form notwithstanding, Cornelia seems to high-light the same elements of discomfort that are often a staple in travel literature. Just like other travel authors, Cornelia amused her audience by contrasting a miserable boat trip to the wonderful vista of castle Maelstede that lay beyond.

The final author in this paper, is the fifteen-year-old Ignatia Geertruida Timmers. In a big, loopy hand she wrote about her leisure trip to the Southern Netherlands in 1729. She journeyed alongside her father Johan (1684–1738), mother Susanna (1684–1732) and her older sister Aletta Johanna (1707–1775), as well as four other gentlemen.[67] She started off her account with a traditional depiction of the sexes. While the men stayed on deck to drink and fire the cannons, the women turned in for the night. Not for long however:

> Somewhere between midnight and one o'clock seven shots were fired. It woke everyone up, even the hens in their cage, except for one of the kind souls of the female sex, who, after draining her wine cup, must have been so overcome with sleep, that she did not notice a thing.[68]

The celebrations on deck continued for a while. This small excerpt juxtaposes the raucous men who stayed on deck to celebrate with the women who stayed away from such an activity. In Antwerp they were kindly welcomed with a cannon shot and returned in kind. Mr Bentinck "fired the cannon himself with unequalled stout-heartedness," Ignatia noted.[69]

Just like most other accounts of leisure trips, Ignatia reports on the buildings and churches of the Flemish cities. In Brussels, for example, she visited the city arsenal, the Temple des Augustins, and the castle of archduchess Maria Elisabeth of Austria (1680–1741), the governor of the Austrian Netherlands. Together with her sister Aletta she rushed to the opera in order to see the archduchess, while the rest of the party observed her arrival.[70] Ignatia also spent her time in theatres, browsed through shops and boutiques, and reported on her many social visits and return visits in the Southern Netherlands. Those social calls take a leading role in her account: In Middelburg she paid a visit to Mrs Radermacher and her six-year-old boy, in Antwerp a social call turned into a wine tasting, and the last day in Brussels was spent visiting all friends and acquaintances. Ignatia also reported on her fellow passengers and the social activities they undertook together. For example, during stormy weather and quiet nights, the group stayed below decks laughing, drinking tea, and playing games. In these descriptions we can tentatively pinpoint an interesting difference between male and female authorship. While men dutifully and concisely noted their visits to friends, Ignatia seems to elaborate on the social aspects of her journey. Instead of focusing on the precise observations of a foreign city, which is often the dominant theme in travel accounts by male authors, she seems to elaborate on the company of family members. In that regard, her account is the direct opposite of the journals of Hinlopen and Van Assendelft, who barely mention their fellow passengers at all. Another interesting feature in Ignatia's account is that the travelling group sometimes splits up. In Middelburg the women visited a local glassworks and in Antwerp they spent hours eyeing lace clothes in the city's boutiques, while the men paid a visit to the local mint. The members of the travelling group seem to be able to pursue their particular interests. Finally, danger is presented in a more traditional way. According to Ignatia's travelogue, the journey to the Southern Netherlands went without a hitch, save for a frightening crossing in Vlaardingen:

> The ladies became very frightened because we had to sail against cross-currents and adverse winds, which made us decide to return to Vlaardingen and visit the home of Mr Convent. The ladies drank a glass of wine with sal volatile [ammonium carbonate] for the shock as well as a cup of tea, and the men had a glass of wine and smoked a tobacco pipe.[71]

When the women had fully recuperated, they made a brief detour and quickly returned to Rotterdam. In her description of a summer jaunt, Ignatia adopted a different perspective: While she observed churches and city halls, she mainly focused on the social aspects of the journey.

Conclusion

Travel accounts of leisure trips can be used to reflect on the new position of women in the study of early modern mobility and are a means to juxtapose male and female observations. Summer jaunts were a new mode of travel and a family activity. Although male travel writers did not always report in detail on their female passengers, the travel account of Cornelis de Jonge van Ellemeet offers an interesting framing of the division of the sexes. Cornelis spent his time and ink on his depiction of his fellow travellers, writing a poetic, almost Petrarchan portrait of his Agatha. At the same time, he used the dangers or supposed dangers on the road to fashion his own masculinity. He depicted the women in his company cowering below decks, while he expressed his masculinity by meeting the brutish border patrol head first. Accounts of female travellers are unfortunately scarce for the eighteenth century, save for the elaborate observations of the seasoned traveller Adriana de la Court. The manuscripts of Timmers and De Vassy are the exceptions to the rule. Cornelia offered a curious, though incomplete travel account in verse, elaborating on the unexpected hardships on their journey. The fifteen-year-old Ignatia adopted a somewhat different perspective, focusing on the social aspects of her journey: Drinking tea with her fellow passengers, visiting acquaintances in Flemish cities, and mocking one of the women who happily kept on snoring while the men on deck continued to fire the cannons. The social and familial aspects of her journey seem to take the forefront in her account. While this article only offers an exploration of the gender aspects of this genre, accounts of leisure trips can be a rich source to investigate family relationships and early modern female authorship.

Notes

1 See for example: Goldsmith, S. (2015) "Dogs, Servants and Masculinities: Writing about Danger on the Grand Tour," *Journal for Eighteenth-Century Studies*: 1–19; Brewer, J. (2013) "Whose Grand Tour?" in *The English Prize: The Capture of the "Westmorland," an Episode of the Grand Tour*. Maria Dolores Sánchez-Jáuregui and Scott Wilcox (eds.). New Haven: Yale University Press: 45–62; Gabbard, D.C. (2003) "Gender Stereotyping in Early Modern Travel Writing on Holland," *Studies in English Literature, 1500–1900*: 83–100; Dolan, B. (2002) *Ladies of the Grand Tour*. London: Harper Collins; Cohen, M. (2002) *Fashioning Masculinity: National Identity and Language in the Eighteenth Century*. London: Routledge; Turner, K. (2001) *British Travel Writers in Europe, 1759–1800: Authorship, Gender and National Identity*. London: Routledge.

2 Gilroy, A. (ed.) (2000), *Romantic Geographies: Discourses of Travel 1775–1844*. Manchester: Manchester University Press; Chard, C. (1999) *Pleasure and Guilt on the Grand Tour: Travel Writing and Imaginative Geography, 1600–1830*. Manchester: Manchester University Press: 34–37.

3 Verhoeven, G. (2009a) *Anders reizen? Evoluties in vroegmoderne reiservaringen van Hollandse en Brabantse elites (1600–1750)*. Hilversum: Uitgeverij Verloren: 152–159.

4 Lindeman, R., Scherf, Y., and Dekker, R. (eds.) (2016) *Egodocumenten van Neder-landers uit de zestiende tot begin negentiende eeuw: repertorium*. Amsterdam: Panchaud; Lindeman, R., Scherf, Y., and Dekker, R. (eds.) (1994), *Reisverslagen van Noord-Nederlanders uit de zestiende tot begin negentiende eeuw: een chronologische lijst*. Haarlem: Stichting egodocument.

5 Muller, K.I. (2001) *Elisabeth van der Woude: Memorije van 't geen bij mijn tijt is voorgevallen, met het opzienbarende verslag van haar reis naar de Wilde Kust 1676–1677*. Amsterdam: Terra Incognita.

6 Stannek, A. (2001) *Telemachs Brüder: die höfische Bildungsreise des 17. Jahrhunderts*. Frankfurt/New York: Campus: 41–55; Stagl, J. (1995) *A History of Curiosity: The Theory of Travel 1550–1800*. London: Routledge: 48–49; Bepler, J. (1994) "The Traveller-Author and His Role in Seventeenth-Century German Travel Accounts," in *Travel Fact and Travel Fiction: Studies on Fiction, Literary Tradition, Scholarly Discovery and Observation in Travel Writing*. Zweder von Mantel (ed.). Leiden: Brill: 183–193.

7 Verhoeven (2009): 153.

8 Dolan (2002): 8–13.

9 Mączak, A. (1995) *Travel in Early Modern Europe*. Ursula Philips [tr.]. Cambridge: Polity Press: 158–180.

10 Verhoeven (2009a): 153–154.

11 Goldsmith (2015); Chard (1999): 34–39. For liminality on the Grand Tour, see: Stannek (2001): 19–23.

12 Warneke, S. (1995) *Images of the Educational Traveller in Early Modern England.* Leiden: Brill: 191–216.

13 Verhoeven, G. (2013) "Foreshadowing Tourism: Looking for Modern and Obsolete Features – or Some Missing Links – in Early Modern Travel Behavior (1675–1750)," *Annals of Tourism Research*: 262–283; Verhoeven, G. (2009b) "'Een divertissant somertogje': Transport Innovations and the Rise of Short-Term Pleasure Trips in the Low Countries, 1600–1750," *The Journal of Transport History*: 78–97.

14 Verhoeven (2013): 272–273.

15 De Vassy, C.C. (1748) *Verslag door Cornelis Carolina de Vassy in dichtvorm van een reis van Middelburg naar Den Haag.* Ms. Utrecht: The Utrecht Archives, FA Martens van Sevenhoven 984; De la Court, A.P. (1742) *De reys na Hamburg.* Ms. The Hague: High Council of Nobility, FA Van Spaen 184; De la Court, A.P. *[Travel Account to the Southern Netherlands]* (1740). Ms. The Hague: High Council of Nobility, FA Van Spaen 183; De la Court, A.P. (1733) *Het jaar 1733 met de heer en mevrouw Snakenburg.* Ms. The Hague: High Council of Nobility, FA Van Spaen 182; De la Court, A.P. (1732) *Het jaar 1732. De reys na Maestricht* Ms. The Hague: High Council of Nobility, FA Van Spaen 181; Timmers, I.G. (1729) *Dag register van de commissi [...]* Middelburg: Archives of Zeeland, FA Schorer 395; Van Assendelft, A.G. (1696) *Journal off dagregister vande reijs [...]* The Hague: High Council of Nobility, FA Van der Lely (van Oudewater) 421; Hinlopen, G. (1683) *Speel-reijs gedaan met schepen Gerard van Lingen [...]* Amsterdam: University Library Amsterdam, coll. hss. VIII E 15[XI]; De Jonge van Ellemeet, C. (1669) *Journaal van een reijse gedaan naar Brussel en Antwerpen.* Middelburg: Archives of Zeeland, FA De Jonge van Ellemeet 92a[III].

16 Verhoeven (2013): 278–279.

17 Idem, 264. For more on that dominant view, see: Towner, J. (1985) "The Grand Tour: A Key Phrase in the History of Tourism," *Annals of Tourism Research*: 297–333.

18 Verhoeven (2013): 267.

19 Hoyle, M. and Verhoeven, G. (2013) "Langs de randen en rafels van Nederland (late zeventiende-negentiende eeuw)" in *Met andere ogen... reizen in Overijssel.* Gerrit Verhoeven and Lydie van Dijk (eds.) Hilversum: Uitgeverij Verloren: 13–34; Verhoeven (2013): 267–269; Verhoeven (2009): 84–92.

20 Verhoeven (2013): 271–275.

21 Hinlopen, G. (1662–1683) *Verscheyde voyagien naar diverse coninckrijcken, landen en steden soo nu als dan door mij, Gerard Hinlopen, gedaan.* Ms. Amsterdam: University Library Amsterdam, coll. hss. VIII E 15[I-XI]. For his journey to Istanbul, see: Oddens, J. (2009) *Een vorstelijk voorland: Gerard Hinlopen op reis naar Istanbul (1670–1671).* Zutphen: Walburg Pers: 29–38.

22 De Jonge van Ellemeet, C. (1666–1669) *Alderhande saaken soo Duijtse als Franse waar onder veele van weijnig importantie,* 5. Ms. Middelburg, Archives of Zeeland, FA De Jonge van Ellemeet 92a.

23 Verhoeven (2013): 275–277.

24 Verhoeven (2009a): 152–159.

25 The compendium of Dutch travel accounts by Lindeman, Scherf and Dekker, which lists 83 and 348 accounts for the seventeenth and eighteenth century respectively, mentions the following female authors: Elisabeth van der Woude (1676–1694), Ignatia Geertruida Timmers (1729), Adriana Petronella de la Court (1732, 1733, 1740, 1743), Cornelia Carolina de Vassy (1748), anonymous (1757), Johanna Constantia Palm (1760), Anna Maria de Neufville (1763), anonymous (1766), anonymous (1774), Anna Maria Verkolje (1776), anonymous (1782), Josina Seegers (1783), Agneta Maria Catharina Boreel (1786), Jacoba Johanna Nagtglas (1787), Antje C.W. van Hogendorp (1787, 1792), Eva Magdalena Gavanon (1791), Jeanette Agnes, baroness van Delen (1797), C.F.J.E. (1798), and Maria Catharina de Leeuw (1799).

26 De Jonge van Ellemeet (1669).

27 Zandvliet, K. (2010) *De 250 rijksten van de Gouden Eeuw: kapitaal, macht, familie en levensstijl.* The Hague: Rijksmuseum Publishing: 54–56; De Muinck, B.E. (1965) *Een regentenhuishouding omstreeks 1700: gegevens uit de privé-boekhouding van mr. Cornelis de Jonge van Ellemeet, ontvanger-generaal der Verenigde Nederlanden (1646–1721).* The Hague: Martinus Nijhoff.

28 De Jonge van Ellemeet, *Journael gehouden van mijn reis als ik naar Vrankrijk gingh Ao. 1666* (1666–1667). Ms. Middelburg, Archives of Zeeland, FA De Jonge van Ellemeet 92a[II].

29 De Jonge van Ellemeet (1669): 149–150.

> Al twee of drie Somers naar den anderen hadden de oude Vrouwen wat Vreugde aan haar Dogters belooft, en al desen tijd hadden de Jonge Juffers haar sinnen meest op een Brabants reijsje gesteld als een Provintie sijnde weerdigh om besien te worden, en in veele dingen en voornamentlijk in maniere van Godsdienst seer veele van ons Hollant verschelende.

30 Verhoeven, G. "Backyard Othering: Framing the Southern Low Countries in Dutch Travel Writing (1585–1750)." *Cultures and Practices of Travel, 1600–1800.* University of Leicester, Leicester. 25 March 2017.

31 De Jonge van Ellemeet (1669): 158–160. "veel konstige beelden en schildereijen."

32 Idem, 159.

33 Ibidem. "het eene off het andere onfatsoenelijke wijf."

34 Idem, 158. "een kleijn, kleijn, kleijn wein beetje."

35 Idem, 168.

36 Idem, 170. "een Vriendelijkheijt in haar aanscheijn die sonder weergae is," "haar albaste tanden," "haare roosen-vervige lippen."

37 Idem 170–171.

> Haar oogen en sijn niet grood, maar soo vol viers en te gelijk vol alderhande aangenaamheden dat het niet te bedencken is, hoe dat soo stercke vierbakens die als flickerende sonnen soo veele gulde stralen van haar schieten die lieftalligheijt die men in haar bespeurt konnen uijtwijsen [...]

38 Idem, 170. "Jae, haare aantreckelijckheden sijn soo veele dat men moeijten heeft haar te kennen sonder op haar verlieft te worden."

39 Zandvliet (2010): 54.

40 De Jonge van Ellemeet (1666–1669): 5. "En in die schoonheijt is geen schoonheijt soo volmaakt / Als d'uwe daar mijn hert alleen van is geraackt."

41 De Jonge van Ellemeet (1669): 167. "een grooten impertinenten beest."

42 Idem: 162. "Dit alles gaff groote ontsteltenis onder het geselschap, en bijsonder munte uijt de schierlijkheijt van Cijltje, die haar al soo wel als haar mamatje bevreest toonden."

43 Idem, 166.

> [...] sijnde onder de derde troup deser geweldenaer dien grootsten Belhamer wederom, die ons twee dagen te vooren het alderonfatsoenelijkste hadde bejegent, en de juffers sulke schrick op den hals hadden gejaagt, dat men al reede ringen en geld begon in de schoenen te steeken.

44 Ibidem

45 Goldsmith (2015): 5–13.

46 De Jonge van Ellemeet (1669): 162

47 Verhoeven (2009a): 153–154.
48 Hinlopen (1683). Cf. Odden (2009): 29–38.
49 Hinlopen (1683): 503–505.
50 Idem, 498–501.
51 Idem, 510. "vrouwvolk"
52 Oddens (2009): 31.
53 Van Assendelft (1696).
54 Verhoeven (2009a): 153–154.
55 Van Assendelft (1696).
56 Ibidem.
57 Verhoeven (2009a): 153–154.
58 Allard de la Court, *Aanteekening ofte journaal van mijn reys naar London met de hr.*
    Florius Drabbe en Johannes Buckingham (1710). Ms. Amsterdam: University Library
    Amsterdam, coll. hss. IV J 10[II]; De la Court, P. (1928) "Dagboek Pieter de la Court,"
    in *De reizen der De la Courts 1641, 1700, 1710.* F. Driessen (ed.) Leiden: Leidsche
    Katoenmaatschappij: 1–31; De la Court van der Voort, P. "Brieven van Pieter de la
    Court van der Voort aan zijne echtgenoote Sara Poelaart," in *De reizen der De la*
    Courts 1641, 1700, 1710. F. Driessen (ed.) Leiden: Leidsche Katoenmaatschappij: 33–
    75. For an introduction to the De la Courts, see: Weststeijn, A. (2012) *Commercial*
    Republicanism in the Dutch Golden Age: The Political Thought of Johan & Pieter de
    la Court. Leiden: Brill.
59 Verhoeven (2009a): 12.
60 Idem, 153–154.
61 De la Court (1733).
62 Idem, 18. "hebbende de gansche reys met schoone weer volmaakt plaisir zonder het
    minste rampje volbragt gehad."
63 De Vassy (1748). Her relation to the Godin family (in turn part of the Martens van
    Sevenshoven's family archives), is uncertain. Most likely she was directly related to
    Johan Bernard Laurens de Vassy, who married Anna Maria Godin.
64 De Vassy (1748): 1.
65 Ibidem. "in d'een of andere hoek," "[…] van dat soet / dat onderweeg ons is
    ontmoet"
66 Idem, 2. "Wanneer men ons sag altemaal / naar sieken voor het hospitaal."
67 Timmers (1729): 1.
68 Ibidem.

> tusschen twaalf en 1 uijren nog seven schooten gelost hebben, waardoor alles
> wierdt op gewekt, selfs tot de hoenders in de kooij, behalve een van de gediensti-
> gen geesten van de vrouwelijke sexe die soodanig door de slaap op t sien drinken
> van pocale overvallen moet sijn geweest, dat daar van niets is gewaar geworden

69 Idem, 3. "met een weergaelose kloekmoedigheyt heeft het canon selfs afgestooken"
70 Idem, 5–6.
71 Idem, 10.

> de Dames seer bang geworden omdat wij tegen stroom en wint voerden het geen
> ons deet resolveeren om weder na Vlaardinge te keeren en na t huijs van de Heer
> Convent te gaan alwaar de Dames een glaasie wijn met salvolaat voor de schrik
> hebben genomen en een koppie tee gedronken, en de Heeren een glaasie wijn en
> een pijp toebak

7 Memsahibs' travel writings

Wifely virtues and female imperial historiography

Ipshita Nath

Travel to India was made easier with the opening of the Suez Canal in 1869, encouraging young European women to make journeys to the subcontinent for matrimonial purposes. Men who had made fortunes in India as officers in the Raj were ideal to many families back home as matches for their marriageable daughters, making the risky enterprise of sea voyages quite worthwhile. Accordingly, women who began arriving in India from the late eighteenth century with the primary purpose of finding husbands amongst the rank of capable officers stationed in India, came to be known as the "fishing fleet" (they were literally fishing for husbands). India was a marriage bazaar where marriages were fixed quickly. And Englishwomen, particularly those belonging to large families with little fortune, not only had greater chances of finding eligible husbands among the several promising bachelors who worked as part of the British Raj, they were also likely to catch a husband very soon after their arrival in India. Thus, by nineteenth century, ships from England regularly arrived bringing in cargo for matrimony. It must be noted that European women came to India for various other reasons as well. Sometimes they came as relatives of families who were already settled here, as travellers, sometimes as missionaries, or even to pursue jobs such as those of teachers or governesses. Within the colonial space, these women functioned under various written and unwritten conventions charted out for the "ideal" Englishwoman in India.

Amongst the several wifely duties women who became wives had, an important one was accompanying their husbands on official tours and travels. Indeed, travel was a salient feature of life in the Raj. Europeans travelled to India to settle here, but due to the expansionist nature of the imperial enterprise, they travelled extensively and frequently within India, making visits/exploring/studying/settling necessary in different places for official purposes as well as for socialising and for entertainment/recreation. Women, although not direct employees of the Raj and without any official roles to fulfil as part of the empire except as wives who would take care of the household, help procreate and produce offspring to legitimise the colonial process by furthering the white race, and help establish the colony through the settlement of British colonies, were expected to fulfil other duties as spouses by assisting their husbands, the sahibs, in their work, or at least accompanying them on official duty wherever possible.

Memsahibs therefore went on extensive tours and travels with their husbands/
brothers who were sahibs, gaining an opportunity to see and experience India
alongside their male counterparts, without however being responsible for any
official imperial work. Yet, they were not merely appendages to the sahibs. Their
labours gained them access to official information, policies and initiatives, and in
the cases of marriages, their marital status accorded them the same social status
as their spouses. They were even known to don men's clothing while on tours,
and "looked" like their husbands, thus blurring the gender divide between the
sahib and the memsahib (wife of the sahib). Indeed then, the term "memsahib"
meant that "connotations of colonial power were being vested upon the wives of
the sahibs as well."[1]

The memsahibs' epistolary writings on their travels are therefore significant as
their female perspective, combined with their knowledge as spouses on official
matters, enabled them to have opinions on the Raj which often differed from the
"official stance" of the empire.[2] Indeed, memsahibs' writings that emerged from
their insider-outsider positions, granted them the distance and perspective necessary to create alternative imperial discourses. And "these varied records of Anglo
Indian women's lived experiences in the Raj reveal them as active agents in
imperial politics."[3] Thus, memsahibs managed to contribute to the Raj, while
operating within the institution of marriage or family. Moreover, by subscribing
to the popular rules on wifely duties they managed to challenge their subordinate
roles by becoming "colleagues" as they often worked in tandem with their
husbands. For instance, sometimes the wives' work was on ad hoc basis, filling
in as needed on a particularly burdensome or time-sensitive job.[4]

Marriage in colonial India was therefore considered the bedrock of the
imperial family that depended on an equal partnership of men and women in
the colonial enterprise, as the "companionate" relationship of husband and wife
augmented the growth of the empire and enabled appropriate governance. For
this reason, spousal relationships in colonial India are interesting to study as they
provide an important insight into the seemingly innocent ways in which the
memsahibs participated in British imperial processes without having direct ways
of exercising power. As far as travel writing is concerned, it must be noted that
the writings of these women provide an insight into the personal narratives of the
Raj which were largely unofficial. However, "they kept a written record of their
stay in India, so invaluable for social historian. It is important that their long-
neglected voices are retrieved."[5]

This chapter, in making a study of memsahibs within colonial India, shall try
to locate the role of spousal behaviour in the mechanics of the empire. Keeping
in mind official as well the imperial discourses on matrimony, wifely duty, and
ideal womanhood, the chapter shall refer primarily to spousal behaviour during
travels that are documented in the writings of memsahibs who contributed to
imperial historiography specifically as a wife of a sahib. In doing so, the chapter
will comment on the larger concepts of marital relationships within the Raj
which were not merely emotional and sexual pairings, but more of partnerships
of spouses who could work together on fulfilling imperial duties. By referring to

instances of camaraderie between Anglo-Indian spouses, the chapter will establish how the empire tacitly acknowledged women as influential agents of the Raj. Furthermore, it will demonstrate how the memsahibs' travel writings display a conflation of wifely duties and duties to the empire. The issue of companionship within conjugal relationships will be thereby be explored, regarding the role of women as wives, as well as historiographers, sharing the "white man's burden" in the Raj. It shall also dwell on the nature of these literatures produced by the memsahibs in as far as their publication process is concerned. When and how was their writing published? Did the women write with the objective of getting published? Was it easy for the women to find publishers? What was the reception of their writing? These are some of the other concerns of the chapter.

Women and empire

Despite the steady influx of women, the British Empire remained a masculine arena. This was crucial to the construction of a British masculine identity amongst the men stationed here particularly in the late nineteenth and early twentieth century. However, the hyper-masculine nature of the empire which denoted martial prowess, administrative expertise, and a spirit of "manly" adventure entailed a domestication of memsahibs in the colonial space. While men were responsible for the supposedly masculine tasks of travelling, ruling, governing – the "outside," women were made responsible for activities such as raising children, supervising the servants etc.[6] Imperial marriages thus focused on harmonious, companionate living wherein both the sahib and the memsahib became equal participants working towards the propagation of the empire in India. However, this also meant that there was disproportion in roles, and unequal division of labour, as each partner within the conjugal relationship was given a certain separate imperial duty to fulfil. Indeed, imperial roles were gendered. A paradox therefore lies in the way despite equal participation of both men and women in the mechanics of the Raj, traditional family structures with nineteenth century had Victorian underpinnings and ultimately relegated women to domestic spaces, excluding them from official Raj work. Thus, even though women were essential to the Raj – the family being an important unit for the healthy growth of the colonising race – they were mainly restricted to conventional feminine roles of housekeeping and motherhood.[7]

Be that as it may, despite the lack of an official status for wives of sahibs, they often worked in close associations with their husbands, challenging set gender divides as far as imperial duties were concerned. Indeed, European women's relationship to domesticity was not conventional as it eschewed several traditional roles that women were supposed to fulfil in the household, allowing them to take up supposedly masculine tasks such as travel and exploration for instance. This was because the abundance of servants and helpers ensured that women did not have to engage in domestic work hands-on, and could instead delegate housekeeping responsibilities, to focus their attentions elsewhere. Moreover, the typical realms of the "home" and the "outside" were blurred considerably also as supervisory duties of the household were carried out by men at times, both married and bachelors, either due to the absence of a spouse, or when the wives were new in a place or away in the hills for the summer. Indeed, for both men and women in India, the work of empire took precedence over gender roles or domestic responsibilities and men often helped women supervise housework as she may not always have known social customs or the language of the place. Cookbooks for instance were often addressed to a mixed audience rather than just ladies. Housework was gendered only to an extent. Thus, the reimagining of duties in the empire in such ways freed Anglo-Indian women from the seemingly inevitable gender associations such as the pairing of women and home, wife and housewife, femininity and domesticity. Relieved of the practical and ideological burdens of housework, Anglo-Indian women could turn their energy and attend to the work of empire both in the home and beyond, according to their will and interest.[8]

It therefore emerges that divisions in work were not inviolable as both men and women were known to trespass into each other's areas of control, and women especially were known to enter "masculine" realms to help their husbands in dispensing official work. However, even as memsahibs are known to have regularly participated in colonial enterprises, they remain ossified in popular imagination as domestic/domesticated individuals who derived authority from their husbands. Margaret Strobel says that "wives of colonial administrators in particular suffered the problems of 'incorporated' status; that is, a wife's own status and position deserved entirely from her husband's place within the hierarchical structure"[9] Furthermore, Nupur Chaudhuri and Margaret Strobel in *Western Women and Imperialism: Complicity and Resistance* have commented that scholarship has reinforced the common beliefs among imperialists that colonies were not for white women and by thus consciously or unconsciously accepting that colonialism was a masculine enterprise, they marginalised women and their writings in the focus of their studies. And those who have not and have included women in their studies, only stereotype them as racist etc. without complicating their role they played in colonial history.[10]

The memsahib's role as an agent of the Raj must therefore be explored cautiously, by taking into account the lived realities of women in colonial India, and by making a study of the alternative personal narratives within their writing that were often eclipsed in official histories. This is because contemporary opinions on the role and agency of women are inadequate as they either celebrate their ability to appropriate power through their partners, or broadly view them as domestic and sexual beings that were mere subordinates. It is in fact essential to acknowledge the importance of spousal duty in the functioning of the empire, and women's participation in the Raj through it, to fully understand the nuances and heterogeneity in women's role and contribution in the Raj. Mary A. Procida in *Married to the Empire* has pointed out that women often advised and helped their husbands with a wide range of tasks or empire such as:

undertaking revenue assessments, typing official reports, decoding secret communiqués in wartime, disposing of routine paperwork, touring the district to foster good relations and the inhabitants and hunting down dangerous animals. Anglo Indian women used their marital connections to participate actively in the practices and discourses of imperialism. They were married not only to their husbands but to the Raj itself.[11]

For instance, "the government of India employed women in positions which were unsuited to men, particularly as inspectors of girls' schools. "Flora Annie Steel, one of the earliest of these female inspectors, recalled that she worked long hours. . . the authorities continued to view them as appendages to their husbands."[12] It is a fact that even though women participated in their husbands' work, "the Raj maintained an old-fashioned misogynistic attitude towards women, generally, and wives refusing to acknowledge their work, or even their presence, in the empire."[13]

Wifely duties: women's roles in conjugal, and imperial order

It must be noted that memsahibs' letters, journals, travelogues that documented their experiences of the Indian subcontinent, were written not only from a European female's perspective – the perspective of an "outsider" in the essentially masculine space, but also from the perspective of the wife/companion of the sahib, taking part in a masculine enterprise of imperialism from a subordinate position. The internal contradictions in their writing, and irregularities in tone and tenor demonstrate their anxiety about their position in society not just as women in an alien space, but also as subordinates; as the alternate agent/voice shaped by their unique perspectives vis-a-vis the female "gaze." Consequently, to trace the memsahibs' claim over power and control, spousal relationships become a point of enquiry for it is essential to understand the way women indirectly, yet tangibly affected the mechanics of the empire, and influenced/ shaped imperial historiography from their supposedly secondary positions as spouses/relatives. The assumptions, beliefs, and sociocultural practices that underlie the gender divisiveness of the colonial space must also be studied through a systematic study of texts that informed the contexts of the empire. Accordingly, a study of memsahibs as women travellers (or travelling women) requires a scrutiny of literary and sociocultural texts that informed their participation in the Raj.

It must be pointed out that travel was a gendered task since touring and exploration were considered masculine endeavours that were supposedly injurious to women[14] due to their inability to travel great distances, and due to their domestic duties, that clashed with such outdoor/public activities. Dedication to the husbands' work, and the empire thus came at a price. It was not always conducive for women, for biological as well as social reasons, to always accompany men. Travel and excessive movement was said to have a direct adverse impact on women's bodily functions. Women as a result were often left alone and felt lonely and neglected. The lonely memsahib is therefore a motif in much of colonial literature. Despite this, it was one of the activities that regularly witnessed active participation of women. For instance, memsahibs had to accompany their husbands on official tours and visits, travel to hill stations during summers to escape the heat in the plains,[15] travel back home to England for their children's education, move to "mofussils"[16] or cities as their husbands were transferred on duty, or simply travel (often great distances or through tough terrain and harsh climate) to make social visits etc. In fact, even if the memsahibs weren't required to travel, many found it in their favour to undertake journeys out of a simple spirit of adventure and exploration.[17] Moreover, not only did women participate significantly in travelling, several memsahibs chronicled their experiences of travelling with men, and wrote extensively on their discoveries and adventures. What is more interesting is that these chronicles often contained discourses that subverted the official discourse on colonialism and India. While at times they buttressed stereotypes of India as savage and barbaric, they also often provided important favourable insights into the culture – something which was often absent in the mainstream imperial discourses. The writings by Emily Eden (1796–1869) are a good example of how women's writings offer alternative discourses to official accounts. Although Emily Eden found travelling undesirable – unlike Fanny Parkes (1794–1875) who undertook travelling as a sport – and was horrified at realising that her brother would be made the Governor of India, she did undertake several journeys across India, albeit extremely reluctantly.[18] Her records of these travels published under the title, *Up the Country* (1866),[19] offer a personal and intimate narrative of her experiences. She thus provides an alternative voice to the official masculine discourse that seldom deviated from the colonial project.[20] And in describing her interactions within India as a woman who was not directly employed by the Raj, she was able to provide a supplement to official histories by offering her own subjectivities.[21] Although her writing does not reveal much about her relationship with her brother or her experience of travelling with him, they do provide an instance of what life of a memsahib was as a companion of a sahib holding an important rank. Since there is a greater focus in her writings on her relationship with her sister, Fanny Eden, who accompanied her on several visits and journeys, rather than case of spousal relationships that advantaged a memsahib, her journal is an example of female friendships between memsahibs that allowed them to understand India and adjust it in better.

A good example to study the role of spousal relationships in travel is that of Lady Anne Wilson (1855–?), who in her work published as *Letters from India* (1911), highlighted the importance of companionate marriage in colonial India. Through her recounting of the various quotidian ways in which she and her husband helped each other in carrying out duties or fulfilling their respective roles in the empire, she is able to highlight her own participation in imperial work. Fanny Parkes is another example of how a memsahib managed to derive authority through her husband. In her journal published originally under the title, *Wanderings of a Pilgrim in Search of the Picturesque* (1850),[22] her sympathetic and resourceful attitude, as well as her patient behaviour and bravery while travelling with her husband, becomes apparent. For instance, in one incident when she and her husband set out to meet Captain A.S., they were robbed of their belongings while they were camped halfway through the trip. Her husband, leaving her "seated by the side of the road," went in pursuit of them, not only displaying confidence in her ability to take care of herself, but also subverting traditional chivalric codes of social behaviour, particularly in the colonial space, wherein a woman must not be left alone in a lonely spot due to the risk of assault and rape. This was particularly necessary in colonial India where an unchaperoned memsahib could arouse undesirable curiosity. Moreover, the fear of sexual assault upon white women was high as it was thought that brown men desired European women. There were also several tales of white women's sexual exploitation at the hands of the "natives."[23] Apart from bravery and cleverness, the feeling of camaraderie between them is conspicuous. Fanny Parkes writes:

> En route there were several parties of fakirs, who said they were going to Jaganath. These rascals had some capital tattoos with them. Several of these men had one withered arm raised straight, with the long nails growing through the back of the hand. These people are said to be great thieves; and when any of them were encamped near us on the march, we directed the *chaukidars* to keep a good lookout, on our horses as well as chattels.[24]

Apart from a general sense of partnership trust, and patience in women, intimacy in married life was also extremely essential in Anglo-Indian marriages. British men and wives needed to provide each other emotional and physical companionship, particularly in lonely posts where European population was sparse. Lady Wilson in her very first letter writes, "Jim did what he could for me; he translated my list of wants at breakfast every day, interviewed the cook, went through every room with me, and ordered the contents to be moved, removed, or destroyed. ..."[25] Her writings demonstrate how the husband and wife made for a unit that embodied authority in the colonised space. Her involvement in her husband's work is apparent throughout her writing as she accompanies him on official duty:

> Jim takes me with him when he visits the dispensaries in the towns, or examines the boys in the schools. Our great ambition is to establish a school for girls, as well as an Indian woman doctor in each of the four towns before we leave the district.

Fanny Parkes writes, "I went with my husband into tents near Alamchand, for the sake of shooting; and used to accompany him on an elephant, or on my little black horse, to mark the game."[26] It is clear how the "Anglo-Indian husbands and wives had much in common with their ideological ancestors in the great landed families of Britain, in which the marital relationship formed the centre of a web of familial, personal, and economic ties."[27]

However, despite a husband's attentions the life of a memsahib could be filled with boredom and loneliness. Adjusting was difficult due to innumerable reasons. Margaret Macmillan in *Women of the Raj* writes that women longed for simple things they had always taken for granted – a visit to the shops, a chat with friends, the sound of a doorbell ringing. Some could not endure the loneliness: They had hysterics (like the bride in Assam who took to her bed and wept for days on end).[28] Lady Wilson writes in her journal, "In these romantic surroundings Jim sits at an office-table disposing of 'files.' That is the insignificant name bestowed on gigantic folios, sometimes printed, sometimes containing in manuscript the opinions written by different officials on some subject."[29] Fanny Parkes too had to undertake her travels without her husband: "My husband proposed that I should go up the Jumna [...] as far as Agra [...] and promised if he could get leave of absence, to join me there to view all that is so well worth seeing at that remarkable place."[30] Although in the latter's case it is contested that she could undertake exploration precisely because of her husband's absence, the question arises whether it was easy for memsahibs to bear with their husband's schedules and their incessant work and/on tours. It was difficult to be a selfless helpmeet, particularly due to the trying circumstances – in the absence of familiar faces and surroundings. Anne de Courcy in *The Fishing Fleet* writes:

> One of the main hazards of married life was loneliness. Girls who married a man whose work was in the *mofussil* – anywhere in country or well away from cities, towns, stations, or cantonments – were often miles from their nearest neighbour, with their social highlight weekly visit to the club, with its leather chairs, month-old newspapers and if enough people came, a Saturday night dance.[31]

However, women had little option but to cope and engage in activities wherever they could manage to, in conjunction with their partners. Some did it out of compulsion while some did it out of keen interest. Lady Wilson writes,

> Meantime, while Jim is writing files, I am writing Hindustani exercises, and cover far less ground than he does by the time my task is accomplished. There are dozens of names for a cow. Jim says differentiations are characteristic of a pastoral people, who might be able to identity their cattle, especially where rivers abound.[32]

Indeed, several women took to understanding Indian cultures and took initiatives in learning local customs and languages. Women who did not have the inclination to or could not manage to settle down and adapt to the new surroundings often made their husbands give up their work and go back to England, or if they couldn't do that, maladjustment in India resulted in melancholy and depression. In other cases, women remained indifferent. However, some were intensely fascinated by the Indian spaces and cultures, so much so that they became self-proclaimed ethnographers, as did Fanny Parkes, who took up the task of touring India, even in the absence of her husband. But what becomes apparent, particularly through Lady Wilson's writings, is that not only was it imperative for the wives to remain forbearing in the face of adverse living conditions or protracted spells of loneliness and isolation, it was also crucial for husbands to remain sensitive to their wives' needs and provide them company and help wherever it was required.[33]

It was for this reason that there were several rules against marriage for men employed by the Raj in India. They were initially advised to not get married at all – to at least put it off until the appropriate age which was thirty. It was considered that a wife and family would impede the mobility of the officer and affect his efficiency. The Raj was an exclusively male domain and women were supposed to be an impediment to imperial duty. "To rephrase a hoary catch phrase... 'the empire was in acquired in a for of absence of mind, so much as in a fit of absence of wives.'"[34] Indeed, marital relationships were given a lot of importance during colonial rule in India and Anglo-Indian couples believed strongly in the ability of spouses to "make or break a man's career."[35] Thus, women were subjected to several social and cultural conventions, literatures on appropriate behaviour, and dictates on feminine virtue and wifely duty. This attitude then shaped a model of a domestic imperial womanhood[36] – and gave rise to the image of the ideal memsahib – where the memsahib's biological/regenerative abilities were considered primary to her legitimate fulfilling of her role in the empire. Women were expected to be adept at managing the household, being good mothers, good hostesses etc. The schema that best describes gender relationships in the Raj, therefore, is that of a "partnership between men and women as imperialists in the masculine mould, rather than one of an antagonist polarity between adventuresome men and ultra-domestic women."[37]

Indeed, women were expected to be good consorts by taking keen interest in their husband's work and by being intellectually inclined towards his duties, and to also be self-sufficient in cases where the husband was unavailable or away. Fanny Parkes writes, "I generally accompanied my husband on his sporting expeditions in the evening, either on foot or on pony, and enjoyed it very much.[38] Lady Wilson, upon meeting a Colonel's wife adept at outdoor activities, says appreciatively, "she is fearless rider, a good shot, an excellent housekeeper, and a skilled musician. She thoroughly enjoys her open-air life and is on good terms with the Indian gentry..."[39] J.E. Dawson in *Englishwoman in India: Her Influence and Responsibilities* has enumerated the various desirable traits in a memsahib. An Anglo-Indian wife was someone who had to relinquish her own dreams and ambitions and subsume her identity into her husband's.[40] Mary A. Procida says that "duty to husband was conflated with duty to empire" and in return for fulfilling these they acquired access and knowledge into the intricacies of imperial work along with the ability to influence their husband's decisions.[41]

Companionship and individualism: alternative/supplementary imperial historiography

As is evident then, traditional roles for both genders remained fluid, particularly for women who regularly transgressed into the "masculine" realms of power, exercising mediated authority,[42] and conducting imperial duty by becoming a partner and advisor to her husband, and by at times helping him in dispensing official work in his absence. This destabilised the fixed social and familial duties assigned to women and consequently upset the binaries that were created with regard to gender roles. Mary A. Procida comments:

> One woman, for example, literally invested herself with her husband's imperial identity and authority. Impatient with his heavy load of official responsibilities and his plodding method of working through official tasks, she had a rubber stamp made his signature and "dealt with the less important (matters) myself." Women's practical assistance to their husbands was by no means limited to such acceptably feminine tasks... Norah Burke, whose father's duties as forestry officer included tracking wild animals that were harassing the local population, recalled that her mother regularly took these hunting duties upon herself.[43]

Significantly then, the extent of women's involvement in their husbands' work freed them from the position of the subordinate and instead empowered them enough to be able to become directly involved with the Raj, albeit unofficially. While official policies regarding women's position remained exclusive, the mundane realities of everyday life in Anglo-Indian households gave women ample opportunity to access power, authority and knowledge, and thereby break free of the tag of being a mere appendage.[44] Despite this, women remained on the peripheries of the Raj, occasionally, and through their own wit and will, managed to make their way into the intricacies of the empire. Anne de Courcy's enquiry into this matter remains relevant:

> Did the Fishing Fleet girls have any real influence on the conduct of affairs in this vast country that was home to so many of them during the time of the Raj? The short answer is no. The Raj was entirely run by men, in the kind of hierarchical fashion that preceded a sudden leap to top by a man of out-standing brilliance who might normally have been considered an outsider... In the Raj, the role of the British female was as wife, helpmeet and mother[45]

Be that as it may, memsahibs managed to carve spaces for themselves in the Raj, and contribute to the Raj, from their own subject positions. Travel was important in this, as it allowed women the kind of access to the colony that the sahibs had. But it was not always easy as the hyper-masculine nature of the empire which denoted martial prowess, administrative expertise, and a spirit of "manly" adventure, resulted in a binary where on one hand, the memsahibs were deemed responsible for the domestic side of the colonial Raj in pursuing activities like raising children, supervising the servants etc., while the men were responsible for the supposedly masculine tasks of travelling, ruling, governing – the "outside." This made the empire a masculine enterprise excluding women from the process of colonialism and depriving them the authority that men could exercise for being able to be explorers and colonisers in charge of the "public" aspect of colonialism. Yet, travel remained an activity that was both desirable and undesirable for women. While excess travel and movement could interfere with their health and safety, travel was needed whenever they had to provide companionship to their male partners, as mentioned above. This basic requisite freed them of the strict Victorian codes of womanhood and femininity and enabled them to liberate themselves of social conventions like in the case of Fanny Parkes. William Dalrymple writes in his introduction to *Begums, Thug and Englishmen* (2002): "The more Fanny wanders, free of her husband, the more outspoken, sympathetic, and independent she becomes."[46]

However, that they were at a secondary position, and were subordinates, aided them in becoming alternate authorities within the Raj. Their writing, for instance, becomes a rich body of literature in the form of letters, diaries, and memoirs that documented various aspects of imperial domesticity which were often overlooked in hegemonic discourses. Indeed, due to their indirect connection to the Raj, memsahibs were not influenced by political agendas as much as the sahibs, and were writing in mostly personalised forms, oftentimes only for private consumption. The genre of epistolary writing itself then allowed them to incorporate as little hegemonic discourses as possible and instead be able to provide their views on those, while often being subversive and counter-hegemonic.

In this, the memsahibs were often writing specifically to be published, and sometimes as an afterthought. For instance, while Flora Annie Steel (1847–1929) wrote novels with the sole intention of publishing them, conducting extensive research for each project, Fanny Parkes began with writing a journal that she later went home to publish as her memoirs of her travels, but which quickly receded from popularity. The Eden sisters however became more popular due to their connections in high places and social standing. Emily Eden wrote novels specifically to publish them, although she did not have to write in order to earn money but merely for her passion for the art. It must be understood that the influence of the memsahibs' writings was not enough to alter hegemonic, official colonial discourses. However, Orientalists understood the value of the literatures produced by female writers such as Steel particularly because of her evocation of folklores in *Tales of the Punjab* (1894). They saw it as an opportunity to further the coloniser's knowledge of, and control over, its colonised subjects.[47] The case of Flora Annie Steel, married to Henry Steel of the Indian Civil Service, may be a good point of enquiry in so far as her writing influenced imperial activities and colonial approaches to India. Steel was not merely a "burra memsahib"[48] by being married to a sahib, her two brothers were serving as civilians in India. She wrote extensively during her stay in India and was well known for her novels, although she has been critiqued for not been accurate or comprehending about the politics of all she wrote about. She however, was not easily accepted into the literary realms, despite her eventual popularity. *On the Face of the Waters* (1896) was rejected by her publisher, Macmillan, but accepted by Heinemann and published to great acclaim; indeed, such was the success of this novel that for a time her popularity and celebrity status were equal to those of Rudyard Kipling[49]

Her joint publication with Grace Gardiner, *The Complete Indian Housekeeper and Cook* (1899) which was a manual on practical ways of living in India, was also well received and became popular amongst memsahibs in India. Ralph Crane and Anna Johnston have said:

> On the one hand she was an ardent supporter of British rule in India, while on the other she made a genuine attempt, in all her Indian writing, both fiction and non-fiction, to interpret the country and its culture using Indo-centric rather than Eurocentric measures. Ultimately, though, it is difficult to escape the sense that in all her writing, her knowledge of India is used to control the natives, to support British rule of a subject race.[50]

Fanny Parkes on the other hand, despite not being as well connected as some of her contemporaries, wrote with the awareness of her advantage over her male con-temporaries writing in the travel genre: Her access to Indian zenanas. In many ways then her text becomes feminist through its preoccupation with women-related themes. The interesting bit about Parkes' text is that during her time, it was criticised by her contemporaries for being overly sympathetic to the natives, while it is now critiqued for its orientalist nature and for exoticising India blatantly. Dalrymple says: "Fanny Parkes' wonderful book is an important historical text for its record of the last moments of this very attractive (and largely forgotten) moment of cultural and sexual interaction, of crossover 'chutneyfication.'"[51]

Women's collusion in the mechanics of the empire however remains a contentious issue. Their status as wives of officials, and their writing, afforded them agency and authority, but they also implicated them in the exploitative colonial structure. Their writing therefore needs to be studied with reference to their marginal position as unofficial "voices" of the Raj which, importantly, often digressed from the official stance. It is equally important that while glorifying their acquirement of power and authority, the tendency to gloss over their possible complicity in the manufacturing of imperial ideology is avoided. The memsahibs' position remains subject to uncertainty as they worked under the hierarchies of class, race, and gender wherein they faced both advantages and disadvantages. Mary A. Procida in *Married to the Empire* has written:

> Varied records of Anglo-Indian women's lived experiences in the Raj reveal them as active agents in imperial politics, a facet of the imperial story generally ignored in the existing historiography. Much recent imperial scholarship, there work of subaltern studies collective being the most prominent, has focused on destabilising accepted interpretations of power relations in the empire.[52]

Ostensibly then, memsahibs were dependent upon their marital connections to participate in the processes of empire building, and their status was determined vis-a-vis their husbands, fixing them in the subordinate position. And yet, there is evidence of them participating equally with their husbands particularly on travels. Their position of power was impaired because they were women, yet they used their subordinate position to their benefit, and derived authority from their husbands as their wives. Indeed, they were privy to official data and information simply by virtue of their connection to the sahibs. Moreover, in having their own adventures and explorations in colonised India, and by harbouring their own interests in understanding India, both of which stemmed from motivations which may or may not be racist/imperialist, they became significant "chroniclers" – at times accidentally and at times deliberately where in some cases they methodically charted other aspects of the Indian society. Their position as "white" but female gave them a certain nebulousness, a certain liminality which allowed them a different perspective on colonialism and colonial India. The entire body of literature produced by them is thus an indispensable source of information on India. And their writings which emerge from the intersection between colonialism, gender, and imperial ethnography, reveal their role in the empire, particularly in imperial historiography.[53]

Conclusion

Was their status as a wife really empowering? Memsahibs may have managed to create spaces for themselves in the Raj, but that, or their status as wives of the sahibs, did not ensure that their authority was fixed or indisputable. In conclusion then it must be said that different experiences that informed memsahibs' various subjectivities need to be addressed through an understanding of their social and political positions that resist typecasting of these women either as liberated individuals who were agents of the Raj, or wives/appendages. This is because viewing these women as "agents" universalises their ability to gain access into official matter, while viewing them as merely spouses and partners or even co-workers eliminates the possibility of understanding their writing as being possibly empowering in being derived from a sense of association and partnership, as also from individualism and independence. Accordingly, while the relationships that they shared with their travel partners, particularly spouses, influenced their subjectivities, their positions as active participant/agent/accomplice or a mere tool/appendage/subordinate need to be traced vis-a-vis their differing experiences.

Indeed then, there was no archetypal memsahib with a specific type of travelling experience. There was also no meta-narrative, but in-fact a plurality of discourses and variation in ideology and experience. Thus, women's self-representations as well as their writings on travel with their partners, in being as variegated as they are, open different avenues of enquiry into gender, imperialism, and travel during the Raj, and provide varying answers. And as this overview has demonstrated, a gendered study of spousal behaviour within Anglo-Indian couples particularly displayed while travelling in colonial India, offers a more sophisticated understanding of the complexities brought in to the development and stability of the empire, and the lived realities and political aspects of conjugal relationships in the larger imperial order. Thus, although the role of women has been overlooked in traditional and official records of imperial practices, their writings on their travels reveal their share of the "burden" of the Raj.

Notes

1   Sen, I. (2002) *Woman and Empire. Representations in the Writings of British India (1858–1900)*. New Delhi: Orient Longman: 10.
2   Procida, M.A. (2002) *Married to the Empire: Gender, Politics, and Imperialism in India, 1883–1947*. Manchester: Manchester University Press: 5
3   Procida (2002): 5.
4   Procida (2002): 48.
5   Sen (2002): 3.
6   James Hammerton in *Emigrant Gentlewomen: Genteel Poverty and Female Emigration, 1830–1914* has commented that "cultivated British women had an "Imperial mission" to perform by bringing their British deals to an abandoned generation of male pioneers who were threatened with alien assimilation; these ideas, furthermore, could only be implanted by women who occupied their "proper sphere" in the colonies as civilised domestic helps, teachers, wives, and mother." Hammerton, J. (1979) *Emigrant Gentlewomen: Genteel Poverty and Female Emigration, 1830–1914*. London: Croon Helm: 48.
7   Margaret Strobel in *European Women and Second British Empire* has said: "In the face of real difficulties, women clung to the models derived from 'home.' Indeed, the tasks of homemaker and mother had even greater implications of preserving 'civilisation' when carried out in the outposts of the empire." Strobel, M. (1991) *European Women and Second British Empire*. Bloomington: Indiana University Press: 17. This is an interesting offside of imperial womanhood which is often not given attention to.
8   Procida (2002): 105.
9   Strobel, M. (1991) *European Women and Second British Empire*. Bloomington: Indiana University Press: xii.
10 Chaudhuri, N. & Strobel, M. (1992) "Introduction," in: *Western Women and Imperialism: Complicity and Resistance*. Bloomington: Indiana University Press: 3.
11 Procida (2002): 30.
12 Procida (2002): 45.
13 Procida (2002): 30.
14 British women in India faced several problems regarding mobility and climate. The climate was harsh and ruthless in the summers and European women found it difficult to cope with the heat and dust. They were often stationed in far-off places and with little scope for entertainment, the women felt lonely and very often bored with life in India. Communication with the locals, as well as the household servants was a challenge due to the language barrier, and because their husbands would frequently be transferred, they often failed to make use of whatever smatterings of the local languages they managed to learn. Furthermore, Indian foods were unpalatable to most and they had the hardest time adjusting and recreating domestic spaces as they knew them back home in Europe. Travelling was a problem, especially for women, due to a lack of proper roads and transportation systems. A lack of medical facilities also often jeopardized the lives of many women.
15 The sultry and harsh weather during the summer was overwhelming for the women and they often sought refuge in the cooler climes of hill stations, while their husbands worked on in the plains. However, despite this being a rather regular phenomenon, such women were often considered selfish. They were also made fun of in popular culture for being spoilt.
16 Term used to refer to remote areas of India, such as places beyond the three capitals of East India Company such as Bombay, Calcutta, and Madras.
17 Indira Ghose in *Women Travellers in Colonial India* has commented: "There was not the woman travellers in India, but a variety of different women – there is no overarching story to be told." Ghose, I. (1998) *Women Travellers in Colonial India*. Oxford: Oxford University Press: 10.

18   William Dalrymple, in his introduction to Fanny Parkes' autobiography titled, *Begums, Thugs, and Englishmen,* has remarked upon how the Eden sisters resented Fanny Parkes as she took advantage of their protection while travelling, and seemed to enjoy it much more than they did. Dalrymple suggests that the Eden sisters were envious because she seemed to "having more fun – and getting to know India much better" than them. Dalrymple, W. (2002) *Begums, Thugs, and Englishmen.* New Delhi: Penguin: 11.

19   Emily Eden's journal especially records her disinclination towards touring in India. J. K. Stanford in *Ladies in the Sun* has said:

> There is in Emily Eden's letters, vivid as they are, a discernible note of boredom and languor, and pity for herself. She suffered much from beaches and fever and said what she calls "spasms," and she clearly hated camp life and the incessant changes of transport, carriages and palanquins and rides on Arab houses and elephants as well as the enormous amount of heavy and formal entertaining which the governor-general had to do whenever he stopped on his progress.
>
> (pp. 85–86)

Stanford, J.K. (1962) *Ladies in the Sun: The Memsahibs' India 1790–1860.* London: Gallery Press: 85–86.

20   Emily Eden wrote on a variety of issues and displayed a knack for details. She was often contemptuous of Indian customs. She derisively writes that ladies came great distances just to be able to curtesy the Governor General, as did Rajas. She is not, however, insensitive in the area which was deemed primary to a memsahib: Domesticity. She was sympathetic towards the servants and forgiving in case of any digressions as she is conscious of their honesty and perseverance. In one incident when a servant gets accused of theft she says, "...The poor wretch came in immediately after, his mouth still covered with flour: he had not been able even to touch it, but he protested his innocence, and I believe in it." Stanford (1962): 74. Further, she is not oblivious to how the servants often go without proper lodging or salary and pension.

21   Indeed, she expressed her honest opinions as a memsahib who was interacting with not just Europeans but also Indians: When she went to meet the Raja of Benares, she detailed the opulence of his lifestyle and how they were treated as officials – her disdain for the Indian way of life, especially the practice of the men keeping more than one wives/women, becomes clear.

22   Her journal has been reprinted under the title, *Thugs, Begums, and Englishmen* in 2002 by William Dalrymple who has omitted several passages from the over eight hundred pages edition of 1850, and has removed inconsistent spellings of names of places and other Indian words. Dalrymple (2002).

23   See Nancy Paxton's *Writing Under the Raj: Gender, Race, and Rape in the British Colonial Imagination 1830–1947* for more details.

24   Parkes, F. (2002) *Begums, Thugs, and Englishmen: The Journal of Fanny Parkes.* New Delhi: Penguin: 39.

25   Wilson (1911): 6.

26   Parkes (2002): 125.

27   Procida (2002): 29.

28   MacMillan, M. (1988) *Women of the Raj.* New York: Thames and Hudson.

29   Wilson (1911): 30.

30   Parkes (2002): 161.

31   de Courcy, A. (2012) *The Fishing Fleet: Husband-hunting in the Raj.* London: W&N: 235.

32   Wilson (1911): 40.

33   Paxton, N. (1999) *Writing Under the Raj: Gender, Race, and Rape in the British Colonial Imagination 1830–1947.* New Brunswick: Rutgers University Press. Lady Wilson writes in her journal how her husband found ways to keep her happy and content: "Jim knowing my interest in strange, out-of-the-way characters, often has them (outcast people, probably gypsies) sent out to the tent. Some of them are wolf-catchers." Wilson (1911): 17.

34   Nevile (1998): 1.

35   Procida (2002): 40

36   Migration as it became a mass phenomenon was increasingly closely tied to ideas around "home," the ultimate motif of domesticity and by the mid-nineteenth century, also of respectability. "Making a new home," became the colonial task given to women, whether planting roses in the withering Indian sun to emulate an English cottage, or braving the winters of the Canadian prairie in log cabins. Levine, P. (2004) Gender and Empire. Oxford: Oxford University Press: 8.

37   Procida (2002): 6.

38   Parkes (2002): 38.

39   Wilson (1911): 256–257.

40   Women often had to choose between their husbands and children as children had to be taken back home or in the hills to be educated. Despite the fact that memsahibs often spent much of their time in India many none the less attempted to balance the periods with husbands and children. "Memsahibs commonly were the most well-travelled members of their families because they were free to migrate between Britain and India as much as family finances and personal inclination permitted, in sharp contrast to their husbands, whose professional responsibilities restricted such movements to periods of long leave" (Buettner 116).

41   Procida (2002): 46.

42   Derived from their husbands.

43   Procida (2002): 47.

44   Janet Finch in *Married to the Job: Wives' Incorporation in Men's Work, Volume 20* has said that at times "married women are still drawn into the helpmeet role, especially where a husband's job is one which is prestigious and important, and where it has particular moral worth attached to it. So, as a man rises through the status hierarchy of an organisation, it becomes increasingly difficult for his wife to fail to act as a helpmeet." Finch (1983) *Married to the Job: Wives' Incorporation in Men's Work, Volume 20*: London: Routledge: 86.

45   Courcy (2012): 307.

46   Dalrymple (2002): 20.

47   Hulme and McDougall (2007): 81.

48   Ralph Crane and Anna Johnston have said in "Flora Annie Steel in the Punjab," "Steel convincingly played the role of burra memsahib to her rapidly promoted husband" (73). Crane, R. & Johnston, A. (2007) "Flora Annie Steel in the Punjab," in: *Writing, Travel and Empire.* Peter Hulme & Russell McDougall (eds.). New York: IB. Tauris: 71–96.

49   Crane, R. & Johnston, A. (2007) "Flora Annie Steel in the Punjab," in: *Writing, Travel and Empire.* Peter Hulme & Russell McDowell (eds.). New York: IB. Tauris: 76.

50   Hulme & McDougall (2007): 74.

51   Dalrymple (2002): 23.

52   Procida (2002): 6.

53   Flora Steel's *The Complete Indian Housekeeper and Cook*, for instance, was a source of information on the everyday.

8 Travelogues by two companions describing Rachel's American *odyssée mortelle* 1855–1856

Rob van de Schoor

When the French tragedienne Rachel Félix, better known as "Mademoiselle Rachel" (1821–1858) visited the United States and Cuba for an eight-month series of performances in 1855 and 1856, her fame preceded her. In French theatres, and later across the whole of Europe, she had already celebrated triumphs for more than fifteen years as the actress whose remarkable performances had breathed new life into the classicist tragedies of Racine and Corneille, which had fallen out of favour in the heyday of Romanticism. Her "romantic" acting – the way she identified with her characters and remained in her role while others were speaking, her "silent acting" – made her a star performer who captivated the Parisian *beau monde* for many years. Her humble origins – she was a poor Jewish child who sang with her sister in the street for money – contributed not a little to her charisma.

Rachel did not need to carry her own luggage on her journey to America. She was accompanied by members of her family – her father, her brother Raphaël, who acted as her agent and "producer," and her three sisters Sarah, Lia, and Dina – and a *troupe* of ten actors and actresses from the *Comédie Française* who took care of all the travel arrangements. Rachel's journey to the New World is documented in the travelogues of two of her male companions, Léon Beauvallet (1828–1885) and Jules Chéry (1817–1910). Their writings tell us about the hardships of travelling in America and their journey from New York to Havana. Rachel is protected from confrontations with the rude and uncivilised and her travelling companions withhold disturbing news from her. Not only is she a delicate woman in declining health, she is also a celebrity who does not always enjoy exposure to the public when offstage.

A glance at the letters Rachel wrote during her trip to America reveals a difference between the observations of her travelling companions and her own worries and fears. She is mainly concerned with her deteriorating health, with her anxiety about the future and – most of all – with the pain she feels at being apart from her children.

On 21 August 1855, aboard the steamer that would dock in New York the next day, Rachel wrote to her mother. Joking about the herculean work awaiting her, it seems as if she is trying to bolster her own spirits:

> Vraiment je serais injuste si je témoignais le moindre regret d'avoir quitté des enfants que j'adore, une mère que je chéris, des amis que j'aime de tout mon cœur. Non, non, Mademoiselle, allez faire cette gentille tournée, et alors seulement vous aurez vraiment gagné le pain de tous les jours de la semaine. Eh bien! ma mère, est-ce trop le payer par un labeur de sept mois en travaillant comme un nègre? Il faut bien que les blancs prennent l'ouvrage, puisque les noirs refusent le service.[1]

At first, Rachel's health did not trouble her. She told her mother that she would be prepared to surrender all the proceeds from her American performances in exchange for continued good health: "Dussé-je perdre à la fin de ma tournée en Amérique l'argent que j'y aurai gagné, je ne me plaindrai pas si ma santé continue ce qu'elle est en ce moment."[2] She was counting the days until she would see her mother and children again, but she was trying to convince herself that it was better to spend that time in the favourable American climate rather than in Paris:

> Eh! grand Dieu! que je suis loin encore de ce moment, 8 mars!!! Mais quoi! ne vaut-il pas mieux passer son temps dans un climat qui me convient si bien, que de souffrir à Paris comme j'ai souffert ....[3]

But her health soon forsook her. She wrote from Boston on 28 October:

> Si les lauriers préservent de la foudre, ils ne préservent pas des enrouements. Voilà ma position. J'ai eu froid en chemin de fer, et, depuis que je suis à Boston, je tousse comme une poitrinaire que je ne suis pas, je vous prie de le croire, malgré mon teint pâle et mon apparente maigreur.
>   A part l'imprudence que j'ai eue de ne point me vêtir assez chaudement, le voyage s'est parfaitement opéré.[4]

In Charleston, and even in Havana, she expected an improvement that would enable her to perform again. The prospects of success in Havana were good: Her twelve scheduled appearances would earn her 60,000 francs. But, as she wrote in a letter of 23 December, the date of her first performance in Cuba had not yet been determined:

> Sais-je seulement si je jouerai et si plusieurs mois de repos ne me sont pas nécessaires ? Quoi qu'il arrive, je me résigne. Avant tout, je veux vivre encore. Si je ne dois plus jouer la tragédie, si cette force me fait défaut, je sens que la force de mon amour pour mes fils grandit à tout moment. Je veux voir des hommes en mes enfants.[5]

Rachel's first performance (*Les Horaces*) was on 3 September at the Metropolitan Theater on Broadway. Ticket sales brought in 26,334 francs (5016 dollars). For the second performance, on 4 September (*Phèdre*), however, the box office take was 19,587 francs, almost 7000 francs less than the day before. *Adrienne Lecouvreur* (in America, constantly misspelled as *Adrienne Lacouvreur*, much to the amusement of the French) went somewhat better: 21,613 francs. The proceeds were disappointing, certainly compared to those of the "Swedish Nightingale" Jenny Lind, whose first American appearance brought in no less than 93,786 francs. While in New York, Rachel fell ill: The cold that she contracted aroused her dormant tuberculosis – she herself speaks of a "poitrine médiocre" (a poor chest) – that would prove fatal in early 1858.

After a series of performances in New York, the company moved on to Boston on 21 October, returning to New York on 3 November and giving their final performance there on 17 November. On 18 November, the "French Company" went on to Philadelphia, where Rachel collapsed after a performance on 19 November. She had to lie down, and a number of performances were cancelled. The doctor who attended her recommended a stay in the southern United States and expressed the expectation that she would never again be able to perform. On 27 November, the company left Philadelphia for Charleston, arriving there on 1 December. On 17 December, Rachel appeared one last time, in *Adrienne Lecouvreur*. She was ill and constantly coughing. She wrote about this unwise appearance, which she had been talked into against her better judgement, on 23 December:

> J'ai voulu essayer ma force en donnant une représentation l'avant-veille de mon départ, priée que j'en étais par bon nombre de charmantes dames. Moi, de me rendre à ce désir.[6]

The day after that performance, the French Company embarked for Havana, arriving there on 22 December. The company was disbanded there on New Year's Day. On 10 January, they began the return voyage to New York and from there back to Europe. Only Rachel remained in Havana, with her *femme de chambre* Rose.[7] It was not until 29 January that she left the Cuban capital, first for New York and then back across the Atlantic, arriving in Le Havre on 25 February.

Three approaches

Chaperonage

This article is about the way men thought they should protect women from the hardships of nineteenth-century travelling. Men's behaviour towards their female travelling companions was an adaption to exceptional conditions of the usual gendered manners, as described in etiquette books. For a proper understanding of the observations in the travelogues we will be studying, it is imperative to consider recent research on etiquette books. In particular, the argument of Jorge Arditi's article "Etiquette Books, Discourse and the Deployment of an Order of Things" is relevant to our investigation on Rachel's journey to America. Looking at etiquette books "as tools to study the emergence, structure and workings of what we might call "cultures of dominance,"" Arditi notices a change from "centeredness" in nineteenth-century American etiquette books to "decentered-ness" in their early twentieth-century successors. The latter present "a number of parallel etiquettes," each demanding a different personality for a variety of occasions. Adaptation to changing life conditions is the key to this modern etiquette, which, for example, provides a traveller with a travel etiquette. Early twentieth-century etiquette books began to be conceived as reference books (the format of these books would hint at such use), in which one could quickly look up how to behave and what to wear on a specific occasion. Their nineteenth-century predecessors, however, were to be read as coherent treatises, centring around one social principle that Arditi unfortunately fails to define. Considering their elaborate discussions of various forms of chaperonage, that principle could perhaps be called "anxiety." Women were to be protected from embarrassing events by their chaperons.

The subject of chaperonage[8] is crucial to this article, because it makes us aware of the differences between French and American social behaviour. What is Rachel to be protected from by her fellow travellers, and what social behaviour of American women strikes Beauvallet and Chéry as extraordinary? Can this perhaps be seen as anticipating the adaptation to travelling conditions that Arditi has observed in etiquette books from 1900 onward, or do the French hold on to nineteenth-century "centeredness," defined as female anxiety, as the guiding principle for their behaviour?

Constructing charisma

Rachel's travelling companions not only had to deal with the delicate, "anxious" nature of a female companion, they also needed to adapt to the fact that Rachel was their employer *and also* an artist. Moreover, she was both ailing and a celebrity, conditions that explained her desire to shun company and to be left alone most of the time. On a very few occasions she left her hotel room or ship's cabin to view the exotic scenery and the inhabitants of America, a continent that became more and more unfamiliar and uncivilised as the company left behind New York, Boston, and Philadelphia and travelled south, towards Cuba.

The question then arises as to whether this withdrawal did not prevent her celebrity from increasing in America. The studies collected in *Constructing Charisma: Celebrity, Fame, and Power in Nineteenth-Century Europe* show the necessity – precisely for female stars – of winning over the public by means of eccentric behaviour and an unconventional love life, stories about which were eagerly peddled by the press. But for Rachel the time had definitely passed when her reply to billets-doux asking "Où? – Quand? – Combien?" was "Chez toi – Ce soir – Pour rien." She simply wanted to act and to play the roles that had made her so famous in Europe. She initially did not even agree to the express request of French Americans to sing the *Marseillaise* again, as she had done in France in 1848.

But did Rachel nevertheless gain the sympathy of the American public? What action did Raphaël Félix take – perhaps in imitation of, or in fact differently to Barnum – to turn Rachel's fame into cash in America, and what did Rachel herself do (or not do) so as to charm the American public?

Cultural colonisation and masculinity

Rachel and her travelling companions utilised various comparisons when speaking about their journey to America. In a letter to a friend in 1857, Rachel speaks of an "*odyssée mortelle*"; in another letter, dated 7 January 1856, she writes that, like Napoleon after his Russian campaign, she had sent her troops home and was preparing to rest her weary head in the Hôtel des Invalides.[9] To Beauvallet, she lets slip that her brother Raphaël, who had insisted on an American tour, was the "Juif Errant" and she was his five cents.[10] Beauvallet regularly compares Raphaël's organization of the tour with the measures that the "showman" P.T. Barnum – founder of Barnum & Bailey Circus, "The Greatest Show on Earth" – had taken in 1850 to make Jenny Lind's American appearances lucrative. The travelling theatre company thus becomes a travelling circus, with Raphaël Félix as the director and Rachel as the main attraction.

Odysseys, campaigns, endless wanderings, circuses: All of these involve ways of travelling especially – if not exclusively – fit for men, requiring them to be away from home for long periods, to embark on adventures, and to yield themselves to the vicissitudes of fortune. A third research question that can be derived from these characterisations concerns the representation of masculinity in the "travelogues" studied here. In this regard, we can find support in Helen Goodman's study "Masculinity, Tourism and Adventure in English Nineteenth-Century Travel Fiction," in which she investigates the way masculinity is presented in such works. Goodman discusses novels by Anthony Trollope, H. Rider Haggard, Joseph Conrad, Rudyard Kipling, and W.H. Hudson. She positions "masculinity" within the colonial discourse and connects it with "Englishness." This particular interpretation of British "imperial manliness" or "imperial masculinity" in the novels studied should not prevent us from searching for a French equivalent. Many of Goodman's observations are applicable to the "travelogues" of Beauvallet and Chéry, who speak about American culture with a certain disdain and view themselves as colonial adventurers with a civilising mission in a backward country, where French culture can only be found every now and again. In the novels of Rider Haggard, it is fortune-hunting that constitutes the primary motive for the male heroes who enter the African wilderness, a motive that they conceal behind more noble ones. This narrative programme is evident in the two travelogues that we are considering here, albeit that it is placed in the hands of the – almost invisible – protagonist Rachel. Goodman cites a definition of the adventure genre that can be effortlessly applied to the texts by the two French actors: "a series of events, partly but not wholly accidental, in settings remote from the domestic and probably from the civilised […], which constitute a challenge to the central character."[11] All in all, it does not seem absurd to consider the reports on the US tour as a narrative of cultural colonisation, including the likelihood of a profitable outcome.

Rachel is virtually invisible in the travelogues by Beauvallet and Chéry, in the same way as the women in the travel literature studied by Goodman. Those novels deal, after all, with "masculine identity interrogated and reaffirmed by travel." On the other hand, masculinity is only fully expressed when contrasted with femininity. Goodman's solution to this problem – the absence of femininity, which is nevertheless visible as a contrast to the masculinity of the travellers – is also interesting for us. She seeks the feminine in "an alternative inanimate form," such as the rugged landscape that must be overcome and that may even take the shape of a woman's body. A minor flaw in Goodman's argument seems to be the problem that the world that is to be discovered by men is supposed to be female, while at the same time this "female wilderness" is supposed to be inaccessible to women. In the travelogues by Beauvallet and Chéry, the absent Rachel manifests herself in their explorations of the foreign country and its people. They tackle it in a "masculine" manner but they constantly wonder whether they shouldn't conceal their discoveries from Rachel. "Anxiety" is interwoven with male bravado. In discussing the two books we will notice various indications of this.

In section, "Rachel performing and travelling in America," answers will be given to the research questions derived from the three approaches above. This discussion of the travelogues by Beauvallet and Chéry is preceded by a Section (I) recounting a travel reminiscence by Rachel at the age of 22. The triptych concludes with a passage from a letter from a year before her death in which she tells of her impressions while travelling in Egypt (III). Framing the American travelogues in this way reveals the antithesis between Rachel's own account of her travels, in the first and third sections, and those of her companions, in the second. But this triptych also shows the evolution in how Rachel travelled: For pleasure, to earn money, and to postpone her death somewhat.

Rachel as a tourist

According to Georges d'Heylli, who edited her letters, Rachel travelled little for pleasure. She was only on the road in order to give national and international performances, with the single aim of "gagner le plus d'argent possible" (earning as much money as possible). D'Heylli is nevertheless able to present us with three letters that she wrote during a brief holiday. The most interesting, to Mme Samson, dates from 20 August 1843, when she was only 22 and was sent from Interlaken. At Montenvers (Chamonix), she had visited the famous Mer de Glace glacier, a visit that she describes excitedly in her letter. She continued, ("Après la grande pièce, la petite, dit-on." [After the big bit, the little bit, one might say.]) by recounting her meeting with a party of French travellers, some of whom believed that they recognised her:

> Dans une auberge sur la cime du Montanvert se trouvait en même temps que nous une société de vrais Parisiens sortis tout chauds du passage de l'Opéra: un gros monsieur, probablement courtier de la Bourse, habitué des Variétés

ou du café Anglais; trois jeunes femmes en costume de voyage pris fort exactement dans le journal des modes; deux jeunes échappés de collège voyageant sans doute pour terminer leur éducation. Une des jeunes femmes crut me reconnaître: "Comme elle ressemble à Rachel!" – 'Mais c'est Rachel elle-même!' répondit un des collégiens; 'je l'ai vue dernièrement dans *Phèdre*, et ses traits sont restés gravés dans mon esprit." – "Allons donc," reprit le vieil habitué du café Anglais: "Rachel est beaucoup moins jolie que cette charmante voyageuse." Je vous fais grâce de la discussion qui, s'échauffant de plus en plus, en vint au point de ne pouvoir se terminer que par une bataille ou un pari. Ce fut ce dernier qui l'emporta, mais vous ne devineriez jamais le pari: un gigot de mouton! ... L'ingénieux courtier se chargea de découvrir la vérité: après une profonde réflexion il accoucha d'un moyen infaillible pour percer mon incognito. Nous étions sortis de l'auberge et, soutenus par les guides, nous nous aventurions, non sans peur, sur la mer de glace. En traversant une crevasse, je me trouve face à face avec mon parieur; il est d'abord un peu embarrassé, puis en détournant la tête il lance cette phrase captieuse: "La nature et l'art, tout est admirable! ..." Si c'est Rachel, avait-il dit, elle sera doucement chatouillée par la délicatesse exquise de ce compliment et elle ne pourra comprimer sa satisfaction. Mais, beaucoup plus occupée du terrain glissant sur lequel je me trouvais que des bons mots du Monsieur, je passai mon chemin bien tranquillement. Alors lui de s'écrier en se tournant vers sa société: "Vous voyez bien que ce n'est pas Rachel! j'ai gagné mon pari!" Ne voulant cependant pas être cause d'une perte aussi considérable que celle d'une gigot de mouton, revenue à l'auberge avant nos Parisiens, j'écrivis de ma belle écriture sur le livre des voyageurs: "Payez le gigot de mouton, Monsieur, je suis Rachel! ..."[12]

What is striking about this anecdote is the behaviour of the gentleman from Paris, who is more interested in revealing Rachel's identity and in the outcome of his bet than in an introduction to the actress. The ill-mannered way he talks about her in her presence – it seems as if the Parisian group assume that the lady who looks like Rachel doesn't understand French – is reminiscent of the rudeness to which celebrities are nowadays treated by their fans when they turn their back on them when asked to take a selfie. Looking back on it, Rachel is able to see the humour of all this, but during her American tour she emphatically wishes to be spared the attentions of intrusive admirers.

Rachel performing and travelling in America

Two travelogues

Le Figaro for 7 February 1856 printed a letter from Léon Beauvallet, one of the actors in Rachel's theatre company, addressed to A.M.H. de Villemessant, "*Rédacteur en chef du Figaro.*" In his letter, Beauvallet reported the return of a number of members of the company and asked the editor to make space available in his newspaper for an account of their tour:

> Maintenant, mon cher monsieur de Villemessant, ne trouvez-vous pas comme moi que l'instant est venu de raconter l'Odyssée de la tragédie française en Amérique? Je reviens de là-bas avec un volume d'anecdotes, d'histoires, de cancans. Un volume entier, vous verrez! Je vous avouerai, du reste, que c'est un peu pour cela que j'étais parti... Je n'avais pas l'intention de faire quatre mille lieues dans une multitude de pays plus fantastiques les uns que les autres, pour me livrer exclusivement aux tirades de ce grand Jocrisse qui s'appelle Hippolyte, et de ce faux marchand de dattes qui a nom Bajazet! – Oh! non! J'ai écrit tout, noté tout![13]

The first instalment of Beauvallet's travelogue appeared in *Le Figaro* starting on 14 February 1856 (pp. 4–5) and the last on 20 March (pp. 5–7) with an overview of Rachel's box-office takings alongside those of Jenny Lind. The travelogue was published the same year in book form, with an English translation appearing in New York before the year was out.

Jules Chéry kept his own travelogue to himself for a long time, presumably because Beauvallet had beaten him to it with his publication. His reminiscences of the American tour were never in fact published (until Anne Martin-Fugier's 2008 edition); the manuscript, dated 1902, is in the library of the Comédie-Française. Chéry's report is less impertinent than that of Beauvallet; it is more nuanced and less sensationalist. He regularly expresses his concern for Rachel and he reports on a heart-to-heart talk that he had with her. Although there would seem to be a certain coyness in his reporting of conversations in which Rachel expressed her worries and feelings, Chéry does seem to have enjoyed her trust.

Chaperonage

Hardly had the company arrived in New York than Pierre and Jules Chéry went off by themselves to explore the city together. Their initial interest was in day-to-day life and the behaviour of people in the street and on the trams. The conductors let everyone get on – except blacks – even if the carriage was already packed full. There was no need to give up one's seat to women; they would do just fine:

> Si c'est une femme qui monte et que toutes les places soient prises, elle s'assoit sur les genoux du premier homme venu et personne ne s'en étonne; que la même chose se fasse à Paris et vous verrez la conduite aussi stupide qu'indiscrète de ceux qui se disent les plus policés du monde.[14]

What Chéry found especially striking was that women could move around freely in public, without a chaperone. Anyone who abused that freedom would find himself called up before the court of public anger:

Au reste, nous avons déjà vu par nous-mêmes, et l'on nous a dit, que la femme était tellement respectée aux États-Unis qu'elle pouvait aller seule partout, dans les promenades, dans les lieux publics, sans craindre aucune inconvenance de la part des hommes; que si un individu se permettait de suivre dans la rue une femme ou une jeune fille en lui tenant des propos toujours déplacés et souvent plus que grossiers, il se ferait lapider par la population: on devrait bien infliger cette punition aux Don Juan qui suivent les femmes à Paris. Ainsi ce peuple, qui n'a pas les raffineries [sic] de nos vieilles civilisations, entend mieux que nous la déférence que l'on doit aux femmes et un homme ne garderait pas son chapeau sur sa tête dans un lieu public, spectacle, concert, réunion quelconque où des femmes se trouveraient.[15]

But women weren't really as well protected in public as Chéry thought. Rachel supposedly feared not only for her jewels but also for her life when she entered a "taxi" and the driver could not find the way.[16]

The company travelled from Washington to Charleston on a train equipped with every comfort. Rachel even had her own private compartment:

Nous voyageons en wagons très confortables, par exemple, et bien aménagés: salle à manger, salon de lecture avec journaux et revues, cabinet de toilette avec linge, water-closet; tout ce qu'il faut pour un long voyage. On circule d'un bout à l'autre du train. Mlle Rachel a un lit dans un compartiment particulier. Elle voyage sans trop de fatigue et elle paraît un peu moins triste.[17]

Chéry also reports that while "wandering" pleasantly around the train, he came across a carriage full of black slaves, a discovery that would have severely limited access to all the carriages for female travellers and adaptation to their sophisticated taste. After talking to the owner of the slaves, a plantation owner from South Carolina who had bought them at a market in Virginia, Chéry visited the carriage in which the "merchandise" was located. The owner had explained to him that the life of a slave wasn't all that bad:

Je suis allé voir, dans le compartiment particulier où ils voyagent, la cargaison de cet apologiste du sort des Noirs. Il y avait quatre négresses de seize à dix-huit ans et autant de nègres leurs maris, quatre négrillons de trois à quatre ans qui ressemblaient à ces belles grosses mûres des bois d'un noir d'ébène. J'ai donné des gâteaux à ces enfants; les pères et les mères m'ont regardé niaisement, en riant, sans montrer aucun plaisir à voir leurs enfants dévorer mes gâteaux. Ces Noirs, d'une vraiment belle race, n'ont pas, je crois, beaucoup de sentiments: il n'ont pas fait une caresse à leurs enfants devant moi.[18]

The mere thought that Rachel had to travel in the same train as black slaves – or with the cynical slave owner, who sang the praises of the "maisons de production de la race nègre" (production houses for the negro race), cannot have been reassuring for someone who was convinced of the need for chaperonage during a journey. When Chéry asked what he meant by "production houses," the plantation owner answered: "Des commerçants ont dix, quinze, vingt négresses et plus, jeunes et fortes, et deux ou trois nègres, également jeunes et forts; dans ces conditions, les naissances sont nombreuses et profitables." (Some traders have ten, fifteen, twenty or more negresses, young and strong, and two or three negro men, also young and strong; under these conditions, births are numerous and profitable.) Chéry's exclamation "Mais ce sont de véritables haras humains que ces maisons de production!" (But those houses of production are genuine human stud farms) was answered with a condescending smile and the assurance that someone who was not American could not judge. When the French actor asked what the slave owner thought of "ce fameux réquisitoire dressé contre l'esclavage par une de vos compatriotes dans La Case de l'oncle Tom" (that famous indictment of slavery by one of your compatriots in *Uncle Tom's Cabin*), he was told that the book contained truths but also misunderstandings and exaggerations.[19] The explanation about the slave-breeding farms and the defence of slavery must have been shocking for a female passenger; it was probably not without a certain relief that Chéry noted the next day that the plantation owner and his slaves had left the train at Wilmington.

The sight of the confined black slaves may not have made the company very cheerful but at least one of them found attending the "negro carnival" in Havana at Epiphany extremely alarming. Chéry and Beauvallet both report on the colourful, exuberant parade of blacks who prowled the city's streets. On the very day when they were told that the tour was being cancelled and they would have to return to France prematurely, they witnessed the festival celebrating the one-day "liberation" of the slaves. Chéry displayed masculine courage in venturing out, because one needed to be bold to face the black slaves who ran wild in the streets, as do the bulls once a year in Pamplona. His views on their dancing betray a professional interest, which was thwarted, however, by his dismay at the lascivious nature of their movements:

> Cette fête s'appelle le carnaval des nègres. Ils sont libres ce jour-là, comme les esclaves l'étaient à Rome un certain jour de l'année. Ici, ils se livrent dans les rues à toutes les extravagances possibles, surtout à la danse. Ils font un tapage infernal, se permettent des libertés avec les personnes qui se hasardent dans la rue, dont ils sont les maîtres absolus.
>
> ...
>
> J'ai suivi une de leurs bandes avec quelques Blancs aussi curieux et aussi imprudents que moi, car ces nègres, ivres la plupart, nous auraient molestés que personne n'auraient pris notre défense: il n'y avait pas de police dans les rues.
>
> Nous les suivons jusqu'à l'hôtel du gouvernement et nous pénétrons avec eux dans une vaste cour intérieure.
>
> Les appartements qui donnent sur cette cour ont un balcon tout le long du bâtiment. Alors une vingtaine d'hommes et de femmes du plus beau noir ont donné une représentation de leurs danses, accompagnée par la musique la plus

hétéroclite et la plus sauvage qu'une oreille puisse entendre. Ces danses et cette musique, ils ne doivent les connaître que par tradition, car ces nègres sont esclaves de pères en fils depuis longtemps à La Havane et il n'en vient plus de nouveaux d'Afrique. Parmi ceux qui formaient le cercle autour des danseurs, il y avait bien une centaine de jeunes négresses d'une très beau type, habillées avec des robes à volants, des fichus, des ceintures de soie; ces jeunes filles étaient certainement femmes de service dans de riches maisons et elles étaient habillées avec les vêtements de leurs maîtresses; par exemple, toutes étaient pieds nus.

Les danses ont commencé aux sons de cette musique à faire hurler tous les chiens de la ville; danses échevelées, lascives, avec des gestes et des intentions d'un cynisme à faire rougir un singe. Des jeunes filles, peut-être les filles du maréchal Concha, gouverneur de Cuba,[20] étaient sur le balcon avec leurs amies et regardaient ces turpitudes comme une chose toute simple.

Mais ce qui montre la passion de cette race noire pour la danse, la force d'impression chez ces natures primitives, l'entraînement de l'exemple, c'est que toutes ces jeunes négresses qui regardaient avaient des mouvements fébriles, qui augmentaient à mesure que la danse devenait plus emportée et la musique plus enragée, et qu'elles ont fini par se lancer dans le tourbillon avec une ardeur extravagante.

Ce carnaval des nègres doit tenir beaucoup, surtout la nuit, des saturnales païennes, et ce n'est pas, il me semble, à l'honneur des Espagnols cubains qui les autorisent.[21]

Chéry found it particularly shocking that the daughters of the governor and their girlfriends watched the lewd dancing without being upset by it: Their indifference did not fit in with his views on female modesty, which needed to be protected against this overt display of lasciviousness. Precisely what he was afraid of took place before his very eyes: The well-dressed black girls at first merely looked on but then eventually threw themselves into the passionate, sexual dancing. What had overcome them could just as well overcome white girls too. Here too, the presence of Rachel – confined alone to her sickbed – is felt: It is only the walls of her residence that protect her against the wild and uninhibited passions on display in the street. Chéry's disapproval of the orgiastic negro celebration is tempered in a concluding paragraph. In it he reports that he had seen an advertisement in a French-language Cuban newspaper – one destined for a civilised, because Francophone, readership! – in which a "spotless" (*sans tache*) black girl of 15 or 16 was offered for sale: "Cela se passe de commentaire." (That [was] beyond words.)

Unlike the more serious Chéry, Beauvallet had an eye mainly for the grotesquery of the negro carnival, for example the ridiculous attire of the revellers: "Ces pauvres diables sont tous affublés des costumes les plus baroques, des travestissements les plus impossibles, qui feraient fureur au bal de l'Opéra." (These poor devils are all muffled up in the oddest costumes and the most impossible travesties, such as would be all the rage at a fancy ball.)[22] He considered that the slaves of Havana, who can indulge in such extravagances, were living a good life compared to their counterparts on the sugar plantations in the interior. Beauvallet also refers to an event at the carnival that Jules Chéry is silent about. Was that perhaps because that bit of service performed in drag detracted from the masculine character with which Chéry wished to endow his exploration of the ominous carnival?

> Un autre nègre, vêtu en blanc et en rose tendre, avec un chapeau de bergère et un masque blanc et rose sur la figure, s'est agenouillé devant les frères Chéry, et s'est mis à essuyer leurs souliers avec un mouchoir brodé, qu'il tenait prétentieusement à la main.[23]

Capitalising on celebrity

The hero's welcome that the company had expected did not greet them on their arrival in New York and after their first relatively lucrative performance public interest in French tragedies was disappointing. The newspapers were full of praise for Rachel but most theatregoers were quickly bored by the performances, which were of course in a language that most Americans could not understand. Nevertheless, the audience turned out to have prepared well for an evening of unintelligible alexandrines: They had acquired copies of the text in English. They read along with what was being declaimed on stage, without of course looking up from the text very much. The communal reading led to a periodic noise like a rainstorm, as hundreds of spectators turned the page simultaneously:

> Le public écoute religieusement les vers de Corneille. Le silence le plus complet règne dans la salle.
> Tout à coup, un bruit étrange, inattendu, vient couvrir la voix des artistes en scène.
> On dirait qu'un orage affreux éclate, et que la pluie vient fouetter avec fureur toutes les vitres de la salle.
> Pas du tout! Il n'y a pas plus d'ondée que sur la main. Ce bruit est tout simplement produit par les innombrables brochures d'*Horace*, traduites en anglais, dont tous les spectateurs tournent en même temps le feuillet terminé.
> Rien de comique comme d'entendre ce sifflement soudain au beau milieu d'une tirade.
> Rien de divertissant surtout comme l'ensemble parfait avec lequel s'agitent toutes ces paperasses.
> On dirait un régiment en habits noirs, exécutant un commandement militaire.
> Mademoiselle Rachel ne trouve pas que ce soit si divertissant que cela.
> Elle réfléchit que ces maudites brochures vont couper en deux ses mots, ses phrases, ses tirades, et cela ne la rassure que médiocrement.[24]

But audiences that read along were not Rachel's only ordeal in New York. She came to realise that others came to watch her like a fairground attraction – and immediately made off again as soon as they had seen her – while some people outside the theatre, but clearly audible to everyone within, made fun of the French Company by crowing like a cock. This acoustic vandalism was probably intended as an allusion to the Gallic cock as a symbol of the French nation.

It was of course natural for Rachel's (male) companions to feel a need to protect the artist from the boorishness of the American public. The solace they offered is to be found in the company's conclusion: America is too far away, too hot, there are too many flies, and the public have too little literary culture.

Les Français de New-York sont enchantés; ils applaudissent avec frénésie.

Quant aux Américains, ils persistent à faire un bruit désastreux avec leurs brochures et à ne pas s'amuser énormément.

Quelques-uns, qui sont venus seulement pour voir Rachel, quittent leurs stalles après son entrée et se sauvent, comme si le diable les emportait. Ils ont *vu* Rachel! Ils pourront dire à tout le monde:

– J'ai vu Rachel!

C'est tout ce qu'il leur faut.

Quant à étudier la tragédie et la tragédienne françaises, ils s'offriront ce plaisir une autre fois. En attendant, ils vont voir, à *Broadway-Théâtre*, une certaine danse de corde qui fait beaucoup de bruit dans le monde dramatique newyorkais.

Ce soir, pendant toute la première scène de Rachel, de mauvais plaisants, cachés dans la rue du Théâtre, s'amusent à imiter le chant du coq.

Hier déjà, à son entrée dans les *Horaces*, ils s'étaient livrés à cette étude de basse-cour.

Le chant de cet oiseau, au milieu des vers de Corneille et de Racine, faisait l'effet le plus désagréable du monde; aussi, a-t-on envoyé à la poursuite de ce faux coq une bande de policemen, qui naturellement n'ont rien attrapé du tout.

A la suite de cette deuxième soirée, malgré le succès obtenu, on fut beaucoup moins satisfait qu'après la représentation d'hier. – Il y avait de quoi. – Et l'on se hasarda à trouver que ce pays était décidément trop éloigné, trop chaud, trop orné de mouches ct pas assez littéraire![25]

Chéry's analysis was more thoughtful. He observed the New York audience before the performance of *Les Horaces*, noting: "*Il était curieux de voir la physionomie d'un public si peu fait et si peu préparé à juger un des chefs-d'œuvre de notre théâtre.*" (It was strange to see what an audience looked like that was so little suited and so little prepared for judging one of the masterpieces of our theatre.) Would Corneille and the performer of his tragedy, Rachel, in fact be able to arouse the admiration of such an audience? Were the latter actually aware of the achievements of the tragedienne, could they analyse the emotions that the play aroused in them? He did not believe so for one minute. The audience were there for the show, to experience the thrill, and they were indifferent to the efforts that the actors and actresses had to undertake in order to give them an enjoyable evening. For his part, Chéry was certainly aware of what was necessary to arouse the audience's admiration. Although he believed that Rachel had everything necessary to appeal to a spoiled and impatient audience, the applause was not as enthusiastic as one would expect from the American public "quand la trompette de la renommée leur a monté la tête" (when the trumpet of fame had gone to their heads):

> Avant que l'acteur parle, il est vu, et la première impression, sans examen, est bonne, indifférente ou mauvaise. Il faut que la figure plaise, que la tenue, la prestance soient bien celles du personnage que l'on attend; que le costume, le maintien, la démarche, le premier geste flattent la vue et l'esprit.[26]

Chéry shows himself sensitive to the demands of a modern audience with little cultural "baggage" who come to the theatre because of rumours regarding world renown but who are soon disappointed and leave, finding classicist tragedies tedious and boring. Beauvallet expresses the same "culture shock" as Chéry, although in his own more vehement tone:

> Dieu! quel succès monstre, quels frénétiques bravos eût obtenus l'acteur qui, au milieu d'une scène de tragédie, se fût mis à marcher sur la tête, à faire le saut de carpe et à avaler son sabre![27]

Masculinity

Beauvallet leaves no room for doubt: Travel is for men. One becomes disorientated and loses one's sense of time and place. America reveals itself to Chéry and Beauvallet like an unreal dream, a "fairy play" in which fantasies become reality and reality a fantastic illusion:

> Quoi qu'il en soit, ces perpétuels voyages ont un attrait qu'on ne peut nier, un charme dont on ne saurait se défendre. – Il est positif que cette éternelle locomotion vous fait éprouver une ivresse véritable. – Les saisons n'existent plus pour nous. – Hiver, automne, printemps, été, tout marche à présent sans ordre et sans règles. – Hier, nous étions couverts de fourrures comme de vrais Esquimaux, demain, nous serons habillés de toile blanche. – Quant à moi, j'ignore totalement comment je vis à présent. – Pour savoir dans quel mois je me trouve, je suis obligé de le demander à mon almanach. – On doit devenir fou très-vite, dans ce pays![28]

In the seventh part of his book – "*En route vers le sud*" (On the way south), Chapter 1, "*où les chemins de fer deviennent de plus en plus impossibles*" (where the trains become more and more impossible) – Beauvallet complains bitterly about the inconvenience and dangers of travelling by rail. Rachel is apparently travelling separately, *à petites journées* (in a series of short trips), so as to avoid the greatest inconveniences. The men then have a quarter of an hour left to explore the American wilderness at Weldon, which reminds them of the novels of James Fennimore Cooper, author of the five *Leatherstocking Tales* (published between 1823 and 1841). There are no Mohicans any more but there are waterfalls, a river, and big trees. So the emptiness of this paradisiacal American landscape has to be ornamented with fictitious "savages," who figure in a fantasy about the hidden history of the French Dauphin.

Their guide, a Louisianan, tells Beauvallet and his companions the story of Eleazer Williams, a Methodist preacher in Albany, who is claimed to be the Dauphin, the son of Louis XVI and Marie Antoinette. He had supposedly been brought up by an alcoholic Indian called Williams, who had ensured that his foster son received a good education. A Frenchman, Bellanger, who had died in New Orleans a few years previously, had stated on his deathbed that he had saved the Dauphin from the hands of the revolutionaries and brought him to America. On a trip to the United States, the Prince de Joinville had visited Williams and talked to him at length; afterwards Williams had declared that he did not in any case wish to become king. This strange story made a great impression on Beauvallet: "I admit that I experienced a strange emotion; a thousand memories arose, and as if in a dream, it seemed to me that all these memories of the past century were alive again and passing before me!"[29]

He stated that he would not have dared to record this history, this fantastic legend, if he had not read the same story in a book by J.J. Ampère, *Promenade en Amérique* (1855).[30] As if in a dream, Beauvallet felt transported to the – French – past, which in America was still a reality. That feeling of being transported to a new world in which space and time are different from the familiar is consistent with the experience of a journey into an unknown parallel universe. Even so, French points of recognition had been installed there for the convenience of the French Company. They came across French people in the unlikeliest of places, for example a restaurateur at whose establishment they could recover for a time from what American cuisine had inflicted on them (fried squirrels!). At Key West they discovered a clothes shop reminiscent of Paris run by a French Jew, who, as they thought befitted a Jew, charged them far too much for light clothing with which to withstand the heat. However the thespians considered that they had quickly made up for this financial loss by fobbing off a pleasant "*nègre*" with two dollars for the abundance of fruit that he offered to the French ladies. Only then does it become clear that there were also women in the party:

> Vendredi 21 décembre, nous abordons à Key West, à l'extrême pointe de la Floride, à dix heures du matin. Le capitaine nous dit que nous ne repartons pour La Havane qu'à huit heures du soir et que les passagers qui voudraient descendre en ville le pouvaient. Nous profitons de l'avis, nous sautons à terre, le bateau touchant au quai, et nous voyons de près les arbres et la végétation des tropiques: [C]ocotiers, bananiers chargés de leurs fruits; des orangers, des citronniers, des grenadiers en plein terre, chargés de fruits et de fleurs; des lauriers-roses gros comme des arbres.
>
> Pierre et moi, nous nous séparons des camarades et nous suivons un sentier à travers les jardins séparés les uns des autres par des haies de cactus,

d'orangers et de citronniers. Les oranges et les citrons jonchent les sentiers comme dans nos campagnes les prunes et les pommes. Nous sommes pour de bon dans un pays qui ne ressemble pas au nôtre. À deux heures, nous revenons dîner sur le bateau. En traversant la petite ville de Key West, nous entrons chez un marchand d'habits dont la boutique et l'étalage rappellent Paris; et, en effet, c'est un bon juif parisien établi à deux mille lieues de la rue Saint-Denis, qui vend des vêtements d'hiver à ceux qui vont vers le nord et des vêtements d'été à ceux qui passent pour aller dans le sud. Nous lui achetons quelques hardes légères; il nous témoigne un grand plaisir de voir des compatriotes en nous vendant très cher ce dont nous avons besoin pour ne pas étouffer de chaleur. Il y a déjà ici trente degrés au-dessus de zéro.

Après dîner, nous allons en bande sur le bord de la mer; nous passons devant une jolie maisonnette dont le jardin, à côté de la maison, est ravissant de fleurs. Nous admirons un oranger qui aurait éclipsé ceux du jardin des Hespérides par la beauté de ses fruits. Nos exclamations attirent le maître de la maison, un nègre, qui nous engage avec force signes et bons sourires à entrer dans son jardin. Il cueille des branches chargées d'oranges et les offre aux dames avec des manières très avenantes. Nous le remercions par une pantomime expressive et nous lui donnons deux dollars qu'il reçoit avec une évidente satisfaction.[31]

Their satisfied conclusion "Nous avons passé à Key West la plus belle journée de notre voyage." (At Key West, we spent the nicest day of our voyage), was followed immediately by an expression of disappointed hope: "Mlle Rachel n'a pas voulu quitter le bateau; elle est restée toute la journée sur le pont, livrée sans doute à de tristes reflexions" (Mlle Rachel did not want to leave the ship; she spent the whole day on deck, doubtless given over to sad reflexions.)[32]

Léon Beauvallet had a different view, writing that Rachel left her cabin for the first time when the ship berthed at Key West.[33] At the arm of the captain, surrounded by her numerous family, she went for a walk in a woodland grove. Chéry's observation that they really were in a country nothing like their own is consistent with Beauvallet's remark that it seemed as if they had ended up in the fifth act of a "fairy play":

Dans le simple but, je le suppose, de voir *de près* ces hôtes légèrement pittoresques, mademoiselle Rachel, qui n'est décidément pas d'une gaîté folle quand elle approche du tropique, consent, pour la première fois depuis l'embarquement, à franchir le seuil de la cabine du capitaine. Bien plus, ô prodige, elle se hasarde, au bras de ce même capitaine, et entourée de sa nombreuse famille, à faire un tour quelconque dans un admirable bois, ma foi, une vraie serre chaude, très-chaude, même, où les palmiers et les cocotiers poussent comme chez eux, où le cactus fleurit avec une facilité effrayante. Là, la grenade s'entr' ouvre d'elle-même devant votre soif; le citron vous tombe tout mûr dans... la bouche; les oiseaux mouches remplacent nos hannetons; les papillons sont gros comme des moines, et les cigales chantent des grands airs d'Opéra.

Quand on se trouve, tout d'un coup, face à face avec cette nature luxuriante, on se figure que ça *n'est pas arrivé*. Vrai, cela vous fait juste l'effet d'un cinquième acte de féerie.[34]

The fairy-tale world that the French actors found themselves in was one without a dark side: Everything was edible or bigger, more colourful and exotic than its counterpart in the Old World. Ladies could look around boldly and taste, without a care, what smiling *nègres* offered them. Nature and civilisation were not at war with one another there, in the way that the French tended to think in the eighteenth and nineteenth centuries. The absence of civilisation with which nature was associated was hostile to women and invoked the masculine urge to explore and exploit. But over there nature revealed itself as an unreal "fairy play."

Rachel's last journey

At the end of September, Rachel left for Egypt, her final long journey, in the hope of restoring her shattered health there. She went for a *croisière* (cruise) across the Nile from Cairo to Thebes, finding it just as little enjoyable as her sea journeys in the Caribbean. She travelled with her *femme de chambre* Rose, a kitchen maid, and a Polish doctor, on a boat fitted out specially for her. Rachel referred to her American journey as an *"odyssée mortelle"*; Georges d'Heylli, who edited and commented on her letters, called the Nile trip a *"calvaire."*

A letter missing from D'Heylli's collection and not published until 16 October 1893, in *Le Figaro*, (and subsequently included in Rachel's *Lettres inédites*, edited by Gabriel Laplane) was written *"à l'ombre des Pyramides"* and shows us Rachel as a performer in the last act of her personal tragedy. In this undated letter to Arsène Houssaye, she writes:

Du bas des Pyramides, je contemple vingt siècles évanouis dans les sables. Ah! Mon ami, comme je vois ici le néant des tragédiennes. Je me croyais pyramidale et je reconnais que je ne suis qu'une ombre qui passe... qui a passé. Je suis venue ici pour retrouver la vie qui m'échappe, et je ne vois que la mort autour de moi. Quand on a été aimée à Paris, il faut mourir. Faites-moi bien vite faire un trou au Père-Lachaise et creusez-moi un trou dans votre souvenir. M'avez-vous oubliée? Moi, je me souviens.

J'écris ceci sans bien savoir ce que je dis, mais je sèche l'encre avec la poussière des reines d'Égypte, c'est ce qu'il y a plus éloquent dans mon billet.

Celle qui s'en va.

Rachel[35]

Conclusion

The three perspectives from which the travelogues of Chéry and Beauvallet have been studied have brought to light various behaviours and observations which, perhaps only half-consciously, were motivated by a form of chaperonage modified for travelling, the desire to turn Rachel's fame into cash, or to open up America for the ailing tragedienne. It would seem very much as if these actors who performed the classicist tragedies on the other side of the ocean – far removed from the stylised court culture within which they had been created and from the traditional ceremoniousness associated with their appreciation by French audiences – also found themselves confronted by a cultural divide in their social interaction. They noticed that American women behaved more freely and independently in public than the French were accustomed to back home. For French audiences, the modernity of Rachel's portrayal of tragic heroines had to do with its free approach to theatrical conventions, but that was a modernity which could not hold the attention of the unconventional American public for very long. Where respect for the French cultural heritage was lacking, the refinement that Rachel had brought to its consumption could arouse but little admiration in America. The struggle with modernity is also apparent from the practical measures taken to earn as much money as possible: In this, America was far ahead of Europe. In France, Rachel's commercial tours had been greeted by indignant criticism but by American standards she was not nearly commercial enough.

Rachel's companions did their best to conceal the rough side of American life from her. The conversation with the cynical slave trader on the train and Chéry's meeting with the slaves whom he was transporting gains additional resonance against the background of Rachel's unseen presence. The same is true of the "negro carnival" in Havana. The journey from New York to Havana was an exploration of a world in which French manners were growing increasingly irrelevant. The sporadic meetings with expatriate French people were like arriving at an oasis. At first, the French company experienced the American wilderness as a void that needed to be filled in with an apocryphal French history, as if the New World revealed the back of the tapestry that had been woven in France. In Florida, however, exotic nature revealed itself in all its abundance and loveliness, like a "fairy play" in which women had nothing to fear. Meanwhile, for someone facing death, the world looks the same everywhere.

Notes

1 D'Heylli, G. (1882) *Rachel d'après sa correspondance. Avec quatre portraits à l'eau-forte gravés par Massard*. Paris: Librairie des Bibliophiles: 208. Translation:

> Truly, I would be wrong if I expressed the slightest regret at having left behind the children whom I adore, the mother whom I cherish, and friends whom I love with all my heart. No, no, Mademoiselle, go off on that nice tour, and only then will you have really earned your bread for every day of the week. Well dear mother, is it too much to pay for it by seven months of labour while toiling like a black [*nègre*]? Whites must take on the work since the blacks [*noirs*] refuse to do it.

2 D'Heylli (1882): 210. Translation: "Even if at the end of my American tour I lost the money I earned there, I wouldn't complain if my health continued as it is at the moment."

3 D'Heylli (1882): 211, letter to her mother dated 25 September 1855. Translation: "Oh! Good God! How far away that moment is, March 8!!! But never mind. Isn't it better to spend my time in a climate that suits me so well rather than to suffer in Paris as I have suffered?"

4 D'Heylli (1882): 215. Translation:

> Even if laurels protect us from lightning, they don't protect us from hoarseness. That's my situation. I was cold on the train, and since I've been in Boston I've been coughing like someone with consumption [tuberculosis], which I'm not – please believe me – despite my pale complexion and my noticeable thinness.
>
> Apart from my rashness in not dressing warmly enough, the journey has gone perfectly.

5 D'Heylli (1882): 216. Translation:

> If only I knew whether I can appear and whether I won't need several months of rest. But whatever happens, I'm resigned to it. Above all, I want to live. Even if I can't perform tragedies any longer, if that strength fails me, I feel the strength of my love for my boys growing all the time. I want to see my children grow into men.

6 D'Heylli (1882): 215. Translation: "I wished to try my strength by giving a performance two days before my departure, begged to do so by many charming ladies. I gave in to their wish."

7 For a brief overview of the American journey, largely based on the travelogue by Chéry, see: Chevalley, S. (1989) *Rachel. "J'ai porté mon nom aussi loin que j'ai pu..."* Paris: Calmann-Lévy: 340–359.

8 On the decline of chaperonage, as reported in etiquette books in the first decades of the twentieth century, see Wouters, C. (1995) "Etiquette Books and Emotion Management in the Twentieth Century, Part Two: The Integration of the Sexes", in *Journal of Social History*, Vol. 29, No. 2: 325–339; Wouters, C. (2004) *Sex and Manners. Female Emancipation in the West, 1890–2000*. London: Sage Publications: 47–85.

9 D'Heylli (1882): 220: "… sans précautions aucunes, j'ai marché devant moi sur cette interminable route qui va de New-York à la Havane, la dernière étape de mon odyssée mortelle!…"; D'Heylli (1882): p. 217: "Je ramène toute ma pauvre armée en déroute sur les bords de la Seine; et moi peut-être, comme un autre Napoléon, j'irai mourir aux Invalides et demander une pierre où reposer ma tête."

10 Beauvallet, L. (1856a) *Rachel et le Nouveau-Monde. Promenade aux États-Unis et aux Antilles*. Paris: A. Cadot: 119:

> Quelle odieuse chose qu'une traversée! La mer est évidemment l'un des plus affreux supplices que je connais. Et dire que Raphaël Félix, qui pouvait parfaitement ne pas faire ce voyage, a voulu l'entreprendre à toute force! Quelle chose bizarre! Je fis cette observation à mademoiselle Rachel. – Que voulez-vous, me répondit-elle, il ne peut tenir en place. – Et elle ajouta avec un sourire: – Mon frère, voyez-vous, c'est le Juif Errant … c'est moi qui suis ses cinq sous.

Beauvallet, L. (1856b) *Rachel and the New World. A Trip to the United States and Cuba. Translated from the French of Léon Beauvallet.* New York: Dix, Edwards and Co.: 363–364, 145.
11 Goodman, H. (2015) "Masculinity, Tourism and Adventure in English Nineteenth-Century Travel Fiction", in: Thomas Thurnell-Read and Mark Casey (eds.), *Men, Masculinity, Travel and Tourism*: 18.
12 D'Heylli (1882): 148–150. Translation:

> We were in an inn high above Montanvert [*sic*] and there was also a group of real Parisians, who seemed to have come straight from the Opera: a portly gentleman, probably a broker on the stock exchange, a regular at the Salon des Variétés or the Café Anglais; three young women, in travelling dress, exactly as depicted in a fashion magazine; two boys just out of school, doubtless travelling to complete their education. One of the young women thought she recognised me: 'Doesn't she look like Rachel!' – 'But that really is Rachel,' said one of the schoolboys, 'I saw her in *Phèdre* just recently, and her features are etched in my memory!' – 'Come on!' said the old habitué of the Café Anglais, 'Rachel is nowhere near as beautiful as that charming traveller.' I'll spare you their discussion, which got more and more heated, ending up at a point when it could only be settled with either a fight or a wager. It was to be the latter, but you'll never guess what the stake was: a leg of mutton! The cunning broker took it upon himself to discover the truth: after thinking hard, he came up with an infallible way of revealing my true identity. We had left the inn and, led by guides, we ventured, not without trepidation, onto the Mer de Glace. Crossing a crevasse, I found myself face to face with the wagerer. At first he was a bit ill-at-ease but then, averting his gaze, he came out with the specious turn of phrase: 'Nature and art, are they not both admirable?' If it is in fact Rachel, he'd said, she'll be gently tickled by the exquisite delicacy of this compliment and she won't be able to stifle her satisfaction. But I – more preoccupied with the slippery terrain in which I found myself than with the well-chosen words of the gentleman – continued quietly on my way. He, however, turned to his companions and shouted: 'You see, it isn't Rachel! I've won the bet!' Not wishing, however, to be the cause of a loss so great as that of a leg of mutton and – arriving back at the inn before the Parisians – I wrote in the guestbook in my very best handwriting: 'Pay for the leg of mutton, monsieur. I am Rachel!'

13 Translation:

> Do you not agree, my dear Mr Villemessant, that the time has come to recount the odyssey of French tragedy in America? I have returned from there with a volume full of anecdotes, stories, and tittle-tattle. A whole volume – you'll see! I must confess that that is a bit of the reason why I left … It wasn't my intention to travel four thousand leagues through a variety of countries, each one more strange than the other, so as to dedicate myself exclusively to the rantings of that great simpleton called Hippolyte and that fake date-seller called Bajazet! O no!
> I wrote it all down, I noted everything.

14 Chéry, J. (2008) *Mademoiselle Rachel en Amérique (1855–1856). Recueil et impressions par Monsieur Chéry de la Comédie-Française.* Édition présentée et annotée par Anne Martin-Fugier. Paris: Mercure de France: 58. Translation:

> If a woman gets on and all the seats are taken, then she just sits on the knee of the most convenient man and nobody is at all surprised. If that happened in Paris,

you'd see behaviour both stupid and indiscreet from those who consider themselves the most civilised people in the world.

15 Chéry (2008): 58. Translation:

> For the rest, we have already seen for ourselves that, as we were told, women are so respected in the United States that they can go anywhere alone, in public places and where people go for a stroll, without fearing any impropriety on the part of men. If someone dared to follow a woman or a young girl on the street to speak to her – something that is always inappropriate and often more than coarse – then he would risk being stoned by the crowd. It would be a good thing to introduce that punishment in Paris for the Don Juans who follow women. So the Americans, who do not have the refinements of our ancient civilisations, understand better than us the respect that is due to women. And a man will never keep his hat on in a public place, at a place of entertainment, a concert, or another meeting where women are present.

16 Brownstein, R.M. (1993) *Tragic Muse. Rachel of the Comédie-Française.* Durham: Duke University Press: 205.
17 Chéry (2008): 95–96. Translation:

> We are travelling in carriages that are very comfortable, for example, and well equipped: a dining room, a reading room with newspapers and magazines, a bathroom with linen, a water closet – everything you need for a long voyage. You can wander from one end of the train to the other. Mlle Rachel has a bed in a private compartment. She is travelling without getting too fatigued and she seems a bit less sad.

18 Chéry (2008): 99. Translation:

> I went to the separate compartment where they were travelling to see the cargo belonging to this apologist for the condition of the Blacks [*Noirs*]. There were four negro women, aged from 16 to 18, and as many negro men, their spouses, and four little piccaninnies [*négrillons*] aged 3 and 4, who resembled those nice fat woodland blackberries, as black as ebony. I gave cakes to these children; their fathers and mothers looked at me inanely, smiling without showing any pleasure in seeing their children devouring my cakes. These Blacks, of a truly beautiful race, do not, I believe, have many feelings: they didn't caress their children while I was there.

19 Chéry (2008): 97–99.
20 José Gutiérrez de la Concha (1809–1895) was Captain General of Cuba in 1856.
21 Translation:

> This festival is called the carnival of the blacks [*carnaval des nègres*]. They are free for the day, as were the slaves in Rome on one day of the year. In the streets here they display all conceivable excesses, especially dancing. They make an infernal racket and allow themselves improper liberties with those who venture out into the street, because it is they who are masters there.
>
> I followed one of those groups, along with some other white people who were just as curious and rash as I was, because these blacks, most of them drunk, could have molested us and nobody would have protected us; there were no police on the streets.

We followed them to the governor's residence and with them we entered the large courtyard.

The rooms looking out onto the courtyard have a balcony across the entire width of the building. About twenty men and women with the most beautiful black skin colour then gave a performance of their dances, accompanied by the strangest and wildest music that one's ears could hear. The only way they can know those dances and that music is through tradition because the blacks have been slaves for generations in Havana and no new ones come over from Africa. Among those who formed a circle around the dancers were a hundred really beautiful young negresses [*négresses*] of a very beautiful type, wearing flounced dresses, headscarves, and silk sashes. Those young girls were certainly maids in wealthy families and they were wearing their mistresses' clothes; but they were all barefoot.

The dancing started to the sound of music that would make all the dogs of the city bark; frenzied, lascivious dances, with gestures and suggestiveness of an audacity that would make a monkey blush. There were some young girls, perhaps the daughters of Marshal Concha, the governor of Cuba, on the balcony with their girlfriends, watching these base goings-on as if they were the most ordinary thing in the world.

But what the passion of this black race for dancing shows – the susceptibility to impressions of these primitive natures, the compelling power of example – is that all the young negresses who were watching were making feverish movements which became ever stronger as the dancing became wilder and the music more furious, until they finally threw themselves into the whirl with extraordinary ardour.

This negro carnival must be very similar, especially at night, to the pagan Saturnalia and I believe that it does no honour to the Cuban Spaniards that they allow it.

22 Beauvallet (1856a): 282–283; Beauvallet (1856b): 363–364.
23 Beauvallet (1856a): 283–284; Beauvallet (1856b): 365:

Another negro, dressed in white and pale pink, with a shepherdess hat and a white and pink mask on his face, dropped to his knees before the Chéry brothers and began to wipe their shoes with an embroidered handkerchief which he flourished pretentiously.

24 Beauvallet (1856a): 107–108; Beauvallet (1856b): 128–129:

The public listens religiously to the Alexandrines of Corneille. The most complete silence reigns in the house.

Suddenly a strange, unexpected noise drowns the voices of the actors.

One would say that a frightful storm had come on, and that the rain was furiously beating against all the windows of the house.

Nothing of the kind! The deluge is all in your eye. The noise is produced merely by innumerable pamphlet copies of *les Horaces*, translated into English, and all the spectators are turning over the leaf together.

Nothing can be more comical than to hear this sudden rustling, just in the middle of a passage.

Nothing can be so diverting as the perfect concert in which all these old papers are hustled.

You would say that a regiment in black uniform was executing a military order.

Mdlle. Rachel does not think this so very diverting.

She reflects that these accursed pamphlets are going to cut in two her words, her sentences, and her passages, and that reassures her only partially.

25 Beauvallet (1856a): 118–119; Beauvallet (1856b): 144–145:

> The French in New York are enchanted; they applaud frantically.
>
> As to the Americans, they persist in making that disastrous noise with their pamphlets, and in not being amused enormously.
>
> Some of them, who came only to see Rachel, leave their seats on her appearance, and hurry away as if the devil were behind them. They have seen Rachel! They can say to everybody:
>
> 'I have seen Rachel.'
>
> That is all they want.
>
> As to making a study of the French tragedy and tragédienne, they reserve that pleasure for another time. Meanwhile, they go to the Broadway Theatre to see a certain tight-rope dance, which is making a good deal of noise in the dramatic world of New York.
>
> To-night, through the whole of Rachel's first scene, a number of blackguards, concealed in the passages of the theatre, amuse themselves by imitating the crowing of a cock.
>
> Yesterday, indeed, on her entree in *Horace*, they were indulging in this barn-yard amusement.
>
> The noise of this fowl, in the midst of the poetry of Corneille and Racine, produced the most disagreeable effect in the world; so they sent in pursuit of this pretended cock a party of policemen, who, of course, found nothing at all.
>
> At the close of this second night, in spite of its success, we were not nearly as well satisfied as we had been the evening before. There was a reason. And we ventured to make the discovery that this country was decidedly too far off, too warm, too full of flies, and not literary enough!

26 Chéry (2008): 61. Translation:

> Before the actor has spoken, he has already been seen. The first impression – aroused without any reflection – is good, indifferent, or bad. The figure must be pleasing, the attitude and appearance must match the character that they are expecting to see. Costume, bearing, gait, the first gesture must please the eye and the mind.

27 Beauvallet (1856a): 114; Beauvallet (1856b): 138:

> Gods! what a monstrous success, what frantic bravos, the actor would have obtained, who, in the midst of a tragic scene, had taken to walking on his head, turning summersets [*sic*], and swallowing his sabre.

28 Beauvallet (1856a): 233; Beauvallet (1856b): 298:

> Say what you will, this perpetual travelling has an attraction which cannot be denied, a charm which you cannot help feeling. Positively this eternal locomotion produces a real intoxication. For us the seasons are no more. Winter, autumn, spring, summer, all come at present, without order. Yesterday we were covered with furs like genuine Esquimaux, tomorrow we shall be dressed in white linen. For myself, I know not how I am living. To find what month it is, I have to refer to my almanac. People must go mad very easily in this country!

29 Beauvallet (1856b): 304.

30 Beauvallet (1856a): 235; Beauvallet (1856b): 300; Ampère, J.J. (1855) *Promenade en Amérique. États-Unis – Cuba – Mexique.* Tome Premier. Paris: Michel Levy: 342–345.
31 Chéry (2008): 105–106. Translation:

> On Friday 21 December, we landed at Key West, at the southernmost tip of Florida, at ten in the morning. The captain told us that we wouldn't be leaving for Havana until eight in the evening and that passengers who wished could disembark and visit the city. We followed his advice and hopped off the ship as soon as it touched the quay. We saw from close up the trees and the tropical plants: coconut palms, banana plants laden with fruit, orange, lemon and pomegranate trees right out in the open, laden with fruits and flowers; oleanders as thick as a tree.
>
> Pierre and I left our companions and followed a path between the gardens, which were separated by hedges of cacti, orange trees, and lemon trees. The paths were strewn with [fallen] oranges and lemons just like plums and apples back in France. We really were in a country nothing like our own. At two o'clock we returned to the ship to dine. Walking around the little town of Key West, we entered an establishment selling clothes. The shop and its display window reminded us of Paris. And yes indeed, the shopkeeper was a real Parisian Jew who had set up shop two thousand leagues from Rue Saint-Denis. He sold winter clothes to those on their way north and summer clothes to those heading south. We bought some light garments from him; he assured us that it was a great pleasure to see compatriots, while charging us over the odds for what we needed so as not to suffocate from the heat. It was already thirty degrees there.
>
> After dinner a group of us went for a walk along the seaside, passing by a pretty little house whose garden, at the side of the house, was full of lovely flowers. We admired an orange tree that would have eclipsed those in the garden of the Hesperides with the beauty of its fruit. Our cries of admiration attracted the attention of the owner, a negro [*nègre*], who invited us into his garden with a lot of gesturing and smiling. He plucked oranges from the branches and offered them to the ladies with very pleasant manners. We thanked him with an expressive pantomime and gave him two dollars, which he received with obvious satisfaction.

32 Chéry (2008): 106.
33 Beauvallet (1856a): 245.
34 Beauvallet (1856b): 314–315:

> With the desire simply, I suppose, of seeing these slightly picturesque hosts close by, Mdlle. Rachel, who decidedly does not manifest any foolish gayety as she approaches the tropics, consents, for the first time since coming on board, to cross the threshold of the captain's state-room. Still more, O prodigious event! She ventured, on the arm of that same captain, and surrounded by her numerous family, to make a sort of journey to an admirable grove, *ma foi!* a regular hot-house, particularly hot, where palms and cocoa trees grow as if they were at home, and cactuses flourish with frightful facility. There the pomegranate opens of itself to your thirst; the lemon falls ripe into your – mouth; there humming-birds replace our cock-chafers; butterflies are as big as warming pans, and grasshoppers sing opera airs.
>
> When you find yourself suddenly face to face with this luxuriant nature, you feel that *something has not yet happened*. Indeed, it has just the same effect upon you as a fifth act of a fairy play.

The translation "something has not yet happened" (for 'ça *n'est pas arrivé*') does not seem entirely correct.

35 Translation:

> At the foot of the pyramids, I contemplate twenty centuries that have disappeared into the sands. Oh my friend! How well do I understand here the nothingness of tragediennes. I thought I was like a pyramid and now I realise that I am nothing but a shadow that passes ... that has passed by. I have come here to recover the life that escapes me but I see nothing other than death around me. When one has been loved in Paris, one must die. Have a hole dug for me soon at Père-Lachaise, and hollow out a hole for me in your memory. Have you forgotten me? Myself, I remember.
>
> I write this without really knowing what I am saying, but I dry the ink with the dust of the queens of Egypt; that is the most eloquent thing in this little note.
>
> One who is preparing to disappear,
> Rachel

9   Companions and competitors

Men and women travellers and travel writing in the mid-nineteenth-century French Pyrenees

Martyn Lyons

The importance of writing

In continental Europe, the genesis of modern mass tourism occurred in the middle decades of the nineteenth century. Significantly, travel writing boomed at exactly the same time, from individual accounts and diaries to commercially available guidebooks. Travel produced a mass of writing, which invites us to view travel in terms of both cultural practices and textual representations.[1] Tourism as a cultural practice always relied on writing to sustain and perpetuate itself. Advertising, newspaper articles and personal accounts publicised attractive destinations and set the fashion for tourists. In France, great writers like Stendhal, Victor Hugo, and Alexandre Dumas among others all tried their hand at writing travel journals. John Murray, Adolphe Joanne, and Karl Baedeker produced successful guidebooks which dictated the itineraries and organised the emotional reactions of thousands of new travellers. Travel and writing about it were inseparable.

For Pyrenean mountaineers, a daring ascent lost most of its value unless it was recorded in writing. Without a written account to establish who made the first ascent, any subsequent climber might claim that he (or she) was the first to conquer the peak. Henri Béraldi, who claimed to have invented the term "pyrénéisme," wrote succinctly at the end of the nineteenth century:

> The ideal Pyreneist must know at the same time how to climb, write and feel. If he writes without climbing, he can do nothing. If he climbs without writing, he leaves no trace. If, as a climber, his account is dry, he leaves a mere document.[2]

Travellers took notes as they travelled, jotting down new sights and sensations which they would later try to recall in the form of a more considered and reflective literary text. *Nulla dies sine linea* was Linnaeus' advice to all botanists – not a day without writing.[3] Sometimes travellers wrote up their diaries in the evening, when they had the time and leisure to reflect on the day just passed, but this practice was at one remove from complete immediacy. Scientists and later anthropologists similarly wrote notes in the field. But when they tried to recall them later, they could easily forget the exact details of the observation they had recorded, as when Alexander von Humboldt wrote a memory of Tenerife which he later realised had actually happened in Madeira.[4] Such travellers could not interpret the world except through the medium of written notes. Most often the written recollections of ordinary tourists were derivative or conventional; their memories were buried in clichés wrapped up in literary references. What interests us, however, are their memories, clichés and all, rather than the concrete details of what, where, and when. What we value here is their subjective impression, not an exact re-constitution of their actions and movements.

It follows that when we ask how men and women travellers reacted to one another en route, and indeed when we ask any question of the travel literature of the past, we can expect an answer on two levels. Firstly, there is the level of what travellers actually did, where they went, what they thought about the places they visited and what they decided to reveal about what felt about each other. Secondly, there is the level of their writing, with all its imaginative constructions of the landscape, mistakes, obfuscations and lack of transparency, inventions, and omissions (deliberate or accidental). In their written accounts, both men and women writers pushed their companions into the distant background. Perhaps the most striking and best-known omission was committed by Victor Hugo, who travelled through the Pyrenees in the summer of 1843, accompanied by his mistress Juliette Drouet. To protect his moral reputation, his account of the trip, published much later, made absolutely no mention of Drouet and gave the false impression that the writer was alone.[5] We must therefore distinguish clearly between practices and representations. Any study of nineteenth-century travel must also be a study of nineteenth-century travel literature, who wrote it, why and for whom.

Travelling to the Pyrenees

This chapter takes the example of travel to the Pyrenees, which attracted many French, Spanish, English, and American tourists during the nineteenth century, although the region's role in mountain tourism history has been unjustly over-shadowed by the conventional focus on the Alps. The Pyrenees enjoyed a milder climate than the Alps, and there were fewer glaciers there. An archipelago of popular spa resorts, such as Cauterets and Bagnères-de-Luchon, attracted thousands of visitors to the Pyrenees from all over the world in the summer season. Sea bathing at nearby Biarritz was a further draw card, especially after Empress Eugénie favoured it with her presence. In the second half of the century, the expansion of the railway network helped to reduce problems of access, making the Pyrenees a significant European tourist destination.

In the Pyrenees, the tourist gaze had multiple faces – romantic, sacred, ethnological among them – but in the case of the Pyrenean spa resorts, mass tourism was prompted by reasons of health. To cite only two among the most illustrious examples, the poet Lamartine came in 1840 for his rheumatism and the painter Delacroix was at Eaux-Bonnes in 1845 for tubercular laryngitis. Each watering place had its speciality, thus the waters at Bagnères-de-Bigorre were reputed to be laxative, diuretic, and good for the digestion, while others treated female infertility.[6] The spas provided a wide range of treatments, from a simple glass of water to total immersion. There were high and low pressure showers, descending and ascending showers and horizontal showers. The *Guides Joanne* gave the tourist a detailed analysis of the chemical contents of the water at each resort. Resident doctors prescribed waters, purges, bleedings, and detailed diets. The Pyrenees were reinvented as a cure for the illnesses of modern life. As a result, they acquired a reputation as a giant sanatorium, a place full of the sick and the frail, and this association was exacerbated after the visions of Bernadette Soubirous turned Lourdes into a world pilgrimage centre and a magnet for invalids worldwide.

Visiting the spa was not of course a full-time occupation, and tourists always had time on their hands. In fact, boredom was their main problem. Henry Blackburn, always a self-conscious Englishman abroad, mocked French tourists for not appreciating the scenery and for constantly complaining of "ennui." He deplored the faded dandies at Luchon, desperate to find a way to fill the interminable gap between *déjeuner* and *dîner*.[7] Despising the French for their laziness and unwillingness to do any climbing was a British obsession.

Tourists did not arrive in great numbers at the spa resorts just in order to improve their health. They went because the resorts were fashionable – some more so than others – and because the railways had made it easier to travel to them.[8] They went to see and to be seen, and there were many opportunities for self-exhibition, at dances, concerts, reading-rooms, the theatre, and the gambling salons. Social groups intermingled, the aristocracy with the provincial middle classes, the Spanish with the French. In the informal ambiance of the resort town, it was hard to exactly pinpoint everyone's social rank. When social distinctions became blurred, it was easier to play a role. Matrons scouted for an eligible husband for their daughter, older men were interested in an affair with a younger woman, and young women fell in love, like twenty-one-year-old George Sand in 1825, enamoured of Aurélien de Sèze in Cauterets. The temporary nature of their stay in the resorts, and their distance from the responsibilities and worries of real life, made "holiday romances" more likely. The spa resorts of Europe, according to Blackbourn, offered tourists a fantasy world; they were a kind of "Disneyland for the upper classes."[9]

I consider travellers to the region and their travel writing over three roughly chronological, but overlapping, stages. Firstly, in the early years of the nineteenth century, the scientific accounts of geologists and botanists were recorded for a male intellectual peer group, and obscured the presence of any woman on the expedition. Then, during the Romantic period, men and women travellers both projected onto the Pyrenean landscape their needs for rapture or horror, the picturesque or the sublime, a meeting with the exotic or the tranquil contemplation of the divine. Travel writing on the Pyrenees became more impressionistic, and the author's subjective responses were central to the account. This version of the genre allowed a space for female authors as well as female readers. Finally, the rising vogue for mountaineering celebrated masculinity and once again relegated female companions to obscurity.

I draw on a number of published travel accounts, by French, Spanish, British, and American travellers to the Pyrenees, focussing especially here on those written by women.[10] Women writers, like many of their male counterparts, often recorded their experiences of the Pyrenees with a small circle of friends and family in mind as their intended audience. But this was not always the case. Several women travellers were already accomplished authors, or if not they soon acquired a literary reputation in the genres in which women authors conventionally excelled (religious writing, travel, novels). Louisa Costello, for example, wrote history and travel books, and published in Charles Dickens' magazine *Household Words*.[11] Selina Bunbury wrote Evangelical tracts, fiction, and travel literature. Her writing career was inspired by the role model of novelist Fanny Burney, to whom she was related. The commercial success of Burney's novel *Evelina* (1778) encouraged Bunbury to become a novelist. Other women travellers were commissioned by a publisher or magazine. Thus the American journalist Amy Oakley, who must have been one of the first women to drive through Andorra in 1923, published seven travel books for The Century Press in New York. She wrote for initial publication, however, in *Harper's Magazine*.[12] Mary Eyre, who visited Andorra much earlier in the 1860s, repeatedly berated her London publisher, Richard Bentley, for sending her to such a place of poverty and hardship.[13] It was not unusual, therefore, for women to travel to the Pyrenees and write about the experience. The handful of women authors just mentioned crossed the frontier of gender expectations in another way: They were exceptional in their role as professional writers, for whom publishing was a career and a main source of income.

I focus on three women in particular. Selina Bunbury, who travelled as a widow in the early 1840s, wrote an account distinguished by her strong sense of British identity and Protestant principles.[14] Georgiana Chatterton travelled one year earlier with her husband, until she was traumatised by her encounter with exotic Spain.[15] My third example, Ann Lister, did not publish her own account. She was a rare female mountain climber, who clashed with her competitor, the Prince of Moskova, when he refused to acknowledge her achievement in climbing the Vignemale in 1838 (3,298 metres). All three stories reveal different aspects of female self-representation in a mountainous landscape, as companions, dependants, or competitors with male fellow-tourists.

From the *voyage savant* to the romantic Pyrenees

In the second half of the eighteenth century, the Age of Enlightenment discovered the Pyrenees. Scientists and surveyors travelled across the mountains to measure the height of the peaks and to collect scientific information. Geologists brought home fossils and rock specimens, while botanists accumulated examples of local flora. What had in previous centuries seemed marvellous but unknowable was in this period subjected to an unprecedented effort to record and classify a range of natural phenomena. The high peaks – and not just the foothills already frequented by the *habitués* of the spa resorts – were elements of a text which had to be deciphered and appropriated. Natural historians – mainly geologists – were conscientious scientists and, unlike later travellers, they were not inclined to indulge in personal recollections or reveal their subjective impressions. What excited them most of all was geological data, which they believed would either confirm or challenge prevailing theories about the early history of our planet. In the *voyage savant*, therefore, the traveller insisted on a scientific approach.

The scientific travellers to the Pyrenees were rivals, but they belonged to a homogeneous scientific community. They built on each other's work and reported to the same peer groups from France's elite scientific institutions. The botanist and mining engineer Bernard de Palassou, for example, reported to the royal Académie des Sciences, which authorised the publication of his work. Under the Republic, Ramond de Carbonnières reported his work to the Institut National. They formed an exclusively male community: When the cartographer François Pasumot made his second trip to Barèges, he was accompanied by Madame de Marnésia, but she only made a fleeting appearance in his account and presumably did not accompany him to the summit of the Pic du Midi de Bigorre.[16]

Their achievements depended on peer review, the financial backing of eminent aristocrats, and royal missions of a mainly utilitarian nature. Unlike later tourists who wrote for commercial purposes and for popular consumption, their audience was composed of fellow-intellectuals. They shared a common cultural capital and attacked similar research questions. When Palassou laced his account with references to Ovid, Livy, or Caesar, he was drawing on a classical culture that would have been familiar to his male educated peers. They frequently cited and criticised each other, operating within a closed network of inter-textuality.

By the early nineteenth century, however, European sensibilities were changing. Travellers now wanted to differentiate themselves from the dry scientific treatises of the geologists. They placed a new value on subjective emotions, and their writing was intended to express their inner feelings. Instead of scientific discourse, they aimed to provide amusing reflections and sentimental asides. Later in the century, visitors produced volumes of anecdotic memoirs whose whimsical nature was advertised in their titles: Fragments, impressions, *arabesques, bluettes* (trifles).[17] They privileged the author's subjectivity. Thus François Albaniac, who travelled with his family from Agen to Bagnères in the summer of 1818, pointed out that "I didn't undertake this journey to study the mountains; so I didn't travel through them with the nervous and erudite curiosity of the mineralogist or the botanist." Geologists were far too serious, whereas Albaniac promised his readers that he would remain in "la domaine de la gaîeté" (in cheerful territory).[18] And yet, in spite of such explicit attempts to sketch a new discourse of the Pyrenean landscape, men's tourist accounts continued to incorporate the scientific representations which preceded them. Even Albaniac, who promised his readers fun rather than science, owned a mineralogical collection.[19]

Romantics of any generation could imagine the Pyrenean forest populated by spirits and mythological figures. A few, who were more practically minded, brought their own. For example, when the Barcelona businessman José Puigdollers travelled with his photographer Pedro Abarca to the valle de Arán in 1902, he imagined a countryside full of nymphs. Then he actually proceeded to photograph them, and the glossy art book they produced contained many images of nymphlike figures.[20] I imagine the ladies concerned were the wives of the two travellers, posing obediently beside rivers and waterfalls or frolicking in the foliage. The author and his illustrator had staged their very own version of the "pinturesco."

In contrast to the exclusively masculine genre of the scientific treatise, the new literary fashions of the nineteenth century opened up a space for women writers and their audiences. The generations of Romanticism experienced "l'éxoticisme des hauteurs" (the exoticism of great heights), and searched for the experience of the romantic sublime and the contemplation of the infinite. Romantic tourists, inspired by the poetry of Byron and Ossian, sought out ruined chateaus and the effects of moonlight upon the snowy slopes. The mountains induced a dreamlike state and a sense of reflective melancholy. The tourists' visit was not complete unless they had experienced the violence of a Pyrenean storm.

Women travel writers in this period were ladies of a social elite, members of the aristocracy or the upper middle class. As a result, asking "Who Carried the Luggage?" in the Pyrenees in the mid-nineteenth century is almost a redundant question. No lady or gentleman of any rank would carry their own luggage: This was the task of servants and mountain guides. The gendered discourse of travel writing in the mountains was always underpinned by a strict sense of social hierarchy. Women travelled with a brother or husband, together with a maid and valet; occasionally a woman travelled with a female companion; rarely, as in the case of Mary Eyre, a woman travelled "alone," that is, accompanied only by a (male) guide. The intrepid Eyre rode over the Pyrenees into Andorra with a male guide but still referred to herself as "a single unprotected woman."[21] It is more pertinent to ask: Over rough terrain, who carried the ladies? One answer was the *chaise à porteurs*, a sedan chair lifted by four strong men, often much admired for their physique and great agility.

Selina Bunbury and the problems of female travel

Selina Bunbury travelled to the Pyrenees in 1843. Her account reveals the frustrations inherent in travelling as a woman forever reliant on male companions. Bunbury was born in Ireland in 1802, the daughter of an Anglican parson. Her two-volume account outlines a very leisurely itinerary. After arriving in Paris from London via Calais, she took a boat ride along the Loire, making random stops at chateaux, and inserting historical anecdotes related to them in her narrative. From Nantes, she took a steamboat to Bordeaux. Hence she did not arrive in the Pyrenees proper until page 164, and she did not leave Pau until page 201. By this time it was late in the season (September–October), but she nevertheless visited the fashionable destinations of Cauterets, Bagnères, and Luchon. There is a story, which is probably fictional, running through her travel narrative: She was invited to stay with friends in Pau but, finding they had left, she went in search of them in a series of Pyrenean spa resorts. This novelistic device is a transparent attempt to counteract the inherently discontinuous nature of travelogues. Bunbury returned to Pau to "discover" that her fictional friends had never left England.

Bunbury published on Irish themes and the evils of "Jesuitism," as well as producing evangelical fiction for the Society for the Propagation of Christian Knowledge. Her travel literature, as this repertoire suggests, was imbued with an earnest Protestantism and Sabbatarianism. She was uneasy about travelling on a Sunday, and her Protestant sensibility took offence both at French anticlericalism and at the "idolatrous worship of the Virgin Mary" which she encountered in France.[22] Her life as a traveller and writer did not conform to contemporary gender expectations: She was a professional woman who supported herself through her prolific writing, and commercial considerations were always paramount in her career.

Bunbury had a series of guides and male protectors on her journey, whom she discreetly (and perhaps fictitiously) named as Monsieur M., Jacques Périgord, and Senhor José. All are chivalrous and considerate towards her, and they habitually defer to whatever Madame wishes. Yet Bunbury is frustrated even by their generosity, because she knows that the freedom it gives her is an illusion; the underlying social reality is that she cannot travel anywhere without male company. She does not analyse the reasons for this, and yet she knows it to be true that in France a woman cannot travel alone.

Monsieur M. was an extremely unprepossessing companion to whom Bunbury felt obliged to attach herself *faute de mieux*. He was elderly, a semi-invalid on a crutch who suffered from rheumatism. Because of his frailty and physical handicap, his ability to act as a protector in any emergency was seriously in question. Nevertheless, he escorted Bunbury from Paris to Pau, and then she persuaded him to continue with her as far as Cauterets to take the waters. M., Bunbury conceded, was always thoughtful, or in the language of the time he "had complaisance for the ladies." He agreed at her insistence that he would not smoke a pipe in her presence.[23]

Bunbury represented herself as a bold and independent traveller, and she occasionally went touring without M.'s company, but this was exceptional and she wrote that "it is something quite unrecorded in the annals of French existence, for a woman to take a walk alone."[24] In Bordeaux, she was surprised when people asked where her husband was: In fact she was travelling as a widow.[25] She thrived on making new discoveries on her own: "How delightful it is," she wrote on arriving in Pau, "to find out beauties unpremeditatedly, or [to] which you are not led by a hired functionary."[26]

Monsieur M. was no hired functionary, but rather a single gentleman who perhaps appreciated her company, but when Bunbury wanted to make excursions from Cauterets, she needed to hire a professional guide. She was unwilling to take a *chaise à porteurs* to the lac de Gaube, and so she enlisted the services of Jacques, who also helped her cross the Tourmalet on a pony, and accompanied her on a walk to St Sauveur. The responsibilities of this male companion were rather different from those of Monsieur M., and certainly demanded more physical exertion. Jacques had to hire and look after the horses and help Bunbury mount and dismount. It was his job to give money to peasants who provided the travellers with shelter and bread to eat en route. He had to disentangle her veil when it caught on some thorny vegetation, he had to grab a bonnet that came off during a ride, and retrace his steps to fetch a cloak that Bunbury had left behind.[27] Bunbury realised that she was a demanding mistress, and wrote:

> We certainly do often try the temper of gentlemen in travelling; for which reason I conjecture few travelling parties lead to a union for the journey of life.[28]

Jacques was of course paid for his patience, and there was never any question that his association with Bunbury was anything more than a temporary working arrangement. After they parted company, Bunbury felt a desperate need to be alone again in her private space.[29] In spite of her companions' attentions and devotion, she felt the contradictions of her position as a female traveller. When planning to ride over the Tourmalet, she first asked Jacques if it was practical for her to do it alone (in other words, with him). He nonchalantly replied "Chacun est libre" (Everyone is free to choose), which irritated Bunbury enormously, because she knew the exact limits of her so-called freedom of choice, writing: "Oh! How ridiculous to declare that every one is free, when the person addressed feels the bondage that never can and never must be cast off."[30]

Her final companion, Senhor José, was courteous and obedient. In fact Bunbury almost tried to convert him to Protestantism. Up to a point, Bunbury respected his Catholic beliefs: When José attended Mass, she simply stayed at home. Bunbury's religious convictions, however, could not easily be submerged. Travelling on Sunday gave her a bad conscience. At Loudervielle (Hautes-Pyrénées), she stopped and took out the prayer book which she always carried with her, and read the Sunday service to herself, which made her feel less homesick for England.[31] At Osse (Pyrénées-Atlantiques), she took José to a Calvinist service in the local Protestant church, but both were disappointed by it. Bunbury concluded that there must be a great difference between English Protestant worship and French Calvinism (or, as she called it, Presbyterianism). José unfortunately would never experience true inspiration unless he went to an Anglican service.[32]

Selina Bunbury was a determined and independent traveller with strongly held religious views. She was well served in the Pyrenees by her male companions, whether casually met or paid to escort her on excursions. They accompanied her, helped her on and off her pony, fetched her clothing and even agreed to attend a Protestant church service. When she asked M. to stop smoking in her presence, he did so. Never, in her account, did any man refuse to do what she asked of him. And yet she resented the relationship, because it was forced upon her unwillingly by social convention. Men wanted to please and obey her, but the freedom they offered her was circumscribed, and she experienced it as a burden and a fraud.

Georgiana Chatterton and the disturbing otherness of Spain

Like Selina Bunbury, Lady Georgiana Chatterton was a novelist and travel writer, but unlike Bunbury, she was sympathetic towards Catholicism and later became a convert. Her account of the Pyrenees, published in 1843, combined elements of several different genres.[33] She began with what she called "carriage notes," which recorded her impressions more or less immediately as she travelled. Hence she longed for a paved carriageway which would give her a smooth ride and allow her to take notes in comfort en route. She wrote in semi-diary format with some dated entries, and her accounts were interspersed with long historical anecdotes about, for example, Gaston Phébus in Béarn or Dame Carcas in Carcassonne. Why do people travel?, she asked herself, responding that it must be for the excitement of new scenes, to get away from the cares of housekeeping and, for those who write, "the hope of amusing and interesting others" – her reference to housekeeping implied a female readership.[34]

She included some of her own sketches, along with poetry which she quoted often, from Ariosto and Tasso, Tennyson or Young's *Night Thoughts*.[35] She knew Italian, and she travelled with Spanish books. She could also converse in French and relied on Froissart's fourteenth-century chronicles for historical information. At the same time, she referred to French and English travel guides. Literature, history, poetry, and travel writing in various languages thus informed her impressions. But none of these resources fully prepared her for her Spanish encounter. As we shall see, her excursion across the border was an emotionally strained experience, which her husband's presence did not alleviate.

Chatterton was normally a very resourceful traveller. She travelled by *diligence* to Bayonne and San Sebastián, she went to the Lac d'Oô on horseback fitted with a side-saddle, she crossed the Port de Venasque by *chaise à porteurs* carried by two men, with two more as relief team,[36] and continued into Val d'Aran by the same method. She also took a *chaise* with four men to visit the lac de Gaube.[37] At Argelès and elsewhere for short excursions, she took a donkey.[38] The energy, vigour, and adaptability suggested by this varied itinerary serves to throw her future prostration into greater relief.

Chatterton travelled in a party of four, made up of herself, her husband William who was referred to almost anonymously as "W." her personal maid and her husband's "man," Bénoit. Her references to these companions expressed their place on the social hierarchy; her maid was never even named in her account. Even her husband had only a shadowy presence for most of the journey. Wherever they sought lodgings (and the search for accommodation is a recurring problem throughout the book), they required five rooms. Chatterton and her husband presumably did not share a bedroom, since we are told at one point that he had his own dressing room.[39] Chatterton wrote using the plural "we," and normally the whole party went on excursions as a group. In Paris, Versailles, Fontainebleau and the castles of the Loire, for example, they all visited the sights together. They went to Mass together and they went shopping in Bayonne together.[40] Even when Chatterton does not specifically mention the presence of her husband, we can therefore assume that he was there.

As Marjorie Morgan usefully reminds us, travellers heading south from Britain who crossed national borders like the Pyrenees had to endure a long list of nuisances, which included: Fleas, bugs, cockroaches, mosquitoes, foreign toilets, seasickness, diarrhoea, checkpoints, customs officials, document delays, currency changes, tea without milk, and unpleasant people spitting on the ground.[41] All of the above, except seasickness, applied in Spain. By disrupting daily rituals and unsettling the tourist, foreign travel made travellers acutely aware of national differences. Their national consciousness was confronted and aroused.

Georgiana Chatterton found the Spanish climate very exacting. In the valle de Arán, she endured scorching sun and a "five hours fly-tormented ride."[42] Chatterton thought the benefits of foreign climates were recklessly exaggerated, writing:

> I do not think the air of France, north or south, or indeed that of Germany, or even Italy, a bit more exhilarating to the spirits than the sweet breezes of our own dear England.[43]

This was admittedly a reflection recorded in her most homesick phase, when she was laid up exhausted in St Sauveur. She went on to conclude that foreign climates were very prejudicial to British constitutions, mainly because they subjected the English to extremes of hot and cold. British travellers' comments on the scorching heat of Spain re-enforce Katherine Turner's insights into nineteenth-century British middle-class travel.[44] Whereas British identity had previously been associated with eccentric individualism, now it was rather embedded in national values of moderation and reasonableness. On the continent, in contrast, the natives were too easily carried away by their passions and were prone to hot-tempered violence.

In the mid-nineteenth century Pyrenees, travellers were often asked to pay a special levy either to their coachmen or the local militia (*miquelets*), to guarantee their immunity from highway robbery. This was protection money, enabling brigands to take their cut without putting themselves to the inconvenience of actually robbing anybody. The fear of bandits persisted, however, as Georgiana Chatterton attested. Approaching the Pyrenees from Pau, she dreamed of Spain as a land of serenades and romantic lovers. She responded, perhaps, to the Carmen-and-Don-Juan stereotyping of Spain which sexualised and orientalised the country's image and which was taking shape in exactly this period.[45] She loved the colourful dress of Catalonia and Aragon, describing local costumes in some detail, the long red caps worn by men in the valle de Arán, their brown jackets and culottes, and their blue stockings with coloured garters. In Aragon, she enthused over the women's high conical hats with wide brims and tassels, the green richly embroidered velvet coats, brocade satin waistcoats, red silk scarves worn around the waist, brown striped velvet culottes, garters, blue stockings, and sandals (*espadrilles*).[46] Spain, for her, was a sartorial feast. But at the same time as she tried to sustain her Spanish fantasies, she had a feeling that bandits were lurking behind every rock.

On the way from Pau to the lac d'Oô, she was alarmed to meet Spanish peasants who had "banditti countenances and long red caps."[47] A little later, at Vielha in the valle de Arán, she had a frightening experience which coloured the rest of her trip. The town was full of blackened ruins from the recent Carlist Wars and, re-enforcing its sinister appearance, locals told her stories of plunder, murder and cruelty in those wars.[48] Perhaps Chatterton had been reading too many Gothic novels, but she felt surrounded in Vielha by a "banditti-looking crowd" which would not leave her party alone. She felt hemmed in and was afraid some violence might be done.[49] The food, she reported, was disgusting and the atmosphere one of "ominous gloom." The fact that she had a male "protector" in the form of her husband is not mentioned and seems irrelevant to her deteriorating state of mind. Attitudes to Spain could be ambiguous and unstable. Chatterton's original excitement turned to a fear of being encircled by bandits. She wrote:

> the intense pleasure I felt at getting safe back into France again cannot be described; and yet I was equally enchanted at setting my foot on Spanish ground when we entered Aragon.[50]

In Chatterton's case, the "tourist gaze" was reciprocated; in Vielha she felt she was being watched, surrounded, and intimidated by the locals. The tourist gaze, as Darya Maoz reminds us, does not travel only in one direction; there is a mutual gaze, in which the locals observe the tourists, and both influence each other's behaviour.[51]

From this moment on, Chatterton started to feel weary and increasingly homesick. The trip to Vielha had left her shaken, and both physically and emotionally exhausted. She travelled on but, at St Sauveur, she felt tired and unwell, took to her bed and did not go on any more long excursions, even missing out on visiting the popular site of Gavarnie, which was a must-see destination for nineteenth-century tourists, and is today part of the Gavarnie-Monte Perdido UNESCO World Heritage site.

Chatterton frequently felt too weak to accompany her husband William, who set off alone to climb various peaks of increasing difficulty: First the Pic de Begons (2068m) and then the Pic du Midi (2877m). Since Chatterton did not feel well enough to accompany him, "W." wrote his own descriptions of these excursions, and Chatterton included his accounts vicariously in her book.[52] Chatterton increasingly suffered headaches and fatigue and, in Ax-les-Thermes in mid-September, she confessed to being depressed and irritable.[53] Clearly traumatised by Vielha, she longed for "the easy and beaten track of Italy," and she now admitted to suffering from "a sort of mountain surfeit."[54] In fact, she even gave up the idea of visiting Italy, and the party returned to Paris from Avignon.

Her account illustrates the way in which the otherness of Spain could be contradictory and problematic. On one hand, it seemed enlivening and enchanting, but at the same time it created fear and insecurity. As for her husband, Chatterton refers quite cursorily to "W," and in her moment of greatest crisis he remains completely absent from her story. Later, their companionship takes the form of co-writing a section of the book, as W. fills in some gaps with accounts of his own ascents and excursions. It would be unfair to consider this as a form of marital plagiarism, since Chatterton always makes it clear where her own text ends and that of W. begins. This is rather a rare case of collaborative writing, brought about only by the extreme circumstances of Chatterton's poor health and prostration.

Mountaineers

In one sense, W.'s ascent of the peaks while his wife stayed in the comfort of the nearest spa resort conformed to a familiar pattern in the mid-nineteenth-century Pyrenees: Higher altitudes were male territory, while women preferred less strenuous excursions in the foothills. Mountaineering, which entered its golden age in the Pyrenees in the 1850s and 1860s, demonstrated masculine values of physical endurance and athleticism. At the same time, the mountains were an arena of intense male competition, as individuals sought the distinction of making the first ascent or "conquest" of those surrounding peaks which still enjoyed "virgin" status. This was the heroic age of *pyrénéisme*. The story of the Pyrenees confirms Michael Reidy's insights into mountaineering in the Alps, demonstrating that gender was codified by altitude.[55] In the Pyrenees, terrain higher than about 1500 metres was masculine territory, and a hyper-masculine discourse informed the genre of the "ascent narrative." Women preferred the foothills and the social life of Cauterets or Luchon.

This is not to say that women never intruded into this masculine world. Feminist historians have been at pains to establish that women *did* climb mountains, defying conventional gender expectations, ignoring medical advice, and going far beyond the conventional routine of taking the waters, enjoying gentle walks, and sketching. Clare Roche, while echoing the literature's undue obsession with Alpine scenarios, has nevertheless successfully brought such independent women into focus.[56] Female climbers were still considered oddities. Even in the 1890s, the *Bulletin Pyrénéen* of the Club Alpin français (Pau section) always noted how many women accompanied each recorded excursion. Although women excursionists were by then commonplace, they were still counted and listed as though they formed an extraneous category. On the occasion of the Club Alpin's national congress in Pau in 1897, delegates were asked to divide into three streams: Firstly, the experienced mountaineers, secondly modest mountaineers, and thirdly cyclists and those who wished to travel by coach. Women (29 attended the congress) were expected to fall into the last category, described by the organisers as "the dilettanti of the mountains, more interested in the search for artistic impressions than the satisfactions of sporting vanity."[57]

Although female climbers could sometimes be encountered at higher altitudes, women rarely wrote about their exploits in the same public way that men considered essential. Much of the correspondence and journals of women climbers was published posthumously, if they were published at all, and this goes a long way towards explaining women's invisibility. The first woman to climb Mont Blanc was a 28-year-old local woman, Marie Paradis in 1809, but because she was a peasant in a world of upper- and middle-class gentlemen amateurs, and because she did not or could not write about her own climb, the event was disregarded by later mountaineers.[58] The difficult experiences of women on the high peaks, and the significance of leaving or not leaving written testimony to their presence there, are fully demonstrated in the Pyrenees by the case of Ann Lister.

Ann Lister was a Halifax heiress who inherited her uncle's wealth in 1826, and went to live in Paris.[59] She made her first visit to the Pyrenees in 1829, when she was 40 years old, accompanied by the British ambassador's wife Lady Stuart. In 1838, she returned with her companion Anne Walker, determined to climb the Vignemale. In Luz she hired two guides for 50 francs per day, and in addition she paid Henry Cazaux, an experienced mountain guide, 20 francs to take her to the summit. The party of four reached the summit and, according to custom, celebrated the achievement with a glass of wine, wrote their names and the date in a bottle and placed it under a stone cairn.

Cazaux, however, was the servant of two masters, and had already been hired to climb the Vignemale by the Prince of Moskova, the son of Napoleon I's ill-fated Marshal Ney.[60] The Prince's party arrived a few days after Lister's ascent, unaware that she had already made the climb, and intending to be the first to reach the summit. Cazaux did not want to lose his fee for a historic climb, and therefore let the Prince believe that Lister had not personally reached the top of the mountain, and that only her guides, including himself, had actually made it to the summit. When the Prince eventually reached the top, Cazaux did not show him the bottle under the cairn which would have told him that he was not, as he imagined, the first to arrive.

The Prince's claim to be the first to climb the Vignemale spurred Lister into action. She refused to pay the duplicitous Cazaux, and demanded a written statement to attest that she had in fact been the first climber to reach the summit. She persuaded Latapie, a lawyer from Lourdes, to draw up a document (*certificat de conquête*) for the Prince to sign, recognising that Lister had reached the top under her own steam. Cazaux's deception had been exposed and he had little option but to sign while another of Lister's guides, Jean-Pierre Charles, witnessed it. Lister was vindicated, the Prince felt humiliated, and Cazaux was finally paid for his services.

The clear difference between men and women climbers lay in the fact that women very rarely wrote about their ascents, whereas men always did; writing a public record of the climb to the summit was an essential part of making the claim to have been the first climber there. Without a publication, their story would always remain open to question, unsubstantiated by an authoritative source. Eventually in 1842 the Prince published his account in Paris in the highly prestigious *Revue des Deux Mondes*. His story gave few details and he did not mention any of his guides, giving the public to believe that he had been the first "conqueror" of the Vignemale. By the time the Prince's article appeared, Ann Lister had sadly died while travelling in the Caucasus. She clearly had little intention of issuing any public documentary record, beyond the certificate that she had been provoked into organising in 1838. Her papers were discovered almost by chance in Halifax Municipal Library by Vivienne Ingham, a retired local historian. Ingham visited the Pyrenees and collected oral evidence from locals which supported Lister's version of the exploit.

Conclusion

The case studies briefly presented here illustrate a variety of relationships between men and women who were fellow tourists, ranging from companionship to frustration and outright hostile competition. Invisibility remained the norm: In their travel writings, men wrote little about the wives, daughters, or mistresses who accompanied them; women recorded only sparse comments about male companions and husbands, sometimes not even naming them. Both barely recognised the presence of their own servants.

The mountain guide was the most invisible traveller of all. He looked after the mules, tipped the locals, advised on the route, gave eyewitness testimony to the success of a climb. He carried the backpacks, the climbing equipment, scientific instruments, and botanical specimens for male scientists, and a considerable amount of clothing and accessories for his female employers. Sometimes, the guide also carried his own employer. Occasionally, writers expressed their gratitude but sometimes their rapport with their guide was less than cordial. A guide could, in extreme circumstances, save a climber's life. For women travellers, his presence was essential – without his assistance, paradoxically, a traveller like Mary Eyre could not claim to travel "alone." Usually, however, his contribution and that of other subordinates were obscured. When the Duchesse de Berry climbed to La Brèche de Roland in 1828, she was accompanied by a retinue of no fewer than 30 followers and servants. When she wished to carve her name in the rock, there was a "secretary" at hand to perform the task.[61] The gendered discourse of mountain travel was always predicated on deep-seated assumptions of social hierarchy, which left lower-class companions nameless and out of sight.

This study has further indicated the gap between practices and representations.[62] Our understanding of gender relations in the course of travel is dependent on what the participants decided to include or to forget in their travel accounts. We need to take account not only of who wrote for whom, but what literary conventions framed their narratives. In the early years of the nineteenth century, male geologists in the Pyrenees wrote dry scientific treatises, which put the rock strata at centre stage and left their women collecting floral specimens in the foothills. Later, women tourists wrote more subjective accounts of their travels, in which husbands like "W." never truly solidified as characters in the drama. Even later, the ascent narrative celebrated masculine ingenuity and fortitude, outlining the dangers and physical hardships endured by mountaineers; although women occasionally emulated them, they published very little to advertise the fact. Writing about it, as Henri Béraldi had intimated, was just as important as actually being there.

Notes

1 Bertho-Lavenir, C. (1999) *La Roue et le Stylo: comment nous sommes devenus touristes.* Paris: Odile Jacob: 13–61.
2 Béraldi, H. (2001–2003) *Cent Ans des Pyrénées,* 7 vols. Pau: Princi Negue. [1898–1904], 1: 6.
3 Bourguet, M.-N. (2010) "A Portable World: The Notebooks of European Travellers (18th to 19th Centuries)," *Intellectual History Review,* 20(3): 380.
4 Bourguet (2010): 399.
5 Hugo, V. (1890) *En voyage: Alpes et Pyrénées.* Paris: Victor Hugo Illustré.
6 Saint-Lèbe, N. (2002) *Les Femmes à la découverte des Pyrénées.* Toulouse: Privat: 57.
7 Blackburn, H. (1881) *The Pyrenees: A Description of Summer Life at French Watering Places.* London: Sampson Low, Marston, Searle & Rivington: 178.
8 Blackbourn, D. (2002) "Fashionable Spa Towns in Nineteenth-Century Europe," in *Water, Leisure, Culture: European Historical Perspectives.* Susan C. Anderson & Bruce H. Tabb (eds.). Oxford: Berg: 9–21.
9 Blackbourn (2002): 15.
10 It is impossible to estimate how many travel accounts of the Pyrenees were written and/or published in Europe and the USA during the long nineteenth century. My own study, which in no way aims at being comprehensive, is based on 58 accounts published between the 1780s and 1927, in English, French, Catalan, or Castilian Spanish, excluding commercial travel guides. Twelve of those, or 20 per cent, were written by women. Whereas, in my study. Accounts by male travellers were fairly evenly distributed throughout the period, accounts by women tended to cluster in the period between 1830 and 1850 – a period closely associated with the influence of European romanticism. See: Lyons, M. (2018) *The Pyrenees in the Modern Era: Reinventions of a Landscape, 1775–2012.* London: Bloomsbury.
11 Stuart Costello, L. (1844) *Béarn and the Pyrenees: A Legendary Tour to the Country of Henri Quatre,* 2 vols. London: Richard Bentley.
12 Oakley, A. (1924) *Hill-towns of the Pyrenees.* London: John Long.
13 Eyre, M. (1865) *Over the Pyrenees into Spain.* London: Richard Bentley.
14 Bunbury, S. (1844) *Rides in the Pyrenees,* 2 vols. London: British Library.
15 Chatterton, G. (1843) *The Pyrenees with Excursions into Spain,* 2 vols. London: Saunders & Otley.
16 Pasumot, F. (1797) *Voyages physiques dans les Pyrénées en 1788 et 1789.* Paris: Le Clère: 90.
17 Tastu, A. et al. (1842) *Alpes et Pyrénées: arabesques littéraires, composées de nouvelles historiques, anecdotes, descriptions, chroniques et récits divers.* Paris: Lehuby; Anon (Alexandre de Metz-Noblat) (1858) *Bluettes: Constantinople, Egypte, Rome, Venise, Espagne, Pyrénées, par un touriste.* Nancy: Vagner & Paris: Douniol.
18 Albaniac, F. (1818) *Voyage pittoresque et sentimental à Bagnères-Adour, département des Hautes-Pyrénées.* Nantes: Mellinet-Malassis: 13–14.
19 Albaniac (1818): 34.

20 Puigdollers y Maciá, J. (1903) *Por los Pirineos: impresiones de un viaje,* illustrated by Pedro C. Abarca. Barcelona: Mercurio.
21 Eyre (1865): 89.
22 Bunbury (1844): 1:209 and 2:96–97.
23 Bunbury (1844): 1:52–53 and 283.
24 Bunbury (1844): 1:97.
25 Bunbury (1844): 1:162.
26 Bunbury (1844): 1:179.
27 Bunbury (1844): 1:248 and 2:25–26 and 42.
28 Bunbury (1844): 2:114.
29 Bunbury (1844): 2:42.
30 Bunbury (1844): 1:296.
31 Bunbury (1844): 2:105–106.
32 Bunbury (1844): 2:278–285.
33 Chatterton (1843).
34 Chatterton (1843): 2:43.
35 Chatterton (1843): 1:275 & 2:159, 163, 292, 299–300, 320.
36 Chatterton (1843): 1:339.
37 Chatterton (1843): 2:100.
38 Chatterton (1843): 2:30.
39 Chatterton (1843): 2:40.
40 Chatterton (1843):182–183.
41 Morgan, M. (2001) *National Identities and Travel in Victorian Britain.* Basingstoke: Palgrave Macmillan: 12.
42 Chatterton (1843): 2:6.
43 Chatterton (1843): 2:43–44.
44 Turner, K. (2001) *British Travel Writers in Europe, 1750–1800: Authorship, Gender and National Identity.* Aldershot: Ashgate: 202.
45 Gabilondo, J. (2008) "On the Inception of Western Sex as Orientalist Theme Park: Tourism and Desire in Nineteenth-Century Spain (On Carmen and Don Juan as Femme Fatale and Latin Lover)," in *Spain Is (Still) Different: Tourism and Discourse in Spain.* Eugenia Afinoguénova & Jaume Martí-Olivella (eds.). Lanham, MD: 19–61.
46 Chatterton (1843): 1:375 & 2:108.
47 Chatterton (1843): 1:329.
48 Chatterton (1843): 2:9–10.
49 Chatterton (1843): 1:378–379.
50 Chatterton (1843): 2:14.
51 Maoz, D. (2006) "The Mutual Gaze," *Annals of Tourism Research*, 33(1): 221–239.
52 Chatterton (1843): 2:55, 75 and 110.
53 Chatterton (1843): 2:73–74 and 215.
54 Chatterton (1843): 2:74 and 99.
55 Reidy, M.S. (2015) "Mountaineering, Masculinity and the Male Body in Mid-Victorian Britain," *OSIRIS*, 30: 158–181; see also Hansen, P.H. (2013) *The Summits of Modern Man: Mountaineering after the Enlightenment.* Cambridge, MA: Harvard University Press, although neither of these works discusses the Pyrenees.
56 Roche, C. (2013) "Women Climbers, 1850–1900: A Challenge to Male Hegemony?" *Sport in History*, 33(3): 236–259.
57 Club Alpin Français, *Bulletin Pyrénéen*, février 1898, no. 8bis, souvenir issue of the Congress, 17.
58 Hansen (2013): 140–141; Reidy (2015): 166; Clark, R. (1953) "Chapter 8" in *The Victorian Mountaineers.* London: Batsford.

59 I draw on two main sources for the Ann Lister story: Feliu, M. (1977) *La Conquista del Pirineo: una historia del pirineismo*; and Saint-Lèbe, N. (2002) *Les Femmes à la découverte des Pyrénées*. Toulouse: Privat.

60 Ney was executed by the Bourbons in 1815 after going over to Napoleon after his return from Elba.

61 Saint-Lèbe (2002): 70–72.

62 Changing representations of the Pyrenean landscape are treated more fully in Lyons, M. (2018) *The Pyrenees in the Modern Era: Reinventions of a Landscape, 1775–2012*. London: Bloomsbury.

10 Enamoured men – confident women

Gender relations and the travel journal of Lilla von Bulyovszky (1833–1909)

Ute Sonnleitner

Lilla von Bulyovszky, born in 1833 in Klausenburg/Cluj-Napoca (Austria Hungary – today Romania), was a famous actress of her time, appreciated for her work, adored for her good looks. After her retirement from stage, she started a second career and translated more than 250 theatre pieces. In 1909 she died in Graz.[1] Bulyovszky's multilingual abilities on stage made her exceptional. Her attempts to establish herself in German-speaking theatres as well as on Hungarian stages (she declared Hungarian to be her mother tongue), started with an extensive voyage. Leaving Pest in 1856, Bulyovszky went to Vienna, Munich, and Paris and returned via Brussels, Hamburg, Berlin, Cologne, and the Rhineland. Her main destination was Paris – or at least the main chapters of her travel description *Mein Reisetagebuch* (*My Travel Diary*) were dedicated to the French capital and to the individuals she met there. From Pest to Paris she travelled alone; Alexandre Dumas accompanied parts of her further journey. In remembrance of that trip, Dumas, who was very much impressed by the young actress, wrote the novel *Ein Liebesabenteuer* (*An Amorous Adventure*).[2] The travelling route had been determined by various sights, which she visited with excitement. In Paris it was the entertainment business that caught her attention; she visited various theatres in all her destinations and met with colleagues like "la Rachel" and Wilhelmine Schröder-Devrient. The latter reinforced her decision to start acting in German. Thus Bulyovszky's travelling intentions were made up of a mixture of – private and professional – reasons.

The travelogue, published immediately after her return to Pest, shows the author's awareness of her position as a working woman.[3] In it, Bulyovszky reflected on her living – and working – conditions when describing her numerous acquaintances. Men and women joined sections of her journey and gender relations occur repeatedly as a negotiated theme. The reports on the meetings were shaped by emotions, in which love enjoyed an especially privileged position.

Reflecting on the fact that in Bulyovszky's days it was not seen as at all appropriate for a woman to travel alone, the question arises: How did movement influence social interactions? Therefore, it is suggested to read the common movement of travel companions as an "other place" in the Foucauldian sense.

Such a "heterotopia" is shaped by special regularities; social conditions are represented in a compact, condensed manner. In this chapter, the interaction of travellers and the impact of "other places'" will be examined. The (self-)perceptions of a working woman and traveller, her interpretations of her companions – and through Dumas' novel a companion's gaze on her – will be investigated and will thus allow insights into contemporary assessments concerning mobility and its intersectional implications.

"Travel-intersections": methodical and theoretical considerations on travel-research, emotions, and gender

> Arguably, we could identify those sharing a train, bus, plane or other journey as a 'community of occasion; [...] enjoyable and tense journeys are often shared experiences that promote emotions and emotional experience between individuals who would otherwise not come into contact with one another.[4]

This quote by Letherby and Reynolds marks one of the rare attempts to examine travellers' interactions while on the move, focusing on gender (and emotions) as a main category of analysis.[5] A few other investigations dealt with encounters among travellers but didn't place an emphasis on the meaning of their shared experiences while on the move.[6]

Compared to the actual movement, travellers' behaviour in their temporary destinations has found much more interest.[7] The gaze on the "Other" was examined and detected as a means of constituting the "self": The persons and cultures described functioned like a mirror that reflected ideas and thoughts, and thereby played an immense role in the process of a writers' self-positioning.[8] Authors like literary scholar and linguist Mary Louise Pratt deconstructed the "European" gaze, and its colonial interlacing.[9] Members of Critical Whiteness studies showed how deeply racialised many descriptions were and how they influenced the picture of the described.[10]

Other focuses seemingly upstaged investigations on interactions of travellers. The lack of research may also be explained by the sources to some extent – or, to put it more explicitly: By the absence of adequate material. Travellers often concentrated on their destinations when they reported on their journeys.[11] When thematising travel-experiences, topics/elements such as landscape and transport vehicles were of greater interest than fellow passengers.[12] However, there are sources that describe travel companions, their behaviour, and the writers' interactions with them. Their shared movement made them a special community. Concentrating on the gaze on the "moving Other" opens new perspectives. It promises new insights, not by fixating on the "exotic native"[13] – and thus perpetuating narratives – but by addressing the "strangers" moving in and through landscapes and examining how they are described in their travel companion's travelogues.

Moving places of gender

Both the person looking (and describing) and the person who is looked at (and described) are travelling, and their common movement creates a special space around them. Sometimes this space is framed by a "real" room or "place" (let it be a railway carriage, the inside of a horse-drawn coach, a bus, a car, and so on), sometimes it is construed by the common locomotion.[14] The changing land-scapes, impressions, and feelings are described to create an exceptional state: An impression of dissolution.[15] Apparently, stable rules are questioned, and undreamt of possibilities emerge in these "heterotopian," "places beyond all places."[16] What consequences arise from that assumption for those who sojourn in these places? How do relations develop under the influence of a shared moving room, what role does the common movement play? What factors were of importance in their interactions?

Peoples' interactions are shaped by a whole range of various and different factors, and categories of social difference in particular play an immense role.[17] It is the aim of this chapter to investigate intersections in the "other place" of shared movement.[18] Additionally "gender," specifically the representation and perception of gender in the mobile "other place" of travel are highlighted, although they are only understandable within the interplay of other factors, such as age, social rank/class, sexual orientation, race, ethnicity, and so on.[19] Emotions are of crucial importance in this context.[20] There is a strong and perpetual intermingling with the diverse categories of difference. The example of "gender" may elucidate these interactions. Both gender and emotions were part of the nineteenth century's dichotomizations: Men were bound to "reason" and "intellect," while women were attached to "nature" and "feeling." It is important to keep this in mind when thinking about women who wrote/female writers. They contradicted (emotional) norms, as the act of creating texts was classically linked to the intellect. Emotions could also be of high importance in their texts: As a means of explanation or as a strategy of legitimisation (of their own behaviour as well as that of others – as will be discussed later).

The division of "intellect" and "feeling" has also been important for research, as emotions have been "heavily censored in the history of social sciences in favour of 'rationality.'"[21] Only in the last decade has an increasing number of studies acknowledged the "power of emotions" in their historical dimensions.[22] It is not the intention of this chapter to prove the "design" of certain emotions and to show their historical boundedness, but to refer to their potency in (social) interactions.

Another bipolarity of the upcoming bourgeois identity, and one of its central aspects, was the division of space into a "male" public sphere (work, politics, etc.) and a "female" private sphere (household).[23] As a consequence, women's mobility was restricted – and the many women who moved nevertheless were suspect for various reasons.[24] Body politics and emotions played a crucial role in this process: The question of access to the public space was connected to aspects of security. Public space was declared unsafe and, thus, dangerous.[25] Women who were described to be weak and delicate therefore shouldn't move on their own – which is: Without male companionship. They were taught to fearfully avoid the frightening public area.[26]

A woman's travelogue

Emotions have an immense significance in *Mein Reisetagebuch* (*My Travel Diary*), the text that forms the main source of this investigation. In it Lilla von Bulyovszky describes various encounters with strangers in the places of stopovers, as well as en route. Bulyovszky uses emotions in order to interpret the behaviour of companions. Moreover, emotions elucidate Bulyovszky's own behaviour as a working woman and female traveller who interacts in the "other place" of shared movement.

Bulyovszky published her memoires shortly after the actual taking place of the journey in 1856. The original version in Hungarian was immediately followed by a translated German version, published in 1858. The book was edited by the publishing house of Gustav Emich in Pest.[27] The travelogue's text alone had a length of 232 pages – the pretext of the German version was counted separately (III–VI).[28]

Women in general were not expected to write and publish texts, nor were they expected to travel on their own. In Hungary, similar to German-speaking parts of "Austria" and a range of Central European regions, a "prevailing atmosphere of oppression" accompanied them.[29] Nevertheless, quite a lot of female writers were well known, as a huge group of women-authors belonged to the literary scene. To publish their work some of them chose a male pseudonym, others used special genres to suit public ideas of adequacy.[30] Travelogues written by women were not common, but Bulyovszky was neither the first nor a singular exception to release her travelling experiences. Her text followed the "typical" criteria of a travelogue: It contained a mix of descriptions concerning "the country and its people" and personal stories of adventures witnessed on the journey.[31]

In using the "Reisetagebuch" as a primary source, it is of course important to engage in source critique: Who wrote when for what reason? To examine the book, methods of qualitative social research were deployed.[32] The text is interpreted as a personal testimonial, a recollection that was written down at a certain state with a certain aim.[33] The text was written immediately after the travel had ended. Nevertheless, memory and all its implications have to be taken into consideration, especially since research has revealed that ego-documents often claim authenticity.[34] Authors pretend to write "true" stories, and readers expect to be presented with facts. This "authenticity" appears to be doubled in the case of *Mein Reisetagebuch*, as Bulyovszky calls it both an itinerary and a journal. Those who write also interpret, describe from their own point of view, and omit or drop episodes. Sometimes they – (un-)consciously – change the course of events in order to obtain certain aims.[35] The strict division of texts into "fiction" and "reality" is therefore not appropriate at all, because fictionality does not mean "das intentionale Abweichen vom Faktischen einer vorgegebenen Realität, sondern vielmehr von dem, was einer Gesellschaft an einem bestimmten geschichtlichen Ort als das Glaubhafte erscheint."[36] Additionally, as Claudia Ulbrich notes: "Auch Machtverhältnisse spielen beim Schreiben eine Rolle. Authentizität ist mit Autorität verbunden. Nicht jedem [und jeder! ad. of the author] wird zugestanden authentisch zu schreiben."[37]

"Mein Reisetagebuch" was the first itinerary Lilla von Bulyovszky published.[38] It is not known why she decided to write it – no personal explanations were given by her.[39] The "Reisetagebuch" remained her only travel description, but Bulyovszky kept writing, and in later years completely changed her profession from actress to translator and author. Therefore, it might have been her wish to express her thoughts by writing, using a medium she had a talent for. In addition, the publication also might have followed a plan to create publicity and thereby foster her career as an actress (abroad). However, whether it was meant as a means of gaining publicity or to express her artistic talents, Lilla von Bulyovszky declared that she would define and shape her memories, and stated her right to act as an independent, sovereign person. In doing so, she burst the widespread tendency of a "male monopoly on memory" (and history).[40]

Before analysing the various acquaintances reported about in Lilla von Bulyovszky's travelogue, the following section provides a short glance into the historical background concerning female artists' movements. It explains Bulyovszky's position and thereby creates an understanding of her behaviour in interactions.

Travelling actress/working woman

Members of performing arts never "fully" belonged to the ideal of a bourgeois society as it was established in the nineteenth century.[41] Men as well as women who acted did not meet the hegemonic gender norms, but acting and performing women fundamentally contradicted middle-class ideals of femininity: Female modesty, domesticity, sedentariness.[42] They were independent and they moved constantly – through spaces and across borders (of states, cultures, languages to name only a few). This was a crucial part of their profession.[43] As it is often investigated, the reason for traveling in Lilla von Bulyovszky's case was a result of a whole bundle of themes. Summing them up, three main causes can be identified: Networking, education, and "classical" holiday sightseeing.[44] During her travels, Bulyovszky did not have working obligations, nor did she make appearances. Nevertheless, she was part of the artists' travelling network. Meeting colleagues shaped her travelling route; recommendation letters functioned as door openers. The status of an acting – and therefore working – woman was of crucial importance to her. It influenced her self-perception but also her interactions "en route."[45] Even the first sentence of the preface of her travelogue is dedicated to her profession – when she explains that the main reason for travelling was "endlich aus den blühenden Kunstgebieten der Franzosen und Deutschen eine oder die andere Blüthe [sic] nach der Heimat zurückzubringen"[46] She positioned herself self-confidentially as an artist and defended this position in a very poised manner.[47]

"Travelling intersections" II: Lilla von Bulyovszky's companionships "en route"

Lilla von Bulyovszky travelled on her own. She started her tour unaccompanied, even though she was hardly ever alone. The destinations were explicitly chosen to meet friends, colleagues or people she hoped to benefit from. While on tour she made various acquaints. With some of them she built up an intense relationship – they shared a "community of occasion" but they were not declared friends.[48] The means of transportation Bulyovszky used were of importance for the development of her acquaintances and the evolving relations. That is why they will be discussed in the following section.

Transport vehicles and places

Lilla von Bulyovszky started her travels in 1856 in Hungary. From the perspective of traffic systems this was a time of change. Infrastructure in Austria and Hungary expanded, especially as the railway network developed. Bulyovszky, for example, carefully described the "Semmering" railway line, which enabled her to make a short side trip from her planned tour to visit Trieste.[49] Although she valued the possibilities of fast transportation, she nonetheless preferred the more classic ways of travelling and went by stagecoach on the majority of her further tours.

> Ich glaube jedermann wird es vorziehen mit guten Pferden und bei schönem Wetter in einem bequemen Wagen zu reisen als auf dem Dampfboot, wo es einem kaum einfällt, dass man reist, oder auf der Eisenbahn, wo der erste Signalpfiff aller individuellen Freiheit ein Ende macht.[50]

She defended her decision to go by coach. Perhaps the security of the closed stage room was of importance for that argument, as it could have been a strategy to emphasise her integrity as a well-situated woman by preferring to travel by stagecoach: Social distinction was probably more likely than on a ship or a train. This type of movement seemed more adequate to her needs: Several times, her travel was interrupted for sightseeing and diverse leisure activities – always carried out with her traveling acquaintances. The transport-vehicles play an important role in the consideration of Lilla von Bulyovszky's companionships. They formed the decor for the first meetings and their specific structure influenced further relationships. The concept of the "other place" is palpable: In the case of Bulyovszky, individuals were haphazardly bound together and, even though sometimes they did not seem to fit together, they very soon built a unit. The travel companionship was extended, and the shared travelling space repeatedly expanded to the room of the coach or railway compartment.

"Auf der Reise wird man bald bekannt," Bulyovszky explained.[51] Her companionships mostly followed a pattern: She got to know the other people on the mode of transport, followed by a brief period of getting acquainted, which was shaped by extensive talks while on the move. Interestingly, farewells were never described – the travel partners simply vanished.[52] In the places where she stopped over, as well as in Paris, the hotel was the only chance to meet strangers (which was another place described as a heterotopian). "Natives," people she met on the street, were described, but interaction with them was rare. Social contacts were practically prescribed, because Bulyovszky knew exactly whom she would meet at her stations: Letters of recommendation opened doors, and thus she was allowed to enter the "better society" and was enclosed in its specific network. Connections to unknown people were established during the journey. Several travel acquaintances were mentioned, talks and interactions reported about. More than once Bulyovszky shared the activities during stopovers with her new consociates and spent much more of her time with them than she would have needed to. A married couple, for example, she even accompanied on an extensive overnight mountain trip.[53] Therefore, it seems plausible to value "the other place" of the shared movement as a constitutive element of relationship and interactions.

To share small, closed rooms was not common for people who did not know each other (neither for mixed nor the same sex). On the one hand, travelling blurred the borders of decency. On the other hand, the "other place" of shared movement provided a secure space – a private public sphere.[54] This was helpful, particularly for women, since a kind of domesticity could be cherished that, in all its ambiguity, helped women to leave behind their bourgeois homes. Reinterpreting the famous picture, one could state that "a room of one's own" was not coincidentally understood to be crucial for emancipation. But more ambiguities may be detected: "For women especially, separate carriages and darkened tunnels were dangerous territories, presenting considerable risks. Not just to their physical and personal safety, but also, as the perfect locale for romantic encounters, possibly their reputations."[55]

Travelling woman: gender, emotion, movement

As mentioned above, Bulyovszky emphasised her status as a working – and therefore independent – woman: "Ich bin Schauspielerin und jeder Künstler hat die Erfahrung gemacht, dass" she explained to a travel companion, and thus fashioned herself a professional – an expert.[56] In addition, this mention of her profession was probably to explain why she was travelling alone. Her theatrical profession could have made her non-serious, and she very much underlined her femininity as well as her respectability when interacting with her acquaintances. Interestingly, she hardly ever mentioned her husband and her child: Perhaps in order not to dim the positive effect by the fact that she had "left her family behind."

To Lilla von Bulyovszky her companions served a specific purpose, namely to bridge time during a stay. She obviously despised being alone, and she quickly felt lonely on her un-accompanied sightseeing trips.[57] While travelling, she socialised with her companions, and was willing to accept disadvantages in order to avoid being alone. Additionally, they fuelled her report with funny, comical, and strange stories. Bulyovszky satirically emphasised little weaknesses. She made fun of male as well as female acquaintances, but she targeted men especially, which was probably her way of symbolizing a certain distance and showing that contacts had not been "too close." Several times, she seems to have used stories of superiority as a narrative strategy. By labelling some of her (male) companions as inferior, she was able to maintain an image of distance and to forestall suspicions of having been in too close contact to any of them. This can be seen as an approach to defuse the indecent "female" travel. At the same time, her writing also subverted social norms in declaring the female writer to be superior.

On her way to Graz she sat opposite to an "English engineer," "der in einem fort den Mund offen hielt."[58] When she arrived in Trieste she did not sleep well, because she dreamed

> von meinem schwärmerischen Mährer, von dem ich nicht erwähnt habe, dass er auf dem Weg Verse auf Hero und Leander dichtete, und dabei von Zeit zu Zeit sich eine Wurst zu Gemüthe [sic!] führte, die mein Geruchsorgan nicht so sehr an die Gärten der Hesperiden als an die der Debracziner erinnerte.[59]

This companion did not keep his promise to visit Trieste with her, because she had talked to another man. "Die Eitelkeit der Männer geht doch noch über die unserige [sic!]," she stated.[60]

Almost all the men she got to know on her journey were funny in one way or another and were not fully taken seriously in Bulyovszky's description. Emotions she mentioned as a main reason for their often rather helpless behaviour – with love playing an outstanding role. It seems evident that Bulyovszky did not believe in the romantic ideal of love, or at least questioned it when she was confronted with her companions' love stories. She acted as an observer and rarely seems to have openly declared her opinion on these matters. She only reflected on them in her travelogue – or added the stories to elucidate her position. On her first stage from Vienna to Linz she shared the coach with a newly-wed couple.[61] The husband, obviously older than his wife, was enraptured by the young woman and did not recognise what seemed conspicuous to Lilla von Bulyovszky: The grief of his spouse. Blind because of his love, he did not feel she did not love him back. A fact Bulyovszky observed with wonder.

The man's clumsiness was described in a comical scene:

> (Er) aber ließ, als er seine Gattin lächeln sah, vor Freude seine Tabakdose fallen, deren umherfliegender Inhalt bei uns unaufhörliches Niesen verursachte.[62]

This "kleine Episode, die durch die Verlegenheit des Seidenhändlers noch komischer wurde," was one of the rare coincidences that happened en route that Bulyovszky mentioned.[63] The impression of amiable bearishness of the man thus increased.

From Paris to Brussels she shared her *coupé* with a young man she described as rather extraordinary. He wore several different layers of clothes (the reason was not mentioned) and – once again – was enamoured.[64] Sighing constantly, he declared that she was desperately unhappy. Nevertheless, he lost her sympathy when he told his story of the two women he loved and between whom he was not able to decide. On the contrary, Bulyovszky reacted rather brusquely, declaring he was a "typical man" and, against her habit, immediately left him after the arrival. She had not felt comfortable from the beginning, because she feared a declaration of love. The young man sitting opposite to her actively sought contact. He wanted to talk and hoped for her advice. Bulyovszky accepted the conversation; she was not afraid but amazed. Following her argumentation, in the case of necessity she would have been able to change her seat.[65] But Bulyovszky was "safe" also in a transferred sense: The "other place" guaranteed security. Even though stages and railway compartments were under suspicion of being potentially dangerous, they nevertheless were socially accepted rooms for a woman. In Bulyovszky's case, it had not been her decision to travel with this man and, according to her story, it wasn't her who had sought contact. Therefore, her behaviour was completely "correct." In addition to this they were talking about emotions, which was an appropriate theme for a woman. Again, an enamoured man had crossed her path, but her acquaintance could not gain any compassion. Emotion was of crucial importance once more: The behaviour of the man wanting two women to be in love with him got her emotionally involved. But what the enamoured man gained was finally not friendly condescension, but rejection.

Even though she tended to make fun of them, Lilla von Bulyovszky commonly was on the side of men. Women in general were presented as powerful. Their behaviour in relationships often seemed to be ridiculous too, but in contrast to their male counterparts, they acted successfully. They sulked and pouted and did not converse. Such a performance was understood to be part of "ideal femaleness": Not to actively speak out against things they disliked. To Bulyovszky it was a type of subversive empowerment – a very effective means for women to get what they wanted.[66]

From Kassel to Frankfurt a young couple from Amsterdam on their honeymoon travelled with her. Appreciating their love, she got to know them more closely. The spouse noticed that Bulyovszky was watching them and the young woman was afraid that their happiness and luck could give her a bad feeling or could make her feel sad because of a loss of someone beloved or an unhappy love.[67] Once more, emotions formed the centre of the relationship between Bulyovszky and her observed companions. There were no further explanations concerning the people, their origins and so on. Not even the language they used for conversation was mentioned. One might suggest it was

French as a lingua franca in these days, but we lack proof of this. Their social rank was insinuated, but not discussed. Although some of her acquaintances were shortly introduced with their profession, perhaps it was all too clear that a certain wealth was necessary to travel like she did, and therefore no further explanations were given.

Gender, emotion, and movement formed a constant triad in Bulyovszky's travelogue. The requirements of the "other place" seemed to exclude other themes. The confined space shared with unknown people potentiated the importance of "gender." Chance and the necessities of travel bound strangers together and created a kind of intimacy that fostered exchange. The knowledge that, after the journey, they would most likely never meet again could have eased the contact.[68] When thinking one step further and wondering why Bulyovszky reported so extensively on that point, one might suggest that to talk about emotions was an adequate topic for a woman. Love especially had an explicitly "female" connotation and was thus an appropriate topic in women's writings. Moreover, her descriptions of enamoured men made them "harmless" (because their passion was directed towards other women) – and even comical. In that sense the "Reisetagebuch" could also be read as a kind of defence, or at least coverage against potential suspicions.

Excluded intersections?

Other categories and signifiers of social difference did not enter that space, despite the fact that they were of crucial importance during the whole trip. Lilla von Bulyovszky only mentioned them when reporting events in the places for stopovers. Nation and nationality (especially connected to colleagues and her profession), age and class then entered the stories. Gender and emotions did, however, not lose their significance. "(G)roße Kunst darf man in Paris nicht suchen"[69] was her conclusion concerning theatre after her stay in the French capital, and later on she declared that the Germans were really different from the French "bei welchen Alles nur auf den Schein berechnet ist."[70] An old officer who drank loads of beer constantly made advances while they were taking their meal, which led her to sum up: "Es ist doch traurig, daß Alter nicht vor Thorheit schützt!"[71] The women rowing the boats on the Bavarian Königssee seemed "rather old and ugly" to her.[72] In Trieste on a boat trip she talked with its conductor and learned that he was desperately in love with a young flower seller. The love failed because of the couple's poverty, which prompted the flower girl's infidelity.[73]

Themes that were not even mentioned when she was en route suddenly appeared in the look on the "exotic," the "strange other." Perhaps she used these stories to create distinguishing features and to be able to present reports on otherness that were somehow expected in a travelogue. Bulyovszky thereby was able to indirectly refer to her travel acquaintances as socially coequal. Thus, the people sharing movement (the "other place") with her were not different in means of rank. The "other place" proved to guarantee safety once more.

"En route" with Alexandre Dumas: final thoughts

Finally, one of Lilla von Bulyovszky's travel acquaintances thoughts and feelings will be questioned. In his novel *Ein Liebesabenteuer*[74] Alexandre Dumas wrote:

> Wir hatten unsere Zweisamkeit wiedererlangt; doch beeilen wir uns hinzu-
> zusetzen dass diese Zweisamkeit seit unserer Abreise einen ungeheuren
> Schritt gemacht hatte. Meinerseits hatte sie sich von verliebtem Verlangen
> zu innigster, doch höchst ehrerbietiger Freundschaft gewandelt, seitens
> meiner Begleiterin von verschämter Furcht zu höchst zutraulicher
> Ungezwungenheit.[75]

Dumas' *Liebesabenteuer* reports about the same travel. This second text written by a man allows comparison in order to question gender differences, even though Dumas used the genre of a novel that reported the author's encounter with a young Hungarian actress, "Lilla." Her second name was not given but Bulyovszky must have been identifiable to everybody who knew her. Bulyovszky never replied in written form, but others reported that she despised Dumas' text.[76]

Emotions in this text were of crucial importance as well, although they were described in rather different stories. It wasn't pure love without any sexual implications that formed its centre. On the contrary, without hesitation Dumas thematised his longing for the young actress. In doing so, he made himself an emotional actor, while Bulyovszky generally narrated others' feelings. The author was able to do so because he chose the semi-fictional form, in which the reader is not advised to read it as facts or fiction, and because it was fitting for a man who felt attracted by a beautiful lady. Love, sexuality, and fidelity were bound to other rules: Here, gendered norms show their impact.

In Dumas' description of encounters, conversation forms an important part too, but he extended the stories and included interactions. Like in the passage cited above, intimacy and his advances were of crucial importance in that context. We do not know whether this was reality or not. In any case a "serious" woman would not have been able to report such an occurrence. Therefore, gender and "allowed" interactions were strongly intertwined, at least society's norms clearly shaped reports.

This becomes especially obvious in an event that appears to have been completely differently reported about when comparing both texts. Travelling up the Rhine, Lilla von Bulyovszky felt indisposed; a terrible sickness tormented her. So far both reports matched, but while Bulyovszky just mentioned that she was ill and lay wrapped in blankets on the deck of the ship all day, Dumas created an exciting story out of it. In his version the scene was set in a hotel.[77] The actress Lilla called him and her illness even made her allow Dumas to enter her hotel room, where he sat beside her bed. "Magnetism" (which nowadays would be described as hands-on healing) is what he called the practice he used to cure her.[78] "Sie zog meine Hand bis zu ihrem Magen hinab, ließ aber das

Leintuch und die Decke zwischen meiner Hand und ihrer Brust," he described.[79] Given the moral norms of their time this scene was completely indecent and scandalous.

Clear signals were given that this relationship had been much more than an acquaintance, that there had been a significant erotic component. For a woman this meant a threat even more so when she was married. Contact between men and women was strictly regulated and bound to specific rules (variably dependent categories of social difference: Especially class, age, ethnicity). Her integrity was bound to an impeccable behaviour, and any suspicion of "amorality" implied a loss of honour for her, her husband, and the whole family.[80] The husband needed to challenge the rival to a duel – which would have rehabilitated his honour but not his wife's. It was simply not possible for a woman to restore reputation when she was accused of sexual "misconduct."[81]

While Dumas could be perceived as a tempter – and in the worst case in a tongue-in-cheek negative way – to Bulyovszky such a story, interpreted as a "real" event, could have meant a "social death."

Conclusion

Dumas and Bulyovszky corresponded in describing a closeness that advanced quickly between travellers. The common movement developed an "other place" that fostered a special kind of relationship based on chance and the knowledge of its short-term nature. Travel companions' interactions (let it be sitting together, talking, etc.) were thus on the one hand relieved from everyday life, but on the other hand its guidelines remained valid. They may have increased or decreased, but they did not vanish. Gender norms kept their relevance – especially in the publications that reported the travellers' experiences: Men were "allowed" to tell different stories than women. Social restrictions required different strategies of storytelling. Dissimilar contents were necessary to gain success (of any kind whatsoever).

The special atmosphere created in the "other place" manifested itself in the negotiated themes. Emotions were of crucial importance, with love playing an especially important role: Relationships between men and women, their constitution and development made up the main content of conversation. On a second level, they were shaping the travelogues' passages concerning companionships and acquaintances.[82] Women were automatically connected to emotions. To them talking about and reporting on feelings was to "move on safe ground" – as long as relationships did not leave prescribed courses or get too close. The "other place" allowed them to get into contact in a socially accepted manner. To avoid any suspicion, Lilla von Bulyovszky additionally, and strategically, chose to write extensively about encounters and to describe them as completely harmless.

Gender influenced the emotional interactions, and thus the "other place" of shared movement as well as the publications on it and vice versa. Paying attention to the triad of travel, gender, and emotions, this may help to broaden the understanding of each phenomenon.

Notes

1 Bulyovszky, L. (1858) Mein Reisetagebuch (German translation; Hungarian version 1856). Pest: Gustav Emich (ed.). *Biographisches Lexikon des Kaisertums Österreich. Zweiter Teil.* Constantin von Wurzbach (ed.): 204–205; Schlossar, A. (1910) "Lilla Von Bulyowsky [Todesmeldung]," in *Bühne und Welt. Zeitschrift für Theaterwesen, Literatur und Musik*, 12 (2): 456; Freiherr von Meysenbug, C. (1910/1911) "Lilla von Bulyowsky," in *Bühne und Welt. Zeitschrift für Theaterwesen, Literatur und Musik*, 13 (2): 74–78; Gragger, R. (1914) *Lilla von Bulyovszky und der Münchener Dichterkreis. Mit ungedruckten Briefen.* München/Leipzig: 2; Reichold, K. & Endl, T. (2011) *Ludwig forever. Die fantastische Welt des Märchenkönigs.* Hamburg: Hoffman und Campe Verlag.
2 Dumas, A. (2014) *Ein Liebesabenteuer* (first edition 1860). Zürich: Manesse Verlag.
3 Bulyovszky, L. (1858) *Mein Reisetagebuch* (German translation; Hungarian version 1856). Pest.
4 Letherby, G. & Reynolds, G. (2016) "Introduction: Making the Journey – Travel and Travellers," in *Gendered Journeys, Mobile Emotions.* Gayle Letherby & Gillian Reynolds (eds.). London/New York: Routledge: 159–164, 159.
5 Three chapters of their book are explicitly dedicated to that theme.
6 See for example Siebert, U. (1998) *Grenz.Linien. Selbstrepräsentationen von Frauen in Reisetexten 1871 bis 1914.* Münster: Waxmann: 88–95.
7 Nevertheless, many aspects of travel – especially when focusing women travellers – are not investigated yet. As an example noble female travellers can be named: Tagungsbericht: Prinzessin, unterwegs – Reisen (hoch-) adeliger Frauen zwischen 1450 und 1850, 21.01.2016 – 22.01.2016 Gießen, in: H-Soz-Kult, 18.07.2016, <http://www.hsozkult.de/conferencereport/id/tagungsberichte-6615> (accessed 8 August 2016).
8 Siebert (1998): 42–47.
9 Pratt, M.L. (1992) *Imperial Eyes: Travel Writing and Transculturation.* London/New York: Routledge; Pratt, M.L. (1991) "Arts of the Contact Zone," *Profession*, 33–40.
10 Walsh, M. (2016) "Gender and Travel: Mobilizing New Perspectives on the Past," in *Gendered Journeys, Mobile Emotions*, Gayle Letherby & Gillian Reynolds (eds.). London/New York: Routledge: 5–18, 7; Johanna Gehmacher & Elizabeth Harvey (eds.) (2011) "Politisch Reisen," in *Österreichische Zeitschrift für Geschichtswissenschaften*, 22 (1).
11 Hunt, K. (2011) "'Whirl'd through the World': The Role of Travel in the Making of Dora Montafiore, 1851–1933," in *Österreichische Zeitschrift für Geschichtswissenschaften*, 22 (1): 41–63, 55.
12 Krauze, J.M. (2006) *Frauen auf Reisen. Kulturgeschichtliche Beiträge zu ausgewählten Reiseberichten von Frauen aus der Zeit 1842–1940.* Hamburg: Kovac: 99.
13 Exoticisms play an important role in travelogues – especially "the orient" was of interest. Its importance is shown when e.g. L. v. Bullyovszky implements stories concerning "Arabic wisdom" in her book, even though her route did not even touch "Arabic" regions. Bulyovszky opened the passage by mentioning an Arab sitting at the shore of the Rhine and smoking. Bulyovszky (1858): 179–183.
14 For concepts on space and room see: Letherby, G. & Reynolds, G. (2005) *Train Tracks. Work, Play and Politics on the Railway.* Oxford/New York: Bloomsbury: 30–39.
15 Rißler-Pipka, N. (2009) "Be- und Entgrenzungen. Theatralität und Räumlichkeit in den Abenteuerromanen Jules Vernes," in *Theatralität und Räumlichkeit. Raumordnungen und Raumpraktiken im theatralen Mediendispositiv*, Jörg Dünne, Sabine Friedrich & Kirsten Kramer (eds.). Würzburg: Königshausen & Neumann: 125–136, 126.
16 Foucault's "heterotopia" describes "a room outside all rooms" that at the same time represents, contests, and turns real places of a culture. Foucault, M. (1990) "Andere Räume," in *Aisthesis. Wahrnehmung heute oder Perspektiven einer*

anderen Ästhetik, Karlheinz Barck, Peter Gente, Heidi Paris, & Stefan Richter (eds.). Leipzig: Reclam: 34–46.

17 For the case of train travels Letherby and Reynolds formulated: "The train space, therefore, is the site of conflict and negotiation in social interactions that are themselves often culturally specific, or even unarticulated in terms of cultural etiquette." Letherby & Reynolds (2005): 8 f.

18 Elliott and Urry point out that "mobilities develop into a distinct field with characteristic struggles, tastes and habituses. It is a sight of multiple intersecting contestations." It seems worth taking up and pursuing the thought questioning conditions and their implementations "on the move." Elliott, A. & Urry, J. (2010) *Mobile Lives*. London/ New York: Routledge: 59.

19 Intersectionality describes a process: Categories of difference do not meet one time and increase their destructive power. Many investigations have proven that categories are intermingling; they are in constant flow and their impact changes constantly: It may increase as well as decrease; its effects may be negative as well as positive. Crenshaw, K. (2000) *The Intersectionality of Race and Gender Discrimination. Backgroundpaper for the United Nations Regional Expert Group Meeting* (21–24. November Croatia, Zagreb, 2000); Lutz, H., Herrera Vivar, M.T., & Supik, L. (2013) "Fokus Intersektionalität – Eine Einleitung," in *Fokus Intersektionalität. Bewegungen und Verortungen eines vielschichtigen Konzeptes*, Helma Lutz, María Teresa Herrera Vivar, & Linda Supik (eds.).Wiesbaden: Springer: 9–31; Kapp, G.-A. (2013) "'Intersectional Invisibility': Anknüpfungen und Rückfragen an ein Konzept der Intersektionalitätsforschung," in *Fokus Intersektionalität. Bewegungen und Verortungen eines vielschichtigen Konzeptes*, Helma Lutz, María Teresa Herrera Vivar, & Linda Supik (eds.). Wiesbaden: Springer: 243–264.

20 Research on emotions increased over the last years. In this text "emotions" are understood not to be constant but variable. They are determined historically and changing perpetually. (There are some affects – like fear or joy – that are stable and part of human being. But even those are connected to cultural surroundings: they ways they are interpreted and perceived change and thus also their repercussions.) Henderson, B.K. (2015) Affekttheorien/Affektbegriff, *KRASS kritische assoziationen. Beweg(ung)en und Verknüpf(ung)en. Glossar* #3: 4–7; Laukötter, A. (2015) "Editorial. Geschichte der Gefühle – Einblicke in die Forschung." via: https://www.history-of-emotions.mpg.de/de (accessed 4 August 2016).

21 Letherby & Reynolds (2016): 1–18, 3.

22 Schnell, R. (2015) *Haben Gefühle eine Geschichte?* Göttingen: Vandenhoek & Ruprecht: 15–17.

23 Hausen, K. (1976) "Die Polarisierung der 'Geschlechtscharaktere'. Eine Spiegelung der Dissoziation von Erwerbs- und Familienleben," in *Sozialgeschichte der Familie in der Neuzeit Europas*, Werner Conze (ed.). Stuttgart: Ernst Klett Verlag: 363–393, Nachdruck in: Hark, S. (2007) *Dis/kontinuitäten: feministische Theorien*. Wiesbaden: Vs Verlag Fur Sozialwissenschaften: 173–196, 191 f.; Hoff, W., Kleinau, E., & Schmid, P. (2008) *Gender-Geschichte/n. Ergebnisse bildungshistorischer Frauen- und Geschlechterforschung*. Köln/Weimar: Boehlau Verlag.

24 Women moved (travelled and migrated) for different reasons: work, love, they had to flee, wished to get to know something new and so on. See: Aufhauser, E. (2000) "Geschlecht und Migration. Zur Konstruktion und Rekonstruktion von Weiblichkeit und Männlichkeit in der internationalen Migration," in *Internationale Migration: Die globale Herausforderung des 21. Jahrhunderts?* Karl Husa, Christoph Parnreiter, & Irene Stacher (eds.). Frankfurt a. Main: Brandes & Apsel: 97–122; Hahn, S. (2008) *Migration-Arbeit-Geschlecht. Arbeitsmigration in Mitteleuropa vom 17. bis zum Beginn des 20. Jahrhunderts*. Göttingen: V&R University Press; Lutz, H. (2008) "Introduction: Migrant Domestic Workers in Europe," in *Migration and Domestic*

Work. A European Perspective on a Global Theme, Helma Lutz (ed.). Aldershot: Ashgate, 1–10.

25 Stevenson, K. (2016) "'Women and Young Girls Dare not Travel Alone': The Dangers of Sexual Encounters on Victorian Railways," in *Gendered Journeys, Mobile Emotions*, Gayle Letherby & Gillian Reynolds (eds.). London/New York: Routledge: 189–199.

26 Ahmed argues that fear is not a "'resonable response' to vulnerability" but is fostered to control bodies. Ahmed, S. (2012) *The Cultural Politics of Emotions*. New York/ London: Edinburgh University Press: 68, 70.

27 Emich, G. (1843–1911) was head of the "Athenäum" publishing house which had been founded by his father. He was known as bibliographer and as an entomologist. Österreichisches Biographisches Lexikon 1815–1950, Bd. 1 (Lfg. 3, 1956): 245.

28 Bulyovszky (1858).

29 Fábri, A. (2001) "Hungarian Women Writers, 1790–1900," in *A History of Central European Women's Writing*, Celia Hawkesworth (ed.). New York: Palgrave Macmillan: 87–109, 97.

30 The formal access of epistulary novels was quite common; as well as all kind of guides (especially cookbooks).

31 Krauze (2006): 55.

32 Müller-Botsch, C. (2008) "Der Lebenslauf als Quelle. Fallrekonstruktive Biographie-forschung anhand personenbezogener Akten," in *Auto/Biografie, Gewalt und Geschlecht*, Johanna Gehmacher & Gabriella Hauch (eds.). *Österreichische Zeitschrift für Geschichts-wissenschaft*, 19 (2): 38–63; Apitzsch, U. & Jansen, M. (2003) *Migration, Biographie und Geschlechterverhältnisse*. Münster: Westfälisches Dampfboot; Jancke, G. & Ulbrich, C. (2005) *Vom Individuum zur Person. Neue Konzepte im Spannungsfeld von Autobio-grafietheorie und Selbstzeugnisforschung*. Berlin: Wallstein Verlag; Schmidlechner, K.M. (1994) "Oral History als Methode der Historischen Frauenforschung," in *Signale. Veröffentlichungen zur historischen und interdisziplinären Frauenforschung*, Karin M. Schmidlechner (ed.). Graz: Graz Gender Studies: 9–24.

33 In any case texts and authors need to get located: Historically, socially, and so on. Ulbrich, C. (2012) *Europäische Selbstzeugnisse in historischer Perspektive – Neue Zugänge*, online: http://www.geschkult.fu-berlin.de/e/fmi/institut/arbeitsbereiche/ ab_ulbrich/media/UlbrichEurop__ische_Selbstzeugnisse.pdf?1350899276: 1–20, 18 (accessed 25 July 2017).

34 For authenticity and its various meanings see: Saupe, A. (2017) Historische Authenti-zität: Individuen und Gesellschaften auf der Suche nach dem Selbst – Ein Forschungs-bericht, in: H-Soz-Kult 15.8.2017, http://www.hsozkult.de/literaturereview/id/ forschungsberichte-2444 (accessed 20 August 2017).

35 Schenk, F.B. (2012) "Ich bin des Daseins eines Zugvogels müde." Imperialer Raum in der Autobiographie einer russischen Adeligen, in *Geschlechtergeschichte global, L'Homme. Europäische Zeitschrift für Feministische Geschichtswissenschaft*, 23 (2): 49–64, 51.

36 (. . .) fictionality does not meen "to deviate from a given reality, but to differ from what a society at a specific historical point believes is plausible." Neuber, W. (1989) "Zur Gattungspoetik des Reiseberichts. Skizze einer historischen Grundlegung im Horizont von Rhetorik und Topik," in *Der Reisebericht. Die Entwicklung einer Gattung in der Deutschen Literatur*, Peter J. Brenner (ed.). Berlin: Suhrkamp: 1989: 50–67, 51 cited after Siebert (1998): 45.

37 "Power relations play an important role in the writing processes as well. Authenticity is affiliated to authority. Not everybody is conceded to write authentically." Ulbrich (2012): 12.

38 She had written two volumes of novellas in Hungarian before and published them in 1855. Gragger (1914): 2.

39 In contrast to her reasons for travelling, which she explained in the book's preface. Bulyovszky (1858): III.
40 Assmann, A. (2006) "Geschlecht und kulturelles Gedächtnis," in *Erinnern und Geschlecht. Band 1*, Meike Penkwitt (ed.). Freiburg i. Breisgau: Jos Fritz: 29–46; Assmann, A. & Friese, H. (1999) *Identitäten. Erinnerung, Geschichte, Identität 3*. Frankfurt a. Main: Suhrkamp.
41 Sonnleitner, U. (2016) "Moving German-Speaking Theatre: Artists and Movement 1850–1950," in *Journal of Migration History*, 2: 93–119.
42 Grotjahn, R. (2011) *Diva – Die Inszenierung der übermenschlichen Frau. Interdisziplinäre Untersuchungen zu einem kulturellen Phänomen des 19. und 20. Jahrhunderts.* Dörte Schmidt and Thomas Seedorf (eds.). Schliengen: Argus; Möhrmann, R. (2000) *Die Schauspielerin – Eine Kulturgeschichte* (1. Auflage 1989). Frankfurt a. Main: Insel Verlag.
43 Changing engagements and guest appearances could be possible reasons for travels. Many actors/actresses were part of wandering theatre companies. So actors/actresses were migrants, travellers, and nomads – very often all of it in one person.
44 Krämer, F. & Haase, M. (2012) *Reisen und Bildung. Bildungs- und Entfremdungsprozesse im jungen Erwachsenenalter am Beispiel von Work and Travel.* Wiesbaden: VS Verlag für Sozialwissenschaften: 21. The educational purpose of travelling makes her outstanding of other actors' and actresses' movement. See diverse reports in biographies of actors/actresses, e.g.: Barnay, L. (1954) *Erinnerungen.* Berlin: Henschel Verlag; Tyrolt, R. (1904) *Aus dem Tagebuche eines Wiener Schauspielers 1848–1902. Erinnerungen und Betrachtungen.* Wien/Leipzig: Wilhelm Braumüller; Durieux, T. (1954) *Eine Tür steht offen. Erinnerungen.* Berlin: Herbig. To visit a theatre on a trip was popular and widespread in all social classes: It is well known from their journals for example that wayfaring journeymen were very interested in that kind of entertainment. Funder, L. (2000) *Aus meinem Burschenleben. Gesellenwanderung und Brautwerbung eines Grazer Zuckerbäckers (1862–1869)*, Ernst Bruckmüller (ed.).Wien/Köln/Weimar: KRAL; John, M. (2015), *Das Tagebuch des Buchdruckerlehrlings Friedrich Anton Püschmann von 1850 bis 1856. Band 1: Die Buchdruckerlehre in Grimma, die Wanderung durch Sachsen, Thüringen, West- und Norddeutschland während der Revolutionsjahre.* Berlin: Trafo Wissenschaftsverlag.
45 See Skinner's reflections on tourism in that context: "Tourism provides us with one of those 'fateful moments,' a space and time for both anxiety and opportunity, a point of transition during which reflexivity and attention of the self and focus apon self-actualization are heightened." Skinner (2007): 339 cited by: Letherby, G. & Reynolds, G. (2016) "Afterword. Destinations Unknown," in *Gendered Journeys, Mobile Emotions*, Gayle Letherby and Gillian Reynolds (eds.). London/New York: Routledge: 201–207, 203.
46 "…finally to bring from the prosperous artistic fields of the French and the Germans one or another blossom back to my homeland (…)" Bulyovszky (1858): III.
47 Bulyovszky (1858): 13 f. Even the last sentence of her book was stating that her patriotism was as mighty as her enthusiasm for art. Bulyovszky (1858): 232.
48 Other travellers declared their travel acquaintances to comrades, but Bulyovszky never was so close to them. Hunt (2011): 61. The German "Kameradschaft" / comradeship is strongly connected to a military context: Wartime comrades or comrades-in-arms are evoked. Therefore this term does not fit. Kühne, T. (2006) *Kameradschaft: Die Soldaten des nationalsozialistischen Krieges und das 20. Jahrhundert.* Göttingen: Vandenhoeck & Ruprecht: 27–78.
49 The no-stop railway track from Vienna to Triest was not opened before 1854. The Semmering-line was kind of a "world wonder" and was built under challenging conditions: The construction but even more so the efforts of the workers – many of them migrants – (quite a huge number of them died) were incredible. The Semmering

railway line was declared a "world cultural heritage." Kaser, K. & Stocker, K. (1986) *Bäuerliches Leben in der Oststeiermark seit 1848. Band 1.* Wien/Köln/Graz: Böhlau: 35.

50 "I believe that everybody prefers to travel with good horses, when the weather is good, in a comfortable coach than to take a steam boat whereat one barely notes he/she is travelling, or to travel on the railway whereat the first signal whistle sets an end to individual freedom." Bulyovszky (1858): 23.

51 "While traveling, one gets to know soon." Bulyovszky (1858): 59.

52 Only one time she mentioned a farewell: When finally parting from Dumas but even then the actual operation was not described. Bulyovszky (1858): 195 f.

53 Bulyovszky (1858): 66–77.

54 Walsh (2016): 7.

55 Stevenson (2016): 189.

56 Bulyovszky (1858): 172.

57 Bulyovszky (1858): 16; 82.

58 "who had his mouth open all the time" (Who talked all the time). Bulyovszky (1858): 4.

59 "of my enthusiastic Moravian, of whom I forgot to tell, that he versified on Hero and Leander and doing that ate sausage which reminded my nose not that much on the gardens of the Hesperides than on those of Debrezin [wordplay: name of a place as well as of a special kind of sausage]" Bulyovszky (1858): 9 f.

60 "The vanity of men is even bigger than ours." Bulyovszky (1858): 16.

61 Bulyovszky (1858): 25–42.

62 "When he saw his wife smiling he dropped his tobacco tin. Its swirling contents caused our incessant sneezing." Bulyovszky (1858): 27 f.

63 "This little episode that became even more funny because of the silk dealer's embarrassment..." Bulyovszky (1858).

64 Bulyovszky (1858): 170–177.

65 Bulyovszky (1858): 172.

66 After a failed trip a spouse sulked for hours in the chain – only the gifts her husband bought for her were able to conciliate her. Bulyovszky (1858): 77 f.

67 Bulyovszky (1858): 198–200.

68 A phenomenon that is known from other circumstances as well: Whitelegg, D. (2016) "When Being at Work isn't Work: Airline Cabin Crew, Emotional Labour and Travel," in *Gendered Journeys, Mobile Emotions*, Gayle Letherby & Gillian Reynolds (eds.). London/New York: Routledge: 133–143, 138–140.

69 "One must not search for great art in Paris."
To many German-speaking members of the performing art Paris represented the centre of stage art and Parisian theatres and theatre business were role models. This enthusiasm never completely vanished during the "long nineteenth century" but clearly changed its character in the last decades. Growing nationalism was – literally – staged in theatre. To Lilla von Bulyovszky "national" divergences explained different styles of acting. She clearly parted "French," "German," and "Hungarian" theatre giving preference to "German" art.

70 "The French are doing everything just in pretence." Bulyovszky (1858): 215.

71 "It's sad that age doesn't prevent from foolishness!" Bulyovszky (1858): 52.

72 Bulyovszky (1858): 78.

73 Bulyovszky (1858): 12.

74 Alexandre Dumas (2014).

75 "We had returned to our togetherness; but let me add quickly that this togetherness had crucially developed since our first encounter. From my point it had changed from enamoured want to intimate but highly deferential friendship. From the point of my companion from bashful fear to trusting informality" Dumas (2014): 159.

76 One of her admirers reported about an encounter with Bulyovszky. In the course of the meeting, he wrote, she had shown her indignation concerning Dumas' stories. Meysenbug, *Lilla von Bulyowsky*, 78.
77 Bulyovszky (1858): 178.
78 Healing magnetism ("Mesmerism" after Dr Franz Anton Mesmer) was intensively discussed throughout the nineteenth century and is practised still today.
79 "She pulled my hand down to her stomach, the sheet and the blanket remained between my hand and her chest." Dumas (2014): 47.
80 Social belonging was of high importance in that context as every class and group had distinct rules how to sanction "misconduct." See Frevert, U. (2011) *Emotions in History. Lost and Found.* Budapest: Central European University Press: 62–65.
81 Frevert (2011): 37–85.
82 Memory as a field that is highly (re-)shaped by emotions shows its evidence. See: Brauer, J. & Lücke, M. (2013) "Emotionen, Geschichte und historisches Lernen. Einführende Überlegungen," in *Emotionen, Geschichte und historisches Lernen. Geschichtsdidaktische und geschichtskulturelle Perspektiven*, Juliane Brauer & Martin Lücke (eds.). Göttingen: Vandenhoeck & Ruprecht Verlage: 11–26, 19f; Schnell (2015).

11 An Italian in Scandinavia
Elisa Cappellis's idealizations of the North

Rosella Perugi

Italians in the Arctic

Throughout the nineteenth century, during the Golden Age of Polar exploration, a number of expeditions were conducted to the Artic area. Primarily the United Kingdom and the United States set out on these travels, in an attempt to discover the Northwest Passage and to reach the North Pole. At the height of these activities was the celebration of the First International Polar Year in 1882, when twelve nations participated in creating twelve stations in the Artic and two in Antarctica.[1] This wave of explorations opened the area to the imagination of a wider public. After it had served as the base of many expeditions during the second half of the nineteenth century, Scandinavia became the target of an ever-increasing number of foreign travellers, the first daring tourists of the area.

Among them were primarily the British, who saw in Scandinavia a more temperate version of the Arctic, and who wanted to relive the Romantic myth of an idyllic country life that had been destroyed in their own country due to the Industrial Revolution.[2] Their presence in the North soon led to the transformation of Scandinavia from a frontier land into a touristic target[3]: British "spinsters" (as female solo travellers were often scathingly called) started to visit Scandinavia and write their travelogues. Famous examples include Henrietta Kent's *Within the Arctic Circle: Experiences of Travel through Norway, to the North Cape, Sweden and Lapland* (1887) and Mrs Alec Tweedie's. The latter visited Scandinavia after Iceland in the winter, crossed Finland by carriage, and consequently became one of the bravest female visitors of the Northern Countries in her times. A final example is Helen Peel, who sailed along Norway heading for Siberia on a steam ship in 1894.[4] After these British forerunners, the redefinition of this area in touristic terms started to attract female travellers of all nationalities. Among them were also Italians who, having been excluded from explorative expeditions so far, headed northwards between the last years of the nineteenth and the first decades of the twentieth century.

Italy was a relatively young country: It had become an independent nation between 1860 and 1870, after a long period of conflicts and negotiations with the powerful, long-lasting neighbouring nations: France and the Austrian Empire. During the Italian Risorgimento women had played a crucial role, hosting political discussions in their *salotti*, backing street upheavals, taking part in secret societies (Le Giardiniere, a female equivalent of the more renowned Carboneria), and following and protecting, at home and abroad, patriots like Giuseppe Mazzini, Giuseppe Garibaldi, Felice Cavallotti, the Cairoli brothers.[5]

However, after the unification, the figure of the emancipated woman, who fought along with men, underwent a radical change. Suddenly, women were forced to resume their role of "angel of the hearth," according to their assumed "natural inclination." The 1865 Code Pisanelli, the new Family Law, put them in a subordinate position to their fathers and husbands. Women were meant to embody the role of mothers and wives, and the long-awaited equality of rights never took place. Nonetheless, gender emancipation was unavoidably taking place in other parts of society. Due to the proliferating industrialization, especially in the North of Italy, an increasing number of working-class women were employed (and exploited) in factories. Although they were excluded from political life at first, thanks to the influence of socialist leaders like Anna Kuliscioff, the first Women Labour Unions were founded later on, which eventually led to the first laws protecting women's (and children's) labour.[6] On the basis of civil rights, the fight for women's suffrage started immediately after the unification, with Anna Maria Mozzoni's pamphlet *The Woman, and Her Social Relationships in Connection to the Review of the Italian Code*[7] (1864); indeed voting, which had been formerly promised, was now denied.[8] However, slowly but unavoidably changes occurred. In 1868, the journal Woman (La Donna) started its publication in Padua. In 1874, women were admitted to high school and university education (but not to professions).

As for professional life, women engaged especially in such "caring occupations" as teaching, education and nursing, considered "suitable for ladies";[9] some of them acquired a temporary reputation, writing books and lecturing; nevertheless, they were soon ignored and eventually disappeared from the cultural scene after a few years.[10] In such a context the woman writer remained an exception, struggling to acquire a recognised status. Few writers enjoyed a limited reputation, and mainly in a gendered field (children's books and books for young women). Eventually, only some actresses and sopranos – that is, professionals in the field of entertainment – acquired international fame.[11] In general, Italian women were certainly not encouraged to emancipate in society or public debate. Instead, they were searching for their own identity, struggling with their paradoxical role of embodying the wife and the mother on the one hand, and taking part in industrial labour on the other, rebuilding a *Terza Italia* which was meant to lead Europe towards a new Renaissance.[12]

On the international scene, Italy was economically weak, but nonetheless aspired to a leading position. Although it was not a colonial power yet, it started to to take part in the "scramble for Africa," as well as other parts of the world.[13] Although Italy was still absent in the organization of the Polar Year of 1882, it did claim a role in various Arctic expeditions. For instance in the last years of the nineteenth century, some officers of the Italian Royal Navy sailed with Nordenskiöld in search of the Northeast passage.[14] Moreover, between 1899 and 1900, Luigi

Amedeo d'Aosta, Duke of Abruzzi, organised an expedition that earned him national (and international) fame: "Sledding to the North Pole, on 25 April 1900, he reached the latitude of 86°33' 49," that remained unsurpassed for 6 years.[15] In addition, in 1880, Paolo Mantegazza and his friend Stephen Sommier visited Scandinavia and wrote a detailed travelogue of the area, which was rich in cultural and environmental features, and can be considered one of the first tourist guides in Italian.[16] However, explorers and scholars travelling for scientific purposes did not involve women in their staff, as they considered them to be too emotional, and therefore unsuitable for scientific projects of any kind.[17] As they were excluded from men's parties, whether professional or scientific, Italian women did not have a valid reason to travel. If they did travel (abroad), it was usually there to accompany their husbands or relatives, and escort them during diplomatic missions or business ventures. Italian women had to wait for the advent of tourism to start travelling on their own – at least without having to account for it.

A journey of one's own: Italian women head northwards

In this atmosphere, at the dawn of the twentieth century, it seems that few Italian women chose the "extreme North" for their journeys. Although these women usually represented a wealthy, educated, international upper class, they all "carried the luggage," as they were the subordinate members of a rigid patriarchal culture. By venturing to the idealised world of the Nordic Countries, they could provisionally escape. Female travelogues remain extremely and conspicuously rare in the field of Italian travel literature, in which male writing was unrivalled.[18]

We cannot speak of these female Italian travellers as "group," but certainly of a minor, elitist trend, a fringe fashion, that started and ended in a few decades. There have only been eight women who travelled northwards and reported on their trips in this period, ranging from the first travellers who visited the North in 1898,[19] and the last who visited that area in 1937.[20]

Elisa Cappelli in Sweden

Elisa Cappelli (Firenze, 1845–?) daughter of Luigi, a goldsmith in Florence, was a teacher and an educational developer. Nowadays her name and her books are forgotten, but in her time, she was a prolific writer of several volumes, covering a wide variety of topics. Her production convered a variety of subjects related to educational methods and were regularly reissued until 1938. Her schoolbooks were used in primary and secondary schools until the 1940s. She was also a translator of French and English. As a teacher at Italian state schools, she was involved in the theoretical debate on education all her life; she was responsible for *Storia universale della pedagogia*[21] (1884, MI-Trevisini), the first Italian translation of J. Paroz's *Histoire Universelle de la Pédagogie* (1867), in which Cappelli introduced and supported Pestalozzi's intuitive method. She took an active part in the educational debate, which was particularly lively in Italy during those years. As a new nation, Italy had to address the problem of the lack of a common syllabus or language, as local dialects still prevailed in everyday communication. Elisa Cappelli was deeply involved in the effort of creating a common language within the educational system. She aimed to spread new models of behaviour and new values among the "new" Italians; this is why her production is so varied and widens from simple textbooks to theoretical handbooks on didactics, from children's books to translations, from her own fiction to, eventually, her travelogue.

Cappelli's detailed travelogue was written in 1898 and published in 1902; at that time she was a lady of 53, and probably the first Italian woman to report her experience in Scandinavia, in times when independent travelling was neither fashionable nor recommended for a middle-aged Italian woman.[22] Cappelli writes a faithful daily report of the events occurred while travelling. Far from creating an imaginary world, or reworking events subjectively, her travelogue aims to describe facts and events.[23] The book's title *In Svezia* (*In Sweden*) simply clarifies the destination of her journey. Interestingly, it is followed by a double subheading. The first, *Impressioni di viaggio* (*Travel impressions*) hints at her subjective impressions. The second, *Libro per la Gioventù* (*A book for the Youth*) states her mission: The book is addressed above all to the young generation, the brand-new Italians that were born after the unification, those same pupils Cappelli used to teach. Although it is never openly declared in the text, she aims at widening young people's minds and offering a glimpse of a distant, attractive country – unknown to most of them, and not at all popular as a touristic destination in those days. Indeed the clarity of the author's aim recalls Braidotti's assertion that "a vision requires a politics of positioning" which, in its turn, "implies responsibility."[24] In the case of Cappelli, her "politics of positioning" can be seen in what she considers her mission, that of widening young Italians' minds by showing how their Swedish peers behave, especially between the two sexes, both in the social and in the family sphere. Writing a travelogue allows her to depict a social system that may influence Italy positively, especially in light of the relationship between the two sexes, and urges the new generation to favour women's emancipation.

By following this line of thought, and thus deliberately neglecting the more consistent descriptive one about the places, cities, and natural landscapes visited, the reader is left with two possible engagements with the text. The first is to investigate Cappelli's descriptions of human relationships, including the people she meets directly and how they welcome and host her. The second possibility, is to focus on the development of relationships among people, described through her eyes as an outsider, all the more impartial as she belongs to a foreign culture.

The idealised North

Apparently, during her transit[25] from Florence to Sweden, Cappelli only travels in feminine company: she and Ebba, her female companion, share the accommodation, their impressions, their opinions; nevertheless, male encounters are very frequent, as all the workers they meet are men, who prove to be essential both for the progression of the journey and to substantiate the writer's remarks. Observation plays an important role in defining the author's "travel impressions," and often substitute a direct interaction that, given her state of a female traveller in transit, is neither possible nor advisable.[26] A striking detail is that, during the entire trip, Cappelli is attracted by the elegant uniforms of coachmen, soldiers, and policemen even before they have reached "the North," as she describes them as early as in Lucerne.[27] In Berlin, again, she is attracted by the physicality of the handsome, broad-chested soldiers, goose-stepping.[28] And then again, in Stockholm she meticulously describes the changing of the guard, where the soldiers are (of course) tall, young men, with a proud posture.[29] In fact, she is quite frequently impressed by people's physical appearance: First the Bavarians, who "...are healthy and strong people, taller than usual, also the women, and with a frank and honest spirit, though a bit rude superficially."[30]

Later, Cappelli praises the first "Nordic" students she encounters, singing in a park in Copenhagen: "that superior crowd of handsome, tall, white-dressed, white-cap youth."[31] These are all examples of how the author tries to apply her theoretical knowledge about physiognomy and phrenology in practice; she shows her interest for, and competence in, the "new sciences," and shares Lombroso's theories on physical types. These theories enjoyed a valid scientific reputation in Italy (and in the whole of Europe) at the time.

When she finally reaches Sweden, the author's appreciation for the Nordic type becomes more and more evident. Tall, blue-eyed, usually "long haired" workers immediately attract her attention.[32] Similarly to descriptions of the Germans, these physical features are considered signs of good temper and high moral values. For example, train conductors in Dalarna are described as:

> handsome and strong, like all the people in charge for public services in Sweden, proceed calm and self-confident, and are of an extraordinary politeness.[33]

At Ludvika, "kind and friendly" workers politely greet her on the road, even though they are walking home quickly and deliberately after a hard day's work; the farmer that leads her and her friend into a small historical house in Ornäs, once Gustav Wasa's refuge, is not only "handsome and strong" but so hospitable as to invite the two women into his humble house for a snack.[34] Additionally, to underscore Swedish men's gentle inclination, Cappelli writes that there are "no bird hunters in Sweden."[35]

Cappelli's direct experiences reinforce her opinion: Swedish people's flawless behaviour depends on the perfect examples given by the Royal family and the representatives of the Lutheran Church. Among her random encounters, one proves to be particularly meaningful: Karl, the Prince of Sweden, son of King Oscar, that she meets —— by chance at the Stockholm station. Here a small crowd is gathering to see him get off a train, where he travels like any of his subjects: He's "tall and thin," but his attitude is "quick and assertive."[36] Dressed in civilian clothes, he politely greets everybody and reaches his carriage. In

Frescati, Cappelli is hosted by a Minister and his young wife; far from being scandalised as a Catholic by a married Lutheran clergyman, she receives the young couple's friendly hospitality, and gratefully describes the man, again by starting with his physical appearance and relating it to his good attitude and morals: "[...] the husband, a Minister, young, light-haired and strong, whose sportive and fair face expressed the purity of his thought and habits."[37] As it was the case with Prince Karl, the Minister's appearance reflects a positive moral attitude. After these experiences, Cappelli feels entitled to draw some striking conclusions: The Swedes are "honest and disciplined" because of the positive examples of the King and the Protestant Ministers, that "proceed in a mutual accord" which lays the foundations for an equal and peaceful society, where people can live a pleasant life.[38] However, the travelogue is not only aimed at persuading her readers of the Swedes' high moral values. Addressing young people, the author tries to amuse them and arouse their curiosity, while relying on rhetoric of equality and peace.

As Cappelli travels in the summer, she has the opportunity to participate in traditional festivities. First of all, Midsummer Night's Eve, that she celebrates in Leksand: Here all the country people, men and women, dance together around the Pole, dressed in their traditional costumes.[39] It is noteworthy that Cappelli includes this performance of "tradition" in her travelogue. She also notices some drunkards, but even in their drunken state, they don't damage the idealised image Cappelli had envisioned: "...their drunkenness lasts a short time and does not damage anyone; it brings a good mood instead!"[40] After midnight, couples continue to dance outside in the meadows, until dawn, which would have been an unthinkable transgression in Italy.[41] Although she is usually full of admiration for Swedish traditions and folklore in every small town or village she visits, Cappelli's encounter with the Laplanders reveals her prejudice against this people: She sees them in Skansen, Stockholm's open air museum, and subsequently dismisses them with the openly despising sentence: "...short and ugly [...] by nature melancholic and suspicious, and we didn't dare speak to them, lest we'd be offended."[42] The author does not consider that these people lived in captivity and were on display like animals within the confines of the open air museum. Instead, she views their hideous physical appearance as an indication for their attitude and character, so that the Laplanders are the only negative people she reports on during her whole stay in Sweden.

However, on matters of gender, she adheres to a more equalitarian view. This view comes to the fore when she expresses her amazement over the equality between men and women, both in the intellectual possibilities they are granted in Sweden as well as their ability to engage in physical activities. In Rattvik Cappelli meets groups of sportswomen trekking, wearing boots and rucksacks, and on the Siljan Lake women are rowing "like men."[43] Her amazement primarily stems from the fact that, in her home country, these activities were considered unsuitable for women. Moreover, she observes groups of university students of mixed sex in Swedish cities like Uppsala and Stockholm. This would be quite unusual in Italy, where separation between sexes was the norm, and university education was considered unsuitable for women.[44] These students are either friends of her host Ebba, or just strangers, relaxing in parks or attending social events. Although it is not emphasised excessively in her travelogue, their mere presence in her description suggests an appreciation of gender equality. While events such as open-air parties, choirs, orchestras, dances, decorate Cappelli's narrative, apparently just ornamentatively, she continuously underscores her admiration to lead a quiet and dignified life in a condition of evident equality.[45] At the end of her journey Cappelli visits the so-called "Society of Work" in Stockholm, where women of all social classes (even one of the Princess' Ladies-in-Waiting) offer their handwork for sale, be it tapestry, knitting, embroidery, under the supervision of the Swedish Court itself, "...and to the women who contribute the gratitude of the whole Country is righteously deserved."[46] Herself a model of independence, she meets women busy both at home and outside. Consequently, she maintains that:

> Northern women's industriousness is unquestioned. In Sweden all ladies work, be they rich or poor, and they do not waste their time with visits or useless gossips. If they go to meet a friend, they take a handwork with them; rich ladies work for the poor, experiencing those true and intimate rewards that are not possible to those who live a fake and superficial life.[47]

Such a statement sounds not only like praise for Northern women, but also like an indirect criticism of the Italian social convention of paying visits and gossiping. More importantly, passages like these reveal how Cappelli discretely (and continuously) submits her readers to issues of women's emancipation.

Enjoying Ebba's company: travelling with "my Swede"

Cappelli's travel is rich in new and unusual relationships. First of all, she travels with a younger female friend, her former student of Italian in Florence, who accompanies and assists her all along the way, and will be her host once in Sweden.[48] As a matter of fact, this woman is never described thoroughly, possibly due to the rules of decency of the times, which recommended a general characterization, rather than a detailed one, when dealing with close friends that could be identified by the readers.[49] Indeed, this travel companion is first referred to by her Christian name only, and only in Chapter 7, when the two women reach Copenhagen: "Ebba (this is my Swede's name)."[50] However, she represents a steady reference point, albeit anonymous; since the first lines of the book, she has been depicted as:

> a Swedish young lady, my former pupil and now very dear friend who, in a bit longer than two years, has learnt Italian so well as to overtake her teacher; and she is now more Italian than Swedish, both because she has lived in Florence for a long time, and because of her feeling.[51]

Later, she is often referred to as "my friend," "my Swede."[52] Very often Cappelli uses the personal pronoun *we*, implicitly including Ebba in her narrative. Ebba is a silent but essential companion: she speaks German and, of course Swedish, so she can arrange all the details of the journey, book hotels or buy tickets, and more generally interact with the natives; until their touching farewell in Hamburg, on Cappelli's way back to Italy:

> And it was time to leave. My good friend took care of everything, she gave me all the necessary information, had thousands of loving concerns for me, and we regretfully separated for good.[53]

As an Italian abroad, Cappelli is the guest of honour in a number of events. The first invitation she receives is in Berlin, where a Swedish friend of Ebba's, married to a famous German painter, welcomes the two women to a picnic in the forest, with a group of friends of hers. The author's description of the hostess is quite conventional, and Cappelli will repeatedly use the same words for most of the Swedish hostesses she meets: She omits the woman's name, defining her as "beautiful and kind, and very nice."[54] The same adjectives characterise women all over the travelogue: Ebba's family members in Goteborg, who learnt some Italian words of welcome; the Swedish extended family in Ludvika; the hosts in Uppsala; the Minister's wife in Frescati.[55]

Cappelli is not just a tourist, fascinated by the beauty of the Swedes; she also has the priviliged opportunity of living within Swedish families, observing the relationships between men and women in this intimate context. She admires the partners' balanced collaboration in a traditional structure, with men functioning as the wise head of the household, and women satisfied with an active, albeit complementary, position. Cappelli never explicitly compares the patriarchical Italian family to the Swedish family structure. Instead, she eloquently depicts the latter, thus providing her readers with a wealth of meaningful examples to enable them to draw their own conclusions. At times she cannot avoid noticing a difference with her home country: in Sweden, middle-class women are first of all wives, and secondly mothers. In fact, they accompany their husbands on scientific or business trips, while the children stay at home with "reliable, honest" nannies.[56]

Social events follow one another along Cappelli's journey with an amazing frequency; since the first occurrence in Berlin she speculates that, to overtake the sombre winter solitude, Northern people take advantage of the short, bright summer days by spending as much time as possible together in the open, for instance by arranging very informal events. Picnics, as well as concerts in parks, soon become a reccuring opportunity to socialise with the locals. Moreover, because of her nationality she is welcomed everywhere as a special guest. Among the Nordic middle-class, educated people she meets, her Italian heritage is perceived as the mark of a refined culture and an illustrious historical past. Since the first picnic in Germany the people she meets are generally "appreciators of the arts and literature"[57] and students, who "praise Italy and express their will to visit it."[58]

As a life-long teacher, Cappelli feels at ease with young people and all the students she meets: She draws some interesting conclusions based on her observations, as well as direct interactions with the local people; ranging from Berlin to Gothenburg, from Ludvika to Uppsala to Stockholm, and describing both public spaces and family's houses, her observations describe a wide range of interactions. One of her conclusions concerns the close relationship of the Swedes with nature, which "explains the Swedes' temperament as excellent workers, however simple and honest in their thoughts and actions, and maybe also happy."[59] Consequently, children are also good natured, and show great respect for the adults.[60] Moreover, nature inspires their creativity: "Fantasy prevails also in children, which is explained with the environment around them."[61]

A visit to Ebba's family friends in Ludvika absolutely assures the author of the Swedes' good and strong nature: this wealthy old couple, living in a beautiful villa, receives her in the friendliest way.[62] The wife is, as are all the women in the narrative, extremely kind and hospitable, and treats the author as an old friend.[63] Her husband, the unquestioned head of the family is an old, handsome gentleman with an assertive countenance, who suffers from a serious heart disease. When the children of the family come to visit their parents, Cappelli notices their "reverent respect," which shows even in the "simplest gestures of everyday life."[64] The husband's behaviour towards her confirms her opinion about the Swedes' extreme decency. When she leaves to continue her journey, the man has reached the final stage of his disease; nevertheless:

> he apologized [via Ebba], as he was receiving me in bed…he, a dying person! [...] I saw him raise [...] and lower his head in a deep and respectful bow.[65]

Cappelli draws her conclusions:

> [...] Such a principled people – I thought – can only be strong and good-natured, and indeed the Scandinavians are, uncorrupted from the climate or the excessive refinements.[66]

Again, the author's indirect allusion to her home country's habits (that is, instead, affected by the climate and the refinements) is clear.

Lastly, she has the opportunity to visit Stockholm Royal Library and some schools, and is able to interact with the Heads of these institutions. The Library Director is a very learned and polite gentleman who speaks Italian: Cappelli is very satisfied, as eventually she can exchange her opinions freely, using her native language. The Director tells her about his visits to Italy, and his amazement in Naples: "Everybody is shouting! – he said – and for us, used to quietness, this is absolutely disturbing."[67] He is very proud of being Swedish, since "Here we are happy – he said – we are peaceful, and we don't have to worry about politics."[68] Cappelli is ready to comment:

Indeed the Swedes, because of their geographical position, their temperament and their educational orientation, are such an ordered people that they reject any disagreement or turmoil.[69]

Again, her comment offers an indirect reference to the confusion, restlessness, and disorganization that prevail in her home country. She visits two schools and meets the Director of one of them in Nääs, near Gothenburg. Here she is received in the most respectful way:

The Director had been informed of my visit and [...] displayed the Italian flag. Hospitality, innate in Northern people, emphasises when they meet Southern people. Because they spend most of the year between snow and ice, they take Italy in the utmost consideration, calling it "the Country of the Sun," and therefore they urge upon welcoming Italians in the most sincere and affectionate way.[70]

Cappelli comments on the syllabuses as well, a subject she is particularly passionate about. She praises the homogeneity of teaching for both boys and girls, as there is no apparent difference in their syllabus in primary schools. She has the opportunity to observe the students, working harmoniously together in vocational schools. She notes that all the students, boys and girls, have to exercise every day between their classes, and that corsets are forbidden for girls. She describes physical activities and loose clothes as allowing them to be particularly healthy.[71]

Conclusion

Cappelli is a scholar and an educator; although in this capacity she is a professional writer, *In Svezia* is her only travelogue and, as the subtitle declares, it is devoted to expose the young generation to a foreign culture and involve them in considering its social values. Therefore companionship is important, presented as an example of peaceful, respectful social and familiar coexistence; whereas the readers' amusement and the description of an exotic environment are only ancillary themes. Indeed, this journey represented a unique opportunity for Cappelli, interested as she is – as a woman, as a teacher and as a scholar in pedagogical studies – in experiencing the differences in social structures and human relationships in Swedish society, both through observations and direct interaction. As she is perfectly aware of her role in society – that of a teacher and educational developer – she is very careful not to shock her readers, and gradually guides them to share her positive opinion about Sweden. To do so, she approaches her destination carefully; not just the real one – the foreign country – but also an ideal one, for what it represents in terms of differences with Italy.

It might be said that she is careful not to reject Italy (perhaps keeping her audience in mind), as its glory, fame, and history are well known and admired by the host people. Rather, she wants to be inspired by that other possible world. I suggest that the implicit message of Cappelli's travelogue, is a highly emancipatory and idealistic one: what if there was a place in Italy's new and still-developing identity for the kindness, politeness, social equality that the Swedish society embodies? In a way, her travelling companion Ebba is a crucial character in this project, and not just because her very presence clearly opens doors up North since they often visit her friends and relatives. Ebba is *both* Swedish and Italian – in fact, as we have seen, she is even called "now more Italian than Swedish, both because she has lived in Florence for a long time and because of her feeling" – and therefore in a sense embodies what Cappelli seems to stand for: a kind of synthesis between South and North, or more precisely, an Italy that remains true to itself but that has adapted what is valuable from Northern models.

Although it is very conventionally written, Cappelli's travelogue is not ordinary and underscores her personal approach. By citing the words of the people she meets and describing their behaviour both in public and private, she indirectly points to a positive example of social coexistence for her fellow country people. She offers a variety of observations, substantiated by physognomic theories – which were considered scientific and reliable in her time. Thus, her observations are "scientifically" justified to serve as evidence for the Swedes' nature and their moral attitude. Moreover, she concludes that the Swedes' attitudes are responsible for the Swedish peaceful way of life, thus openly expressing her personal approval of this (exotic) sensibility. By providing a wealth of observations of harmonious coexistence, she indicates a positive example for her target readers, namely students and young people in general: the image of a country where men and women live in harmony and equality.

Notes

1 https://www.pmel.noaa.gov/arctic-zone/ipy-1/index.htm; http://www.ipy.org/; Malaurie, J. (2001) *Ultima Thulé*, 2nd edition. Paris: Chêne; Berton, P. (2001) *The Arctic Grail: The Quest for the Northwest Passage and the North Pole, 1818–1909.* Toronto: The Lyons Press.

2 Fjagesund, P. & Symes, R.A. (2003) *The Northern Utopia: British Perceptions of Norway in the Nineteenth Century.* Amsterdam: Rodopi.

3 Taylor, B. (1857) *Northern Travel. Summer and Winter Pictures of Sweden, Lapland and Norway.* New York: G.P. Putnam; Kassis, D. (2015) *Representations of the North in Victorian Travel Literature.* Cambridge: Cambridge Scholars Publishing; Hansson, H. (2009) "The Gentlemen's North: Lord Dufferin and the Beginnings of Arctic Tourism," *Studies in Travel Writing* 13: 1, 61–73.

4 Birkett, D. (1989) *Spinsters Abroad: Victorian Lady Explorers.* Oxford: Blackwell Publishing; Foster, S. (1990) *Across New Worlds: Nineteenth Century Women Travellers and Their Writings.* New York: Harvester Wheatsheaf; Birkett, D. (2004) *Off the Beaten Track: Three Centuries of Women Travellers and Their Writings.* London: National Portrait Gallery; Leavenworth, M. L. (2010) "Exotic Norths? Representations of Northern Scandinavia" in S.H. Kent's "Within the Arctic Circle and Bayard Taylor's Northern Travel," *Nordlit*, 26; Hansson, H. (2007) "Henrietta Kent and the Feminised North," *Nordlit,* 22.

5   Doni, E. (2011) *Le donne del Risorgimento*. Bologna: Il Mulino. With examples of the manifold role of women in the *Risorgimento*.

6   In 1902, a law was issued that forbade working in mines and limited the daily timetable to twelve hours (Carcano Law, or 242/1902 Law)

7   Mozzoni, A.M. (1865) *La donna e i suoi Rapporti Sociali in Occasione della Revisione del Codice Italiano*. Milan: Tipografia Sociale.

8   Some States in the Italian peninsula had already granted women's participation to local elections (the former Lombardo-Veneto; the Grand Duchy of Tuscany); in 1861 women from Lombardia presented in vain a petition to Italian Parliament. Galeotti, G. (2006) *La sconfitta di Atena*, in *Storia del voto alle donne in Italia*. Rome: Biblink. Even in 1912 the PM Giovanni Giolitti refused the vote to women, defining it a "leap in the dark." Eventually, Italian women voted in 1946.

9   Opinions on women's intelligence witnessed the belief of her inferiority. As an example, Paolo Mantegazza wrote: "woman is shorter, and her brains are lighter (la donna è più bassa [...] il suo cervello ha minor peso)." Mantegazza, P. (1893) *Fisiologia della donne*. Milan: Edizione Studio Tesi: 13; "Oppression in itself, in which woman is bred, is not enough to justify her inferiority (L'oppressione, in cui fu tenuta fino ad oggi la donna, non basta a spiegare la sua inferiorità)." Mantegazza (1893): 269.

10 The advent of Fascism played an important role in erasing women from the Italian cultural scene. The most famous example is Maria Montessori, still well-known abroad, where her educational programme is followed in many schools, but is recognised in Italy only at the elementary level. De Grazia, V. (1993) *Le donne nel regime fascista*. Venice: Marsilio.

11 In 1877 Ernestina Puritz, of Russian origins, received a university degree in medicine; Rina Monti, in 1907 was the first female professor in an Italian University. The most famous actresses were Eleonora Duse, Lyda Borelli, and Francesca Bertini; writers Matilde Serao, Sibilla Aleramo, Carolina Invernizio, and Grazia Deledda (who won the 1926 Nobel Prize in Literature, but even nowadays is underestimated and mostly ignored in school textbooks); sopranos Luisa Tetrazzini and Lina Cavalieri.

12 Although this will be the leit-motif of Fascist culture, the idea is already very popular in post-unitary Italy, supported, among the others, by Giuseppe Carducci, the "*Vate della terza Italia*," one of the most authoritative poets and scholars of the period and winner of the Nobel Prize in Literature in 1906. Armellini, G. & Colombo, A. (1993) *La letteratura italiana*, vol. C1. Bologna: Zanichelli: 323–364; De Grazia (1993).

13 Bandini, F. (2014) *Gli italiani in Africa. Storia delle guerre coloniali 1882–1943*. Res Gestae; Corradini, E. (3 December 1919) *Report to the First Nationalist Congress*. Florence; Abbondanza, G. (2016) *Italia potenza regionale. Il contesto africano dall'Unità ai giorni nostri*. Rome: Aracne; Pascoli, G. *La Grande Proletaria si è mossa,* speech held in Barga (Lu) 11–11-1911.

14 The most important was Giacomo Bove, 1878–1880.

15 Nencioni, G. (2010) *The Italians in the Arctic Explorations*. Umeå: Umeå University.

16 Carcreff, A.O. (2014) *Paolo Mantegazza e Stephen Sommier in Lapponia*. Monaco: Liber Faber; Puccini, S. (2003) *Bozzetti lapponici. Il viaggio in Lapponia di Paolo Mantegazza e Stephen Sommier, antropologi*. Manziana: Vechiarelli; Mantegazza, P. (1881) *Un viaggio in Lapponia con l'amico Stephen Sommiers*. Milan: Clinamen.

17 Möebius, P.J. (1900) *Über den physiologischen Schwachsinn des Weibes*. Vol. 3, Chapter 3. Leipzig: Hall, who maintains that women are less intelligent than men because their brains are lighter; on women's inferiority, see also Lombroso, C. & Ferrero, C.G. (1893) *La donna delinquente, la prostituta e la donna normale*. Turin: L. Roux.

18 In the second half of the nineteenth century few Italian women ventured abroad and wrote about their journeys; among these, Cristina Trivulzio di Belgiojoso

wrote about her journey to Palestine, deepening her permanence in Turkey; Amalia Nizzoli wrote about Egypt, where she accompained her husband in a diplomatic mission. The first wrote in French, while the second had very little, if any, follow-up.

19 Possibly there are more diaries, which were never published.

20 Elisa Cappelli, an educationist and teacher from Florence, wrote a detailed report on her journey to Sweden in 1898. Maria Savi Lopez, a scholar of folklore and an anthropologist from Turin, narrated about Norwegian landscapes, legends, and traditions. Giulia Kapp Salvini, from Ancona, Stefania Türr from Rome, two wealthy noblewomen, and Ester Lombardo, a Sicilian reporter, sailed on cruises along the Scandinavian coasts in different periods: The first visited the Baltic area in 1904 and took part in the launching cruise to Iceland the following year; Stefania Türr achieved her childhood dream, visiting Norway and the Svalbard Archipelago in 1924; Ester Lombardo was the last Italian woman to write a report of her cruise northwards in 1926. Luisa Santandrea, a writer and translator from Milan, undertook an introspective journey that led her onto the meanders of Norwegian fjords – and of her own psychological malaise – in 1924. Maria Albertina Loschi and Anna Maria Speckel, two representatives of the Fascist Party, visited the Baltic and the Finnish area as members of diplomatic delegations: The first to report about Finnish culture and its assumed similarities with the Italian in 1924, the second to spread Italian culture to the far North in 1935.

21 All the translations from Italian in this paper are by the author, unless otherwise specified.

22 However, during the same years two other Italian women set their writings in Scandinavia: Giulia Kapp Salvini, that cruises to Iceland; and Maria Savi Lopez, a scholar of folklore and a forerunner of ethnology in Italy, who transcribes Nordic legends and writes fictitious novels on the foreground of the extreme North.

23 Martens, L. (2009) *The Diary Novel*. Cambridge: Cambridge University Press.

24 Braidotti, R. (2011) *Nomadic Subjects: Embodiment and Sexual Difference in Contemporary Feminist Theory*. New York: Columbia University Press.

25 I use the term "transit" as defined by Leed, E.J. (1991) *The Mind of the Traveler. From Gilgamesh to Global Tourism*. New York: Basic Books: 13.

26 As early as 1889, Lillias Campbell Davidson recommended first of all "coolness and self-possession" to women travellers on their own. Campbell Davidson, L. (2011) *Hints to Lady Travellers (at home and abroad)*. London: Elliot & Thompson.

27 Cappelli, E. (1902) *In Svezia: Impressioni di Viaggio: Libro per la gioventù*. Firenze: R. Bemporad & Figlio: 10.

28 Cappelli (1902): 23.

29 Cappelli (1902): 170.

30 "I Bavaresi sono gente sana e robusta, di altezza non comune, comprese le donne, ed anche di animo schietto ed onesto, quantunque un po' ruvidi in superficie." Cappelli (1902): 31.

31 "quella schiera eletta di giovani belli, alti, tutti vestiti di bianco, col berrettino parimenti bianco" Cappelli (1902): 31.

32 Cappelli (1902): 74.

33 "belli e forti, come tutte le persone addette ai servizi pubblici in Svezia, vanno calmi e sicuri, e sono di una cortesia straordinaria." Elisa Cappelli (1902): 59.

34 Cappelli (1902): 111, 64.

35 Cappelli (1902): 73.

36 Cappelli (1902): 171.

37 "Il marito, un pastore, giovane, biondo e forte, sulla cui faccia gioviale e serena era scritta la illibatezza del pensiero e del costume" Cappelli (1902): 177.

38 Cappelli (1902): 176.

39 Cappelli (1902): 82.

40 "…la loro ubriachezza è momentanea e non reca danno a nessuno; anzi mette di buon umore ed essi e chi li vede." Cappelli (1902): 84.

41 Cappelli (1902): 86

42 "…piccoli e brutti […] per natura tristi e diffidenti, non osammo rivolgere loro la parola per timore di ricevere un mal garbo." Cappelli (1902): 164–165.

43 Cappelli (1902): 74, 87.

44 Willson, P. (2009) *Women in Twentieth-Century Italy.* London: Palgrave MacMillan.

45 Cappelli (1903): 30–31; 48; 135–137; 142; 197.

46 "…e le donne che vi contribuiscono col loro lavoro, hanno un titolo alla riconoscenza di tutto il Paese." Cappelli (1902): 181.

47 "L'operosità della donna del Nord è proverbiale. In Svezia le signore, ricche e povere, lavoran tutte, né perdono tempo in visite e chiacchiere inutili. Se vanno a trovare un'amica, portano il lavoro; e le ricche lavorano per i poveri, provando così quelle soddisfazioni intime e vere che non son date a chi vive di vita fittizia e superficiale:" Cappelli (1902): 57.

48 The end of the nineteenth and the first decades of the twentieth century see a deep interest from the Nordic countries for Italy, especially as for figurative arts. Bottai, M.S. (2009) "Perché vai in Italia?" – Artisti finlandesi in Italia e la rinascita della pittura murale in Finlandia tra Otto e Novecento (Ph.D. diss., University Roma La Sapienza). Probably Ebba is one of these Nordic people, interested to learn about Italian Arts and history.

49 The same attitude can be noticed in another contemporary woman writer, Giulia Kapp Salvini, that hints at her travel companions using only the first letter of their surnames.

50 "…Ebba (è questo il nome della mia Svedese)" Cappelli (1902): 31.

51 "… una signorina svedese, già mia alunna ed ora carissima amica, la quale, in poco più di due anni, ha imparato così bene l'italiano, da superare la sua maestra; ed è più italiana che svedese, sia per la consuetudine dell'aver abitato per molto tempo a Firenze come per il sentiment." Cappelli (1902): 1.

52 Cappelli (1902): 4, 14, 19, 22, 29, 30.

53 "E venne l'ora della partenza. La mia buona amica provvide a tutto, mi dette le istruzioni necessarie, ebbe per me mille pensieri affettuosi, e con vivo rincrescimento ci lasciammo." Cappelli (1902): 211.

54 Cappelli (1902): 19.

55 Cappelli (1902): 39; 95–99; 135, 141; 171

56 Cappelli (1902): 127.

57 "cultori di arte e di lettere," Cappelli (1902): 20.

58 "Fu inneggiato all'Italia ed espresso il desiderio di visitarla." Cappelli (1902): 20.

59 "Così spiegasi l'indole del popolo svedese, lavoratore per eccellenza, e perciò semplice e onesto nel pensare e nell'operare, e forse anche felice" Cappelli (1902): 48–49.

60 Cappelli (1902): 19, 119, 120.

61 "Il senso del fantastico predomina anche nei bambini, il che è spiegato dall'ambiente che li circonda." Cappelli (1902): 130.

62 Cappelli (1902): 94.

63 Cappelli (1902): 98.

64 Cappelli (1902): 120.

65 "…mi fece chiedere scusa [via Ebba] per esser costretto a ricevermi in letto, egli, un moribondo! […] lo vidi sollevarsi, e farmi con la testa un profondo e reverente inchino…" Cappelli (1902): 133.

66 "Un popolo che ha tali principi – pensavo- non può che essere forte e buono, e tali sono gli Scandinavi, non corrotti dal clima o dale raffinatezze soverchie." Cappelli (1902): 120.

67 "Tutti gridano! -esclamava- e per noi avvezzi alla quiete, ciò produce grande impressione." Cappelli (1902): 158.
68 "Qui siamo felici -mi diceva;- abbiamo la pace e le questioni politiche non ci preoccupano." Cappelli (1902): 158.
69 "In fatti gli Svedesi, sì per la loro posizione geografica come per l'indole e per l'indirizzo dato alla loro educazione, sono un popolo talmente disciplinato che rifugge da qualunque dissidio o turbamento." Cappelli (1902): 158.
70 "Il Direttore era stato avvisato, e per far onore a un'italiana che andava a visitare la sua scuola, aveva messo fuori la bandiera tricolore. Il senso dell'ospitalità, innato nei nordici, si accentua di fronte agli abitanti del mezzogiorno. Essi che passano buona parte dell'anno fra le nevi e i ghiacci, hanno un vero culto per l'Italia che chiamano 'il paese del sole' e perciò sentono il bisogno di festeggiare gl'Italiani nel modo che più si confà al loro animo schietto e affettuoso." Cappelli (1902): 195–196.
71 Cappelli (1902): 198.

12 Goddess and Leader

Conflict and companionship in Agnes Herbert's hunting travelogues

Tara Kathleen Kelly

"I think steamer travelling is most enjoyable – that is, unless one happens to be married, in which case there is no pleasure in it, or in much else for the matter of that."[1] So wrote Agnes Herbert, a wealthy English widow who had just undertaken an African safari accompanied by her cousin Cecily Baird, in her book about their adventure, *Two Dianas in Somaliland*. ("Diana," a reference to the Roman goddess of the hunt, was a common term for women hunters at the time.) Published in 1908, the book proved so popular that Herbert quickly received a contract for a sequel from her publisher John Lane. She and Baird chose Alaska as their next destination – but there they did things differently, because they invited two men to share the journey with them. Herbert's account of that trip, *Two Dianas in Alaska,* is at once companionate and contentious, a story of what it meant to seek adventure as a woman traveller in the sometimes supportive, sometimes fractious company of men.

Two Dianas in Alaska challenges common conceptions of Edwardian[2] travel and travel literature – and not only that written by women, but also by men, because the book includes contributions from one of Herbert's male companions. The conventions surrounding adventure writing by Edwardian men appear to have been remarkably stable overall: The historiography finds them consistently presenting themselves in print as the heroic embodiments of masculine virtues such as courage and control. In British narratives, such a persona was often framed as an imperial hero, while in American writing he was usually presented as a devotee of the strenuous life or as an emulator of the pioneers. In either case, narratives of adventure and travel appear to have embodied (in Monica Anderson's words) "masculine power, authority and autonomy" for readers.[3] This in turn meant that Edwardian women writers had to negotiate with a well-established discourse that associated travel, especially adventurous travel, with the heroic, masterful male. Women responded to that challenge in a variety of ways: Mary Louise Pratt has argued that some of them adopted the persona of the "sentimental narrator" in order to conjure reassuring associations with the private sphere, while Sara Mills has found others using self-effacement to deal with their "uneasiness" with the heroic voice.[4] But hunter-writer Agnes Herbert did neither of these things. Instead, she pushed the limits of gendered discourse for women in her era, even as her male coauthor supported her narrative and, in doing so, complicated the seemingly stable figure of the male adventure hero. Their experiences together in Alaska, the ways they chose to describe them, and the book's reception, all raise provocative questions about our current understandings of gendered discourses of travel in the Edwardian world – especially, but not exclusively, in narratives focused on hunting and adventure.[5]

Grouping travelogues with hunting narratives immediately raises two larger questions, however: How common was it for men and women to travel and hunt together at the beginning of the twentieth century, and why should hunting narratives be considered as part of travel literature? There is a great deal of evidence with which to answer the first question. Between 1880 and 1914, hundreds of narratives that combined hunting with travel were published in the English-speaking world. Most of the writers were men and many of them were accompanied on their journeys by women, usually their wives, daughters, or sisters.[6] American big-game hunter Dall DeWeese took his wife on an 1899 hunting trip to Alaska, for instance, explaining in a letter to his friend Theodore Roosevelt that he "wanted her to see what had at that time never before been a woman's pleasure... myself, wife and party killed four [mountain] sheep, two of which were killed by my wife," while Prentiss Gray included a photograph in his hunting journal of his wife in camp with the caption: "Laura Sherman Gray, center, makes plans to hunt elk. Guides think she is the Goddess Diana."[7]

While many women were travelling and, sometimes, hunting with man, far fewer women than men published accounts of their trips. Despite that, those women who did publish often ended up with bestsellers, perhaps because their narratives appealed strongly to female as well as male readers.[8] Josephine Peary and Grace Gallatin Seton were among the most popular American women writers who travelled and hunted: Peary's *My Arctic Journal* chronicled a year spent in Greenland with her famous husband, while Seton's *A Woman Tenderfoot* described her adventures as an East Coast elite woman experiencing the American West – hunting, certainly, but also camping, horse-packing, and riding in a rodeo.

The considerable overlap between travelogue and hunting narrative was rooted in the identities of these writers. Most were members of the middle or upper classes, with enough wealth to be able to travel in order to hunt. Agnes Herbert belonged to this group. Born in the 1870s and raised on the Isle of Man, she had been privately educated and then had been married and widowed before she began hunting abroad with her younger cousin Cecily.[9] (Her uncle sponsored the two women's expedition to Somaliland, another indication both of familial wealth and of male approval of women's hunting at the turn of the century.) Nor was Herbert's choice to hunt far from home anomalous: Rather, it was a necessity. Trophy animals, or "big game," were vanishingly scarce in the British Isles by the early nineteenth century, and by 1900 were also becoming rare in the continental United States. This meant that elites, whether from American urban centres or from Britain, had to travel in order to hunt, and when they wrote about their adventures they also described the landscapes, animals, and people they encountered. Meanwhile, even conventional travel writers often included incidents of hunting: Shooting a buffalo on the American Plains, for instance, was virtually a requirement in mid-nineteenth-century travel stories about the West. By 1900 the two genres were overlapping to the point that hunting narratives often functioned as a subset of the travel genre, offering somewhat formulaic tales of good companions setting off to exotic destinations, and including not only information on hunting but also descriptions of experiences that might be had by any visiting tourist.

This was certainly the case with *Two Dianas in Alaska*. While on the very first page Herbert warns readers that, "should you regard all forms of taking life as unwomanly, read no more... We went to Alaska to shoot, and – we shot"[10] both the contents and illustrations rank this book with others that combine travel with hunting. Chapters such as "On Kodiak Island" and "Dutch Harbour and Its Environs" describe what any tourist might expect to see, including landscapes, shorebirds, and "the prettiest of little shingly beaches."[11] The book also includes 29 photographs. Two of the authors in native dress (Herbert's portrait serves as the frontispiece while her coauthor's is buried on page 140), ten depicting trophies, and 16 showing living animals, Alaskans and their towns and villages, and scenic vistas such as forests and waterfalls (Figure 12.1).[12]

What made *Two Dianas in Alaska* different from the majority of travelogues, however, even those focused on hunting, was that it not only told the story of a party that included both women and men, but gave each gender a voice in the

THE TOWN OF KODIAK

Figure 12.1 A typical photograph from *Two Dianas in Alaska*. For many readers, these would be some of the first images of Alaska they had ever seen.

structure of the narrative. Six of the 19 chapters were written by one of Herbert's male companions, identified in the book only as "the Leader" (actually a wealthy widowed British Army officer, Major Charles Radclyffe).[13] This meant that competing and sometimes contested points of view on gender were on constant display, to the apparent enjoyment of the many readers who made the book popular. Those readers would have been well aware of the personalities involved before picking up the book, however, because the Leader had played a role in Herbert's previous adventure in Somaliland – and in that book both the man himself, and the whole idea of companionate travel, had been a major source of *conflict*. Almost every reader coming to the Alaska book thus would have known the "backstory" of these travellers from *Two Dianas in Somaliland*, and it's worth examining here for several reasons: it established Agnes Herbert's authorial voice for readers, it set up the personalities for *Two Dianas in Alaska*, and its reviews reveal some of the expectations surrounding women's travel at the time.

Most readers of the Alaska book would have been introduced to Herbert's voice in *Two Dianas in Somaliland*, where her wit was exercised most often on the topics of men, love, and marriage. Typical is her response to her cousin's observation that if she didn't marry soon:

> she'll be left on the shelf, but one can see a lot from a shelf, provided it is high enough. Of course she'd be unpopular. Old maids always are. And this is just because a man sees in every unmarried woman a walking statistic against his irresistibility.[14]

Her targets were not always so general, however, for Agnes and Cecily quickly found themselves competing against two male hunters, whom Herbert dubbed "the Opposition Shoot." The men are British Army officers whom they first meet on the boat to Somaliland; the elder member, "the Leader," is never named in the text, but the younger, Ralph Windus, is Herbert's distant cousin.[15] Ralph begins to flirt with Cecily, only to be discouraged by his companion, who explains, unaware that Herbert is listening, that he doesn't want the two women to "tack on to our show" since they will doubtless be poor hunters.[16] He then further endears himself to Herbert by trying to get her to sell him her rifle. "I don't know how I was meant to be able to get along without it," Herbert tells readers, "but I suppose he didn't think that mattered."[17]

Far from "tacking on," the women set off on their own safari. The two groups continue to encounter each other and eventually the men ask to join the women, but, after forcing the Leader to concede that the women are having better hunting than the men, Agnes and Cecily decline the offer. Herbert mainly uses her discussions of the men to emphasise her own safari's success by comparison, although she does admit that, on further acquaintance, she feels bad for having initially mocked the Leader's height, assuring readers that in fact "he was not by any means a midget."[18] This may seem to add up to a thoroughgoing rejection of the Opposition Shoot, but that conclusion is belied by the book's dedication: "To the Leader of the Opposition Shoot: Soldier, Shikári, and Sometime Misogynist."

(Shikári is a Persian word for "hunter" and was often used to describe English big-game hunters as well as talented non-white hunters, especially African gunbearers.) The dedication implies that the Leader was considerably more important to Herbert than the book suggests and yet shifts the blame for any conflict onto the shoulders of the "sometime misogynist." If he had wanted kinder literary treatment, one might infer, he should not have assumed that Agnes Herbert couldn't hunt well.

From the beginning, then, companionship and conflict were intertwined, both in print and in person. Readers moving from the first to the second book would doubtless have enjoyed a frisson of anticipation: What would result from these conflicting personalities attempting to travel, and to write, together? The prior history of *Two Dianas in Somaliland* also complicates Herbert's use of the term "the Leader" for her coauthor, since in Africa she had applied the title to him rather sarcastically, at least at first. And she and her cousin, of course, are Dianas: Whether goddesses outrank leaders is left for readers to decide. Radclyffe himself, however, clearly had no problem either with the appellation or with going on a trip to Alaska with Herbert, aware that she would be writing about him again.

Two Dianas in Somaliland also offers a glimpse into the publishing history and the critical reception of women who chose to travel, to hunt, and to write about it during this period. Herbert's publisher, John Lane, had branches in both London and New York, and in the 1890s his house, the Bodley Head, had embraced political and nonconformist women's writing. By 1900, however, Lane was becoming more conventional, and by the time Herbert became one of his authors in 1908 he was publishing Kenneth Grahame's children's books and G.K. Chesterton's Father Brown mysteries, as well as hunting tales with titles such as *Rifle and Romance in the Indian Jungle*.[19] All this must have made him a natural choice for Herbert: open and welcoming to women writers, and yet known for publishing popular hunting travelogues on both sides of the Atlantic.

The audiences for such narratives in both Britain and the United States were overwhelmingly white and middle or upper class, and the transatlantic publishing houses that catered to them ensured that they were exposed to writing by both British and American hunters.[20] Herbert, like many British writers, celebrated the reach of the Empire in her hunting travelogues and, while that must have enhanced her appeal to English readers, it seems not to have discouraged American audiences. *Two Dianas in Somaliland* quickly went through three editions, making it a profitable investment for Lane. (While much has been made of the ways that Americans like Theodore Roosevelt mobilised the rhetoric of the frontier in describing their hunting, the healthy sales of Herbert's book, and of many other British hunting books published by transatlantic presses, suggest that American readers were more than willing to dispense with references to the frontier as long as the story was exciting.)[21]

Reviewers were also enthusiastic about the book, and none of them seemed disturbed that Herbert and her cousin had launched a safari on their own while refusing an offer of companionship from two countrymen. Most reviewers recommended it without reservation, *The New York Times* lauding it as "vividly described and very exciting."[22] The reviewer for the popular British magazine *The Spectator* had a complaint, however: that Herbert's "bravado" was "irksome at first, when it is only a few simple conventions which the Dianas are defying." This reviewer didn't find the women's safari unconventional *enough*, although he (or she) endorsed the book overall, praising Herbert as "the most genuine of sportsmen."[23] There was nothing in the book's reception to discourage Herbert (and her publisher) from forging ahead.

Two Dianas in Alaska begins much the same way as the previous book, with Herbert and Baird setting off from England. The original plan is for another all-female trip (although that may be a bit disingenuous[24]), but the women run into Ralph Windus and the Leader in Montana and the idea of travelling to Alaska as a foursome is presented as a happy inspiration. Herbert makes it clear that serendipity had little to do with it – Ralph and Cecily conspired to meet up – but her own initial encounter with the Leader is described as an unambiguous pleasure. Up until that moment, Herbert had been rather unimpressed with her trip, in part because of its lack of novelty: "A trip across America is so familiar to most people that there really isn't much that is new to say about it," she sighs.[25] (By 1908 descriptions of cross-continental train travel would in fact have been overly familiar to most armchair travellers.) Her mood changes when she encounters the Leader, however, replaced by the sense of being "contented... He caught my meanings so quickly, he loves the same things that I do, the humorous, the playful, the joyous, the pitiful, the pathetic, the imaginative."[26] Clearly, Herbert yearns for the pleasure of travelling with friends who understand her.

This sense of camaraderie is of course based on more than chance friendship; Herbert is meeting someone of her social circle, class, and country, connections that run deep. The shared trip to Alaska is only the most visible marker of everything these four people have in common, but, as they journey northward, eventually making their way into the wilderness, their shared experiences only deepen those connections. Descriptive passages abound, for example, but, like many travellers, this group finds that the most memorable sights are best appreciated in company. Radclyffe, on shipboard, conveys the beauty of the vista through his companions' reactions: "[T]he ladies appeared with Ralph, and universal delight was expressed by everyone at the magnificent scenery with which we were surrounded on every side."[27] In the wilderness one night the men, who are sleeping rough, call the women out of their tent to view the aurora borealis; they watch the display together until dawn. "Marvel of the world, how exquisite!" Agnes says of the experience.[28]

Travelling in company also means that a variety of distractions are possible. The foursome play whist and patience, they read aloud to one another, and on shipboard they play cricket "on sloppy decks."[29] On shore, the Leader and Herbert hike together for miles at a time, take it in turns to paddle "energetically upstream"[30] in a canoe, and the women carry their own packs, for "we meant to do our share."[31] There is no hint that the women are anything other than game companions, and Herbert in particular appears to have boundless energy. "Agnes...will always spend her time climbing to the highest point she can reach..." Radclyffe notes; Herbert for her part explains that "climbing is very exhilarating if one is in the mood."[32] Nor are the women always dependent on the men for company. The foursome hunt in pairs, often separating for up to a week at a time, and, while sometimes Agnes and the Leader pair off, Cecily and Agnes also go hunting together, leaving the men to their own devices. The women choosing to travel and hunt apart from the men is presented as entirely natural, while hunting in mixed pairs provides an opportunity for shared experiences both in camp and in the field.

Radclyffe takes the women's enthusiasm for strenuous activity for granted, but Herbert makes a point of it. One of their Aleut servants is openly skeptical of the women's hunting ability but, after they successfully shoot a grizzly, he finally:

> treated us with the same consideration and respect which he accorded the masculine element of the expedition. And wherefore not? Were we not dressed alike, in the quaintest of fur *parkas* [sic]...? and did we shirk damp, danger, or dismay?[33]

Herbert stakes a claim to respect in part on the women's readiness to match the men in all things and to persevere without complaint (Figures 12.2 and 12.3).

All of this travel is for a purpose, of course, and, while much of the book is given over to travelogue, two of the central moments involve bear attacks.[34] These are not only the most dramatic moments in the narrative, but also the places where traditional gender roles are most visibly defied or disregarded, and where companionship moves beyond playing whist to life-and-death dependence on one another.

The first episode is narrated by Radclyffe.[35] Hunting together, he and Herbert wound a grizzly that escapes into the brush. It was (and is) the height of bad sportsmanship to allow a wounded animal to suffer, so he asks Herbert to wait while he tracks the bear. She states simply that she is going with him. "I was fully prepared for her laconic reply," he writes, "Agnes Herbert does not waste words on such occasions..."

They are moving through thick brush when the wounded animal rises barely two yards in front of him. He freezes. "Just for a moment I stood irresolute... even now the scene comes vividly back to me of seeing Agnes raise her rifle, and ere yet my inert muscles could obey the brain's command, a shot rang out..." The bear falls dead, so close to Radclyffe that he has to jump aside to avoid being crushed.

As he realises that he has been saved by:

> ...the cool courage of a woman... the magnitude of my debt to her arose clear in my mind... thereby possibly awakening sentiments which hitherto I had done my best to despise...
>
> ...as she held her smoking rifle in one hand, I took possession of the other, and looking squarely into her brave eyes I said, "Little woman, you have saved my life, and for that I pay thee toll."
>
> What the nature of the toll was is left for you to conjecture.

AGNES HERBERT IN NATIVE PARKA DRESS

Figures 12.2 and 12.3 While Herbert mentions that the foursome wore native parkas, these images look like studio shots; it's impossible to know if these are the clothes they wore while hunting or costumes rented at the studio, a common convention of the day. Note also that both hunters pose with their weapons.

Those words end the chapter, and that section of his narration.

The second attack is narrated by Herbert.[36] She and the Leader are charged by a mother grizzly with a cub. Agnes tells him to take the shot, "hardly knowing the tone of my own voice, it was so huskily excited." He takes aim but his gun jams:

THE LEADER OF THE EXPEDITION IN NATIVE PARKA DRESS

Figures 12.2 and 12.3 (Cont.)

...the cartridge would not rise into the magazine.

"Kill her!" said the Leader laconically, with the greatest *sang-froid*.

Of course it had to be. I was using my old 12-bore – best of friends – a terrifically hard-hitting, heavy weapon, and had just time to get in a shot at a near thing of thirty yards... as I danced backward she crashed over... A brave and gallant beast!

Herbert is excited by the experience but distressed to have killed a female bear; her distress increases as the cub approaches and stands with his mother's blood trickling over his feet. Herbert takes out her "very grimy handkerchief. 'You aren't going to cry about it, Agnes, are you?' the Leader asked apprehensively." But when she explains she is going to wipe the blood from the cub's feet, he laughs at her:

> "What a woman you are!... Killing one minute, and healing the next. I wonder how you have acquired your wonderful collection of trophies at all."
> "You're jealous," I said calmly.
> We played "You're another" until we managed to catch the little cub... As soon as the Leader saw that I did indeed mind very much having helped to make an orphan of the cub, he gave over chaffing, and did all he knew to comfort me. It was the truest fellowship.

Comparing the two events is telling. It was standard in hunting narratives for men to be praised for coolness under pressure, but here the tribute is paid not only by Herbert to the Leader, but in reverse: Both are "laconic." The word links the two incidents (separated in the text by about 40 pages), creating parallels between the authors both as laconic hunters and as writers describing one another. In both attacks the drama is stretched to the last possible moment, and in both the comradeship is absolute. Radclyffe's initial desire to protect Herbert from the dangers of tracking a wounded grizzly yields to the kind of trust he would have for a male companion; by the second attack, he is not afraid that she will miss the bear, he is only frightened by the idea that she might cry in front of him. And these expectations of her – of her capability and courage, but also that he would be shocked by tears from her in such a situation – are as unexpected for an Edwardian gentleman-soldier as is his own admission that he froze in the moment of peril.

There is also an overtly romantic element and a sexual subtext. After the first attack, Radclyffe succumbs to romantic feelings. It is tempting to read this as an attempt to reassert masculinity, or to place Herbert back into a more traditional position in relation to him, but he did not have to tell the story the way he did; there was no reason for him to let readers know that he froze. And he takes nothing away from her in the telling. Rather, her "cool courage" allows him to admit that his feelings for her are more than platonic. (All this makes it only more interesting that Herbert left the narration of the experience to him; it may have been a diplomatic move on her part, giving him control over how the attack, his actions, and the aftermath were presented in print.) The second attack has its Freudian moments: Agnes' husky, excited voice, the impotent gun with its cartridge failing to rise, and the implications of "all he knew to comfort me." While the moment when she accuses him of jealousy strikes a discordant note, the next lines immediately soften the exchange, as Herbert pushes past their short argument into the side of his character that matter most to her: His knowledge of her, his sympathetic understanding, the true fellowship he offers her.

The travelogue and hunting aspects of *Two Dianas in Alaska* cannot be easily disentangled and, for readers at the time, there would have been little reason to do so. The framework of companionate travel gives meaning to the hunting scenes. The Leader's growing feelings for Herbert and the tensions underlying their exchanges give the bear attacks their drama, not just because the reader cares about whether the narrator is killed, but also because they advance a human story that overshadows the interactions with the animals. At the same time, the hunt is the place where traditional gender roles are most often defied or disregarded; it is Cecily and Agnes' desire to shoot that has brought them to the wilderness and it is the place where they least conform to traditional ideals of women's roles. It is also, interestingly, where the Leader fails twice in situations of mortal danger. Hunting is where this book most strains against expectation, but that in turn raises the question of whether these people – and perhaps some of the dozens of other women and men who went on hunting trips together – defied expectations because they hunted, or whether hunting was a place where the disruption of gender roles could be made visible to readers in a way that was less possible in more traditional travel narratives. As noted earlier, in *Discourses of Difference* Sara Mills has argued that late nineteenth-century travel writing, especially that involving adventure, was the prerogative of male narrative voices centred around "a position of mastery" – and that, since such a voice was difficult or impossible for most women to assume, their narratives often reveal them resorting instead to self-effacement and deflection.[37] Neither Radclyffe nor Herbert fit this description of men's and women's discourses, however. Were these two hunter-writers unaware of the traditional discourses, or did they choose to ignore them, or, perhaps, did the discourse of the masterful male and self-effacing female simply bear no relation to the actual situations with the grizzlies that they experienced together?

Historians Mary Zeiss Stange and Angela Thompsell have both suggested that, rather than choosing straightforwardly between rejecting or embracing male discourses, many women in this era instead adapted, engaging with social expectations and literary conventions only to change them in the process.[38] *Two Dianas in Alaska* certainly highlights such adaptation on the part of Agnes and Cecily, but it also raises the fascinating question of whether men may have engaged in the same dynamic – whether traditional *masculine* discourses were flexible enough to be adapted by individual men rather than adopted unquestioningly. And going one step further to examine how Radclyffe and Herbert dealt with other expectations and common conventions of their time confirms that such adaptation was constantly at work: for Radclyffe, in terms of discourses surrounding masculinity and the wilds; for the women, with long-standing conventions about female domesticity; and for all of them in their engagement with constructions of white, and imperial, superiority.

A great deal has been written by historians about discourses of manliness and masculinity in this period, especially in relationship to travel and hunting. It is widely accepted that at the turn of the century both British and American elite men suffered from fear of a loss of masculine virility. Outdoor adventure, what

Theodore Roosevelt famously called "the strenuous life," was held up as one solution, and hunting trips have been seen as the ultimate example of this impulse.[39] Men's historians in particular have framed hunters in this era as fleeing not just modern life, but modern women – as seeking, in Michael Kimmel's words, "a more pristine earlier world where men were men and women virtually nonexistent."[40] This discourse centred around reclaiming masculinity through strenuous exercise, wilderness adventure, and association with all that was neither "modern" nor "female."

Radclyffe unquestionably partakes in many of these social anxieties. He notes that "even in these effete days of modern luxury men may still be found to fearlessly forsake the fleshpots of Egypt and wander, for sheer love of adventure, amidst... icebound lands..."[41] This seems to be as clear a contrast between effete luxury and masculine adventure as it's possible to write, and yet three pages later he and Ralph watch from the boat while Cecily and Agnes stalk a bull walrus on the beach. Manliness for Radclyffe seems disconnected from needing to take the lead in the hunt, while fears of effeteness bear no relationship to fears of the modern woman, or of women at all: women crying might scare him, but women with guns make for a grand trip. Moreover, the icebound land that proves that Radclyffe is a real man is one that he is only visiting because women invited him there. Through his actions, he complicates the established discourse constructed around masculinity and travel in the wilderness, even as his rhetoric invokes some of its most familiar elements.

On the women's side, for all their shooting and hiking, Agnes and Cecily also perform domestic camp chores with every evidence of pleasure. They declare a washing day and rinse everyone's clothes, and they cook, stewing wild berries and, later, making porcupine stew for the group.[42] Historian Phoebe Kropp has pointed out that many women who camped in this era prided themselves on their ability to deploy their domestic skills in the wilds, and that seems to be the case here.[43] Nor, despite their willingness to don parkas, do the women abandon an interest in fashion. Cecily hunts a fox, ignoring the Leader's warning that its fur is moulting: "[A]las! 'tis ever thus with women," he informs readers, as she returns chagrined without the makings of the fur collar she covets.[44] With the same mixture of amusement and resignation, however, he tells of a bored Agnes insisting on salmon fishing with a boathook when her bear hunt is delayed: "[S]ince Agnes had come out with murderous intent, she needs must slay something to while away an hour," he explains, as if this were the most natural feminine behaviour in the world.[45] Throughout the book, neither author feels the need to reconcile the seeming contradictions between domesticity and murderous intent and, by never raising the question, they present this as one way that women can be in the world: cooks and killers, followers of fashion and gaffers of fish. It's a beau ideal of its own kind and may have presented as unreachable an aspiration to female readers of the day as did the image of the Victorian hearth angel: Being able to face down grizzly bears and also make very passable strawberry preserves implies a rather wide-ranging skill set.

That said, at times other facets of identity were invoked as well. While gender draws attention in *Two Dianas* because it is the focus of the verbal play between the two authors and of the spark between them, these four people also belonged to a privileged class of white British travellers. There were well-established discourses of imperialism and racial domination on which they drew with far less "play" or adaptation, especially when non-white peoples were concerned.[46] Radclyffe conforms unswervingly to the rhetoric of imperial domination, reminding readers that "Beneath the skin of a native lies the heart of one born to be ruled by a superior hand."[47] And Herbert (at least in Alaska) appears to agree.[48] At one point he attempts to bully some Alaskans into working for them and Herbert celebrates his masculinity in describing the event: "[T]he more difficulties... set in the way the more resolved seemed the Leader to overcome and overthrow them. As a real leader should do... a man fitted by nature to lead and govern others..."[49] The Leader is truly a leader to Agnes Herbert, when it comes to the native Alaskans.

Such moments serve as reminders that, even as gender remained playfully contested, there were deep commonalities that bound these four to each other, and to their readers as well. Agnes and Cecily shared, as the phrase had it, "birth, blood, and breeding" with their male companions; so, too, their readers would have been overwhelmingly white, Anglo-Saxon, and of the middle or upper classes. It can be easy in discussions of gender to lose sight of the many other aspects of identity, but here those aspects form the preconditions for companionship against which the drama of gender stands out in vivid relief. That drama is central to the book, however, a choice made by both authors in their writing and their experiences. While their contacts with the Alaskans are never more than passing incidents, the story really begins when the four meet, the relationship between Radclyffe and Herbert is the emotional heart of the book, and it ends when they all separate – but not into the pairs in which they began.

By the end, the Leader has won Herbert over. He asks her to slide down a dangerous slope: "Would I not, for such a leader?"[50] They still bicker, but she assures readers that it amounts to little: "[W]e were not capable of paying each other off, for there was no antagonism between us... Are we human beings capable of hurting what we love in our inmost hearts?"[51] In the final chapter, "The Precipice Matrimonial," Ralph and Cecily marry, with Agnes giving the bride away. The book ends with her returning alone to her hotel room.

> ...Were the most wondrous trophies in all the world worth the price of so great a loneliness?
> ...the Leader of the expedition that was stood in the doorway. His eyes were smiling, smiling.
> Perhaps, perhaps, I'm not so very lonely after all.[52]

This ending may feel reductive – Herbert may seem to have relinquished her cynical views on men and marriage – but the book itself belies any simple idea of surrender to tradition. It does so in its existence as Herbert's book, with her coauthor anonymous; in the 13 out of 19 chapters in which her voice dominates; and in its real-world finale: Reader, she didn't marry him. Although Agnes Herbert did remarry eventually, it was not to Radclyffe.[53]

Overall, reviewers were as enthusiastic about *Two Dianas in Alaska* as they had been about the previous book. Much of the discussion focused on the descriptive passages: "[W]e are introduced to great beaver-dams," one reviewer exclaimed, while another praised the "graphic descriptions of the scenery and semi-savage races of the wild north-west."[54] The photographs drew attention as well. "Bright and amusing," noted *The Illustrated Sporting News*, "the illustrations are remarkably good."[55]

Reviewers also seemed unsurprised by the women's ardent hunting. One reviewer actually criticised the Leader over a passage where he pondered whether or not the moose he shot deserved its fate:

> one of the authors – the masculine one – [falls] a-moralising... sentiment, sufficiently indulged in, would prove fatal to future trips of the Dianas. But we observe that Miss Herbert's only remark on the occasion was, 'Why, oh why, did you not shoot at the other beast [as well]?'[56]

Here Herbert is being praised for her *lack* of sentiment. Discussing the first of the two bear attacks, however, the readings become more conflicted. One reviewer notes accurately that this "thrilling episode" involved "the authoress rescu[ing] her male ally from very imminent danger" but another misreads the moment, claiming that "The leader pauses in his shot for fear of the risk to his fair fellow-huntress." That is not what happened, but that reviewer, while saving face for the Leader, takes nothing away from Herbert, "who, however, does not pause at all, but shoots the bear and saves the leader's life..."[57] Nor did any reviewer express surprise that Herbert used her own name, or that her co-author did not, while periodicals framed it as Herbert's book, not as a shared narrative. "WOMEN HUNTERS IN ALASKA" was the review title in *The Observer*, which placed it immediately after a review of a book by a woman mountaineering with her husband in the Arctic Circle, classing Herbert with other travelling women writers.[58]

In the end, *Two Dianas in Alaska* is both more and less revolutionary than one might expect. On one hand, it challenges many assumptions about the discourses that characterised and constrained women's travel and women's travel writing. Much of that challenge revolves around hunting. In *Nature's Altars*, Susan Schrepfer has identified a trope in women's travel writing in this period that emphasised their connection to the warmth and "life force" of nature.[59] Agnes and Cecily's response to any animal large enough to contain nature's life force was to shoot it. This may seem to be claiming a male role or male power, but, while Herbert gave every evidence of loving the hunt, she insisted that she did so as a woman. At one point, after allowing a female caribou to pass unshot, she explains, "I like not to war with feminine things. They have enough to contend with as it is. Let her go, and my blessing with her."[60] The equivalent comment cannot be found in narratives by male hunters, and yet the refusal to shoot female animals was an essential element of Edwardian sportsmanship. Claimed as a virtue by many male hunters, in Herbert's hands it also becomes a moment of female solidarity. She insists that she is both a goddess and a sportsman.

She also disrupts gendered readings of travel literature, as does her coauthor, each in her or his own way. As noted earlier, Mills has shown that many female writers felt unable to claim the hero role, but Herbert embraces it, even as her male companion steps back from it. And yet there are other ways to see their claims, as both weave in and out of conventional discourses. Radclyffe, both in his romancing of Herbert and in his attempted domination of the Alaskans, as well as in the language of emasculation and wild restoration that he invokes, conforms closely to some of the traditional masculine and racial discourses of his day. Herbert, too, may not always be the outlier that she seems: Angela Thompsell has cautioned historians to remember that "[a]uthority was never solely a masculine privilege," pointing out that wealthy British women were expected to manage and dominate servants, particularly non-white servants.[61] Discourses have great social power, but they are also filtered through the lives and actions of individuals, and inflected by those lives. Both Herbert and Radclyffe seem to have regarded traditional gender conventions as a buffet that they could browse, claiming some elements, contesting others in a series of enjoyable arguments, adapting still others to fit their circumstances. In doing so, they raise the question of whether they were exceptional or whether the discourses as identified so far do not accurately describe the full range of choices open to Edwardian travellers, both male and female.

And in its own way, *Two Dianas in Alaska* may have expanded that range. In turning her adventure into a book, Herbert created literature that female readers could view as aspirational. Certainly not every reader, whether male or female, would necessarily want to stand down a charging grizzly bear, but the book also made it clear that companionate travel, marked by friendly competitiveness, could hold many pleasures. It may also have suggested to male readers that having women travel with them could add an extra dimension of enjoyment to the experience; Mary Zeiss Stange has shown that outdoor magazines sometimes urged women to take up camping because their husbands wanted their company, and male readers may have identified with the Leader's pleasure in this journey.[62] Readers of the time, after all, would most likely have understood this as a story in the end about friendship – about mornings spent marvelling at the views and relaxing nights around the campfire. That is the story implied by the fact of the trip itself, by all the parts of the book where the coauthors agree on the beauty of the scenery and the camaraderie of the group, and by the photographs, which show readers the scenes that the travellers gazed at together. This does not obscure the gender complications that emerge in the narrative as much as it suggests that such challenges need not be resolved in order for men and women to travel companionably together – that a little friction might have its pleasures as well. It also highlights once again that men and women who shared social position, the wealth and leisure to travel, and the privilege of being Anglo-Saxon in an imperial age, had far more in common than they ever had separating them.

That said, *Two Dianas in Alaska* does pose a profound challenge to current understandings of how women in particular wrote about travel and of what it was acceptable for them to write about. Both Mills and Anderson have shown that women's travel writing was often received with ambivalence or even disdain by critics, and that as a result some women writers self-censored, leaving out moments where they might seem overly courageous or defiant of gender norms.[63] The Dianas series seems to fall totally outside these descriptions, however, nor was its reception ambivalent by any measure. And while it may be tempting to dismiss *Two Dianas in Alaska* as an anomaly rather than as a genuine challenge to such well-established historiographical readings, it seems worth remembering that in her own day *The Spectator* felt that Herbert was not unconventional *enough*.

In the end, the experiences of these travellers, and the book that recorded them for posterity, raise far more questions than can be easily answered, but a careful consideration of them may lead to a better understanding of travel and gendered discourse at the beginning of the twentieth century. In the past scholars have positioned women travellers as courageous anomalies or as sentimental narrators, even as their male counterparts were seen as suffering from crises of masculinity and assuaging those fears in womanless wilds. More recently new images, stories, and discourses have been emerging, as historians have begun to realise how often men and women travelled together, and to explore the ways they chose to describe those experiences. *Two Dianas in Alaska* offers a glimpse into the new history that may yet emerge as we begin to explore the pleasures men and women found in travelling together, in conflict and companionship.

Notes

1   Herbert, A. (1908) *Two Dianas in Somaliland: The Record of a Shooting Trip.* London & New York: John Lane Company: 8.
2   Edward reigned from 1901 to 1910, but the term is often used more generally, as it is here, to indicate the period from the 1890s to the Great War.
3   Anderson, M. (2006) *Women and the Politics of Travel, 1870–1914* (first edition 1993). Madison, NJ: Fairleigh Dickinson University Press: 24; for the male hero image, see Anderson, also Mills, S. (1993) *Discourses of Difference: An Analysis of Women's Travel Writing and Colonialism.* London: Routledge: 76–77; Thompsell, A. (2015) *Hunting Africa: British Sport, African Knowledge and the Nature of Empire.* London: Palgrave Macmillan: 111, 116; MacKenzie, J. (1987) "The Imperial Pioneer and Hunter and the British Masculine Stereotype in Late Victorian and Edwardian Times" in *Manliness and Morality: Middle-class Masculinity in Britain and America 1800–1940*, Mangan, J.A. & James Walvyn, J. (eds.). New York: St Martin's Press.
4   Pratt quoted in Mills (1993): 75–76; Mills (1993): 78.
5   Some of those questions have already been raised by historians of women's hunting: Czech, K.P. (2002) With Rifle and Petticoat: Women as Big Game Hunters, 1880–1940. Lanham: The Derrydale Press; Zeiss Stange, M. (2004) in her foreword to *Two Dianas in Alaska*. Mechanicsburg: Stackpole Books, where she focuses on Herbert's hunting and offers a sketch of her life.

6   Fuller discussion can be found in Kelly, T.K. (2007) *The Hunter Elite: Americans, Wilderness, and the Rise of the Big Game Hunt.* Ann Arbor: UMI Publishing: 188–197.

7   DeWeese quoted in Cassidy, C. & Titus, G. (2003) *Alaska's No. 1 Guide: The History and Journals of Andrew Berg 1869–1939.* Soldotna: Spruce Tree Publishing: 22; Gray, P.N. (1994) *From the Peace to the Fraser: Newly Discovered North American Hunting and Exploration Journals 1900–1930.* Missoula: The Boone and Crockett Club: 106.

8   Classifying "bestseller" in this period is somewhat tricky; I use the term for books that went through several editions, made the annual "best sales" list in *The Bookman*, and/or enjoyed copious reviews, advertising, and recommendations as "must-buys" to libraries.

9   Czech (2002): 67–68.

10 Herbert, A. & Shikári, A. (2004) *Two Dianas in Alaska.* Mechanicsburg: Stackpole Books: 1; originally published in London by John Lane the Bodley Head, 1909.

11 Herbert & Shikári (2004): 28.

12 If you're curious to see what Radclyffe looked like under the parka, his grandson Nick has a lively blog about him that includes a photograph of his tattooed back: See http://foxdentonestate.co.uk/news/news/edwardian-tattoos

13 As far as I know, I'm the first historian to identify the Leader conclusively. In 2004, Stange tentatively identified him as Radclyffe based partly on a careful comparison of images from an earlier book of Radclyffe's with pictures in *Two Dianas in Alaska*. Recently, however, a copy of the book has come up for auction bearing an inscription from Radclyffe to his mother that confirms that he's the Leader. A screenshot of the auction page is in my possession.

14 Herbert (1908): 273.

15 Since they ended up marrying, one hopes that Ralph and Cecily were cousins of Herbert's on different sides of the family, but with the British upper class in this period one never knows.

16 Herbert (1908): 19.

17 Herbert (1908): 33.

18 Herbert (1908): 270.

19 *Rifle and Romance* and other hunting books advertised in endpages of Herbert & Shikári (2004); other information from "John Lane Company, Organizational History," Harry Ransom Center, University of Texas at Austin, accessed 17 June 2017, http://norman.hrc.utexas.edu/fasearch/findingAid.cfm?eadid=00207

20 Ohmann, R. (1996) *Selling Culture: Magazines, Markets, and Class at the Turn of the Century.* New York: Verso: 174.

21 For discussion of British narratives in the North American publishing marketplace, see Kelly, T.K. (2018) The Hunter Elite: Manly Sport, Hunting Narratives, and American Conservation, 1880–1925. Lawrence: University Press of Kansas, ch. 7.

22 "Women Hunters in Africa: Two Dianas in Somaliland," *The New York Times*, 9 November 1907, BR270.

23 "Current Literature," *The Spectator*, 16 November 1907, 749–750. The term "sportsmen" was commonly used for women.

24 Considering the short time between trip and publication, Herbert would have negotiated with her publisher before leaving England, and her co-author would probably have been involved in that.

25 Herbert & Shikári (2004): 3.

26 Herbert & Shikári (2004): 9.

27 Herbert & Shikári (2004): 48.

28 Herbert & Shikári (2004): 242.

29 Herbert & Shikári (2004): 34.

30 Herbert & Shikári (2004): 131.
31 Herbert & Shikári (2004): 201.
32 Herbert & Shikári (2004): 201; Radclyffe (2004): 166; Herbert (1908): 220.
33 Herbert & Shikári (2004): 67.
34 Some readers may prefer to think of this as an attack by people on bears, which is fair enough.
35 To save on footnotes: This incident and all quotes from it take place in Herbert & Shikári (2004): 107–111.
36 Herbert & Shikári (2004): 134–138. They attempted to care for the cub but it died after several days.
37 Mills (1993): 76–78, quote 80. Mills reviews the work of many historians who have contributed to this understanding of gendered narrative voice, while noting that there was sometimes room for women to negotiate with dominant discourses.
38 Zeiss Stange, M. (2003) "Introduction," in *Heart Shots: Women Write About Hunting*, Mechanicsburg: Stackpole Books: esp. 4–6; Thompsell's chapter "An Imperial Femininity" discusses Herbert and other women hunters, and argues that women transformed rhetorics of imperial mastery into a new discourse that linked imperialism to both femininity and sport.
39 Jones, K.R. (2015) *Epiphany in the Wilderness: Hunting, Nature, and Performance in the Nineteenth-Century American West.* Boulder: University Press of Colorado, claims sport hunting by both British and Americans was a response to a drawn-out "crisis of masculinity" (37).
40 Kimmel, M. (1996) *Manhood in America: A Cultural History.* New York: The Free Press: 188. This assumption underlies many other discussions of the so-called "masculinity crisis": Dubbert, J. (1980) "Progressivism and the Masculinity Crisis," in *The American Man,* Joseph & Elizabeth Pleck (eds.). Englewood Cliffs: Prentice-Hall, sees men as going to the woods to act out a yearning for "natural male fulfillment" (311).
41 Herbert (2004): 156.
42 Odds are good this refers only to the foursome; it's incredibly unlikely that Herbert and Baird would have washed their Aleut servants' clothing, although they did cook for the whole camp.
43 Kropp, P. (2009) "Wilderness Wives and Dishwashing Husbands: Comfort and the Domestic Arts," Journal of Social History 43(1): 10.
44 Herbert & Shikári (2004): 165.
45 Herbert & Shikári (2004): 101.
46 The racial and imperial discourses of the day have been well documented in many books including, as related to British hunting, John MacKenzie's *Empire of Hunting* and, in relation to travel, Mary Louise Pratt's *Imperial Eyes: Travel Writing and Transculturation.* I am not suggesting that these discourses were ever separable from gender. Many of the authors to whom I refer discuss this aspect of travel in depth, including MacKenzie, Pratt, Mills, and Anderson, while both Thompsell and Stange (in her foreword) discuss it specifically in relation to Herbert.
47 Herbert & Shikári (2004): 88.
48 Length limits and the desire to cover new ground on Herbert have kept my focus on companionate travel, but her attitude toward race, and especially her friendship with her Somali headman in Africa, was complex; Stange and Thompsell both offer excellent discussions.
49 Herbert & Shikári (2004): 195.
50 Herbert & Shikári (2004): 240.
51 Herbert & Shikári (2004): 258.
52 Herbert & Shikári (2004): 316. It's worth noting that Agnes manages to work a final comment on her outstanding collection of trophies into this tender moment.

53 Stange (2004) "Foreword," xxiii, notes Herbert married a Commander in the Royal Navy in 1913. While Radclyffe is called "the Leader" in the book, the cover and title page describe him as "A Shikári." Why he chose to remain anonymous is unknown to me.
54 Beaver-dams, "Two Dianas in Alaska," (28 November 1908) *The Academy*, 7 November 1908, 448; savage races, "Two Dianas in Alaska," *The Illustrated Sporting and Dramatic News*, 506.
55 "Two Dianas in Alaska," *The Illustrated Sporting and Dramatic News*, 28 November 1908, 506.
56 "Books in Brief: Women Hunters in Alaska," *The Observer*, 18 October 1908, 4.
57 "Ally," *The Illustrated Sporting and Dramatic News*, 508; "Pauses," *The Academy*, 448.
58 *The Observer*, 4.
59 Schrepfer, S. (2005) *Nature's Altars: Mountains, Gender and American Environmentalism*. Lawrence: University Press of Kansas: 6; her book explores yet another discourse that women travellers mobilised to justify their entry into the wilds.
60 Herbert & Shikári (2004): 214.
61 Thompsell (2015): 114.
62 Stange (2003) "Introduction," 11.
63 Mills (1993): 121–122; Anderson (2006): On reception 20–23, on self-censorship 28.

13 "My luggage and my ladies were unloaded"

Companionship in Cyriel Buysse's *De vroolijke tocht*

Tom Sintobin

"Travelling by car, as a gentleman accompanied by three ladies, all through France without a driver, it is no small thing."[1] This is how the I-narrator of *De vroolijke tocht* (*The Happy Trip*, 1911) by the Flemish author Cyriel Buysse evaluates his trip to France. The travelogue is clearly autobiographical. Buysse had indeed toured France the year before, for three weeks, with one of the two cars he owned, a four-cylinder from the Belgian brand Minerva Motors. He was accompanied by three female passengers, which Buysse's biographer identifies as "the Tromp-girls."[2] They were the three daughters of Nelly Tromp-Dyserinck, the widow he had married in 1896. Their names were Inez, Mary, and Thea, and they were 24, 20, and 19 years old respectively. According to Van Parys it was highly unlikely that Nelly took part in this road trip, because she insisted on comfort and suffered from poor health. Interestingly, the I-narrator never specifies his relationship with the women: The reader is left to wonder how a man could travel with three young women in those days without risking public outcry. The narrator never mentions their age, nor their names. He systematically calls them "my ladies" instead, occasionally "the ladies," so they are usually represented as a collective, acting and reacting as if they are one. The limited number of times that they are not treated collectively, they are either anonymous or receive numbers: "[O]ne of my ladies," "my second lady," "my third lady," "the second of our ladies."[3] The second lady has a kind of epitheton ornans: She is the one "who tends to be distracted sometimes," but that is the only characteristic the reader gets from any of the women.[4]

The "I" sometimes speaks as a collective "we": "We hobble and jump through a city: Dendermonde," "then we saw the man come back," "the road on which we drive," "We are on the road from Bouillon to Sedan," "Now that we are approaching the German border," "Thus we were struggling in Nancy, to find the way to Dijon," "Thus we drove the entire day, along the river between the mountains," "we reached the far end of our trip and finally go back," "suddenly we see something coming"...[5] These quotes demonstrate that the "we" is mainly, although not exclusively, used for "factual" information: To indicate where the company is located at a certain moment, or to superficially describe the surroundings. However, when evaluating or reflecting upon what they (have) encounter(ed), the narrator tends to switch to the first person. A few examples: "This time, I want to preserve just one impression of Avignon in me"; "I have never seen the Mediterranean Sea so blue, the coast so fresh and green, the long rows of mansions, houses and hotels so glistening sweet and beautiful..."; "I can't help it, but it [Les Baux] did not impress me much. A plain, old-Italian village looks far more picturesque, nicer to me. What struck me most was the deadly-desolate silence in those oppressively-narrow winding roads [...]"; "I could not help it but I found Nîmes rather insignificant."[6] The I, not the we, is the one to evaluate or interpret the places they visit. After they left Burgundy, the narrator explicitly states that the ladies were unable to do what he did, namely enjoy the landscape and its history:

> And my ladies, my sweet ladies, who only half enjoyed the sultry affluence of the Burgundy-region the day before [...] again were enjoying and cheering, reviving.[7]

One of the few times that the ladies do get to interpret a scene, the narrator immediately makes clear that they are doing so at the wrong moment. This happens, for instance, on an evening when one of the tires explodes and the narrator needs to replace it. Such an incident is nothing to worry about, he says, provided one has the time to replace it. This time, however, it is already getting late, "you need to hurry, get nervous, ask the ladies to stand up to get something from underneath their seat" – it takes ages before he is ready:

> With dirty hands you are behind your wheel again, panting and sweating, and with a worrisome face you stare in the air and at the sky, that is already showing its evening colours. It's beautiful, an orange-red evening sky like that above a darkening river and the blueish mountains that are fading away. The ladies are delighted, enjoy. Ladies are very susceptible to enjoyment, by the way. But the driver who is late and responsible surely is unable to join them. He thinks of the many kilometres left to drive on unknown roads, and every light that reflects in the water and is found to be so poetic and nice by the ladies, stings him like a fire awl in the eyes.[8]

The narrator is the active one in this scene. He replaces the flat tire, whereas his female companions do nothing but sit and enjoy the view, without realising how problematic their situation can turn. This does not mean that the narrator is unable to appreciate beauty, but he knows when and where to do it. Two other striking differences between the narrator and his female companions become clear in this passage. The first is the fact that the narrator clearly has a body: He sweats, he gets his hands dirty. The ladies never do that, on the contrary: They are described as obsessed with cleanliness on multiple occasions. In the first luxurious hotel they stay in, they take not one but two baths:

> They take a bath, and, since one does not know in what kind of hotel one will end up tomorrow, barely dried, another bath, as provision for later...[9]

There is no mention of the narrator himself making use of the bathing facilities. Elsewhere in the text, the I-narrator even aestheticises dirt:

> Never before had I seen something so dirty like these villages. The houses, – miserable slums – no longer have a colour; stinking dung heaps lie in front of every door and the streets are puddles of manure and mud. But it is picturesque-dirty.[10]

It is interesting to bear in mind that the incident on the road was caused by an earlier scene, in which somebody entered the restaurant to inform them that a trumpet had been stolen from their car. The narrator explicitly admits that he would have preferred to continue his dinner to chasing the thief, but his companions insist on him doing just that.[11] Time and time again, he mentions that he had rather forgotten about the trumpet altogether, lamenting that, consequently, his food went cold, and moreover complaining:

> that we did not use the trumpet a single time during the entire trip [. . .] we lost and found her time and time again, she bored and annoyed us, so it would have been better if we had left it from the very beginning

and that the whole affair caused them to lose so much time that they nearly got into trouble in the evening.[12] In other words: The narrator knows when to act and when to let go (of sentimental objects), in contrast to his companions, whose lack of *savoir faire* eventually brings them in a potentially tricky situation.

The second difference becomes clear from the narrator's remark that he has to move the women to be able to reach under their seat. Clearly, they are depicted as passive, as opposed to the hard working narrator. The latter repeatedly compares them, tongue in cheek, to their luggage: "I smile because they fit so nicely together in the car: the ladies and their luggage. One cannot imagine one without the other, they complement one another, are one."[13] And: "My luggage and my ladies were unloaded."[14] Besides passive, they are also depicted as limited to a very well-defined space. Even when the ladies dream of exploring mountains and rivers, they only imagine doing so while seated:

> they did not ask whether it was possible to drive all the way through to the violet and pink mountains, and they would have loved to sail the blue water of the Rhône, all the time comfortably sitting in the car, that would have turned into a vessel.[15]

Time and time again, this travelogue stresses their limited mobility, as well as naiveté and poor decision-making. For example, when they visit the casino in Monte Carlo, the ladies spend the entire day inside at one of the tables gambling and losing all of their money, despite numerous invitations by the narrator to join him to explore the charming village and its expensive restaurants "at the expense of the bank" – since he himself has already won, and was clever enough to stop in time.[16] Moreover, the few times that they do go out and act independently, things go wrong. When they order sandwiches for lunch, the narrator makes clear that they were given huge breads, mockingly stating that it was "enough to satisfy an entire cavalry division." The narrator's thoughts on this: "I paid the bill this morning in a hurry, without looking at the details. I found it a bit expensive already." He forgot to check his ladies and now has to bear the consequences. In another scene, one of the ladies is not even able to find the right dining room on her own. She ends up "in a room where real people – and they were very cheerful – were eating" but calmly takes a seat at a table anyway.[17] After a while, she is informed that she is in the staff room, where "les chauffeurs et les femmes de chambre" have their meal. And when the car breaks down in southern France, while the narrator has it repaired, the ladies take a cab and a train to see Fuenterrabia, a mountain village, on their own. In the evening, they come back, "terribly ripped off, cheated upon, robbed, with hardly enough money left to buy third class tickets back."[18] When the narrator is on his own, however, (evidently) all goes well. A telling scene earlier on in the story is the description of their visit to Lourdes:

> No, the beautiful, nor the romantic, nor the miraculous aspect of Lourdes does not lie in Lourdes itself, but all around it. It is delightful, wherever one goes, and everything looks so fresh and green, with white and red houses in the green mountains. While I was taking a walk, as far as possible from the sadly-banalised basilica and grotto, through the small, old, steep streets of the village, there suddenly was the very soft and melodic sound of horns. I stopped and saw a very plain freight cart emerge from an alley, with a man on top, that was playing wonderful music. I thought he was inviting tourists to join him on a scenic drive through the mountains. No, it was a plain porter, collecting rags or similar rubbish. He disappeared between the green hills and his beautiful music echoed away among the grey rocks. It was as if the tough heroic soul of Roland and the mystically yearning soul of the shepherdess Bernadette were evoked in one single praise song. I would have loved to join that man into the mountains.[19]

The most striking feature of this scene, is the complete absence of the women. They evidently did not join him on his adventure away from the conventional centre of this tourist site but stick to the limited space conventionally granted to tourists, and consequently miss what, in the eyes of the narrator, is the very essence of the place, which can only be found *off the beaten track*. Repeatedly, the narrator shows how the women stick to this tourist script: They want to visit the sites all tourists visit, which, in fact, is a second way in which their space is limited. A good example is when they are driving from San Sebastian to Biarritz and want to visit "the famous Fuenterrabia."[20] The I-narrator does not object, but when they keep failing to find it, he suggests they skip it altogether:

Fuenterrabia no longer exists, I replied with a serious face. Really, I have recently read that it no longer exists. But there will always be postcards. Let's buy those here, we will have seen it nevertheless then! I received a blow on the head with an umbrella. – Turn around immediately![21]

The holy grail of tourism – "authenticity" – shall not be ridiculed, the beaten track shall not be left behind. The narrator eventually is the only one to not visit this village and seems to be proud of it: "And this is how I did *not* see Fuenterrabia."[22] Another interesting scene in this respect is when they run out of spare tires one evening. He does not want to risk driving all the way to Bordeaux and suggests that they spend the night in a small village called Castel-Jaloux – and is pretty excited about this prospect: "Ladies, I cheer, this misfortune is a blessing! We will not get to Bordeaux tonight, we will spend the night in the heroic country praised by your favourite poet, yes, we stay in the country of Cyrano," with a reference to *Cyrano de Bergerac* by Edmond Rostand.[23] His ladies, however, could not care less. They mostly complain about the modest hotel they have to stay in ("It's awful here!"), much to the surprise of the narrator: "My ladies are ungrateful, unable to value the heroic-poetic aspect of the situation."[24] They flee to their rooms and the narrator stays downstairs, as "the only guest in the hotel."[25]

There clearly is a pattern here, as the ladies and the narrator are systematically opposed to one another. The three women form a largely deindividualised group, as opposed to the eccentric narrator. Their space is limited, both literally (the seat of the car) and metaphorically (the conventional itinerary they stick to), whereas his is unlimited. They are passive and obsessed with comfort, while he is adventurous and willing to get his hands dirty.

In relation to this, it is striking that the travelogue opens with the praise of the car:

> a free bird, able to fly and sit, with phantasy or vision, a runner or a dreamer, a poet or a worker [...] All roads, or almost all roads, lie enticingly open for him. He is never tied to the geometrical-straight line of two rails.[26]

A car is, "as it were, the stronger, faster brother of the tramp."[27] Notably, this is precisely the identity the narrator constructs for himself. Whereas the ladies want to visit the "must see" sites, the narrator prefers wandering and a happy go lucky approach – pretty much like a vagabond. His car allows him to travel where no man has gone before, off the beaten track: "The great, great gift of the car," he claims, is that it brings you to places where you would never come making use of the railroad system. It should come as no surprise, then, that the narrator is perfectly happy at the end of the book, when the ladies have left him to take a train (!) to Paris to avoid the sudden bad weather.[28] The narrator found himself a new companion, his car, who he describes as a trusted friend from which he will never separate, and who even gets to speak a few words in direct speech.[29]

Off the beaten track

What happens in Castel-Jaloux is, in fact, a very recognizable scene from tour narratives in general. The anthropologist Eduard Bruner argues that the tourist stories "most cherished are those about experiences outside the regular itinerary that lead to improvisation as they introduce spontaneity and unexpected elements of adventure"; one of his examples is a traffic jam that allows the tourists to visit a family that is not used to meet tourists.[30] Such an occasion gives one a unique opportunity to escape the beaten track and spice up the trip (and the post-tour narrative afterwards), and allows a person to brand himself as an adventurous "traveller," a man or woman of the world, as opposed to a "tourist," unable and even afraid to deal with anything outside the tourist script. Applied to our text: The narrator depicts himself as such a traveller, and places himself in sharp contrast with his female "touristy" companions. In doing so, he places himself in an old discourse. For centuries, travelling people have shaped their own identities at the cost of their fellow travellers. Paul Fussell, in his book *Abroad. British Literary Travelling between the wars*, reconstructs three categories to distinguish between people on the road: The explorer, who "seeks the undiscovered," the tourist, who seeks "that which has been discovered by entrepreneurship and prepared for him by the arts of mass publicity," and the traveller, who has an in-between position:

> If the explorer moves toward the risks of the formless and the unknown, the tourist moves toward the security of pure cliché. It is between these two poles that the traveler mediates, retaining all he can of the excitement of the unpredictable attaching to exploration, and fusing that with the pleasure of "knowing where one is" belonging to tourism.[31]

These categories are easier to understand as discursive constructs than as realities. As an example Fussell presents a mid-nineteenth century traveller who lamented the obliteration of "every trace and trait of the individual" of the "droves" of tourists he sees when visiting Italy. Jim Butcher, in his book *The Moralisation of Tourism. Sun, Sand... and Saving the world?* on what he calls New Moral Tourism, reduces this typology to two categories: The "tourist" and the "traveller." His analysis helps to further understand the way "travellers" tend to look at "tourists," and their motivations. According to Butcher, the distinction finds its roots in the period when aristocratic participants of the Grand Tour increasingly had to deal with customers of Thomas Cook and other travel agents – "the capitalist class" which included more and more members of the working class.[32] The former looked down upon the latter, showing "a common brand of elitism, with the more privileged trying to differentiate themselves from the uncultured masses."[33] The Grand Tourist claimed the newcomers to be uncultured, lacking individuality and adventurousness, industrial instead of in touch with nature. He travels by train, like "a living parcel,"[34] for "consumption" only, not for educational purposes or for "culture"[35]: He is unwilling to work on the road, as a real traveller (from the French *travailler* – to work) does. Evidently, there were counter discourses, like when Cook claimed his customers "could be identified by their 'courteous and joyous fraternization,'" in contrast to the "'independent' tourists who paid up to three times the cost for the privilege of thus sitting solitary in a crowd of free and elastic spirits,"[36] but they were not numerous and unable to drastically alter the discourse. As Butcher convincingly shows, the stereotypes from the early nineteenth century kept informing tourism discourses long after the Grand Tour and aristocracy were forgotten and replaced by new elites, who kept claiming their identities as travellers in similar terms. Although nowadays class distinctions seem to have lost their dominance in this discourse, modern "travellers – backpackers, trekkers, ecotourists, gappers" still perceive themselves as:

> [T]he "thinking" tourist – someone prepared to strike out, experiment with different ways of life, and not be a part of a packaged product put together by global companies.[37]

It is not difficult to recognise many of these traits in Buysse's travelogue, with the narrator's depiction of the ladies as a passive collective, conforming to tourist norms, travelling by train even – he sees them as tourists, as opposed to his own more adventurous, dynamic self. Interestingly, however, in this case the opposition between tourist and traveller does not follow class lines. The four characters clearly belong to the same class: They have enough leisure time at their disposal, they can afford a trip like this, they are all able to speak French, they are referred to as "gentleman" and "ladies." They are upper class, as becomes clear from the "hilarious" scene in the restaurant when one of the ladies ends up in a dinner room of the wrong class. (This was the case in reality as well: The Flemish industrial family Buysse stemmed from was wealthy, as was his wife from The Hague. Buysse would eventually be raised to the nobility in the 1930s but passed away too early, after which the honour was given to his widow.)

Although they belong to the same class, there are clearly power relations at work. To begin with, the ladies are in fact pushed into their passive position. After all, they do not get to drive the car so there is nothing else to do other than sit and watch. They do not seem to have their own money either: It is the narrator who pays for the sandwiches, and in the casino they come to ask him for more money several times.[38] This is a pattern, by the way: When they are given money, they lose it (in the casino) or get robbed (in Fuenterrabia). Last but not least, the ladies hardly get a voice. The I-narrator's level is extradiegetic and thus controls the entire narrative. He grants himself over 28.000 words, whereas the women only get to speak 274 words in direct speech – and evidently, it is the narrator who decides when they do. Some of their words portray the women as obsessed with cleanliness and comfort.[39] They also seem a bit naïve, for instance when they express their belief that they have discovered a system to win at casinos, or ask a local whether it is allowed to visit the house of a famous writer. He shakes his head, "just like one would do when asked by a child whether it was allowed to visit heaven."[40] The narrator gives the word to one of the women when she makes a ridiculous mistake. When he points at the pine trees along the road, "Les pins du Midi," she thinks he is talking about the homonymous *pain* (French for bread) and replies: "Pain du Midi! Where do you see that? Do they have a special kind of bread here?"[41] The *inquit*-formula the narrator uses to introduce the women's direct speech is at times very marked (by an affective overflow): "[S]he asked, passionately," they "cry, horrified," "they cry, in a tone of reproach," "they cried, unanimously," "they cried, annoyed," "they lamented," "sighed one of my ladies," "my ladies lamented, dismayed."[42] With only a few exceptions, the narrator introduces his own replies with a more modest, subdued formula, such as "I said with a smile," "I replied," "I repeated, undisturbed."[43]

Clearly, the man describes himself as a very different type of speaker than his companions – and as an entirely different human being as well. The women only seem to be capable of two types of feelings: They are either delighted/enjoying themselves, or irritated/not enjoying themselves. The narrator, on the other hand, has access to a much broader spectrum of feelings. He can sense joy or irritation, too, but his mood is usually imperturbable. He is always observing the world around him with a smile, never in a malicious way but always benevolently. He is never rude, and he is well read and humble – pretty much like one would expect from a "gentleman," *gentilhomme* in French (or: "friendly man"). "The true definition of a gentleman," writes *The Derby Mercure* on 16 March 1831:

> implies one who is courteous, obliging, polite, free, and easy in his manners, honourable, humane, forgiving, humble-minded, devoid of all conceit or vanity and virtuous.[44]

Buysse's narrator builds in some distance, which one could call mildly ironical – the tone of much of his work. He does not spare himself, as becomes clear from several scenes in which he writes tongue-in-cheek about his own behaviour. The women, on the other hand, are never ironic, or reflective of their situation. Again, this attitude turns them into tourists, whereas the narrator reminds us, to a certain extent, of a very early version of a "post-tourist": a tourist who is aware of the constructed nature of the spectacle tourists are offered, but participates never-theless, with an air of playfulness and irony that allow him to keep his dignity: "The post-tourist is above all self-conscious, 'cool' and role-distanced."[45]

Conclusion

The least we can say about the relationship between the male narrator and his female companions in Buysse's text, is that it is ambiguous. Although he himself raises the suggestion that his position and way of travelling is the superior one, he needs his female companions to be able to shape his own identity, just like a traveller needs "droves" of tourists to prove his own superiority. The reformulation along gender lines of what was once a dichotomy based on class distinction, is remarkable. Further research will show whether this was standard practice in travelogues in Dutch from the interwar period.[46]

Notes

1 Buysse, C. (1911) *De vroolijke tocht*. Bussum: Van Dishoeck: 3.
2 Van Parys, J. (2007) *Het leven, niets dan het leven. Cyriel Buysse & zijn tijd.* Antwerpen: Houtekiet/Atlas, 2007: 385.
3 Buysse (1911): 13, 13, 13, 32.
4 Buysse (1911): 32, 41.
5 Buysse (1911): 5, 9, 18, 22, 28, 34, 42, 114, 115.
6 Buysse (1911): 42, 50, 80, 84.
7 Buysse (1911): 41.
8 Buysse (1911): 16.
9 Buysse (1911): 31.
10 Buysse (1911): 25.
11 Buysse (1911): 9.
12 Buysse (1911): 15.
13 Buysse (1911): 4–5.
14 Buysse (1911): 20.
15 Buysse (1911): 41.
16 Buysse (1911): 63.
17 Buysse (1911): 32.
18 Buysse (1911): 113.
19 Buysse (1911): 101–102.
20 Buysse (1911): 108.
21 Buysse (1911): 111.
22 Buysse (1911): 114.
23 Buysse (1911): 119.
24 Buysse (1911): 120, 119.
25 Buysse (1911): 121.
26 Buysse (1911): 1.
27 Buysse (1911): 2.
28 Buysse (1911): 127.
29 Buysse (1911): 133.
30 Bruner, E. (2005) *Culture on Tour. Ethnographies of Travel.* Chicago & London: The University of Chicago Press: 23.
31 Fussell, P. (1980) *Abroad. British Literary Travelling Between the Wars.* New York & Oxford: Oxford University Press: 39.
32 Butcher, J. (2003) *The Moralisation of Tourism. Sun, Sand… and Saving the World?* London & New York: Routledge: 35.
33 Butcher (2003): 33.
34 Ruskin as quoted in Butcher (2003): 35.
35 Butcher (2003): 36.
36 Cook as quoted in Butcher (2003): 33.
37 Butcher (2003): 41.
38 Buysse (1911): 60, 62, 65.
39 Buysse (1911): 14, 119–120.
40 Buysse (1911): 62, 106.
41 Buysse (1911): 41, 42.
42 Buysse (1911): 62, 97, 104, 109, 111, 113, 120, 120.

43 Buysse (1911): 62, 104.
44 Galakof, A. (s.d.) *The Figure of the Gentleman in 19th Century Victorian England: The Re-Fashioning of a Manhood Ideal*. Buzz… littéraire – http://www.buzz-litter aire.com/the-gentleman-figure-in-19th-century-victorian-england-the-re-fashioning-of-a-manhood-ideal/ [last checked on 7/7/2018]
45 Urry, J. & Larsen, J. (2011) *The Tourist Gaze 3.0*. Los Angeles etc.: Sage: 115.
46 A good example to start with would be *Naar waar de appelsienen groeien* (To where the oranges grow) by the Catholic author Felix Timmermans (1926), in which a male narrator describes his trip to Italy with three women. Another example is *Wat wij in Spanje en Marokko zagen* (What we say in Spain and Marokko), again by Cyriel Buysse (1929).

14 Comrade Lisa

Spousal labour and family branding in Colin and Lisa Ross's travel media[1]

Joachim Schätz and Katalin Teller

"When Colin Ross talks about work, he always says 'we'. With that, he means his wife and travel companion who is busily typewriting at the moment." This scene unrolls for a Viennese journalist of *Volks-Zeitung* who paid a visit in May 1940 to the hotel room of the famous German travel writer, lecturer, and filmmaker Colin and his wife Lisa Ross. A moment later, 17-year-old son Ralph enters and Colin Ross informs the journalist what language his offspring and wife are each currently learning: "'The family has to divide up the languages,' Dr Colin Ross smiles. 'One person alone couldn't master the necessary variety.'"[2]

This portrait of the happy family as a work unit masks as much as it reveals about the actual division of labour that allowed Colin Ross to become, arguably, the most popular and widely read German travel writer of the interwar years.[3] In some regards, the article captures Lisa Ross's position in her husband's travel media enterprise in a nutshell. On the one hand, the constant collaborative efforts of Mrs Ross are frequently acknowledged, on and off the record, albeit uncredited on book covers, on newspaper pages, or in film titles. On the other hand, this unpaid conjugal labour is often absorbed into the harmonious image of a bustling family treating every journey like an exciting vacation.

Chummily referred to as "my comrade" throughout her husband's writings, Lisa Ross arguably was three comrades at once. Over the span of more than three decades of married life and of two joint travel projects, she looms large as 1) a real-life organizational and editorial presence behind the scenes; 2) a crucial character fulfilling an array of functions within Colin's writing (be it the author's *confidante* or his point of reference for thoughts on gender relations or family); and 3) a key ingredient of the distinct brand that "Colin Ross" became in a crowded marketplace for travel media. This brand's main pillar, apart from a strong bent towards the German pseudoscience of geopolitics, was Ross's mode of travelling "*mit Kind und Kegel*" (with kith and kin), taking his wife, daughter Renate (born in 1915), and son Ralph (born in 1923) with him to every continent except Antarctica from 1919 onwards.

In this chapter, we draw on Colin Ross's published writings, media coverage, and unpublished archival documents, as well as what little secondary literature on the Rosses has already been written, to tease out the threefold significance of "comrade" Lisa to this immensely popular, if by now virtually forgotten body of travel writing. Although we focus on Lisa's image, due to the asymmetrical range of source materials, its reconstruction inevitably remains an indirect one. Lisa Ross did not document her travelling publicly and, thus, she can hardly be approached through interpretive models that have been introduced in scholarly literature on women's travel writing since the late 1970s. The lack of first-person sources and, at the same time, the crucial role in her husband's career, makes her case particularly challenging. In contrast to Emmy Bernatzik, for instance, who accompanied her spouse Hugo on his ethnographic expeditions and published a number of texts about them, Lisa Ross did obviously not intend to be acknowledged as a fellow producing travelogues. Still, her existence in the background did not remain traceless. Photographs, film sequences, contextual documents and, above all, her husband's and son's written legacy, offer a body of materials that allows for shedding a light on a particular mode of cotravelling devised in interwar Germany.

For this purpose, we aim to contextualise the gender positionings of Lisa Ross both in public and behind the scenes against the backdrop of Weimar era mass culture, with its new liberties as well as conservative *bürgerliche* conceptions of gender and family. This aspect of *Bürgerlichkeit* is all the more important as Colin Ross, a proponent of racialist geopolitics, is rightly considered a prominent representative of the so-called reactionary modernism that preceded National Socialism's rise to power in Germany.[4] In 1933, Colin Ross converted to National Socialism, changing gears in the following years towards openly propagandistic treatises. On 29 April 1945, one night before Adolf Hitler's suicide, Ross killed his wife and committed suicide with a gun.[5] Archival documents suggest that Lisa Ross had shared her husband's shift away from their previously more noncommittal right-wing outlook.[6]

Married to the Job: Lisa Ross, 1889–1945

Lisa Peter met Colin Ross, four years her senior, while studying in Heidelberg, where they both obtained their doctorates from national economist Eberhard Gothein. They were married in 1911, the same year she submitted her dissertation on female servants in England, having previously studied in Cambridge and London as well as Munich.[7] Both Lisa and Colin Ross came from solid bourgeois backgrounds, her father being a banker in Karlsruhe, and his father a German electrical engineer who resided in Vienna for much of his professional life.[8] Family property and connections would provide important advantages in the Rosses' eventual success. Most important in this respect was Colin's brother Fritz, who had married into the prominent publishing family Ullstein, which proved to be a dependable employer for the couple, giving Colin Ross commissions as a travel writer and filmmaker that implied Lisa's added labour force.[9] But as far as sources suggest, the Ross family's economic situation was determined less by inheritance and entitlement than by a freelance economy that was labour-intensive and, until the mid-1920s, involved considerable personal financial risk which was exacerbated by the economic turmoil of Germany's years after World War I.

This was borne out by the first journey Colin Ross undertook with his wife and daughter after his start in newspaper journalism and the lecturing circuit with his reports from the Balkan Wars, the Mexican Revolution, and the Great War, and his participation as an officer in the failed German Revolution of 1918/19.[10] In leaving for South America in 1919 with Renate and Lisa, he planned to emigrate for good and eventually build up a career as a foreign correspondent for German newspapers. He had also made a loose arrangement with, as it turned out, a rather uncommitted Auswärtiges Amt (Office of Foreign Affairs) in Berlin to send secret reports about the situation in South America in exchange for monetary compensation. Ross, who had participated as an officer in the failed German Revolution of 1918/19, showed a republican bent in his writing and comments in South American newspapers that scandalised the predominantly monarchist German expat communities in Argentina and Chile. They mostly shunned him, and his request for a diplomatic post in Bolivia remained unanswered by his contacts in Berlin as well. For stretches of the stay the family had to depend for their livelihood on Lisa Ross giving English lessons, while Colin pressed German officials for further payments.[11]

After returning broke to Germany's runaway inflation in the spring of 1921, the Rosses' fortunes only turned for the better with the publication of Colin's reports from South America in a volume the same year: its success initiated a solid, supportive partnership with renowned publishing house Brockhaus.[12] For his next journey Ross went to Central Asia by himself, a dangerous undertaking he endured with a slight budget. This was the first time he travelled with a film camera to document his encounters in moving images besides his article writing. Ross would later explain his move towards film from a need to attain financing for his trips and make the most of his travel experiences by developing diverse opportunities for revenue.[13] Ross's breakthrough as a multimedia travel reporter came with the film made from his next, more ambitious trip through the United States and East Asia, *Mit dem Kurbelkasten um die Welt* (*With the Cranking Box around the Globe*) [1925], undertaken together with Lisa.[14]

Ross's graduation at this point from a well-regarded travel reporter to a popular figure within German and Austrian mass culture is due in large part to Lisa Ross's collaboration[15]. As he travelled customarily without a professional camera operator, Colin Ross had to rely on her to crank the camera handle in the numerous shots when he himself entered the frame to interact and give proof of his presence, sporting a scout hat and suit, next to exotic sites. Starting in 1925, Lisa Ross would be recorded in the released films as well, and from the Rosses' next trip, on which they took their children to Africa for a thirteen-month stay in 1926/27, the family members' presence would be more systematically highlighted in the films and books. The publication of Colin Ross's *Mit Kamera, Kind und Kegel durch Afrika* (With Camera, Kith and Kin through Africa), in 1928, started a veritable subfranchise of more anecdotal family-oriented Ross books, the phrase "Mit Kind und Kegel" returning in three more book titles.

Within this family enterprise, Lisa Ross had a great number of tasks, some more publicly acknowledged than others. In Colin Ross's writing and their son

Ralph Colin Ross's travel account *Von Chicago nach Chungking* (From Chicago to Chungking) [1941], much is made of her function as a teacher, homeschooling the children on journeys that often lasted for over a year.[16] Lisa Ross's involvement in filming and photographing during the trips is evident from images of her husband's presence, while newspaper reports find her joining him on press appointments or closely collaborating in the films' post-production.[17] While her husband acknowledged Lisa's importance in decision-making, going so far as to suggest that she was the driving force behind their trip to Australia in 1929, the minutes that publisher Brockhaus wrote about their management's meetings with Mr and Mrs Ross between 1927 and 1943 reveal the full weight of her editorial work.[18] It is on Lisa Ross's insistence, for instance, that Colin overhauled two finished manuscripts about their trip to the South Sea before submitting *Haha Whenua – das Land das ich gesucht* (Haha Whenua – the country I have been looking for) [1933] to Brockhaus. (Her criticism of earlier versions were concerned with both the quality of the writing and protecting the anonymity of some of the people appearing in the text.)[19] Likewise, Mrs Ross was the one who engaged the publishers in discussions about the layout and retouching of the photographs.[20] The minutes also identify her as the author of the photo captions for Colin's books. Moreover, it was apparently within her power to decline another publisher's offer in his name.[21] Finally, the Brockhaus minutes give a clear assessment of the physical cost of the strenuous travellers' life as they report on several occasions on finding Lisa Ross's suffering from infections caught on different trips.[22]

The roles of mother, adviser, and assistant suggest a rather traditional model of unpaid and uncredited conjugal labour – a model made to seem all the more traditional in the contemporaneous public eye by the fact that Lisa Ross's tasks as caregiver and support are publicised, while her importance as a decision maker in the Ross work unit/household is mostly witnessed by internal documents. Going beyond the model of conjugal labour, the collapsing of distinctions between the private and the public, family life and work, behind-the-scenes-labour and family-as-team publicity that the Rosses performed, suggests a specifically modern context of spousal and family labour, which was identified by media scholar Markus Krajewski as the economy of "project-making." Colin Ross can be counted among the number of enthusiastic semi-professionals and freelancers who, according to Krajewski's research, started in the early twentieth century to develop "world projects," be they world histories of technology or efforts at introducing world standards of measurement.[23]

The Rosses' different trips would only coalesce into a more holistic endeavour of capturing "the world" around 1930, at which point Colin aspired to graduate from travel writing to a Spenglerian cultural philosophy. But from the start of their post-war family journeys, the Rosses' work is grounded in the three premises that distinguishes Krajewski's world project makers: they depend on and celebrate an already existing infrastructural grid of overlapping communication and transportation technologies (rather than stressing the more heroic travel writing model of the explorers of uncharted territory)[24]; they position themselves between disciplines and institutions, looking for funding and legitimating associations while defining themselves as in-between them (with Colin going so far as to declare himself a "dilettante"[25]); and – last, but not least – they depend on exploiting the family as a workforce within this precarious economic model.[26] This frame of reference throws the contributions of Colin Ross's wife and children to "his" media production into sharper relief, not only as stars or (later) authors of texts or film shots, but also as integral parts of a branded method of investigating faraway places via domesticity, spending months at a time "embedded" in a suburb of Sydney or weeks in a diamond rush town in South Africa.[27]

Travel Companion and Co.: Lisa Ross as a character and her female counterparts

Although the guidebook for emigrants, the outcome of the first joint trip to South America before the more successful travel report *Südamerika, die aufsteigende Welt* (*South America, the Rising World*) [1922], does not mention Lisa Ross explicitly, this tiny handbook is more than instructive of how Colin assessed the role a woman and the family could play in the context of the colonization of a foreign country. When providing information about the expected living and labour standards in a number of South American countries, Ross gives a word of advice to married and unmarried men as well as fathers. He does so by considering not only the household or climatic conditions, but also and foremost, the economic advantages and disadvantages emigrants would face.[28] His arguments suggest an image of the family as a fundamentally economic association of men, women, and children. Nonetheless, Colin Ross complements this conclusion with the Biblical notion that "It is not good that the man should be alone; I will make him a helper fit for him."[29] The combination of the patriarchal, traditionally religious family structure and of the economic equality in production implies the framework of what would become the basic model of the Rosses' specific travel enterprise. That Lisa Ross's role in her husband's subsequent travel books is thus "cast" in the mould of a handbook's guidelines should alert us to the fact that this essay now changes gears from a historical reconstruction of Lisa Ross's tasks in her husband's travel media business to the murkier waters of Lisa Ross as a character in his writing (edited, among others, by her). Given the purposely muddled position of the nineteenth- and twentieth-century travelogue between fiction and the more rigid truth claims of autobiography and journalism, this character can neither be completely extricated from what we believe the historical Lisa Ross's tasks and experiences to have been nor narrowly identified with her.

The figure of Lisa Ross acquires sharper contours in the first "kith-and-kin-book" following the African journey of the now four-headed family, in 1928. Here Lisa is portrayed as a guarantor of travel safety who not only solves logistical challenges, but also takes care of the children's health and the smooth management of the household.[30] In addition, and this in turn shifts the emphasis to her role as the "comrade" of the famous travel writer, she contributes to the report itself by visiting, for instance, a harem that is inaccessible to her husband. Or, when he becomes exasperated with the organizational difficulties of an elephant hunt and with the daughter's illness, his wife is the one who persuades him not to abandon his original plans to set out for the hunt and, by implication, not jeopardise the success of the future travelogue book and film.[31]

Significantly, it is this hunting episode, embedded in the adventurous book's narration, which features Lisa in her *own* words. Colin Ross not only quotes "the brave woman's" letter that reports on a dangerous nightly visit of a rhinoceros and assures the father of the safety of the kids,[32] but he also tells the subsequent events of an equally menacing elephant visiting the tents through *monologue intérieur*, a rare narrative device in Colin Ross's books:

> The heart of the mother was a single silent scream, a single wild prayer: "It can not and must not be. We shouldn't have dared too much when we took the children with us. And if so, let it turn out well just this time." Nearer and nearer came the beast [...] Breathing ceased, the heartbeat stopped.[33]

Curiously enough, a remark in the 1934 book *Mit Kind und Kegel in die Arktis* (*With Kid and Kith into the Arctic*) puts this episode into perspective, as far as it questions the "copyright" of the scene description: the commentary says that Lisa was not able to talk about this threatening experience for a long time, having been shocked by the incident.[34] The fact that the *monologue intérieur* is used in the Africa report can probably be attributed to the overall tone of the book. As outlined in the book's preface, the adventurous plot fundamentally mediates the intimacy of a family journey with all of its throwbacks and confident moments that stem from the strong ties between family members.[35] In this respect, Colin's faculty of projecting Lisa's thoughts and fears, hard as they are to express by herself, would strengthen the impression of a spiritual unity between the couple and, additionally, would comply with the genre of the adventurous travelogue intensifying the effect of suspense. The use of this specific device is, however, a rare case in Ross's narration in general which is dominated by an utmost traditional rhetorical design preferring first-person singular. Thus the above scene can be viewed as a well-made experiment to portray the "comrade" and to integrate this portrayal into a risky setting.

On the trip to Australia, where Lisa is again described as "brave," Colin foregrounds his wife's sobriety and logistical talents.[36] After a discussion about the overweight of luggage through the continent's desert journey, Lisa turns out to be right, as a sand storm breaks over the family and the car is stuck in a dune because of the overweight.[37] This episode, however, does not imply that Lisa is frightful or overcautious; on the contrary, it is always a mixture of rational argumentation, her belief in some esoteric signposts, and the spirit of adventure that makes her collaboration with the travelogue writer so valuable. For instance, while sailing the South Sea, the couple – disregarding the captain's advice – leaves the ship and their sleeping children for an island to secretly listen to a "dance party in the full moon" and satisfy their curiosity.[38] In other travel episodes, in which Lisa is quoted directly in one of the few dialogues between the spouses, it is she who emerges as the more reasonable person. She pokes fun at the writer's exaggerated fascination with the South Sea and a "wish boat" that mysteriously seems to follow them; in Africa, she advances stronger arguments for leaving the village of the Kavirondos in the face of a menacing situation caused by religious fanaticism.[39]

Her disciplining and antisentimental impetus is effective in taming the husband's erotic projections, too. While there occur a number of erotic incidents, or at least some potentially flirtatious encounters, on Colin Ross's unaccompanied trips, the voyeuristic and erotically charged scenes during the Australasian excursion are significantly weakened by Lisa's empathic and balancing presence.[40] For instance, Colin Ross's emotionally stirring encounter with Jutta Hall, the beautiful English wife of a German settler, is doused by Lisa's cautious but accurate, critical remarks.[41] Accordingly, the somewhat solemn, but pathetically formulated concluding statement of the book suggests the couple's consensus that the external satisfaction of longings is by no means the royal road: "Haha Whenua [i.e. the cipher for heaven on earth], the country I have been looking for, cannot be found anywhere on earth unless you have recovered it from the murky depths of your own heart before."[42] From this perspective, Colin Ross's somewhat disconcerting phrasing in all his books that mention his wife can be better understood: He refers to Lisa with the masculine "*Kamerad*" (meaning comrade, companion, or mate) along with the masculine pronoun "he" that this noun governs, although a feminine form of this noun is available. Of course, gendering, or more precisely "masculanising" Lisa's figure in this way sets up a framework primarily defined by the view of the narrator: It refers to a basically equal standing between man and woman, but from a masculine point of view, and granted by a male narrator.

How distinctive the presence of his wife and/or his family is becomes evident in two contrasting episodes in Africa and in Papua New Guinea. In Africa, after a tough negotiating session with tribe members, Colin Ross takes his camera to a female circumcision ritual. The scenes, both in the book *Die erwachende Sphinx* (*The Awakening Sphinx*) and in the film of the same title (1927), impress with their voyeurism and the inexorability of its strained objectivism, even if they can be viewed as an exotic spectacle.[43] No wonder that the outcome of recording these scenes in the absence of the family was intended for an adult audience. *Haha Whenua*, in contrast, describes a scene of exposed female bodies with increasing restraint: While watching young women in Hanuabada playing cricket, Ross is entranced by the sight of the bare-breasted women. But descriptions of Renate's and Ralph's activities help the narrator to downplay the eroticism of the display.[44]

Against the background of such a relationship with the wife and the family, the images and the explicit or implicit assessments of foreign women are reasonably heterogeneous: The circumcised natives of the African village are portrayed as pure objects of the camera and the writing hand. Another group of women is also depicted as a mere object and, in addition, explicit racist arguments come to the fore: A "female bastard" (Bastardin), the daughter of a European colonist and an indigenous woman, serves as a surface for contrast and projection. "The women looked at me stupidly and without understanding. No human expression was recognizable on their stolid faces." In the eyes of the handsome "female bastard," however, Ross says, a spark of communicativeness arouses, which makes him imagine how she could be recivilised again:

> This beautiful mixed-blood maiden still bore in herself the mystery and the impulse of her noble white blood, whose share could have lifted her far beyond this sphere of misery and distress, in which she now had to live as spellbound and enchanted. If she were taken out of this world, washed and dressed, and transferred to the other, in which she at least half belonged, would it not be very attractive to experience how this blood, now condemned to degenerate, slowly unfolded itself, and all those things that lay now dull and unresolved in her and weigh on her like a heavy dream were developed?[45]

The argument that the black population of Africa is determined by its race to live in an animal existence is not to be overlooked here but, with regard to further sections of the book, needs to be specified: Ross depicts the racial tensions in Africa as a problem of failed colonization and, to a certain degree, expresses his empathy towards the empowerment of the indigenous people. Still, three years later racism plays a much less important role in Madurai, especially when considering matters of female emancipation: Colin Ross, in a brief travelogue passage in his geopolitically inspired overview of India, describes with despair how female minors are forced to marry in front of a temple in which the "old, bloody goddess" Kali is revered. And he poses the rhetorical question of whether the liberation of India from the colonial power of Britain would not be a relapse into the old barbarism with its widows' incantations and the total reverence for the "old, bloody deities."[46] However, even the "white" civilization has its underbelly: In the cinema, next to the mentioned temple, "excited-looking coloured men" are staring at half-naked white dancers accompanied by a bad Broadway melody. "The unscrupulous American rationale of business spreads this image of white civilization like pestilence over the world."[47]

Judging from the way female figures are depicted in Ross's later books, one might venture the statement that while the "comrade's" presentation remains constant, an increasing empathy towards Aborigines and other indigenous peoples becomes noticeable over the course of time. As in India, Colin Ross seems to develop a sense for the destinies of women who are now depicted either as bearers of venerable traditions of the foreign countries or as protective subjects.[48] The trip to the Arctic, which Colin Ross undertakes with Lisa and Ralph in 1933, proves to be particularly significant in this regard. The travel reporter is deeply impressed by the naturalness of family life in which, under the most difficult climatic and economic conditions, a consistent egalitarianism is lived in a self-evident manner. While observing a female Inuit and the way her husband communicates with her, Colin Ross reflects on his lack of knowledge, which is, by the way, a rare case in the course of his career:

Apparently, she counts as much as the men, and, apparently, I have to learn a lot more to fully understand the way of thinking of the "men of the North."[49]

In this case, the appreciation of native life seems triggered less by the association of the north with culture than with its relation to a Canadian landscape that Ross perceives as fundamentally empty and waiting to be settled by Europeans, using the Inuits' tried-and-true techniques.[50] A couple of years later, on his last trip to Central America in 1935, Ross recalls his experience with the combatants of Pancho Villa by remarking how self-evident the presence of the "*soldadera*" was, i.e. how the female soldiers fulfilled serious military tasks side by side with their husbands, at the same time having the "*chamachos,*" their soldier children, on their side.[51]

This shift in emphasis with respect to the assessment of the female figures can be traced back to the changing perspective of Colin Ross himself: The exotic view loses its importance in favour of a more prominent emphasis on family associations in different countries. This modification is in line with Colin Ross's growing interest in geopolitical issues, in which demographic "lines of force"(*Kraftlinien*)[52] play a significant role. Thus, the empathy expressed in Ross's writing is not to be mistaken for a universalist outlook. Fuelled by the impotence of defeated Germany in a post-World War I world order, the tenets of German geopolitical thinking made room for ethnopluralism (to each their own) and cultural learning (i.e. from Inuit families), while keeping the dominance of one's own – German, or European – race the unquestioned political priority. Africa had to be subjugated by Europe, Ross wrote in an especially candid instance of his brand of geopolitical particularism in 1934: Not because its native population was in any way inferior to Europe's, but because Europe needed the resources.[53]

The Ross Bunch: domesticity on the move

Even if the link between the family's specific functions and global population problems is not made explicit in Colin Ross's writings, it is worthwhile to take a look at his further remarks in order to specify the status of the family, and within it that of Lisa, against the background of his own reflections and the prevailing contemporary discourses about family life.

According to literary scholar Walter Erhart, the image of the family at the beginning of the twentieth century was dominated by two models of secular modernism complying with the social and economic requirements of mature capitalism: In the conflict between individualism and community it was either an authoritarian entity or the guarantor of the "private," a greenhouse for the formation of the individual. For both opposing models, however, the figure of the father was decisive – either as a patriarch or as a psychoanalytic compensation to the wife and mother. In the first case, the old-way hegemony of the head of the family was maintained, in the second, a more cooperative and caring figure arose. However, case studies show that the image of the family, with its clear role assignments, is more of an ideal-typical projection surface than a model applicable to individual cases.[54] As far as our sources are concerned, the Ross family, at least through the prism of the father and the son, can be seen as a mixture of father-centred corporation and maternal pragmatism. The parents approximately provide the same degree of intimacy and purposeful rationality, without being clearly classified into one of the extremes.

In this perspective, the framework of politically and economically induced developments can serve as a more instructive interpretation for the way the Ross family functioned and, within it, to what position Lisa was assigned. The Rosses attest not only to the decline of the size of the family due to industrialization and urbanization, effective at least from the beginning of the nineteenth century,[55] but also to the ideas on equality which were formulated in bourgeois reform educational programs as well as in similar recommendations of the workers' movement. The German Social Democrats stressed the necessity to replace the diverse forms of forced marriage by the so-called "*Kameradschaftsehe*" (comradeship marriage) with the simultaneous maintenance of a small-size family; the abolition of authoritarian and patriarchal structures was a central concern for the bourgeois camp, too.[56]

These discourses and economic conditions seem to be applicable to the Rosses, but the real stake of this special family enterprise might be overlooked, if we do not consider that Colin and Lisa ran an association that is to be seen as a late descendant of the entrepreneurial family, too. As social historian Jürgen Kocka has pointed out in a short but illuminating essay, the individual economic success during the early phase of industrialization in Germany could only be guaranteed by large family enterprises. Here, as later in the nuclear family, a contractual relationship between the spouses and further kinship was established in order to gain economic (and partial political) power.[57] In it, the role of the wife, as later in the 1920s, was in a pragmatic and economic sense substantially equivalent to that of the husband. While significantly linked to the old-school entrepreneurial family of their publisher Ullstein via Colin's brother Fritz Ross, the Ross family embodied a more scaled-down version of this pragmatic-economic model, attuned to freelance media production. This modernised form entails a combination of staged intimacy and interest-focused cohesion that could be excellently marketed within the Weimar Republic's mass culture as well as in that of Nazi Germany, for both were open to the integration of progressive social ideas and traditional bourgeois images of smaller and larger communities.[58]

Within this basic constellation, however, the positions of Colin Ross, as they appear in his travelogues and his so-called "worldview books," gain a special note. On the one hand, the family with equal parents is used as an ideal unit for the colonization of foreign lands, thus creating a mirror image of the travelling Ross family. As in the guidebook to South America, the travel report on the Arctic upgrades the family-based conquest activity. Just as the Eskimos travel and live with "kid and kith," the Germans, making plans of colonization in the Arctic, are encouraged to emigrate only in a family association in order to ensure the projected success.[59] Ross's pragmatism comes to the fore in a further dimension. While in the debates about family life in the nineteenth century the long breastfeeding periods were supposed to serve the emotional saturation of family relations,[60] for Colin Ross they merely are a means for natural birth control. Eskimo women, giving birth in an autonomous and uncomplicated way, breastfeed their babies for years, thus preventing economic shortages and the overpopulation of the continent.[61]

On the other hand, such rational arguments would be put into a framework that was inspired as much by Oswald Spengler's *The Decline of the West* as by Otto Weininger's *Sex and Character*. While in Colin Ross's long-standing bestseller *The World in the Balance* (1929) human coupling is thought of as a result of compromises achieved by self set laws that point to a certain rhythm in the relationship,[62] his next book in this category, *Der Wille der Welt* (*The Will of the World*) [1932], would propose a more concrete model. Here, the ideal form of cohabitation is that of an association between men and women on the basis of their ideal androgyny. However, it is the female part that proceeds in this direction in a more apparent way, as far as her "limited sexuality" turns her into a "comrade," which is welcomed by the man who increasingly lacks his own sexuality.[63] In what way this project would have been realised in Ross's private family and sexual life cannot be established, but it seems that the couple's public appearance was built upon an analogous model. By combining the traditional image of the "*bürgerlich*" family with the modern image of a travelling enterprise and balancing the family functions with regard to their gendered semantics, a certain equilibrium between intimacy, domesticity, and profit-oriented activities could be maintained and marketed.

There were several popular travel writers and filmmakers contemporaneous to Colin Ross who were accompanied by their spouses (for instance, Hugo and Emmy Bernatzik or Aloha and Walter Wanderwell),[64] and a few among them who, such as famous filmmaker couple Martin and Osa Johnson, made their travel companionship a crucial part of their media texts and branding.[65] But apart from outliers like Norwegian sailor and writer Erling Tambs (1888–1967), the Rosses were rather unique in their time for travelling with their underage children and exploiting this fact in marketing the results of those travels.[66] When he returns from Africa in 1927, Colin Ross prominently discloses this mode of travel. His writing on the matter reads as a balancing act between boasting a unique selling point and protecting himself from accusations of irresponsible sensation mongering.

In the preface to the first "kith-and-kin-book" *Mit Kamera, Kind und Kegel durch Afrika* Ross claims that he is only grudgingly giving in to respond to rumours about travelling with his wife and children, not wanting to expose his family. He is at pains to go on record that he only brings them along so as not to be separated from them for the extended, often year-long trips, rather than as a publicity ploy.[67] Here, as in some of his articles of the same time, their trips are presented, first and foremost, as pragmatic and logistically feasible solutions to the challenges travel poses to a devoted family man.[68] On the other hand, often only chapters or even sentences later, Ross cannot resist describing in detail the astonishment with which his three-year-old son was received in remote African villages, while at the same time not hiding the dangers that he exposed his children to.[69]

This push and pull between presenting quaint family life and courting adventure is also dealt with in a Ross article about the family embarking on an Australasian trip in late 1928. Having chronicled the many Christmases the family has spent abroad, the article ends on a note pitched between the ominous and the uplifting:

> We have tested on earlier trips what we dare to do, and I know that this journey means going to the limits of what we can risk, or rather beyond them. But why shouldn't we trust our lucky star this time around, which has helped us in difficult situations many times so far?[70]

Few contemporaneous reporters expressed distaste for the Rosses exposing their offspring to faraway dangers as part of his livelihood. One of the critical voices, a reviewer of a lecture held in Vienna in 1928, doesn't so much articulate outrage as poke fun at Colin Ross's rhetoric of domesticated adventure. In contrast to many travelling tellers of tall tales, he jibes, Ross purposefully "scales down the perils and exertions" to his family, making the journey through Africa seem like "a rather pleasant affair" despite the occasional "impolite elephant" almost killing his wife and children.[71]

Colin Ross's portrayal of his wife, examined in the previous section, as both a clear-headed caregiver to her family and a level-headed partner keen on adventure is a crucial component of the balancing act Ross is trying to pull off in his presentation of the travelling family. While son Ralph was the breakout star of the family, spreading the appeal of Ross's books to a younger target group,[72] the character of comrade Lisa is utilised both to leaven the burden of responsibility the author bears for taking his children along and to assuage worries for their well-being.

Lisa Ross is often described taking care of the trips' logistics – discussing with her husband how to pack the car before a trip to the Australian inland,[73] or sending her husband to get tickets for the next passage on a ship.[74] In this way, she also plays a pivotal role in Colin Ross's vision of travel within a world that he presents – like his fellow project makers since 1900 –[75] as closely connected by grids of trade, transportation, and communication.[76] Lisa Ross, while keeping her family on track, is presented as a transitional figure in some regards, no longer the organiser of a logistically sophisticated expedition into the unknown, but not yet the mother of mass tourism who simply packs the suitcase and books transportation and accommodation.

In the media coverage, the Rosses' journeys are occasionally associated with tourism, demonstrating that the world is getting safe for family travel.[77] But despite fanciful comparisons of his journeys to a Berlin family's weekend jaunt,[78] they were a reporter's tours, and as early as the preface of *Mit Kamera, Kind und Kegel durch Afrika*, Ross stresses that his family's presence is, besides a pragmatic necessity, beneficial to his reporting. Their company means that he doesn't have to hurry from one place to the next, but can make his home wherever he is and get to know foreign cultures more thoroughly:

> to say nothing of the insights that a woman companion can provide you with, especially in regions of the orient, where the male stranger is completely barred from domestic and family life, the woman's domain.[79]

Some of the most lively observational passages in Ross's writing stem from his family's experiments in "going native." For instance, the uniform middle-class life in a Sydney suburb with a single-family home, a car, no servants, and a weekend that already starts on Friday evening is described by Ross with an incredulous fascination that betrays the exoticism of this way of life to an upper middle-class German in 1929.[80]

This kind of domesticity on the move became a persistent part of Ross's brand, cited more than a decade after the Sydney sojourn in an article in Vienna's *Das kleine Volksblatt*: "He doesn't observe a country through the globetrotter's glasses, but experiences it as a fellow citizen."[81] Lest this sounds too cosmopolitan for 1940 Nazi Germany, the article avers that travelling with his family is also what enables Colin Ross to stay in his native land even when on foreign soil. This contradiction is already emphasised by the article's title: "The call of the homeland follows him everywhere. Colin Ross, a world traveller – and a good German."[82]

Conclusion

This rather laboured assertion of patriotism suggests the growing pressure of legitimization that even a traveller as loyal to the regime as Ross found himself under in Nazi Germany early during World War II. But it also refers to the white supremacist and belligerent core that was part and parcel of the Rosses' geopolitical outlook ever since at least 1926. This was the vision of a world made smaller, not only by infrastructural grids, but also by its populations' violent struggle for finite space and resources.[83] The basic premise of German interwar geopolitics is the assumption of a strong bond between a population and the geography it inhabits: Settlers can "earn" their soil, make it part of their nation, by cultivating it in a way specific to them. (This belief held obvious attractions to revisionist Germans looking to reclaim lost possessions in Eastern Europe, to say nothing of colonies in Africa and the South Sea, after being defeated in World War I.) In this sense, the Ross family is not so much a band of curious globetrotters trying on different cultures for size, but rather emissaries of a German can-do ethos asserting itself the world over, proving the German people's ability to both "go native" and carry Germany with them. Reactionary modernist thinking both before and after 1933 saw Germany's racial supremacy tied to the family unit, seeing a woman's main tasks in reproduction and care for her offspring.[84] When Ross, in the preface of *Mit Kamera, Kind und Kegel durch Afrika*, praises life in the lonely African outback for making his family grow together more strongly than they ever could within civilization,[85] this is only one step removed from finding his own travelling family mirrored in the Inuit families making life in the Canadian snow, in *Mit Kind und Kegel in die Arktis*, and them foreshadowing future German colonisers.[86]

Lisa's portrayals, smartly assembled with that of other female figures, evoke the image of an emancipated woman who, at the same time, acts to embody the idea of a new National Socialist comradeship. The diverse gendered and non-gendered roles she takes on become, in the end, subordinated to this very objective.

Notes

1　This chapter presents some findings from our interdisciplinary research project on Colin Ross (*Welterkundung zwischen den Kriegen: Die Reisefilme des Colin Ross, 1885–1945*, see http://colinrossproject.net/) carried out at Ludwig Boltzmann Institute for History and Society in Vienna with Nico de Klerk and Kristin Kopp.

2　Anonymous (16 May 1940) "Der Mann, dessen Heimat die Welt ist. Colin Roß' Herz aber gehört seinem Vaterland Deutschland," in: *Volks-Zeitung*, 86 (133): 5.

3　Hahnemann, A. (2010) *Texturen des Globalen. Geopolitik und populäre Literatur in der Zwischenkriegszeit 1918–1939*. Heidelberg: Universitätsverlag Winter: 93–94; Baumunk, B.M. (1997) "Ein Pfadfinder der Geopolitik. Colin Ross und seine Reisefilme," in: *Triviale Tropen. Exotische Reise- und Abenteuerfilme aus Deutschland 1919–1939*, Jörg Schöning (ed.). Munich: Cinegraph: 85–94.

4　Herf, J. (2003) *Reactionary Modernism. Technology, Culture, and Politics in Weimar and the Third Reich*. Cambridge: Cambridge University Press: 1–17.

5　Anonymous (30 June 1949) "Wir dürfen nicht verlieren," in: *Der Spiegel*, 10(1): 11.

6　"Colin Ross. 17.5.33," *Brockhaus minutes* (State Archive Leipzig, 21083 – F.A. Brockhaus, Leipzig, I. Num. 790), 4.

7　Baumunk, B.C. (1999) *Colin Ross. Ein deutscher Revolutionär und Reisender 1885–1945*. Re-edited MA thesis from University of Tübingen, Berlin, 1999: 6.

8　Baumunk (1999): 6; Von Popp, F. (1918) "Ing. Friedrich Ross †," *Zeitschrift des Österreichischen Ingenieur- und Architekten-Vereines* 31: 343–344.

9　Baumunk (1999): 42–43. In summers, the Ross family resided at a farmhouse in Lower Austria called "Thorhof" that was family property from Colin's father's side; Baumunk (1999).

10　His books compiled of partly re-edited articles and additional essays: Ross, C. (1913) *Im Balkankrieg*. Munich: Martin Mörikes Verlag; Ross, C. (1916) *Wir draußen. Zwei Jahre Kriegserleben an vier Fronten*. Berlin and Vienna: Verlag Ullstein & Co.; Ross, C. (1913) *Der Balkankrieg 1912–1913. Bilder von der untergehenden Türkenherrschaft in Europa*. Cologne: Schaffstein; Ross, C. (1925) *Fahrten- und Abenteuerbuch*. Leizig: Verlag der Büchengilder Gutenberg; Ross, C. (1938) *Vier Jahre am Feind. Meine Erlebnisse im Feld*. Leipzig: Brockhaus. On his role in the German Revolution 1918/ 19 cf. Baumunk (1999): 24–40.

11　Baumunk (1999): 42–52.

12　Ross, C. (1923) *Südamerika, die aufsteigende Welt*. Leipzig: F.A. Brockhaus; Baumunk (1999): 54–56; "Colin Ross, 30.8.32," *Brockhaus minutes*, 5.

13　Ross, C. (1 November 1940) "So kam ich zum Filmen. Colin Ross mit der Kamera durch das neue Asien," *Angriff*, 265, s.p.

14　This trip was undertaken without their children. Ross, C. (7 June 1927) "Als Dreijähriger durch Afrika. Die Afrikareise meines Sohnes Ralph Colin," *Berliner Illustrirte Zeitung* 36 (23): 939–940, 939.

15　That Ross's likeness became more well-known is suggested, for instance, by the portrait sketch accompanying the review in the *Berliner Morgenpost*. K. Gl (4 January 1925) "Mit dem Kurbelkasten um die Erde," *Berliner Morgenpost*. In the following years, Ross is popular enough to be referenced in both the Irmgard Keun novel *Gilgi – eine von uns* (1931) and satirical magazine *Fliegende Blätter*. Cf. Baumunk, *Colin Ross*, 1; Anonymous (3 January 1929) "Die unberührte Wildnis Australiens," *Fliegende Blätter* 85/170, 74.

16 Ross, C. (1933) *Haha Whenua – das Land, das ich gesucht. Mit Kind und Kegel durch die Südsee*. Leipzig: Brockhaus: 178–183; Ross, C. (1941) *Von Chicago nach Chungking*. Berlin: Verlag die Heimbücherei: 27–28, 54–62, 195.

17 Anonymous (6 December 1940) "Dr. Colin Roß sprach in Leipzig," *Film-Kurier* 287 s.p.; Mildner, H. (1940) "Ein Fest, das alle Klassen vereint. Kirschblütentage in Tokio," *Neues Wiener Tagblatt*, 74 (229): 9.

18 Ross, C. (31 December 1928) "Wir reisen fürs 'Tempo' nach Australien," in: *Tempo*, s.p.

19 "Besuch Dr. Colin Ross und Frau in Leipzig 10./11.2.31," *Brockhaus minutes*, 2; "Colin Ross, 30.8.32," *Brockhaus minutes*, 5.

20 "Dr. Colin Roß, 6.8.35 [I]," *Brockhaus minutes*, 3; "Dr. Colin Ross und Frau bei FB Jä von 11–12.30 Uhr, 7.2.33 [I]," *Brockhaus minutes*, 5.

21 "Colin Ross, 11.12.35 [I]," *Brockhaus minutes*, 1.

22 "Ross, 18.2.1940," *Brockhaus minutes*, 1.

23 Krajewski, M. (2006) *Restlosigkeit. Weltprojekte um 1900*. Frankfurt am Main: Fischer Taschenbuch: 11–22. Thanks to Michael Wedel for the reference.

24 Krajewski (2006): 23–28; Ross, C. (1934) *Auf deutschem Boden um die Erde. Erinnerungen eines Weltreisenden*. Cologne: Hermann Schaffstein Verlag: 3–6.

25 Ross, C. (1932) *Der Wille der Welt. Eine Reise zu sich selbst*. Leipzig: Brockhaus: 7; Krajewski (2006): 175–182.

26 Krajewski (2006): 169–174.

27 Ross, C. (1930) *Der unvollendete Kontinent*. Leipzig: Brockhaus: 137–141; Ross, C. (1928) *Mit Kamera, Kind und Kegel durch Afrika*. Leipzig: Brockhaus: 29–67.

28 Ross, C. (1921) *Südamerikanisches Auswanderer-ABC. Praktische Winke und Ratschläge für Auswanderer nach Südamerika auf Grund von Reisen und Studien in Argentinien, Brasilien, Chile, Uruguay und Bolivien in den Jahren 1919–1921*. Stuttgart: Verlag Ausland und Heimat Aktiengesellschaft: 4–6, 27. The travelogue *Südamerika, die aufsteigende Welt* is partly written in first-person plural, but it basically continues to expand on the main topics of the guidebook and adds to them geopolitical and historical considerations as well as sceneries.

29 1.Mose 2, 18, cf. Ross, *Südamerikanisches Auswanderer-ABC*, 25.

30 Ross (1928): 60, 79, 118.

31 Ross (1928): 89–90.

32 Colin Ross praised his wife's letters while Lisa criticised her own writings, cf. "Colin Ross und Frau in Leipzig, 28.11.1940," *Brockhaus minutes*, 9. Unfortunately, no correspondence between them has come down to us.

33 Ross (1928): 175.

34 Ross, C. (1934) *Mit Kind und Kegel in die Arktis*. Leipzig: Brockhaus: 167–168.

35 Ross (1928): 8–9; see also the statement of an interviewer on the charming way of Colin Ross's speaking about his "comrade" in C. O. (22 May 1935, MB) "Colin Roß fünfzig Jahre," *Neue Freie Presse* 25393, 6.

36 Ross, C. (1930) *Der unvollendete Kontinent*. Leipzig: Brockhaus: 99.

37 Ross (1930): 69–107.

38 Ross (1933): 192–200.

39 Ross (1933): 123–125; Ross (1928): 136–137.

40 Ross, C. (3 November 1912) "Wie ich zu einem Gaul kam," in: *Münchner Neueste Nachrichten*, 65(561): 1; Ross, C. (1923) *Der Weg nach Osten. Reise durch Russland, Ukraine, Transkaukasien, Persien, Buchara und Turkestan*. Leipzig: Brockhaus: 98.

41 Ross (1933): 52–59.

42 Ross (1933): 289.
43 Ross, C. (1927) *Die erwachende Sphinx*. Leipzig: Brockhaus: 263–269.
44 Ross (1933): 134–139.
45 Ross (1927): 70–71.
46 Ross, C. (1931) *Umstrittenes Indien*. Berlin: Verlag Reimar Hobbing: 24–26.
47 Ross (1931): 26, 28.
48 Ross (1933): 36–40, 44.
49 Ross (1934): 150.
50 Pissowotzki, N. (1 March 2009) "Colonial Fantasies, Narrative Borders, and the Canadian North in the Works of Germany's Colin Ross (1885–1945)," in: *Nordlit: Tidsskrift i litteratur og kultur*, 13(1): 81–98
51 Ross, C. (1937) *Der Balkan Amerikas. Mit Kind und Kegel durch Mexiko und Panamakanal*. Leipzig: Brockhaus: 101.
52 Hahnemann (2010): 26.
53 Ross, C. (July 1934) "Amerika und das schwarze Weltproblem," in: *Zeitschrift für Geopolitik*, 11(7): 399–409.
54 Erhart, W. (2001) *Familienmänner. Über den literarischen Ursprung moderner Männlichkeit*. Munich: Wilhelm Fink Verlag: 24–122; similar arguments are brought up by Koschorke, A. et al. (2010) *Vor der Familie. Grenzbedingungen einer modernen Institution*. Konstanz: Konstanz University Press: 12–21.
55 Mitterauer, M. & Sieder, R. (1994) *Vom Patriarchat zur Partnerschaft. Zum Struktur-wandel der Familie*, 4th ed. Munich: C.H. Beck: 64–65, 109.
56 Gestrich, A. (1999) *Geschichte der Familie im 19. und 20. Jahrhundert*, in: Enzyklopädie deutscher Geschichte, Lothar Gall (ed.). Oldenbourg: Oldenbourg Wissenschaftsverlag: 7–8; Sieder, R. (1987) *Sozialgeschichte der Familie*. Frankfurt/M.: Suhrkamp: 214–219.
57 Kocka, J. (1982) "Familie, Unternehmen und Kapitalismus. An Beispielen aus der frühen deutschen Industrialisierung," in: *Die Familie in der Geschichte*, Heinz Reif (ed.). Göttingen: Vandenhoeck & Ruprecht: 163–186.
58 Föllmer, M. (2016)*"Ein Leben wie im Traum." Kultur im Dritten Reich*. Munich: C.H. Beck: 95–96, 267.
59 Ross (1934): 8.
60 Sieder (1987): 135.
61 Ross (1934): 212–213.
62 Ross, C. (1929) *Die Welt auf der Waage. Der Querschnitt von 20 Jahren Weltreise*. Leipzig: Brockhaus: Ch. 10. English translation: Ross, C. (1930) *The World in the Balance: an Analysis of World-Problems After Twenty Years' Travel About the World*, Winifred Felkin [tr.]. London: Routledge.
63 Ross (1932): 182–190, 196–197. On the debates between Ross and Brockhaus, who first did not want to publish the book, and on the following corrections cf. "Colin Ross, 30.8.32," *Brockhaus minutes*, 2–3.
64 Faber, M. & Pfitscher, M. (2014) "'. . . das Afrika, wie ich es so sehr liebe . . .'," in: *"Die herrlichen schwarzen Menschen." Hugo Bernatziks fotojournalistische Beute-züge in den Sudan 1925–1927*, Monika Faber and Walter Moser (eds.). Vienna: Paper Book: 11–21, 11–12; Eagan, D. (date unknown) "The Long Journey of Aloha Wanderwell." filmcomment.com, http://www.filmcomment.com/blog/the-long-jour ney-of-aloha-wanderwell/ (accessed 17 October 2016).
65 Johnson, O. (1997) *I Married Adventure: The Lives of Martin and Osa Johnson*. Tokyo: Kodansha Globe.
66 Anonymous (27 March 1932) "Ein Baby Weltumsegler," in: *Berliner Illustrirte Zeitung* 41(12): 348–349.
67 Ross (1928): 3–9.
68 Ross, C. (7 June 1927) "Als Dreijähriger durch Afrika. Die Afrikareise meines Sohnes Ralph Colin," in: *Berliner Illustrirte Zeitung*, 36(23): 939–940, 939.

69 Ross (1928): 4; Ross (7 June 1927): 939–940; Ross, C. (18 December 1927) "Eine Reise durch Afrika. Mit Frau und Kindern durch die Wildsteppe," in: *Berliner Illustrirte Zeitung*, 36(51): 2103–2105.

70 Ross (31 December 1928).

71 K. (17 May 1928) "Mit Kind und Kegel in Afrika," in: *Wiener Zeitung*, 225(115): 5.

72 "Besprechung Dr. Ross und Frau, Jä, FB am 10.2.31," *Brockhaus minutes*, 1.

73 Ross (1930): 72–74.

74 Ross (1933): 178.

75 Krajewski (2006): 23–29.

76 Ross, C. (18 February 1925) "Der letzte Forscher: Zu Sven Hedins 60. Geburtstag," in: *Vossische Zeitung*, s.p.; Ross, C. (July 1931) "Die Fiktion der Weltwirtschaft," in: *Zeitschrift für Geopolitik,* 8(7): 562–566.

77 Moll, E. (26 July 1925) "Der Reisefilm in volkswirtschaftlicher Bedeutung," in: *Der Kinematograph,* 962: 9–10.

78 H.P. (15 November 1930) "Der neue Colin-Roß-Film," in: *Vossische Zeitung*, s.p.

79 Ross (1928): 9–10.

80 Ross (1930): 142.

81 Anonymous (16 May 1940) "Der Ruf der Heimat folgt ihm überallhin. Colin Roß, ein Weltwanderer – und ein guter Deutscher," in: *Das kleine Volksblatt*, 9.

82 Anonymous (16 May 1940).

83 Ross, C. (26 September 1926) "Die schwarze Gefahr in Südafrika," in: *Berliner Illustrirte Zeitung*, 35(39): 1237–1238; Roß, C. (10 April 1930) "Die olivfarbene Gefahr: Australische Beobachtungen," in: *Vossische Zeitung*, s.p.; Ross, C. (May 1933) "Kolonien?", in: *Zeitschrift für Geopolitik*, 10(5): 257–269. For this core aspect of geopolitics in interwar Germany, see Murphy, D.T. (1997) *The Heroic Earth. Geopolitical Thought in Weimar Germany, 1918–1933*. Kent/Ohio, London/ England: The Kent State University Press: 24–42. While he is inconsistent over the course of his career, Ross usually argues for white supremacy less out of a sense of inherent racial superiority than for strategic reasons of protecting Europe's place in the world. For Ross at his most liberal (and, at the same time, politically cynical) in matters of race, see: Ross (July 1934).

84 Gestrich (1999): 8–9; Herf (2003): 56–57.

85 Ross (1928): 8.

86 Ross (1934): 8–9; Pissowotzki (1 March 2009).

15 The not-so-solo traveller

Mary Pos, Dutch writer and journalist

Babs Boter

Introduction

In the autobiographical account of her first journey abroad, at the age of 23, Mary Pos recounts how she became seasick on her way from Rotterdam to London. Luckily, a kind steward accompanied her to a lady's cabin, and offered drinks. "How thankful one is when travelling abroad on one's own, when someone is lending a hand," Pos' young "I" gratefully told the steward.[1] The latter, however, instantly responded to the young woman's favourable remark by pronouncing that not long ago another lady had appreciated his assistance so immensely that she had offered him a two-and-a-half-guilder coin. The autobiographical narrator tells the readers of the Christian women's journal that she had only given the "smart fellow" a shilling and had explained to him that she simply had a whole week ahead of her and no money to spend on such generous tips. Thus, although she must have seemed vulnerable as a young female traveller becoming seasick during her first voyage, as the narrator she shows her readers that she has not at all lost her wits.

The remainder of the travel account, published a year after the 1927 journey, continues to confirm the ambivalent character of the young woman traveller, and seems to have served different kinds of readers and attended to different kinds of gender expectations. On the one hand, Pos presents her travelling self as a naïve, innocent and unexperienced young female passenger: The article features a travelling "I" who intuitively believes the honest face of a tobacco smuggler, pays a taxi-driver much more than she should, leaves her umbrella in a taxi, and forgets her gloves on the ship that takes her back to the Netherlands. On the other hand, the story brings forward an autobiographical character who is independent and autonomous, smart and witty, and who never experiences any anxiety. It is the story of an "I" who forcefully keeps to her own agenda and dissociates herself from others (journalists, travellers, tourists) – a motif that would become central in Pos' written work. Although she is sent to London by the Dutch advertising firm she works for as a secretary, to visit an advertising exhibition, she seems to prefer a solo exploration of the city. One night, unaccompanied, she takes the Underground to discover London, and returns to an utterly dark and quiet apartment building where she has to feel her way to her second floor room.[2] On another night, when travelling by bus on her own, the I narrator describes the night as being lovely and quiet, and not cold at all. She notes the strange mysteriousness in the streets where during the day it had been hectic: "The moon lit the large, dark buildings beautifully. [...] I enjoyed being on top of the bus."[3]

Pos' travel text also recounts her "I" as feeling comfortable when meeting up with strangers: Invited to visit the home of Harry Gordon Selfridge, the millionaire owner of the London-based department stores, the young traveller acknowledges that she is considerably underdressed. The other Dutch guests have left her standing there on her own, upon which she decides to slowly and ceremoniously walk into the mansion, "just as if I looked magically chique [...]." Invited to a luncheon at Hever Castle, hosted by Lord and Lady Astor, the young woman appears to be the only one in a crowd of 200 female visitors who is not made up. Still, she resolves to enjoy the visit: "I did feel like the odd-one-out, but I did not eat the less for it."[4]

Apparently, for this article, "Een zakenmeisje in Londen," [A business girl in London], published in *Christelijk Vrouwenleven* in 1928, Pos wanted to feature herself as visiting upscale places. In another travel account of this first journey to London Pos relates that, inspired by her father's missionary work, and driven by her wish to write about the London poor, she had omitted parts of the London exhibition program to wander along the homes of misty East End. There her travelling self found her way to the Salvation Army which assisted her in finding an asylum where she could sleep among the poor.[5] Thus, Mary Pos showcases ambivalent autobiographical characters *within* one travel narrative, and she features different "I" travellers in accounts of the same journey. It seems as if, even at this early stage in her career as a travel journalist, she creatively and resourcefully negotiated different gender roles available to her at the time.

This essay will examine the ways in which, in her travel writing, Pos presented a travelling self that was able to tackle the logistical, financial, physical, and psychological challenges she faced while being on journeys she undertook on her own, and confront the sociocultural and religious pressures when transgressing traditional constructions of femininity.[6] In order to be able to do so the author borrowed from a mix of discourses on hand, such as those of gender, travel writing, tourism, colonialism, religion, class, charity work, and Dutch journalism. Sources used will consist of correspondence with relatives, friends, lovers, admirers, sponsors, and politicians; Pos' published travel writing such as books, and newspaper and magazine articles; manuscripts, written lectures, reviews, personal notebooks, and photos.

The first female travel journalist

Mary Pos (1904–1987) grew up as the oldest daughter in an orthodox Protestant Dutch family in Zaandam and Purmerend, the Netherlands. Inspired by her father's practice as an evangelist among poor peasants in the province of North Holland, and her uncle's work as a missionary in the Dutch East Indies, Pos developed an ambition, to a great extent supported by her family, to make a career as a world traveller, writer, and cultural mediator. Between the 1920s and late 1970s she ventured out on numerous journeys in all five continents to explore other cultures, as well as Dutch immigrant cultures and missionary settlements. Mary Pos declared herself to be the first Dutch female travel journalist, which she was. In the US and the UK there were earlier examples of women reporters who went on trips abroad, but in the Netherlands during the interbellum she was a rare case.[7] She published accounts of her journeys in thirteen book-length travel narratives and countless articles in newspapers and magazines of a mostly Protestant Christian background. In addition, she presented thousands of lectures both abroad and in the Netherlands, where she showed slides, sang and recited poetry, and was regularly dressed in ethnic costumes. She also offered travel stories to listeners of national radio programs. In addition to her travel work, Pos published young adult novels, short stories, and biographical essays. Among her readers and listeners were men and women of various age groups, urban and provincial backgrounds, more or less educated, and mostly but not only middle-class Protestant Christian inhabitants of the Netherlands, the Dutch East-Indies, Suriname, the Dutch Antilles, and Dutch individuals living overseas.

Having grown up in an orthodox Protestant Christian family in the 1910s and 1920s, Pos certainly ventilated conservative ideas, such as those related to colonialism, race relations, and Jewish culture. However, she also featured a rather free-spirited stance, and showed emancipatory views concerning the Protestant religion, women's roles, and social issues. In addition to her wish to contribute to intercultural understanding, she hoped to be able to lobby for better working and living conditions for women, the poor, and other underprivileged groups. Pos perceived of herself as a bridge builder and instructed her audience not to think as Dutch subjects, nor as Europeans, but as global citizens.

In her own words, in one of her 1930s diaries, Pos devotedly and without any trace of irony asserts that the aim of her wanderings is to be able:

> to meet exemplary people, role models for us, to give us courage and help, doctors, nurses, missionaries and social workers. To enter the wide, merry world as a woman on my own, an enterprise that asks for a large dosis of courage, even in this civilised and cultivated world. This is demanding for a man in terms of energy and endurance, but even more so for a woman who naturally and in various ways is the weaker compared to men.[8]

But then again Pos had other, less idealistic matters on her agenda. Implicitly she supported a nationwide project that encouraged the Dutch to emigrate to countries such as South Africa, Australia, and Canada. Secondly, her written work discloses that Pos felt a strong personal urge to explore the world to find self-space and independence. In letters to close friends she writes about the "itch" for travelling.[9] The sources studied for this essay do not allow for a definitive answer to the question whether this "itch" prevented Pos from getting married, or whether there were other reasons for not marrying.[10] In her diary entry of 9 March 1932 Pos asserts that she had been interested in "the problem of married life" since the age of 17.[11] In 1939, when she is no longer engaged to Anne Gerrit van der Horst, her second fiancé, she writes in a letter to a female friend that she is being courted by many men, but is unable to proceed and start a serious relationship. She claims that she would have to sacrifice so much and concludes: "It really needs to be worth it."[12]

Consequently, Mary Pos was free from the duties and responsibilities associated with being a wife and mother, but also had no husband to support her travels financially. Neither did she come from a wealthy family. Pos was able to act on her travel "itch" because she had saved up money she had earned working as a secretary since the age of 16, and she kept her travelling costs low by staying with friends and acquaintances, or with organizations such as the Salvation Army. Later on she paid for her trips by selling articles and short stories to magazines and newspapers. In addition, Pos was a paid lecturer, and organised sponsoring money from ministries, such as the Ministry of Education, the Arts, and Science, and several firms, such as Heineken, Wybertjes Drop, and KLM. She was one of the first Dutch journalists who was sponsored by commercial businesses, and in that sense, she was a pioneer. Some colleagues criticised her for not being an independent journalist. In a published interview from the 1970s Pos claims that she was aware that colleagues were jealous of her, but that she did not really take notice because she went a lonesome road and hardly had contact with other journalists.[13]

Gracefully sliding down the gangboard

In the anecdote about seasickness referred to above, I showed how, in the 1920s, the young Pos presented her travelling self (whom I will call "Mary" to distinguish from Pos, the author) as innocent and unexperienced, but also as robust and resilient. This dual quality of the self-fabricated character runs as a red thread though Pos' published and unpublished writing. *Ik zag Amerika* (I saw America), published twelve years after her London reportage, still displays that subtle, double characterization of her travelling self: Courageous, witty, and somewhat self-righteous, but also blundering and clumsy. Reporting of her arrival at the harbour of New York, in November 1937, Pos' narrative I relates that before the passengers of "De Volendam" even reach the harbour, a party of custom officers, reporters, and photographers has come on board. They submit the travellers to a list of "peculiar" questions. When asked by reporters who would pick her up, Pos has her I-figure boastfully and cleverly pronounce the name of Mr de Young of Avenel, a former US Vice-Consul in Amsterdam who has read her work.

Mary also wittily retorts questions about the white flower she is wearing ("I just like to wear flowers!") and about her buttoned-up shirt with a collar and tie ("Is that of any importance for you or your readers?"). When one journalist inquires how De Young and Pos will recognise each other, Pos just counters that she will look out for the man who looks happiest and most cheerful.[14] After reporting on these interrogations, Mary appears to triumphantly tell the readers of *Ik zag Amerika* that the journalists were not satisfied with her answers. When subsequently Pos has Mary undergo an inspection by immigration officers who inquire about her reasons for travelling to the US, the young woman responds by declaring: "writing, [...] but the truth and nothing but the truth!"[15] This supposedly causes the officers' amusement, and Mary proclaims that she passes through the examination swiftly and laughingly.

This episode does not necessarily offer a transparent reflection of what has occurred, but is an entertaining and informative reconstruction of a young woman's arrival at the port of entry that Pos serves her readers. It presents her travelling self (Mary) as sassy, astute, and good humoured, as taking risks, as connected to distinguished individuals, and as independent and successful in both the performance of travel and the (global) public sphere. Engaging with religious, professional, gender, and other discourses in her work, Pos here offers us an autobiographical subject who moves away from her upbringing in an orthodox Protestant family in a North Holland town, away from the restrictions of office work and 1930s Dutch journalism, and beyond the gender boundaries of her time.

So far, we recognise in this self-confident Mary the young woman who travelled to London in 1927. In addition, the blunders that were made then (inanity, misplaced belongings) happen again. When Mary disembarks from "De Volendam" she plans to "slide down the gangboard gracefully and cheerfully, with just my handbag under my arm, in order to be able to greet my relative, as my suitcases had already been taken down." However, this scenario will not be acted out at all. Her "caring steward" pats Mary on the arm and informs her that some of her belongings have remained in her cabin. Subsequently, as none of her accommodating stewards is to be found, Mary stumbles down the gangboard, bent down under the full load of three coats, her binoculars, camera, and typewriter, and an open handbag filled up to the rim. Red from strenuousness she walks straight into the man whom she had meant to wave at nonchalantly and cheerfully with the bright-coloured hand-kerchief. Once ashore, this slapstick-like scene is over and Mary has full control over her situation again, as is imperative for anyone travelling on her own: As soon as she has declared that she is carrying "no iota of contraband" the custom officer pays no heed to the suitcases, which Mary calls "my three friends," and even calls for a porter.[16]

The above episodes suggest that, as a character in Pos' autobiographical writing, Mary requires other (male) characters (the London millionaire, the taxi driver, the New York harbour reporters, the immigration officials, the former Vice Consul, and the ship's steward) in order to be fleshed out as a persona. Parallel to this, as a travelling author serving her readers, Pos needed the company and assistance of others, especially men, as I will show below. This need is symbolically reflected in the caption of Figure 1: "You never carry along your heaviest suitcase." The cartoon-like image accompanies Pos' article

"Waarom reizen Hollandsche meisjes niet vaker alleen?" (Why do so few Dutch girls travel on their own?), to which I will turn next.

"Why do so few Dutch girls travel on their own?"

In the Christian journal *De Jonge Vrouw* (The Young Woman), which appeared from 1918 to 1935, and which was aimed to prepare young Dutch women for their domestic and societal tasks, Mary Pos published the illustrated article "Why do so few Dutch girls travel on their own?" The travel writer provides a long list of the advantages that solo travel offers the young woman: She will not have to go through the difficulties of finding a companion, nor will she feel irritated or distracted by the behaviour of a fellow traveller; she will not be forced to make any necessary compromises; she encounters all kinds of surprises, acquires new knowledge, and builds up fine memories; she is certainly offered kind assistance and finds friendship and acquaintances with individuals who may become future pen pals and hosts; in contrast to those travelling with others, the solo female traveller is able to distance herself from the Dutch atmosphere, immerse herself in another culture, and learn or practice another language. She is able to take her time, and experience serene moments of her own. She will return to Holland refreshed and cheerful.[17]

In addition to this list of gains, Pos offers advice to the young and female solo travellers. She encourages them to use their common sense, and to adapt and not offend. Of course, as Wilson and Little, writing in 2008, have critically argued, such accommodating strategies should be "unpacked and problematised under a gendered lens."[18] But Pos, writing at the beginning of the twentieth century, felt obliged to offer young women travelling by themselves advice about good judgment and accommodation. Pos herself resists the "geography of fear" that Wilson and Little problematise, which I will show later. In addition, she further instructs the young women to "anticipate," and to pay tribute and offer money to those who are friendly and helpful, such as servants and subordinates. They should never carry along their heaviest suitcase but save their energy by paying 10 cents to a porter. They should be resilient, vigorous, and spontaneous Dutch youngsters, giving the impression to others that solo travelling is just one of their routines. Pos concludes her article by stating that:

> Although as a solo traveller you need to be independent, autonomous, and make decisions on your own, you should remain feminine and grateful for the help and friendliness that you receive from others. You need to be aware of strangers, of differences between southern and northern mentalities and temperaments, and always be mindful of local customs.[19]

A quick intersectional analysis of these admonitions, of course, allows us to see how Pos' instructions, published in a Christian journal for young Dutch women of (mostly) middle-class background, intertwine issues of religion, class, gender, age, and nationality.[20] Solo travelling involved much more than moving about on your own: It involved many components of the young journal reader's identity. Secondly, Pos' references to sociocultural adjustment, respect for domestic help and assistants, and an alertness to cultural others, varying attitudes and local customs, demonstrate that the writer borrows from, and negotiates with, the (gendered) colonial, national and class discourses of her time. Finally, the textbook characterization of the solo traveller evidently evokes the I-figure that Pos manifested in her autobiographical work: The daring and dauntless Dutch and Christian-cheerful role model who is down-to-earth, amiable, and feminine. It is also a reflection of how the press described Pos. In a review of *Ik zag Amerika* Pos is portrayed as revealing a clever and adventurous way of exploring, showing a certain feminine daintiness, and positioning herself as a supposedly typical level-headed Dutch woman who assesses all she encounters from a deeply rooted Calvinist view of life.[21]

Contentment, bliss, and despair

The aforementioned emblematic level-headed Dutch female and Christian-cheerful traveller time and again shows up in Pos' published and unpublished work, which straightforwardly confirms the joys of solo travelling. In a letter to her friend Jet Pos notes that travelling on her own enables her to work hard, enjoy herself, study, and make a little money here and there.[22] Some writings reveal references to moments of quiet contentment, others to spiritual bliss, and still others to moments of despondency. The latter are unsurprisingly only disclosed in her private correspondence and diaries.

Many of the published travel accounts studied culminate in a variation of the following finale on the last page of a reportage on women in France:

> In the almost tactile quietness of that evening, in which now and again I stopped to stand still and experience [everything] as intensively as possible, I strolled homeward bound, with a cheerful heart because of so much peace around me.[23]

Pos' inexplicit reference to "everything" is literally echoed in a letter to her friend Piet, in which she professes: "You know I have travelled a lot! Everything on my own, and I have experienced tremendous interesting things."[24] The superb incidents or events she refers to here may have included a spiritual immersion in a larger scheme of life, but she is not explicit. Apparently, it was difficult for Pos to find the time and inspiration to fully describe her private experiences, as she explicates in a diary entry written during a trip to Copenhagen, in September 1932. Pos conveys that the evening was beautiful, and that she enjoyed the "lovely moon" and "mild weather." She especially appreciated being on deck in the evening: "I wish I had time to write down all these delightful impressions, especially what the sea looked like in the evening and what the moon looked like during storms or mist."[25] Significantly, all three examples (the published account, the letter, and the diary entry) seem to point out that Pos/Mary found self-space and contentment in her travelling, and did not seem to yearn for companionship, nor for the possibility of sharing her experiences in great detail.

The quiet contentment referred to above alternates with states of transcendence. In a number of travel books Pos portrays Mary as experiencing the sublime. On her way to the United States in 1937, the I-narrator witnesses the glittering effects of phosphor, as if chunks of stars had fallen down, around the ship. "[T]he ocean sparkled like emerald."[26] By showcasing her personal exultation and bewilderment when crossing the Atlantic, the narrator positions herself as even more physically apart from the other passengers than she does in the aforementioned instances. She fabricates a travelling self that withstands a storm while on deck, her clothes soaked in ocean water, her lips tasting of salt, and her hair covered in foam fluffs. Noting "space, space" around her Pos' Mary seemingly becomes one with the natural environment.[27] This solo experience of euphoria and delight is, we deduce as readers, very different from that of her fellow travellers whom she knows are not on deck, and are either seasick, resting, or having their dinner.

Travelling back to Europe at the end of her visit, she does enjoy the atmosphere on board of the Red Star Line "Westernland," and dines with fellow travellers, but she prefers her personal contact with the Atlantic surroundings over the crowd of fellow passengers whom she portrays as lethargic.[28] When Mary is not on the ship's decks, bow or poop, she retreats to the gym and drawing room. Pushing the boundaries of the ship's passenger space she descends into the ship's machine room to make friends with the crew.[29] In a parallel move, travelling to California in the late 1940s, she stretches the boundaries of her own role as a solo travelling journalist by taking the lead in setting up a Christmas celebration on board, as no minister nor pastor appears to be on the ship. All passengers, despite their differences in nationalities and goals of travel, join the singing of Christmas carols.[30] This means that while Mary situates herself as physically and emotionally separate from the other passengers, she also assumes the more contiguous role of minister and master of ceremonies. In a more general sense, throughout all of her writings, both published and non-published, we see that whereas the Dutch travel journalist continuously poses as typically *unaccompanied*, she also presents herself as being with travel companions – a stance that, of course, truly fits a character that aims at building bridges.

Mary also adopts other social roles: She becomes a mother-like and playful figure to the forty children on board whose parents, "displaced persons" and emigrants, are for reasons of mental and physical health not taking care of their children.[31] This matches author Pos' frequent references, in her travel books and interviews, to her love of children. One of her short stories of travel is entirely based on her friendship with a 5-year old boy from Capri: "Il mio piccolo amico (mijn kleine vriend)."[32] In an interview Pos claimed: "On the photos that I keep you always see me with little Indian children, Chinese children, Japanese children, and so on and so on, as I am crazy about children."[33] (in Figures 2 and 3 the young and older Pos position themselves as child-loving visitors of Capri and Japan).

Thus Pos' travel accounts disclose private moments of existential bliss as well as collective experiments, and experiences in which boundaries of age, class, nationality, and religion are explored and crossed. Of course, we should not take this complex reportage at face value. From Pos' letters to her Swiss lover Walter, and from her personal diary, we learn that when she retreated to the ship's gym, as echoed in the published text, she was actually feeling depressed and desperate, and struggling with a heartache as Walter had gone home to his wife. In addition, she had been sexually assaulted by the ship's captain who had first tried to woo her. In a letter to her lover Pos declared that she had angrily "told the captain the truth" and had retreated to the ship's gym to write and work.[34] This does not rhyme with narrator Mary's report, in Pos' travel book, that she had accompanied the captain for an exploration of the ship, had joined him for evening strolls and had listened to his stories of his seafaring adventures.[35]

Pos' feelings of loneliness and depression also speak from the letters she composed in her New York hotel room, a few weeks earlier, in December 1937. "Ich bin so allein," Pos wrote to Walter:

> think of me for a moment when celebrating New Year's Eve, while I am wandering far from Home [sic] and while I long for Peace and Quiet [sic]. While I cannot find it. Pray for me, as I can no longer do it. I hope to be able to stay courageous.[36]

She informed him that she was tired. She did not know how to finish the articles she was to send to Dutch newspapers.

> Here in New York City, all alone, every day anew you have to find your way, collecting impressions, visit people, noting down all impressions and in the meantime write articles and take care of my own clothing. If you are not feeling well, as I do today, it is really too heavy for a young woman.[37]

Pos concludes her letter with a typical disheartened proclamation, switching to Walter's native language: "[...] wie schwer machen die Männer mir doch das Leben."[38]

Pos' love ache for Walter, and her traumatic experience with the ship's captain, were only two of the hardships that travel produced. Whereas her published work portrays her as jolly, audacious, and tough, resourcefully compensating her travelling alone during Christmas by embellishing her ship's cabin with decorations, sweets and photo portraits of her loved ones,[39] her letters and diaries emphasise that her travelling included hard work, feeling restless and homesick, insecure, and depressed. A diary entry about her cruise trip to Copenhagen in September 1932 states that she would have enjoyed to go on a walking tour in the capital city "with a nice person," but that it was difficult to find fitting acquaintances on board: The Dutch passengers stuck to their own group of friends, and on top of that Pos was engaged and did not frequent "dancings" in the evening. Pos felt "miserable" for being unable to dance, and confides to her diary, "I believe that it greatly tittilates."[40]

Pos' orthodox Christian Protestant upbringing did not merely hinder her, however. Her family had looked at hard times as challenges to face courageously, and Pos' adagio, during her travels, was to never pity herself. The biographical portraits of prominent figures that she integrates in her travel books all contain instructions that summoned her readers to show endurance, self-discipline, and self-sacrifice. Pos likewise builds a persona of herself as never opting for a comfortable life. In 1955, a Dutch national newspaper featured a Heineken advertisement in which Pos, dressed up in a Peruvian costume, is introduced as "continuously aware of the risks, especially where good hygiene is lacking" (Figure 9). The journalist's pleasant surprise in the "jungle," the ad states, is hermetically sealed authentic Heineken beer.[41] Reviews as well as announcements of Pos' travel books, which at times read as adventure novels, refer to the "risks that must be taken by a woman travelling entirely alone."[42] Pos defied and triumphed over a severe infection of the leg resulting from a wound contracted in the jungle, an automobile accident in Latin America, poisoning, Malaria Tropica, and other mishaps. But she also relates of great anxieties when getting lost during a hiking trip through the jungle of the Dutch East Indies, and when experiencing a car breakdown in the wilderness of Suriname.

At times Mary Pos lied about her feelings of fear. At the beginning of the Second World War, when she was no longer able to travel abroad but delivered lectures throughout the country, she wrote to one of her (female) admirers:

> I don't experience anxiety, and certainly not when I explore a new country; there are friendly people everywhere who wish to be of service, often more than in your own country, just because you are a stranger, and on every spot in the world, no matter how far removed and remote, one can easily pray.[43]

The following section will focus on the friendly people she refers to.

Male service

Not only in correspondence, but also in published articles and diaries Pos wrote about her dependence on the "little bit of friendliness" she receives from others.[44] In fact, Pos' extensive hints at friendly people's assistance suggest that although she advertised her travelling self as "always travelling alone,"[45] she constantly and strongly depended on others, as the following example illustrates. Pos' travel book *Veelbelovend Rhodesia en machtig Tanganyika* has Mary arrive in the city of Beira, in what was then Portuguese overseas territory and is currently Mozambique. She is very disappointed that "Mr. Schippers," the head of the "Zuidafrikaanse Handelshuis" (South-African trading company) is absent during the first days of her stay. None of the other Dutch are able to introduce her to the Portuguese authorities, and she has to work with information received from third parties and from what she witnesses herself. "As soon as he arrived everything changed."[46]

Pos was continuously dependent on (mostly) male service. A mere look at Mary Pos' diary entries of April 1935, when she has travelled to Rome for a personal interview with Mussolini, discloses the fact that technically her travels were never journeys "of her own." Wishing to visit the Dutch ambassador while in Rome, Pos has this arranged thanks to a letter of reference written by Dutch Prime Minister Colijn.[47] In a different sphere, a young man called Hubert helps her purchase a train ticket. A second young man helps her find another seat when, once on the train, Pos is being harassed by a male lawyer who continues to ask her out. Subsequently, two male passengers let her sleep on several seats whereas they just sit in their chairs.[48]

Mary Pos seems to have had no scruples to be pampered and courted by Fascist and Nazi men – which may fit with the finding that in the late 1920s and early 1930s quite a few Dutch artists and notables were appreciative of Mussolini.[49] Reporting on her stay in Freiburg, in the Summer of 1934, she boasts in a letter to a friend that she was revered by everyone. On the first of May, during the German "Nationaler Feiertag des Deutschen Volkes," which she calls Labour Day (in Dutch), she was offered "a car with two S.A. [Sturmabteilung] men, and a press officer, all for myself."[50] The young woman does not specify how she spent the day, nor does she reflect on the political implications of her involvement with the men in question. In April 1935, Pos writes in her personal diary of her Italian lover Edie, a uniformed military officer who works for Mussolini and lives in the latter's fascist camp. Edie offers all kinds of logistical services to Pos, teaches her Italian, gives her driving lessons, and pays for all Pos' expenses, even the postage for her letters to Holland. Following their joint visit to Ostia, Pos writes in her diary that she has to be "grateful for this" and "he is very sweet."[51] When Edie has left town to visit with another lady friend, Pos sends him an angry note written on her business card.[52] They make up later, and Pos sardonically concludes the diary entry as follows:

> as long as he can play the role of St. Nicolaas, and be generous, and could do as he pleases in the company of a kind woman he was happy.[53]

Here Pos seems to position herself as the dependent and receiving woman-child; in no way does she problematise her relationship to Mussolini's military officer.

These young men in Freiburg, Rome and other places, were part of a gendered structure of informal and formal services that Pos depended on. This structure conceivably fitted with the gender expectations of Pos' time, but otherwise did not match the ways in which Pos also seemed to transgress gender boundaries by being a financially independent and fearless freelance journalist who enjoyed smoking, drinking and free sexual relations, and who travelled the world for most of her life. During Pos' entire travelling career, countless men of a great variety of class, age, racial-ethnic, and national backgrounds offered Pos a helping hand and a listening ear. Fellow travellers brought her drinks on deck, paid for her wine, beer, dinners, and taxi; waiters and loyal hut stewards gave her free drinks, comforted her, provided assistance and advice, and information and attention; taxi drivers conversed with her, gave free tours of the neighbourhood, and helped her hunt for available hotel rooms. When Pos asked for directions, local men and visiting strangers accompanied her to where she wished to go.

De Leugen van Moskou (The lie of Moscow) features a Mary who becomes seriously ill during her visit to Russia's capital city. The hotel staff is unable to be of assistance due to language barriers and lack of equipment, but luckily an American man of Russian descent lends a hand. Although Mary proclaims that she usually prefers to venture out on her own when she needs to visit official organizations, by this time she gratefully accepts his offer.[54] Several years later, Pos by chance reunites with the same Russian American in the US who offers her food, entertainment and the company of his friends. The man, it turns out, is part of Pos'aforementioned structure of male service.[55]

Not just a little bit of friendliness

It is important to note that this gendered system of male service is not merely a simple system of courtesy. Various (gendered, colonial, and other) interests play a role. I will illustrate this by focusing on what I have labeled the suitcase service. In her diaries, Pos details the occasions when men help carry her suitcase(s), how much she pays porters, and the hassle of transporting her suitcases without any assistance.[56] She confides in her diary how one man, "Mr B," who is her boss and who would soon become her lover, offered to carry her suitcase as a way of reconciliation after a disagreement. Disembarking from a train, ahead of "Mr B," Pos almost collapsed under the weight of her suitcase but managed to walk completely erect. While on the platform she realised that her boss and an acquaintance were just behind her, so she walked to a bench and pretended to frantically search for something in her purse in order to to let them pass. The boss ended up being "very sweet" and "almost begged to make up. [...] Then he said, you have such a heavy suitcase; I was planning taking a taxi anyway, I will take you home first."[57]

A second example of the complexities of the suitcase service can be found in Pos' travel book about California where the I narrator encounters a "redcap" whose family originates from Suriname. Whereas Mary associates the "negro porter's" face with the protagonist from the nineteenth century slave novel *Uncle Tom's Cabin*, the porter recognises her from her articles about Suriname, which his family in Suriname had forwarded to him. The man offers Mary a speedy and special delivery service for her luggage and arranges the best seat for her on the train. As he accepts no fee Mary offers the black porter her hand, an interracial gesture which, she notes, surprises her fellow passengers. Later on Mary sends him a postcard, and concludes, "This was also a Dutchman who no matter his different skin colour paid homage to the honour of our country, far from his beloved Suriname."[58] Pos' suitcase anecdotes indicate how the practice of travel must be viewed as

situated in a complex context involving, among many other issues, social/
fiscal, sexual/gender, and racial/colonial structures and expectations.

Pos was aware of the ways in which porters, stewards and fellow passengers
overly pampered and indulged her. On her way to Copenhagen in September
1932, she writes in her diary "I enjoyed myself, there were two waiters who both
spoilt me shamefully. The entire table laughed about it." All she was doing, Pos
writes, was being friendly, not more than that. It would be unfair and too
gratuitous, perhaps, to relate this statement to her comment, in the same
paragraph, on what she was wearing (a "yellow satin dress") and her observation,
later on, that wine and cigarettes had produced her "temperamentful" mood.[59]
However, we also know that Pos was well aware that some of her outfits, and her
New Woman–like habit of smoking, were attractive to men. In a letter to her
lover Walter, for instance, she described an ensemble she had just bought as
feminine and eye-catching.[60] In her diary of 1933 she included a lengthy entry
about women's smoking. Modern working women who smoke, she wrote,
exerted a pull on men.

> A married man whose wife is completely absorbed in her household will
> enjoy the amicable contact with an energetic and working woman. And I
> believe that I, particularly, must watch out not to cause anything that would
> arouse certain feelings in a man.[61]

Thus, the little bit of friendliness that Pos refers to above is at times an evident
understatement. To a friend she reports that she had enjoyed a flight back from
Paris to the Netherlands.

> I was with fourteen gentlemen who were all very courteous. I have become
> acquainted with quite a few pilots; after my arrival in Paris I had a friendly
> dinner and a nice evening with the pilot. After the return trip I also had
> dinner with another pilot whom I had become acquainted with before. We
> had a very nice farewell dinner in Amsterdam.[62] (Figures 4–6).

Pos' use of the words "courteous" and "friendly" are telling. It indicates, in her
correspondence with her friend, where she draws the line of tolerability. But this
line was also dependent on her moods and tastes. Whereas at the Waldorf Astoria
Hotel Mary delightedly receives flowers and chocolate from the executive
manager, another rich gentleman who sends flowers and compliments is
dismissed.[63]

We have seen above how Pos cautioned young female travellers to use their
common sense when travelling solo. In the two examples given above, the exact
mechanisms of Pos' common sense are unclear. At other times, however, Pos'
motivations are well-defined: Fellow passengers or local men whom she did not
trust she tried to avoid.[64] This restricted her movement, but Pos did not seem to
suffer from any "geography of fear."[65] In Rome, Pos felt irritated by the
flirtatious habits of the men she met on her ways – she wrote to the wife of the

Dutch ambassador about five Italian men who were eyeing her up – but she was also successful in using "tricks" to get rid of them.[66] One of those we could label the Sunday trick: Pos wrote in her diary that she had to avoid becoming too intimate with people who helped her out. "Sunday I was alone on purpose."[67] Another trick could be called "no fuss." When one man who accompanied her during her wanderings through Rome "made a fuss," Pos instantly indicated that she did not want to be more than friends. Upon this, she wrote down, he behaved amiably. Intriguingly, however, this matter-of-fact report of her prompt action and agency is followed by a sentence which confirms Pos' dependent attitude towards men, and relates it to an alleged lack of professionalism: "I am of course a big child and will not be a good journalist because my need for affectionateness is too great and I am too sensitive."[68] This is one of her very rare references to her status as a reporter and author. Pos predominantly wrote about her practice of travel, not her work as a journalist.

Pos' need for affectionateness comes up in an interview when she is in her seventies. She pronounced that she had had plenty of romantic encounters, but had always kept one thing in mind:

> I had only one body and I needed to be careful. But I am not made of stone, and especially when you are lonely during your journeys....; then you would think, once in a while, it would be nice if I could love this or that person. Fortunately, with me, it would take a while before I would hook up with someone [...] that I would want to spend my whole life with.[69]

In addition, Pos explained, she was always in transit. In case she noticed "a tremendously charming bloke" he would have disappeared within an hour, "behind the horizon so to speak," and Pos would reason that she had possibly forsaken a chance. But she would be pleased and relieved, she stated, that she could continue travelling on her own.[70]

Tour guides and a fiancé

Travelling on her own, we have seen, also involved many encounters with other travellers and local people. Pos at times joined sightseeing trips with tourists. However, in several instances Pos ridicules these holidaymakers, such as the Australian tourist ("stingy," "black moustache and eyes the colour and size of currants," "atheist," "making sinister jokes") who has joined Pos' group that visits the Genoa graveyard. Tired of the group's quick pace and hasty way of going through the "quiet realm of [...] great beauty" Pos physically distances herself from the group in order to be able to fully appreciate the site.[71] Thus she positions herself as a traveller, unlike the mass tourists. We also see this in Figures 7 and 8 where Pos seemingly detaches herself from the group of tourists at Pompeii.

In some countries, though, Mary Pos is compelled to rely on the know-how and assistance of (male) tour guides. In her book on her Australian journey, she has Mary portray an aboriginal tour guide. Just as Pos' travelling self had, in New York, likened the Surinamese American porter to Harriet Beecher Stowe's literary character Uncle Tom, in Australia she associates the aboriginal boomerang vender and tour guide with an image she remembered from her family's Dutch boardgame Ganzenbord (Game of the Goose): "Australia" had been symbolised by a wild character carrying a bow and arrow and wearing nothing but a loincloth. The racialised image, making up part of her national/cultural frame of reference, had both attracted and deterred her.[72] In trying to negotiate with this ambiguous figure of her tour guide, Mary and the man construct a fascinating double trade-off. Mary buys a set of three boomerangs from the vender, and only resigns herself to his high price when he develops into an especially valuable tour guide and in addition demonstrates the art of boomerang tossing and whistling with a eucalyptus leaf. When the guide presents Mary with a brooch of a wooden kookaburra, asking in return a postcard from her next destination, she takes a special effort in selecting one out of the ordinary.[73]

Mary is rather outspoken about her assessment of her local guides, whose names she often lists. She comments not only on obvious features, such as their fluency in English and helpfulness, but also on the way they behave, look, and use their voice, their patience, intellect and intuition, and their racial and ethnic background. Her favourite guides are men who intuitively know when she wishes to be on her own. When she enjoys her guides' company, she describes them as friends (191), and even seems to implicitly substitute one for a lover: In her travel book on Egypt she features a narrative I strolling along with her guide Abushnaff:

> Sometimes we just walk on, through the moon light, without speaking. [...] he asks me whether I am not too cold in the cool nocturnal wind.[74]

Pos' own fiancé Anne Gerrit, of course, could not take care of her. He was in Haarlem, awaiting her return. From that distance Anne Gerrit took care of her administration and advised her on what to ask Hitler when she was on her way to Germany. Pos' private correspondence and diaries reveal that she constantly had to negotiate with her fiancé Anne Gerrit about her planning. Whereas suggesting in a letter that she carries out her travels after thorough consultation and full agreement with Anne, she also uses manipulative techniques during those negotiations, as is indicated by comments such as "If you think I am taking too much time I will certainly and directly return to Holland," and by telling Anne that if she will return sooner she will have to pay extra expenses.[75] Taken into a New York hospital (for reasons not indicated in the archival papers), her fiancé Anne tells her to:

> watch out and stay away from that grime that exists in the sewers of the world, such as cities like New York. Och Rietje, why did you ever leave in order to wander around on your own, on one hand courted but on the other hand so lonely.[76]

Conclusion

During her stay in New York at the end of 1937, Mary Pos took up the plan to visit the neighbourhood of Harlem. Most of her acquaintances, narrator Mary states in *Ik zag Amerika*, had expressed their surprise, but she had persisted.[77] Thus she presents herself as the young, white woman who bravely and on her own explores this allegedly unsafe terrain – a naïve and unexperienced, yet open-minded, European adventurer. But we also notice Mary's dependency on the two African American (male) guides she has recruited: One a minister and the other the chief editor of a black newspaper. The latter takes her on a tour; Mary can hardly keep up with his quick strides. In addition, we notice Mary's utter vulnerability when, at one of Harlem's public schools, she faces students who have completely misunderstood the specificities of Dutch and European geography and history, or when, visiting their schoolyard, she feels as if she is being attacked by a group of students when she is taking photographs.

The I-narrator's overall helplessness and awkward position as she travels through the new environment cannot fully be compensated by the pompous quality of the reportage, nor by her condescending and at times glaringly racist assessments of the neighbourhood and its inhabitants. These assessments evidently echoed the racial/racist, class, and national/colonial discourses that were on hand at the time and which author Pos had internalised. In addition, Pos drew from, and had to negotiate with, other discourses from the 1920s and 1930s, such as ideas regarding gender roles, Protestant Christian ideas, conversations she had picked up at the small businesses she had worked for as a secretary, discussions with fellow Dutch journalists, and social texts on poverty and health. Pos did not fully reject the restricting gender, class, and other codes of her time, nor did she sheepishly follow the trajectory of marriage, motherhood, respectability, and sexual repression. She seemed to have found a way of combining various roles and rules.

This was hard work. Pos had a complex personality and suffered from a strong need of attention from others. She had to contend with an oftentimes sick body, and professional and financial restraints and other hurdles. Although her published and private writing presents her as economically, socially, and sexually emancipated, her personal archives also suggest that she continuously suffered from sombre moods. However, Pos was ambitious, resourceful, and enduring, and had a wilful, stubborn, and tough character.[78] She was not just pretty but also witty, and thanks to her independent and resilient character she was able to set up a personal and professional network of (mostly male) notables, diplomats, politicians, business men, relatives, and acquaintances, both at home and abroad, in which she manoeuvred more or less independently. As an independently operating female travel writer and journalist Mary Pos' life-work attests to the limitations and biases she faced, but also to her ingenuity and talents. An analysis of that work contributes to a larger project of reconstructing transnational lives and the various ways in which twentieth century women travellers of diverse backgrounds handled gender expectations and roles.

Notes

1 Pos, M. (1928) "Een zakenmeisje in Londen" [A business girl in London], in: *Christelijk Vrouwenleven*, 12 (9): 272–278. From Pos' correspondence to "Mr. Kas" we know that she returned to the Netherlands from the trip to London on Saturday, 23 July 1927. She writes to Kas that she had had no trouble to find her way during her stay in London. The British were extraordinarily kind and courteous and helped her whenever they could. "I went out on my own, without looking for the Dutch who were also visiting London." Mary Pos Papers, Vrije Universiteit Amsterdam, University Library. Collection Historical Documentation Centre for Dutch Protestantism. Collection number 529, Folder 2, Correspondence 1920–1927.

2 Pos (1928): 277.

3 Pos (1928): 278. For a discussion of Mary Pos' enjoyment of travelling on top of a bus, when she seems to be the "monarch of all I survey," see Boter, B. & Geerlings, L. (2016) "Neerkijken en rondzien: Twee reizigers uit Nederland portretteren en presenteren Harlem," in: *Tijdschrift voor Geschiedenis*, 129 (3): 393–413.

4 Pos (1928): 275. Pos also noted that of all visitors she is the one who has to sit in the last car that takes the guests to the luncheon, because "they had not counted on [her]." Mary Pos Papers, Folder 2, Correspondence 1920–1927, letter to Mr. Kas, 23 July 1927.

5 Rik Felderhof (20 December 1979) interview with Mary Pos, *Rozegeur en prikkeldraad*, NCRV. In the interview Pos states that she visited the asylum as a young girl. It is possible that she conflated her 1927 and 1934 visits to London: In a letter to a "Dear Friend," dated 9 July 1934, Pos offers an account of a recent trip to London during which she stayed at the plush Victoria Hotel, but also took lodgings at an asylum for homeless girls. Mary Pos Papers, Folder 7, Correspondence 1934.

6 Gilmartin, P. (1997) "The Dangers of Independent Travel: A Century of Advice for 'Lady Travellers,'" in: *Journal of Interdisciplinary Gender Studies*, 2 (1): 1–13.

7 Houttuin, S. & De Weerd, F. (17 July 2017) interview with Huub Wijfjes for Dutch radioprogramme VPRO OVT (Fall 2018).

8 Author's translation. Mary Pos Papers, Folder 64, Interviews, undated typescript; no title.

9 Mary Pos Papers, Folder 7, Correspondence 1934, letter to Jet Christen-Boorsma, 27 December 1934.

10 In 1928, at the age of 24, Pos ended her engagement of more than two years with Mr. Dikkers. From 1929–1937 Pos was engaged to Anne Gerrit van der Horst. They never married. Van der Horst was a student of Dutch Literature and had some minor teaching jobs, but did not yet earn enough to start a family. According to Pos, Anne was not as energetic as she was, and did not have the whip behind him as she did. In 1959, at the age of 55, Pos married an American professor of History, Eber Malcolm Carroll (1895–1959). Her second marriage, when she was 56 years of age, was with Ernest William Dowdeswell (1900–1990), a British engineer.

11 Mary Pos Papers, Folder 40, Diary ["ongelezen verbranden als ik dood ga"], 9 March 1932. This diary was written in short-hand, although a few entries were typed up in Dutch. On its cover Pos had written that it should not be read, but burned after her death.

12 Mary Pos Papers, Folder 12, Correspondence 1939, letter to Mieke, 20 October 1939.

13 Lammers, F. (1975) "Mary Pos zoekt avontuur nu op de de Gooise heide," *Trouw* 24 October, n.p. In: Mary Pos Papers, Folder 64, Interviews. Pos did have friends among journalists, and she was a member of a Protestant Christian network of journalists: The Verbond van Christelijk Letterkundige kringen. However, she was criticised by quite a few colleagues. Her work was considered to be too subjective and sentimental, and too much a collection of moralizing anecdotes, superficial, and cliché-ridden impressions and naïve and dated stories.

14 Pos, M. (1940) *Ik zag Amerika*. Amsterdam: Allert de Lange: 16.
15 Pos (1940): 16.
16 Pos (1940): 16.
17 Pos, M. (1935) "Waarom reizen Hollandsche meisjes niet vaker alleen?" in: *De Jonge Vrouw*, 17 (12): 444–447.
18 Wilson, E. & Little, D.E. (2008) "The Solo Female Travel Experience: Exploring the 'Geography of Women's Fear'," in: *Current Issues in Tourism*, 11 (2): 167–186, 181. See also Wilson, E. (2004) "A 'Journey of Her Own'? The Impact of Constraints on Women's Solo Travel." PhD dissertation, Brisbane: Griffith University. Offering a feminist analysis of solo travel Jordan and Aitchison employ the term of self-surveillance. See Jordan, F. & Aitchison, C. (2008) "Tourism and the Sexualisation of the Gaze: Solo Female Tourists' Experiences of Gendered Power, Surveillance and Embodiment," in: *Leisure Studies*, 27 (3): 329–349.
19 Pos (1935): "Waarom reizen Hollandsche meisjes," 444.
20 Crenshaw, K.W. (1991) "Mapping the Margins: Intersectionality, Identity Politics, and Violence Against Women of Color," in: *Stanford Law Review*, 43 (6): 1241–1299.
21 Mary Pos Papers, Folder 61, Reviews of books and lectures: "Op vleugels naar Zuid-Afrika" 1941–1944, 20 March 1941. Van Garrel, B. "Ik protesteer tegen de verwording: De hartstochten van Mary Pos," in: *Haagse Post* n.d., 11. Figure 10 shows Pos going on board of the Holland America Line. Date unknown. Source: https://ilibrariana.wordpress.com/2012/01/04/mary-pos-1904-1987-de-eerste-vrouwelijke-reisjournaliste/.
22 Mary Pos Papers, Folder 7, Correspondence 1934, letter to Jet Christen-Boorsma, 27 December 1934.
23 Pos, M. (1953) "Vrouwen in Frankrijk," in: *Moeder: Vakblad voor moeders*, 8: 382–385.
24 Mary Pos Papers, Folder 7, Correspondence 1934, letter to Piet de Vink, 29 October 1934.
25 Mary Pos Papers, Folder 40, Diary ["ongelezen verbranden als ik dood ga"], 20 September 1932.
26 Pos (1940): 9; see also Boter, B. (2013) "Heavenly Sensations and Communal Celebrations: Experiences of Liminality in Transatlantic Journeys," in: *Tales of Transit: Narrative Migrant Spaces in Atlantic Perspective, 1850–1950*, eds. Michael Boyden, Hans Krabbendam, & Liselotte Vandenbussche. Amsterdam: Amsterdam University Press: 179–195.
27 Pos (1940): 9, 13.
28 Pos (1940): 317, 322, 324.
29 Pos (1940): 320–321.
30 Pos, M. (1955) *Californië: Dwars door Amerika op zoek naar Nederlanders*. Wageningen: Zomer & Keuning: 9–12, 19; see also 204–205.
31 Pos (1955) *Californië*: 12.
32 Pos, M. (1937) "Il mio piccolo amico (mijn kleine vriend)" in: *Kleuterland: een bundel verhalen vol zonneschijn en blijdschap uit het wonderland van de twee- tot vijfjarigen*. Greet Gilhuis-Smitskamp (ed.) Wageningen: Zomer & Keuning: 2nd part: 119–137. The boy's features seem to be based on the adult sailor whom Pos met in 1934, and who took her on a rowing trip to the caves at Capri's coast. See Figure 11. For a discussion of the trip and the photo, see Mary Pos Papers, Folder 9, Correspondence 1936, letter to Mrs. Patijn [wife of the Dutch ambassador in Rome], 28 March 1936.
33 Van Garrel in Mary Pos Papers, Folder 64, Interviews with Mary Pos. n.d.
34 Mary Pos Papers, Correspondence 1938, Folder 11, letter to Walter, 23 January 1938.
35 Pos (1949): 297, 299–300.
36 Mary Pos Papers, Folder 10, Correspondence 1937, letter to Walter, 15 December 1937.
37 Mary Pos Papers, Folder 10, Correspondence 1937, letters to Walter, 2 and 3 November 1937.

38 Ibidem.
39 Pos (1955) *Californië*: 10.
40 Mary Pos Papers, Folder 40, Diary ["ongelezen verbranden als ik dood ga"], 17 and 20 September 1932.
41 https://ilibrariana.wordpress.com/2012/01/04/mary-pos-1904–1987-de-eerste-vrouwe lijke-reisjournaliste/
42 Mary Pos Papers, Folder 62, Suriname 1947, undated, incomplete document, no title ["When we called on Mary Pos"]. Similar document in Folder 64, Interviews, *Leiden Post*, 11 July 1947, typescript.
43 Mary Pos Papers, Folder 13, Correspondence 1940, letter to Mrs. van Hoogstraten, 31 December 1940.
44 The quote comes from Pos, M. (3 March 1956) *Moeder: Vakblad voor moeders*, 3: 146.
45 Mary Pos Papers, Folder 55, Typescripts of articles and lectures, n.d.
46 Pos, M. (1955) *Veelbelovend Rhodesia en machtig Tanganyika*. Wageningen: Zomer & Keuning: 117.
47 For another reference to letters of introduction see Pos (1940): 27. Pos' interview with President Roosevelt, held in December 1937, was most probably arranged by Mr. De Young, who picked her up when she arrived in New York in November 1937. See Mary Pos Papers, Folder 9, Correspondence, letter from Dirk P. De Young, 20 November 1937.
48 Mary Pos Papers, Folder 41, Diary ["Aanvulsel. Alleen voor mijzelf van eenig belang"], 10 April 1935.
49 Huberts, W. (2017) *In de ban van een beter verleden: Het Nederlandse fascisme 1923–1945*. Nijmegen: Vantilt.
50 Mary Pos Papers, Folder 7, Correspondence, letter to a friend, 9 July 1934.
51 Mary Pos Papers, Folder 41, Diary ["Aanvulsel. Alleen voor mijzelf van eenig belang"], 28 April 1935.
52 Figure 1.
53 Mary Pos Papers, Folder 41, Diary ["Aanvulsel. Alleen voor mijzelf van eenig belang"], 29 April 1935.
54 Pos, M. (1937) *De leugen van Moskou*. Nijkerk: G.F. Callenbach: 14.
55 Pos (1940): 31.
56 Mary Pos Papers, Folder 40, Diary ["ongelezen verbranden als ik dood ga"], 21 June 1932.
57 Mary Pos Papers, Folder 40, Diary ["ongelezen verbranden als ik dood ga"], 23 June 1932. Later that year, in September of 1932 when Pos will go on another journey, Pos' boss tells her he will miss her and gives her a dressing case with travel necessaries as if to extend their contact, and his support, during her travels. Diary 15 September 1932.
58 Pos (1955) Californië: 38.
59 Mary Pos Papers, Folder 40, Diary ["ongelezen verbranden als ik dood ga"], 17 September 1932; 20 September 1932; 22 September 1932.
60 Mary Pos Papers, Folder 10, Correspondence, letter to Walter, 15 December 1937. I have found no information about Mary Pos mirroring herself in the New Woman or Gibson Girl images presented in Dutch and foreign magazines of her time. She must have been aware of those icons, as she sometimes published in the very same publications, but she does not explicitly refer to them.
61 Mary Pos Papers, Folder 40, Diary ["ongelezen verbranden als ik dood ga"], 7 March 1933.
62 Mary Pos Papers, Folder 7, Correspondence, letter to "Lieve Vriendin" [Dear Friend], 27 December 1934. Pos left us a series of photo portraits in which she poses with airline and ship crews. Some of the ones in front of airplanes were taken as part of an agreement with the sponsor KLM.

63 Mary Pos Papers, Folder 10, Correspondence 1937, letters to Walter, 15 and 21 December 1937. Figure 12 shows Pos at the Zanzibar café, being entertained and treated by the owner of the bar.

64 Mary Pos Papers, Folder 40, Diary ["ongelezen verbranden als ik dood ga"], 17 September 1932, Copenhagen.

65 Wilson & Little (2008): 168.

66 Mary Pos Papers, Folder 7, Correspondence 1934, 15 November 1934 and 27 December 1934; Folder 9, Correspondence 1936, 28 March 1936; Mary Pos Papers, Folder 41, Diary ["Aanvulsel. Alleen voor mijzelf van eenig belang"], 4 April 1935.

67 Mary Pos Papers, Folder 41, Diary ["Aanvulsel. Alleen voor mijzelf van eenig belang"], 6 April 1935.

68 Ibidem, 9 April 1935.

69 Felderhof (1979).

70 Ibidem. Pos had many lovers when travelling abroad. In 1942, one of her Dutch lovers, Bert, wrote to Pos' female friend Gon: "Almost every country provided a lover." Mary Pos Papers, Folder 15, Correspondence 1942, 8 October 1942.

71 Pos, M. (1935) "Op het wereldberoemde kerkhof te Genua," *Christelijk vrouwenleven*, 19 (4): 114–116.

72 Pos, M. (1948) *Door de lucht naar Australië: Land van de toekomst*. Amsterdam: A. De Jonge: 133.

73 Pos (1948): 135.

74 Pos, M. (1950) *Sprong naar het land der pharao's*. Wageningen: Zomer & Keuning: 53.

75 Mary Pos Papers, Folder 8, Correspondence 1935, letter to Ida and Arjen van der Horst, "End of December," 1935, 2. Pos also writes to Anne that she may have to come back so as not to annoy her parents-in-law for leaving him alone. Mary Pos Papers, Folder 9, Correspondence 1936, letter by Mary Pos to Anne Gerrit van der Horst, 17 May 1936.

76 Mary Pos Papers, Folder 10, Correspondence 1937, letter by Anne Gerrit van der Horst to Mary Pos, 20 November 1937. Anne Gerrit advised Pos on where to travel and what to ask during interviews; he also took care of her administration back home in the Netherlands.

77 Pos (1940): 87.

78 Boter, B. (2017) "First Female Travel Journalist Meets First Lady: Mary Pos and Eleanor Roosevelt Speak on Women's Roles and Intercultural Understanding," in: *Special Issue: "A Transatlantic Public Diplomat? Recent European Scholarship on Eleanor Roosevelt,"* eds. Dario D. Fazzi & Anya Luscombe. *European Journal of American Studies*.

Index

For Product Safety Concerns and Information please contact our EU
representative GPSR@taylorandfrancis.com
Taylor & Francis Verlag GmbH, Kaufingerstraße 24, 80331 München, Germany

www.ingramcontent.com/pod-product-compliance
Ingram Content Group UK Ltd.
Pitfield, Milton Keynes, MK11 3LW, UK
UKHW021011180425
457613UK00020B/900